Criminal Law in Poland

Criminal Law in Poland

Wojciech Jasiński
Karolina Kremens

This book was originally published as a monograph in the International Encyclopaedia of Laws/Criminal Law.

General Editor: Roger Blanpain
Founding Editor: Frank Hendrickx
Volume Editors: Frank Verbruggen & Vanessa Franssen

Wolters Kluwer

Published by:
Kluwer Law International B.V.
PO Box 316
2400 AH Alphen aan den Rijn
The Netherlands
E-mail: international-sales@wolterskluwer.com
Website: lrus.wolterskluwer.com

Sold and distributed in North, Central and South America by:
Wolters Kluwer Legal & Regulatory U.S.
7201 McKinney Circle
Frederick, MD 21704
United States of America
Email: customer.service@wolterskluwer.com

Sold and distributed in all other countries by:
Air Business Subscriptions
Rockwood House
Haywards Heath
West Sussex
RH16 3DH
United Kingdom
Email: international-customerservice@wolterskluwer.com

Printed on acid-free paper

ISBN 978-94-035-1324-9

e-Book: ISBN 978-94-035-1360-7
web-PDF: ISBN 978-94-035-1391-1

This title is available on www.kluwerlawonline.com

Printed in the United Kingdom.

The Authors

Wojciech Jasiński, PhD works as an Assistant Professor at the Department of Criminal Procedure at the Faculty of Law, Administration and Economics, University of Wrocław, Poland and as a Member of the Research and Analyses Bureau of the Polish Supreme Court. He is also a Member of the Legal Expert Group of Stefan Batory Foundation, one of the leading NGOs, which mission is to build an open and democratic society in Poland.

Wojciech Jasiński received Master in Law degree and Master in Political Science degree from the University of Wrocław, Poland in 2004 and PhD in law from the University of Wrocław, Poland in 2008. In 2011 he was awarded a French Government Scholarship (Université Paris 1 Panthéon-Sorbonne) and in 2015 a Minister of Science and Higher Education Scholarship for Outstanding Young Researchers. Dr Jasiński is also a recipient of 2011, 2013, 2014 Vlamssee Government Scholarship (Belgium). He lectured at the City University of London, UK (2010, 2012), Universidad de Castilla-La Mancha, Toledo, Spain (2013, 2014, 2016) and Universidade de Santiago de Compostela, Spain (2017).

Dr Jasiński participated in national and international research projects financed i.a. by the Polish National Science Center, European Commission and COST. Currently he is leading a project on compensation for wrongful deprivation of liberty financed by the Polish National Science Center.

His research focuses mainly on Polish and comparative criminal procedure, law of evidence and human rights in criminal proceedings.

Karolina Kremens, LL.M., PhD works as an Assistant Professor at the Department of Criminal Procedure at the Faculty of Law, Administration and Economics (University of Wrocław, Poland). She received her Magister in Law degree from the University of Wrocław (Poland) in 2004, Master in Laws (LL.M.) from the University of Ottawa (Canada) in 2007 and PhD in Law from the University of Wrocław (Poland) in 2008. She served as an Assistant Prosecutor at the Regional Prosecutor's Office in Wrocław (2009-2012).

Dr Kremens is the recipient of the 2016-2017 Fulbright Scholarship (University of Connecticut Law School, USA),

2006-2007 Edward Barry McDougall Scholarship (Canada) and 2013 and 2014 Vlamssee Government Scholarship (Belgium). She lectured at the Aberystwyth University, UK (2013), University of Exeter, UK (2014), University of Toledo, Spain (2016) and University of Bologna, Italy (2017, 2018). She also teaches regularly Comparative Criminal Procedure at the University of Ottawa (2014, 2016 and 2018).

She led and participated in many national and international research projects. Currently she finishes the project on the Role of the Prosecutor in Criminal Investigation and leads a project entitled "Reasonable Search - Between Effective Investigation and Rights of Individual" both funded by the Polish National Science Center. She also leads the Polish team in a grant project "Knowledge, Advisory and Capacity Building Information Tool for Criminal Procedural Rights in Judicial Cooperation" (CROSSJUSTICE) funded by the European Commission (Justice Programme 2018).

Her research focuses mainly on comparative and international criminal procedure as well as the role of the prosecutor in criminal proceedings.

Wojciech Jasiński:

- General Introduction § 1, § 4
- PART I – CH 1, 3, 7
- PART II – CH 1§1 and CH 3 and CH 4§2, §3 I-II and CH 5 §1,2 and 4
- PART III – CH 4

Karolina Kremens:

- General Introduction § 2, § 3
- PART I – CH 2, 4, 5, 6
- PART II – CH 1§2, 3, 4, 5 and CH 2 and CH 4§1, §3 III-IX, §4-7 and CH 5 § 3
- PART III – CH 1, 2, 3,

Table of Contents

The Authors 3

List of Abbreviations 15

General Introduction 17

§1. The General Background of Poland 17
I. Geography and Climate 17
II. Population 17
III. Economy 18
IV. Political System and Administrative Structure 18
V. Judicial System 21

§2. Criminal Law, Criminal Justice and Criminal Science 27
I. Definitions of Criminal Law 27
A. Criminal Justice System 27
B. Criminal Law 28
C. Criminal Procedure 28
D. Criminal Offences 28
II. Overview of the Criminal Justice System 29
A. The Police 29
B. The Prosecution Service 36
C. Trial Courts 39
D. Prison System and Probation Service 40
E. The Bar 41
F. Statistical Overview 41

§3. The Historical Background 42
I. Historical Criminal Law 42
II. Interwar Period 43
III. Communist Period (1945–1989) 45
V. Criminal Law after 1989 and the Codes of 1997 47
VI. Latest Reforms 47

§4. Sources of Criminal Law 49
I. Introduction 49
II. International Sources of Criminal Law 51
III. National Sources of Criminal Law 53
A. The Constitution 53

B. Statutes 54
C. Regulations 55
D. Court Decisions 56

Part I. Criminal Law 57

Chapter 1. General Principles 57

§1. Introduction 57

§2. The *Nullum Crimen Sine Lege* Principle 57

§3. The *Nulla Poena Sine Lege* Principle 61

§4. The *Lex Severior Retro Non Agit* Principle 62

§5. The Principle of Individual and Personal Criminal Responsibility 62

§6. The Principle of Guilt 63

§7. The Principle of Humanitarianism 63

Chapter 2. Scope of Application of Criminal Statutes 65

§1. Principles Concerning the Applicability of Criminal Statutes with Respect to Time 65
I. Principle of Non-retroactivity 65
II. Retroactivity of a 'Milder' Statute 65
III. Time of Commitment of an Offence 66

§2. Principles Concerning the Territorial Applicability of Criminal Statutes 67
I. The Territorial Principle 67
II. Extraterritorial Criminal Jurisdiction 68

§3. Principles Concerning the Personal Applicability of Criminal Statutes 70

Chapter 3. General Principles of Criminal Liability 73

§1. The Notion of an Offence: Types of Offences 73

§2. The Material or Physical Element (*Actus Reus*) 74
I. An Act Committed by a Human Being 74
II. The Unlawfulness of an Act 76

III. The Punishability of an Act 77
IV. The Social Harm Presented by an Act 78
V. The Unity and Multiplicity of Acts 78
VI. The Concurrent Application of Provisions of a Criminal Law Statute 79

§3. THE MORAL OR MENTAL ELEMENT (*MENS REA*) 81
I. Guilt 81
II. The Intentional or Unintentional Nature of a Prohibited Act 82
A. The Intentional Nature of a Prohibited Act 82
B. The Unintentional Nature of a Prohibited Act 84

Chapter 4. Justification, Excuse and Other Grounds of Impunity 85

§1. GENERAL PRINCIPLES 85

§2. GROUNDS OF JUSTIFICATION 86
I. Self-Defence 86
A. Notion of Self-Defence 86
B. Requirements 87
C. Exceeding the Limits of Self-Defence 88
II. Necessity 89
A. The Notion of Necessity 89
B. Conditions of Necessity 89
C. Exceeding the Limits of Necessity 90
III. Actions Taken Within One's Authority or in Fulfilment of One's Duties 90
IV. The Consent of the Victim 91
V. Justified Risk 92

§3. GROUNDS OF EXCUSE 92
I. Insanity 92
II. Diminished Sanity 93
III. Insobriety and Intoxication 93
IV. Error of Fact 94
V. Error of Law 95
VI. Error Relating to Grounds of Justification or Excuse 95

Chapter 5. Forms of Criminal Offence 96

§1. GENERAL PRINCIPLES 96

§2. INCHOATE OFFENCES 96
I. Overview 96
II. Preparation 97

III. Attempt 98
IV. Attempting the Impossible 99

§3. Parties to Criminal Offences 100
I. Overview 100
II. Forms of Perpetration 101
A. Direct Perpetration 101
B. Complicity 101
C. Directing the Commission of an Offence 102
III. Instigation and Aiding 103
A. Instigation 103
B. Aiding 103

Chapter 6. Classification and Survey of Criminal Offences 105

§1. General Classification of Criminal Offences 105
I. Statutory Dichotomy of Criminal Offences 105
II. Intentional and Unintentional Offences 106
III. Offences Involving a Commission of an Act or Resulting from a Failure to Act 106
IV. Offences of Result and Offences of No Result 106
V. Offences Subjected to Public or Private Prosecution 107

§2. Survey of Criminal Offences 107
I. Offences of the Criminal Code 108
A. General Introduction 108
B. Offences in the Special Part of the Criminal Code 108
C. Military Offences 133
II. Criminal Offences in Special Criminal Laws 135
A. Drug Offences 135
B. Other Offences in Special Criminal Laws 136

Chapter 7. The Sanctioning System 138

§1. General Overview 138

§2. Penalties 139
I. The Nature and Catalogue of Penalties 139
II. The Penalty of a Fine 140
III. The Penalty of the Restriction of Liberty 141
IV. Penalties Involving Imprisonment 143

§3. Penal Measures 144
I. The Nature and Catalogue of Penal Measures 144
II. Deprivation of Public Rights 145
III. Prohibition from Engaging in a Specified Occupation, Profession or Business 145

IV. Prohibition from Engaging in a Business Relating to Nurturing, Treating or Educating Minors, or from Taking Care of Them 146
V. Prohibition from Associating with Specific Social Groups or Frequenting Specified Kinds of Places, Prohibition from Making Contact with or Approaching Specified Individuals, Prohibition from Leaving a Specified Place of Stay Without the Court's Consent 147
VI. Prohibition from Entering a Mass Event 148
VII. Prohibition from Entering Gambling Facilities and Engaging in Gambling Games 150
VIII. The Obligation to Temporarily Leave Premises Occupied Together with an Aggrieved Person 151
IX. Prohibition from Operating Vehicles 152
X. Pecuniary Payment 153
XI. The Publication of a Sentence 154
XII. Fulfilment of a Penal Measure 155

§4. COMPENSATORY MEASURES 155

§5. FORFEITURE 158

§6. PROBATION MEASURES 159
I. General Overview 159
II. Conditional Discontinuation of Proceedings 160
III. Conditional Suspension of the Enforcement of a Sentence 162
IV. Parole 166

§7. PROTECTIVE MEASURES 168

§8. SENTENCES AND OTHER MEASURES OF PENAL RESPONSE 171
I. The Principles and Directives of Sentencing in Criminal Cases: General Background 171
II. Extraordinary Aggravation of a Penalty 173
III. Extraordinary Mitigation of a Penalty 175
IV. Refraining from the Imposition of a Penalty 176
V. Not Being Subject to a Penalty 177
VI. Crediting a Period of Application of Coercive Measures Towards a Penalty and Other Measures of Penal Response Imposed 177

§9. AGGREGATE PENALTY 178

Part II. Criminal Procedure 181

Chapter 1. Principles, Institutions and Stages 181

§1. THE JUDICIAL ORGANISATION 181
I. Trial Courts 181

A. Jurisdiction of Criminal Courts 181
B. Composition of the Adjudicating Panel 184
II. The Prosecutor 185

§2. THE STAGES OF THE CRIMINAL PROCEEDINGS 186

§3. THE PRINCIPLES GOVERNING CRIMINAL PROCEEDINGS 188
I. General Issues 188
II. The Principle of Material Truth 189
III. The Principle of Impartiality 190
IV. The Presumption of Innocence Principle and *in dubio pro reo* Rule 190
V. The Principle of the Right to Defence 191
VI. The Principle of the Free Evaluation of Evidence 194
VII. The Principle of Conducting Proceedings Ex Officio 195
VIII. The Principle of Legality 196
IX. The Principle of Accusatorial Proceedings 196
X. The Principle of Adversarial and Inquisitorial Proceedings 198
XI. The Principle of Direct Examination of Evidence 199
XII. The Principle of Transparency of Proceedings 200

§4. THE LEGAL POSITION OF THE ACCUSED (SUSPECT) 201
I. The Notion of the Suspect and Accused 201
II. The Rights of the Accused (Suspect) 202
III. The Defence Lawyer 204

§5. THE LEGAL POSITION OF THE AGGRIEVED PARTY 205
I. General Issues 205
II. The Legal Counsel of the Aggrieved Party 207

Chapter 2. Preliminary Proceedings 208

§1. GENERAL REMARKS 208
I. The Notion and Objectives of Preliminary Proceedings 208
II. Forms of Preliminary Proceedings 208
III. Participants Involved in Preliminary Proceedings 209
A. General Issues 209
B. Criminal Justice Authorities Involved in the Conduct of Preliminary Proceedings 210
1. The Prosecutor 210
2. The Police and Other Criminal Justice Bodies 212
3. The Role of the Court 213
C. Parties 214

§2. COMMENCEMENT OF PRELIMINARY PROCEEDINGS 214
I. Information on an Offence and Its Verification 214
II. Decision to Initiate Preliminary Proceedings 216

III. Decision Refusing the Initiation of Preliminary Proceedings 217

§3. Conduct Of Preliminary Proceedings 218
I. General Issues 218
II. Duration 220
III. Charging a Person with an Offence 221
IV. Disclosure and Access to the Dossier 223

§4. The Decision To Prosecute And Other Forms Of Conclusion Of Preliminary Proceedings 224
I. General Remarks 224
II. Filing an Indictment 226
III. Filing an Indictment with a Motion to Convict the Defendant Without a Trial 229
A. General Observations on Negotiated Justice 229
B. Procedure 230
IV. Filing a Stand-Alone Motion to Convict a Defendant Without a Trial 232
V. Filing an Motion for the Conditional Discontinuation of Proceedings 233
VI. Filing a Motion for the Discontinuation of Proceedings and the Imposition of Protective Measures 233
VII. Discontinuation of Preliminary Proceedings 234

Chapter 3. Court Proceedings and Remedies 239

§1. Court Of The First Instance 239
I. Parties and Their Statutory Representatives 239
A. Public Prosecutor 239
B. Subsidiary Prosecutor, Auxiliary Prosecutor, Private Prosecutor and Their Legal Counsels 239
C. The Defendant, Defence Lawyer and Statutory Representative 240
II. Bringing a Case to Court and Preparations for Its Adjudication 241
III. Simplified Forms of Case Processing Before First Instance Courts 243
A. Conviction Without Trial 243
B. Voluntary Assumption of Criminal Liability 246
C. Conditional Discontinuation of Proceedings 247
D. Penal Order Proceedings 247
III. Trial Before the First Instance Court 249
A. Preparation for a Trial 249
B. Public Character of a Trial 250
C. The Adversarial Character of a Trial 251
D. Participation of Parties, Defence Lawyers and Legal Counsels in a Trial 251
E. The Course of a Main Trial 253

F. Shortening of Proceedings at a Main Trial 256
IV. Accelerated Procedure 257
V. Discontinuation of Proceedings and Application of a Protective Measure 259
VI. Private Prosecution 260

§2. Appeals and the Remedies 262
I. Introductory Remarks 262
II. Appeal 263
A. Summary 263
B. Entities Authorised to File an Appeal 263
C. Extent of an Appeal and Pleas Raised 264
D. Procedure for the Submission 266
E. Judicial Examination 267
F. Limits of an Appellate Court's Examination of a Case 269
G. An Appellate Court's Authority to Adjudicate a Case 271
III. Objection 272
IV. Interlocutory Appeal 273
V. Cassation 274
VI. A Motion for the Reopening of Proceedings 276
VII. A Complaint Against the Excessive Length of Criminal Proceedings 278

Chapter 4. Coercive Measures 281

§1. General Overview 281

§2. Arrest and Detention 282

§3. Preventive Measures 287
I. General Grounds for Imposing Preventive Measures 287
II. Detention on Remand 290
III. Financial Surety (Bail) 293
IV. Surety of a Community Organisation 294
V. Surety of a Trustworthy Person 294
VI. Police Supervision 295
VII. Order to Temporarily Leave the Premises 296
VIII. Suspension in the Execution of Official Duties 296
IX. Prohibition to Leave a Country 296

§4. Pursuit of the Defendant and the 'Wanted' Warrant 297

§5. Letter of Safe Passage 298

§6. Procedural Penalties 298

§7. Security Against Property 300

Chapter 5. The Rules of Evidence 302

§1. Principles of Evidence 302

§2. Initiative in and Rules of Evidence-Taking 305

§3. Means of Proof 308
I. Classifications of Evidence 308
II. The Statement of a Defendant 308
III. The testimony of a Witness 309
IV. The Opinion of an Expert Witness 313
V. Documents 315
VI. Search and Seizure 316

§4. Improperly Obtained Evidence 318

Part III. Execution and Extinction of Sanctions 321

Chapter 1. Notion and Sources 321

Chapter 2. Fundamental Principles 325

Chapter 3. The Prison System 326

§1. Organisational Structure 326
I. Prison Administration 326
II. Types of Prisons and Organisational Regimes 326

§2. Penitentiary Treatment 329
I. The Scientific Personalisation System 329
II. Classification of Inmates 329

§3. Penitentiary Regime 331
I. Introduction 331
II. Aspects of Living Conditions 332
A. Healthcare 332
B. Communication 332
C. Work 333
D. Security and Disciplinary Regime 334
E. Leave from Prison 335
F. Other 336

§4. Judicial Control 337

Chapter 4. Extinction of Criminal Liability 339

Table of Contents

§1. Introduction 339

§2. Expiry of a Limitation Period for the Prosecution of an Offence and Enforcement of a Sentence 340
I. Expiry of a Limitation Period for the Prosecution of Offences 340
II. Expiry of a Limitation Period for the Enforcement of a Sentence 342

§3. Abolition and Amnesty 343

§4. Pardon 343

§5. Expungement of a Conviction 346

Index 349

List of Abbreviations

AISA	Act on the Internal Security Agency and the Foreign Intelligence Agency of 24 May 2002
APA	Attorney Act of 26 May 1982
ca.	approximately
CAB	Central Anticorruption Bureau
CABA	Central Anticorruption Bureau Act of 9 June 2006
CC	Criminal Code of 6 June 1997
CEC	Criminal Enforcement Code of 6 June 1997
CCP	Code of Criminal Procedure of 6 June 1997
CSA	Customs Service Act of 27 August 2009
CT	Constitutional Tribunal
EAW	European Arrest Warrant
ECtHR	European Court of Human Rights
e.g.	for example
ECHR	European Convention on Human Rights
EPRs	European Prison Rules of 11 January 2006
EU	European Union
EUR	euro
FA	Forests Act of 28 September 1991
FIOCA	Fiscal Inspection Offices and Chambers Act of 21 June 1996
HA	Hunting Act of 13 October 1995
ICCPR	International Covenant on Civil and Political Rights
Ibid.	Ibidem
i.e.	that is
J.L.	Journal of Laws of the Republic of Poland (*Dziennik Ustaw*)
LLA	Legal Advisors Act of 6 July 1982
No.	number
OEC	Office of Electronic Communications
OSNKW	Official Bulletin of the Supreme Court (*Orzecznictwo Sądu Najwyższego Izba Karna i Wojskowa*)

List of Abbreviations

OTK ZU	Official Bulletin of the Constitutional Tribunal (*Orzecznictwo Trybunału Konstytucyjnego. Zeszyt Urzędowy*)
PA	Police Act of 6 April 1990
para.	paragraph
paras.	paragraphs
PLN	Polish zloty
Prok. i Pr.	Prokuratura i Prawo Journal
PSA	Prosecution Service Act of 20 June 1985
subpara.	subparagraph
SC	Supreme Court
TA	Telecommunications Act of 16 July 2004
v.	versus
Vol.	volume

General Introduction

§1. The General Background of Poland

I. Geography and Climate

1. The Republic of Poland (*Rzeczpospolita Polska*) is a country in Central Europe. It is bordered by Germany to the west, the Czech Republic and Slovakia to the south, Ukraine and Belarus to the east, Lithuania and Russia (Kaliningrad Oblast) to the north. The length of the national borders is 3,511 km, 440 km of which is its Baltic Sea border in the north.

2. The territory of the Republic of Poland is 322 575 km^2. Its land area (including inland waters) covers 311,888 km^2, its internal waters are 2,005 km^2 and its territorial sea is 8,682 km^2. The total administrative area of the country is 312,679 km^2. Poland is the ninth biggest European country.

3. The landscape of Poland is dominated by lowlands, which cover over 75% of state territory. The average elevation above sea level is only 173 m. The south of Poland is covered by mountains (the Sudeten and Carpathian ranges). The highest point is mountain *Rysy* – 2,499 m above sea level. Due to glacial action the north of Poland is rich in lakes. The greatest number of lakes is located in the northeastern part of the territory, and is known as the Masurian Lake District.

4. Poland's climate is moderate. Due to its location in Central Europe, diverse air masses – maritime, arctic and subtropical – collide over the territory. According to the Koeppen-Geiger classification, there are two climate zones in Poland: Cfb Climate (in the western part of the country) and Dfb Climate (in the east). Average temperatures (2013), excluding mountain regions, range from 7.1 °C (in the north-east) to 9.4°C (in the south-west). Annual precipitation is about 600 mm.

II. Population

5. The population of Poland is estimated at 38,479,000 inhabitants (31 December 2014). Poland is the ninth most populous country in Europe (sixth in the EU). The population density is 123 persons per km^2.

6. 51.6% of the population are women. Over 60% of the population lives in urban areas, while less than 40% live in rural areas. The most populous cities are: Warsaw (1,724,400), Kraków (759,000) Łódź (711,300), Wrocław (632,100) and Poznań (548,000).

7. About 6,943,000 people are of pre-working age, 24,230,000 are of working age and 7,305,000 are of post-working age.

8. Poland has a very homogeneous population. Over 95% are Polish and speak Polish. Almost 90% of the population declare themselves to be Roman Catholic. The biggest national minorities are German, Ukrainian and Belarusian.

III. Economy

9. According to the World Bank, the Gross Domestic Product (GDP) of Poland is estimated at about USD 548 billion (USD 14 422.8 per capita). The annual growth in GDP amounted to 3.4% in 2014, 1.7% in 2013 and 1.8% in 2012. The agriculture sector's share of GDP is approximately 3.7%, industry is 32% and services have a 64.3% share (2014). Poland has, when we consider GDP, the largest economy in Central Europe and the eighth biggest in the EU (2014).

10. Poland do not belong the Eurozone. The currency in Poland is the złoty. The złoty can be divided into 100 groszy. Exchange rate of 1 euro is approximately 4.3 złoty.

11. The Central Statistical Office of Poland estimates that in 2014 there were 17,428,000 economically active people. About 15,862,000 were employed and 1,567,000 were unemployed. The annual average unemployment rate in 2014 was 9%, which was below the EU average. This represented a decrease in comparison to the 2013 figure of 10.3%. Approximately 57.9% of employed persons work in the service sector, 30.3% in industry, and 11.6% in agriculture.

12. Poland's leading trade partner, both in terms of exports (26%) and imports (22%), is Germany. The biggest foreign investors in Poland are Germany, the Netherlands and France.

IV. Political System and Administrative Structure

13. Article 2 of the Constitution stipulates that the Republic of Poland is a democratic state ruled by law and which implements the principles of social justice. Poland's political system is based on the division and balancing of powers exercised by the executive, legislature and judiciary. Legislative power is held by the Parliament comprising of the *Sejm* and the *Senat*, executive power is shared by the President of the Republic and the Council of Ministers, while judicial power is exercised by courts and tribunals (Article 10 of the Constitution).

14. The *Sejm* comprises 460 deputies. Election to the *Sejm* is universal, equal, direct and proportional, and conducted by way of secret ballot. The *Senat* comprises 100 senators. They are elected in a universal and direct election, conducted by way of secret ballot. Both the *Sejm* and the *Senat* are elected for a four-year term.

15. Every Polish citizen who has the right to vote and has attained the age of 21 on or before election day may be elected as a *Sejm* deputy. Every Polish citizen who has the right to vote and has attained the age of 30 on or before election day may be elected as a Senator. A person loses his or her right to be elected if he or she has received a final prison sentence for an intentional offence prosecuted by public accusation. Candidates for the role of deputy and senator can be nominated by political parties and voters. The mandate of a deputy or senator is free: elected persons are not bound by any instructions from voters. Deputies have parliamentary immunity. The *Sejm* and the *Senat* convene in sessions.

16. The President of Poland is the supreme representative of the Republic of Poland and the guarantor of the continuity of State authority. The president ensures observance of the Constitution, safeguards the sovereignty and security of the state and the inviolability and integrity of its territory (Article 126 paragraphs 1 and 2 of the Constitution).

17. The President of the Republic is elected in a universal, equal and direct election conducted by way of secret ballot. The president serves for five years and may be re-elected only once. In order to become president, a candidate must receive more than the half of validly cast votes. If in the first round of the presidential election none of the candidates obtains the above majority, the two highest-ranking candidates take part in the second round. Every Polish citizen who has a full electoral franchise in the Sejm elections and has attained the age of 35 on or before election day may be elected president. A presidential candidate maybe nominated by at least 100,000 citizens who have voting rights in Sejm elections.

18. In the Polish constitutional system, the powers of the president are limited. The Council of Ministers plays the key role among the executive bodies. The president, however, has a number of powers, including the right to veto laws (statutes) enacted by the Sejm and the Senate. In order to override a presidential veto, the Sejm must re-enact a vetoed law by a three-fifths majority of votes, in the presence of at least the half of the statutory number of deputies.

19. The Council of Ministers conducts the internal affairs and foreign policy of the Republic of Poland, and also manages government administration. The powers granted to the Council of Ministers include: ensuring the implementation of laws, issuing acts of secondary legislation, coordinating and supervising the work of State administration bodies, protecting the interests of the State Treasury, adopting a draft state budget and implementing the budget, ensuring the external and internal security of the state, and ensuring public order, exercising general leadership in relations with other States and international organisations, concluding international agreements that require ratification as well as accepting and renouncing other international agreements, exercising general leadership in the area of national defence.

20. The Council of Ministers consists of the Chairperson of the Council of Ministers (prime minister) and ministers. One or several deputy chairpersons (deputy prime ministers) may be appointed to the Council of Ministers. Ministers lead relevant departments of government administration (e.g., justice, internal affairs, foreign affairs) or perform tasks delegated by the prime minister.

21. The President of the Republic designates the prime minister, who then proposes the composition of the Council of Ministers. Then the president appoints the prime minister together with other members of the Council of Ministers, who ask the Sejm for a vote of confidence. The Sejm passes the vote of confidence by an absolute majority of votes, in the presence of at least the half of the statutory number of deputies.

22. Province governors (*wojewodowie*) are representatives of the Council of Ministers in provinces (*województwa*) – the largest administrative regions of the country.

23. Pursuant to Article 11 of the Constitution, the Republic of Poland ensures the *freedom of creation and operation of political parties*. However, the law prohibits the functioning of political parties and other organisations whose programmes are based upon totalitarian methods and operational practices of nazism, fascism and communism, as well as those whose programmes or activities sanction racial or national hatred, the use of violence for the purpose of obtaining power or to influence state policy, or maintain secrecy in their structures or their membership. Political parties operate according to the principles of voluntary participation and the equality of Polish citizens, and their purpose is to democratically influence the formulation of state policies. The financing of political parties must be open to public inspection.

24. Over the last decade, the Polish political scene has been dominated by two parties. The first is the Civic Platform (*Platforma Obywatelska*), a liberal and conservative centrist movement, and the other is the conservative Law and Justice (*Prawo i Sprawiedliwość*). A contemporary feature of the Polish political scene is the absence of a strong social democratic party. In the 2015 elections to the Sejm and the Senate, for the first time in the history of post-Communist Poland (post 1989), a single party (Law and Justice) won the majority of seats in both parliamentary chambers. Before 2015, parliamentary majorities were formed by a coalition of at least two political groupings. In the parliamentary terms of 2007–2011 and 2011–2015, Poland was ruled by a coalition of the Civic Platform and the Polish People's Party (*Polskie Stronnictwo Ludowe*).

25. Poland is a unitary country. There is a three-tier system of administrative division in Poland. The country is divided into *16 provinces* (sometimes referred to as voivodships, Polish: *województwa*), *380 counties* (or poviats, Polish: *powiaty*) and *ca. 2,500 communes* (or municipalities, Polish: *gminy*). Provinces, counties and communes are also the units of local government. Both local government and state bodies perform public tasks (both their own and those delegated to them). Units of local government have legal personality. The independence of these units is safeguarded by the courts. Local government has two sources of financing: its own revenue (e.g., from local taxes and levies) and an allocated portion of public revenue (e.g., a percentage of national personal and corporate income tax), the value of which should be sufficient to cover local government's expenditures associated with the tasks it performs.

26. In Poland, the public has relatively limited impact on the development state policies on a day-to-day basis. However, Article 125 of the Constitution of the Republic of Poland states that a *national referendum* may be held in respect of matters of particular importance to the state. Such a referendum may be ordered by the Sejm, in a resolution taken by an absolute majority of votes, in the presence of at least half of the statutory number of deputies, or by the president with the consent of the Senate expressed by an absolute majority of votes, in the presence of at least half of the statutory number of senators. The result of a national referendum is binding and conclusive if more than half of the eligible voters take part in it. This requirement does not apply to a referendum that approves an amendment to the Constitution, separately regulated in Article 235 paragraph 6 of the Constitution. Only a few national referenda have been held in Poland since 1989. The only one that produced a binding result (apart from the constitutional referendum of 1997) took place in 2003 and concerned Poland's accession to the EU. It was supported by nearly 77.5% of the participating voters.

27. In addition to a national referendum, a *local referendum* may be held. A local referendum may be conducted among residents of a unit of local government and address matters that are crucial to a local community. This type of referendum can be initiated by the legislative body of a given unit of local government (commune council, district council, province assembly) or upon the motion of at least 10% of the eligible voters in a commune or a district, or 5% of the eligible voters in a province.

V. Judicial System

28. Pursuant to Article 173 of the Constitution of the Republic of Poland, **courts and tribunals** are a separate and independent branch of power. This means that the principle of the division of powers has been particularly emphasised in the Constitution in respect of the judiciary. This emphasis was made by the Constitutional Tribunal (CT) itself, which ruled that *since judicial powers may be exercised only by courts of law, the remaining branches may not interfere with the judiciary or participate in the exercise of judicial powers (..). In the case of the judiciary, any exceptions from the principle of the division and balance of powers (..), which are otherwise acceptable in relations between the other powers, are out of the question.*

No other branch may interfere in the matters of the structure, composition or operations of the judiciary unless such interference is allowed in exceptional cases described in the Constitution. In the context of the judiciary, the principle of division and balance of powers should be interpreted in a way which underscores that the special position of the courts and tribunals is based on the principle of judicial independence and jurisdictional monopoly for the exercise of judicial powers, understood as the authority to ultimately determine rights and duties of individuals or legal persons.[1] Obviously this does not mean that the division of powers is absolute. There are functional ties between the executive and the judiciary, which manifest themselves above all in the president's authority to appoint judges and in the power of the Minister of Justice to have administrative supervision over the operations of the judicial system.

29. The judicial system in Poland comprises *common courts, military courts, administrative courts and the Supreme Court.* An extraordinary court (*sąd wyjątkowy*) may be established only in a time of war.

30. The common court system comprises more than *300 district courts* (*sądy rejonowe*), *45 regional courts* (*sądy okręgowe*) and *11 courts of appeal* (*sądy apelacyjne*). Common courts have jurisdiction in all matters that are not covered by the jurisdiction of administrative courts, military courts or the Supreme Court. A district court is established for one or more communes. In some specific situations, several district courts can be created for a single commune. District courts have different divisions. Each has a criminal and civil division. If a need arises, additional divisions may be created: a family and juvenile division, labour and employment division, social insurance division (or an employment and social insurance division), commercial division, land and charges registry division and other divisions. A regional court is created for the area of jurisdiction of at least two district courts. A civil and criminal division is always established within the structure of a regional court. Additional divisions may also be created: labour and employment division, social insurance division (or a labour and employment and social insurance division), commercial division, telecommunication data access division (it reviews relevant motions filed by the police and special services), and other divisions. The Regional Court of Warsaw also has the following divisions: the division for competition cases, energy sector, telecommunications and rail transport regulatory matters (the competition and consumer protection court), the division for the registration and protection of community trademarks and industrial designs (the Community trademarks and industrial designs court). A Court of Appeal is created for the area of jurisdiction of the judicial circuits of at least two regional courts. It comprises a civil, criminal and a labour and employment and social insurance division. Other divisions may be established too.

1. Judgment of the CT of 15 Jan. 2009 (Case No. 45/07, OTK-A 2009, Vol. 1, item 3).

31. Military courts established within the Armed Forces of the Republic of Poland have jurisdiction in criminal cases to the extent stipulated in statutory law and adjudicate other cases covered by their jurisdiction pursuant to separate statutes. There are two types of military courts: regional military courts (*wojskowe sa̧dy okręgowe* – two in the country) and garrison military courts (*wojskowe sądy garnizonowe* – seven nationwide).

32. Administrative courts, above all, review the functioning of public administration (which in principle, means reviewing the legality of its activities). Administrative judicial review includes, among other things, adjudication on the statutory compliance of resolutions adopted by local government bodies and the legality of normative acts issued by local branches of government administration. Administrative courts are also tasked with resolving jurisdictional disputes between bodies of units of local government, local government review boards (*samorządowe kolegia odwoławcze*) and also disputes between such bodies and bodies of government administration. The system of administrative courts comprises the Supreme Administrative Court and provincial administrative courts. As a rule, provincial administrative courts hear administrative cases in first instance. The Supreme Administrative Court oversees the adjudication of the provincial administrative courts in the manner determined by statutory law. It is particularly responsible for taking decisions in respect of appellate measures submitted against the rulings of provincial administrative courts, adopting explanatory resolutions on points of law and hearing other matters covered by its jurisdiction under separate laws.

33. The Supreme Court is the judicial body obliged to supervise the legality and uniformity of the jurisprudence of common and military courts. It also hears appeals in cassation and resolves other appellate measures, as well as adopting resolutions on the points of law. The Supreme Court also performs a key role in the election process: it resolves electoral protests and confirms the validity of elections to the Sejm and the Senate as well as presidential elections and national and constitutional referenda. Moreover, the Supreme Court presents opinions on drafts of statutes and other normative acts that provide the basis for the adjudication and functioning of courts, and on other laws, if it deems it purposeful to do so. The Supreme Court is divided into four chambers: 1. Civil; 2. Criminal; 3. Labour and Employment, Social Insurance and Public Matters, and 4. Military Chamber.

34. In the exercise of their office, *judges* are independent and subject only to the Constitution and statutes. They may not belong to a political party, a trade union or perform public activities incompatible with the principles of the independence of the courts and judges. Judges are appointed by the President of the Republic, upon the motion of the National Council of the Judiciary of Poland, for a life tenure. As a rule, judges are not removable. A judge may be recalled from office, suspended or transferred to another location or position against his or her will only by virtue of a court ruling and only in the cases prescribed in a statute. Judges in Poland are protected by immunity. This means that a judge cannot be held criminally responsible or deprived of liberty without the consent of the court designated in a statute. A judge cannot be detained or arrested, except when he or she is apprehended in the act of committing a crime and provided that the detention is required to ensure the proper conduct of the proceedings. The president of a local court must immediately be notified of the detention of a judge; the former may order the immediate release of the detained judge.

35. Apart from judges, *associate judges* (*asesorzy*) also work at courts. Associate judges have full judicial powers, but may not apply detention on remand in preliminary proceedings or conduct insolvency and restructuring proceedings. They are appointed for five-year terms. The office of an associate judge is designed to constitute a trial period during which their ability to work as a judge is reviewed and assessed.

36. Judges and associate judges are tasked with the exercise of the judicial function. The judicial function, traditionally termed 'the administration of justice', is defined by both the scholarship and jurisprudence of the Constitutional Tribunal as the *activity of the state that involves adjudication, or the binding resolution of disputes about the law, in which at least one party is an individual or a similar entity.*[2] Non-judicial functions, or 'legal protection functions', may also be performed by court referendaries (*referendarze sądowi*). Court referendaries are employed at district courts and regional courts. Court referendaries are entrusted with the performance of certain procedural acts as a means to streamline court proceedings and reduce judges' workload by removing time-consuming but legally uncomplicated administrative and organisational duties that fall outside the judicial function within the meaning of Article 175 of the Constitution of the Republic of Poland.

37. In Poland, judicial function is also performed by non-professionals. In district and regional courts and in regional military courts, *lay judges* (*ławnicy*) take part in adjudication. This happens in the categories of cases described by procedural laws (the Code of Civil Procedure, the Code of Criminal Procedure, etc.). Lay judges adjudicate together with professional judges. There is no jury in the Polish legal system. In order to become a lay judge in a common court, a person must satisfy the following requirements:

a) they must have Polish citizenship and fully exercise civil and citizen's rights;
b) they must be of impeccable character;
c) they must have attained the age of 30;
d) they must be employed, carry out a business activity or live within the locality of the relevant court for at least one year;
e) they must be younger than 70;
f) they must be physically capable of performing the duties of a lay judge;
g) they must have at least secondary education.

The following persons may not serve as lay judges:

---

2. Judgment of the CT of 13 Mar. 2012 (Case No. 39/10, OTK-A 2012, Vol. 3, item 26) and the references (incl. case law) cited there.

a) employees of common courts or other courts and the prosecution service;
b) members of bodies that issue decisions which may be challenged in court proceedings;
c) police officers and other persons who take positions related to the prosecution of criminal offences and petty offences;
d) attorneys and trainee attorneys;
e) legal advisors and trainee legal advisors;
f) clergymen;
g) military personnel on active duty;
h) prison service officers;
i) commune, county and province councillors.

Lay judges of regional and district courts are elected in a secret ballot by commune councils from the areas covered by the courts' jurisdiction. The term of lay judges of regional and district courts is four calendar years following the year of their election.

38. There are two special judicial bodies in the Polish legal system: *the Constitutional Tribunal* (*Trybunał Konstytucyjny*) and *the Tribunal of State* (*Trybunał Stanu*).

39. The Constitutional Tribunal's primary function is adjudication on the conformity of statutes and international agreements to the Constitution, the conformity of statutes to international agreements whose ratification require prior consent granted by a statute and the conformity of legal enactments issued by central state bodies with the Constitution, ratified international agreements and statutes. A review of the conformity of normative acts to higher-ranking acts can be initiated in three ways. First, authorised entities (e.g., the President of the Republic, the Speaker of the Sejm, the Speaker of the Senate, the prime minister, fifty deputies, thirty senators, the President of the Supreme Court, the President of Supreme Administrative Court, the Prosecutor General, the President of the Supreme Audit Office, the Commissioner for Human Rights) can request a review of a given normative act, which may be either preventive and already occur at the legislative stage (this power may be exercised only by the president), or reactive ('an *ex-post* review'), that is requested after a legal instrument is enacted. Second, every court may present a question of law to the Constitutional Tribunal, requesting the review of a normative act's conformity with the Constitution, ratified international agreements or a statute, provided that the resolution of a case pending before a court depends on the answer to the legal question. Third, a constitutional complaint can be submitted by anyone (e.g., a natural or legal person) whose constitutional rights or freedoms have been violated. A complaint may include a request for the constitutional review of a statute or another normative act on the basis of which a court or public administration body has made a final resolution on a complainant's rights or freedoms, or a complainant's duties defined in the Constitution.

40. The Constitutional Tribunal is also responsible for reviewing the constitutionality of the objectives or operations of political parties (see *supra* paragraph 23).

The Constitutional Tribunal also resolves jurisdictional disputes between central constitutional bodies of the state and is authorised to determine that there is an impediment to the president's ability to perform his or her duties.

41. The Constitutional Tribunal is composed of fifteen judges selected by the Sejm for nine-year separate terms of office from among persons with exceptional knowledge of the law. Judges of the Constitutional Tribunal may not be re-elected. The President and Vice-president of the Constitutional Tribunal are appointed by the President of the Republic from among candidates presented by the General Assembly of Judges of the Constitutional Tribunal. In the exercise of their office, judges of the Constitutional Tribunal are independent and subject only to the Constitution.

42. Rulings of the Constitutional Tribunal are universally applicable and final. They are made by a majority of votes. Rulings are effective as from the date of notification, however the Constitutional Tribunal may designate another time frame after the expiry of which a normative act loses its binding force. Such a time frame may not exceed 18 months (for statutes) or 12 months (for other normative acts). A ruling of the Constitutional Tribunal declaring that a normative act, on which a final court ruling, administrative decision or another resolution was based, is contrary to the Constitution, a ratified international agreement or statute, serves as grounds for the reopening of proceedings, or the revocation of a decision or resolution, on the terms and in the mode laid down in the laws governing the proceedings in question.

43. The Tribunal of State (*Trybunał Stanu*) is a special judicial body whose primary role is to adjudicate in matters of constitutional responsibility, and – to a certain extent – also on those of criminal responsibility (*infra* paragraph 478) of the highest state officials. Pursuant to Article 198 paragraph 1 of the Constitution of the Republic of Poland, the following persons will be held constitutionally accountable before the Tribunal of State for violations of the Constitution or of a statute committed in connection with their office or within the scope of their functions: the President of the Republic, the prime minister and members of the Council of Ministers, the President of the National Bank of Poland, the President of the Supreme Audit Office, members of the National Broadcasting Council, persons to whom the prime minister has granted powers of management over a ministry and the Commander-in-Chief of the Armed Forces. Also, Sejm deputies and senators who violate the statutory prohibition against engaging in a business that involves receiving a benefit from the property of the state or local government or acquiring such property are held constitutionally accountable before the Tribunal of State.

44. The Tribunal of State is composed of the chairperson, two deputy chairpersons and sixteen members – selected by the Sejm – who are not deputies or senators, for the duration of the parliamentary term. Deputy chairpersons and at least half of the members of the Tribunal of State should hold qualifications required for holding judicial office. The Tribunal of State is chaired by the President of the Supreme Court. In exercising their role as judges of the Tribunal of State, the members of the Tribunal of State are independent and subject only to the Constitution and statutes.

45. The National Council of the Judiciary of Poland (*Krajowa Rada Sa ̨downictwa*) is an important body that safeguards the independence of courts and judges. The Council is composed of the President of the Supreme Court, the Minister of Justice, the President of the Supreme Administrative Court, an appointee of the President of the Republic, fifteen members selected from among the judges of the Supreme Court, common courts, administrative courts and military courts and four members selected by the Sejm from among the deputies as well as two members selected by the Senate from among the senators. The term of office of the elected members of the National Council of the Judiciary of Poland is four years.

46. The powers of the National Council of the Judiciary of Poland include in particular:

a) reviewing and assessing candidates for judicial offices,
b) presenting applications for judges' appointments to the President of Poland,
c) adopting and enforcing the observance of a code of judicial ethics,
d) issuing position statements in matters concerning the judiciary and judges,
e) presenting opinions and proposals with regard to the drafts of normative acts that concern the judiciary and judges,
f) adopting resolutions requesting the Constitutional Tribunal to review the constitutionality of those parts of normative acts that concern the independence of courts and judges,
g) appointing ethics commissioners (*rzecznicy dyscyplinarni*) for judges of common courts and military courts,
h) expressing opinions on the appointment and recall of presidents or deputy presidents of common courts and military courts.

§2. Criminal Law, Criminal Justice and Criminal Science

I. Definitions of Criminal Law

A. Criminal Justice System

47. Polish law uses the term 'criminal justice system' (*wymiar sprawiedliwości w sprawach karnych*). However, this term is defined not by the thematic areas the system deals with, but rather by bodies that perform, albeit not exclusively, the function of criminal justice. At this point reference should be made to Article 175 paragraph 1 of the Constitution. This provision stipulates that the judicial function in the Republic of Poland is performed by the Supreme Court, the common courts, administrative courts and military courts. Also, the public prosecution service and – sometimes – the police are, quite intuitively, included into the category of criminal justice system bodies although this inclusion is somewhat incorrect, given the strict constitutional definition of the term. Irrespective of the above, under Polish law the notion of the criminal justice system may extend equally to matters of substantive criminal law, and also the law of criminal procedure and executive criminal law.

B. *Criminal Law*

48. The Polish legal system follows many other continental law systems and does not really use the notion of 'criminal law' as an umbrella term referring to both substantive and procedural criminal law. It is a concept that reflects the perception of criminal law as a certain whole, which discusses types of criminal acts, penalties for such acts and rules governing authorities' actions that aim at identifying and judging perpetrators of criminal acts. As a rule, however, these notions are used separately, and the branches of law regulating these matters are treated as independent thematic areas that are clearly strictly linked to each other but are not subordinated or dependent. This is also manifested in the structure of the law (separate codes) and that of legal education in Poland: substantive and procedural criminal law are taught as different subjects at universities. As a matter of custom, criminal lawyers in Poland specialise in either field (but not in both at the same time), and this also affects the structure of Polish law faculties, which traditionally comprise a department of criminal law (*katedra prawa karnego*) and a department of criminal procedure (*katedra postępowania karnego*).

49. Criminal law (*prawo karne*), sometimes also referred to as the substantive criminal law (*prawo karne materialne*), is defined as the law describing the acts that constitute criminal offences and principles of criminal responsibility for the commission of such offences, and also types of penalties and penal and protective measures, as well as the rules governing the imposition of such penalties and measures. The basic source of criminal law is the Criminal Code of 6 June 1997 (J.L. 1997, No. 88, item 553, as amended), which entered into force on 1 September 1998.

C. *Criminal Procedure*

50. The law of criminal procedure (*prawo karne procesowe*), also known as 'criminal procedure rules', includes all legal norms regulating the proceedings set up to enforce the substantive criminal law. It determines the rights and duties of criminal justice bodies, parties and other participants in criminal proceedings, and also the course of activities that aim at detecting an offence and its perpetrator, resolving the issue of a perpetrator's responsibility for the offence and enforcing a penalty. The basic source of rules of criminal procedure is the Code of Criminal Procedure of 6 June 1997 (CCP) (J.L. 1997, No. 89, item 555, as amended), which entered into force on 1 September 1998.

D. *Criminal Offences*

51. The notion of *criminal offence* (*przestępstwo*) is used in Polish criminal law. There is no legal (statutory) definition of a criminal offence, which means that the Parliament has decided against explicitly defining this term in the provisions of law. However, a definition of a criminal offence can be interpreted from the language of

Article 1 §§ 1–3 CC, the provision that determines who assumes criminal responsibility. According to this definition, *a criminal offence is an act committed by a human being, which is prohibited under a statute and carries the penalty as a felony or a misdemeanour, is illegal, culpable and presents a higher than negligible degree of social harm.* Notably, not every prohibited act (*czyn zabroniony*) is an offence – it may, for example, turn out not to be culpable. This rule is expressed by the Parliament i.e. in the case of insanity (*niepoczytalność*), understood as the absence of culpability on the part of a perpetrator: Article 31 § 1 CC states that in such a case 'no criminal offence shall be committed'.

52. On the contrary, Polish law does not differentiate between the terms 'an offence' and 'a crime': it may be assumed that these notions can be used interchangeably.

53. The main criterion that allows for the classification of *criminal offences* (*przestępstw*) in Poland is the *gravity of an offence* (*waga przestępstwa*). According to Article 7 CC, offences in Polish criminal law can be divided to *felonies* (*zbrodnie*) and *misdemeanours* (*występki*). A *felony* can be defined as a prohibited act punishable by a penalty of not less than three years of imprisonment (Article 7 § 2 CC). A *misdemeanour* is a prohibited act punishable by a fine of above 30 daily rates or above 5 000 PLN, the restriction of liberty of not less than one month and a penalty of imprisonment not less than one month (Article 7 § 3 CCP).

54. Apart from criminal offences, the law has created the category of *petty offences* (*wykroczenia*), or acts that are subject to a penalty no harsher than that imposable for misdemeanours. It must be remembered, however, that the Criminal Code exclusively describes felonies and misdemeanours while petty offences are regulated in the Petty Offences Code (*Kodeks wykroczeń*) of 20 May 1971 (consolidated text in J.L. 2015, item 1094). Also, the procedure used for the determination of criminal responsibility of petty offenders is governed by a separate set of legal rules, namely the Petty Offences Procedure Code of 24 August 2001 (consolidated text, J.L. 2008 No. 133, item 848, as amended).

II. Overview of the Criminal Justice System

A. The Police

55. The police (*Policja*) is one of the most important state institutions responsible for detecting criminal offences, petty offences and prosecuting their perpetrators. The legal status of the police is regulated in the Police Act (PA) of 6 April 1990 (consolidated text, J.L. 2015, item 355). Pursuant to the Act, the police is a uniformed and armed formation whose purpose is to serve society, protect the safety of the public and maintain public safety and order. The police is a body of the executive branch.

56. The Polish police is a relatively homogeneous and hierarchical organisation. The police comprises three branches: criminal (investigative), prevention (patrol) and auxiliary (organisational, logistical and technical support) (Article 4 paragraph 1 PA). The operational structure of the police also includes specialised subdivisions: crowd control units, emergency tactical response units, court security police, the National Police University, training centres and police academies and research institutes (Article 4 paragraphs 2–4 PA). The police is headed by the Chief Commissioner of the Police (*Komendant Główny Policji* – Article 5 paragraph 2 PA).

57. Article 1 paragraph 2 PA describes the tasks of the police, which include:

- the protection of human life, health and property against unlawful attacks on those interests;
- the protection of public safety and order, and in particular keeping the peace at public places and in on public transport, and on highways and waterways that are accessible to the public;
- the initiation and organisation of actions with the purpose of preventing the commission of criminal offences and petty offences and crime-related phenomena and working in partnership in these actions with state and local government bodies and social organisations;
- the detection of criminal and petty offences and the prosecution of their perpetrators;
- the supervision of specialised armed formations, exercised within the scope of separate provisions of law;
- the review of compliance with procedural and administrative rules related to public activities or applicable in public places;
- collaboration with police forces of other countries and international organisations of police forces, as well as with the bodies and institutions of the European Union, in accordance with international treaties or agreements and separate provisions of law;
- the collection, processing and transfer of criminal intelligence;
- the maintenance of databases with information on recorded fingerprints, unidentified fingerprints taken from crime scenes and results of DNA tests, gathered by authorised bodies.

58. The responsibilities of the police include the following types of activities, undertaken in order to identify, prevent and detect criminal offences and petty offences: operational and intelligence-gathering activities, investigative activities, and administrative and organisational activities (Article 14 paragraph 1 PA). The first type, *operational and intelligence-gathering activities*, are extrajudicial actions that are performed e.g. in order to verify a report of the commission of an offence or obtain information about a new offence. In conducting these activities, the police has the statutory authority to materially interfere in civil rights and freedoms in the following ways:

- by performing identity checks of persons;

- by detaining persons in the manner described in the Code of Criminal Procedure and other laws;
- by detaining persons deprived of liberty (inmates) who, on the of permission of relevant authorities, have left a detention (remand) centre or a prison but have not returned within the designated date;
- by detaining persons who clearly pose a threat to the health and life of other people, or a threat to property;
- by taking fingerprints or oral mucosa swabs from persons;
- by taking fingerprints or biological samples from unidentified human corpses;
- by searching persons and premises in the manner described in the Code of Criminal Procedure and other laws;
- by video monitoring and recording images from the premises of detention centres, sobering stations, police remand homes for children, transition facilities or temporary transition facilities;
- by performing body searches or searches of baggage at seaports, riverports and airports and train and bus stations, and on means of land, air and water transport, if there is a reasonable suspicion that a prohibited act has been committed.
- by video monitoring and recording images of events that occur in public places, and in the case of operational and intelligence-gathering actions, and administrative and organisational actions conducted under a statute, and also sound that accompanies these events;
- by demanding necessary assistance from state authorities, bodies of central and local government administration, and business organisations that provide public utility services; the above-mentioned authorities, bodies and organisations are obliged to provide such necessary assistance, within the scope of their operations and to the extent required by law;
- by requesting necessary assistance from other business organisations and social organisations, and – in case of an emergency – also by requesting any member of the public to provide assistance on an ad hoc basis, to the extent required by law;
- by using the means of physical coercion (e.g., chemical incapacitating agents, police batons, service dogs or horses);
- by using firearms in order to repel a direct attack on the life or health of police officers;
- by applying covert investigative methods (officially termed *kontrola operacyjna,* literally 'operational control') such as the secret inspection of correspondence and parcels or the wiretapping of telephone conversations;
- by making covert purchases, sales or acquisitions of items (jointly referred to as 'controlled purchases');
- by conducting what is known as the 'covert supervision of parcels', which may involve e.g. the covert supervision of the manufacturing, transfer and storage of, or the dealing in objects of criminal offences;
- by secretly obtaining, collecting, processing and using data, including personal data.

59. Another type of police activity is *investigative action,* namely procedural act undertaken during the course of criminal proceedings, either on the police's own initiative or ordered by a public prosecutor or the court. However, court-ordered investigative actions appear very rarely in the Polish criminal process. Finally, *administrative and organisational action* is related to police activities performed, for example, as part of the proceedings for issuing on-the-spot fines.

60. A specialised department within the police, the *Central Bureau of Investigation* (CBI, Polish: *Centralne Biuro Śledcze*), was created in 2000 following the merger of the police Bureau for Counteracting Organised Crime and the National Police Headquarters' Bureau for Drug Crime. The CBI is designed to operate as the Polish equivalent of the FBI. The CBI was established as an investigative service tasked with identifying, preventing and tackling organised crime in Poland (Article 5a paragraph 1 PA).

61. Pursuant to the Polish rules of criminal procedure, not only the police, but also other state bodies, are authorised to conduct preliminary proceedings and – in rare cases – appear as public prosecutors in criminal cases (see *infra*, paragraphs 657–662). The following are the examples of bodies that perform investigative functions in the Polish criminal process:

(1) the Border Guard;
(2) the Internal Security Agency;
(3) the Central Anticorruption Bureau (CAB);
(4) fiscal inspection offices;
(5) fiscal inspection inspectors;
(6) the Customs Service;
(7) the Military Police;
(8) the Trade Inspection Authority;
(9) the State Sanitary Inspection Authority;
(10) the President of the Office of Electronic Communications (OEC);
(11) the Forestry Guard;
(12) the State Hunting Guard.

62. *The Border Guard* (*Straż Graniczna*) is a uniformed and armed organisation tasked with protecting Poland's land and sea borders and controlling border traffic. It operates under the Border Guard Act of 12 October 1990 (consolidated text, J.L. 2014, item 1402, as amended). The responsibilities of the Border Guard related to the conducting of criminal proceedings include identifying, preventing and detecting criminal and petty offences covered by the Border Guard's jurisdiction and the prosecution of perpetrators of such offences. The Border Guard's jurisdiction extends to the criminal offences and petty offences that relate to the legality of the crossing of Polish borders, are connected with the crossing of Polish borders or the transborder movement of goods and products that are subject to excise duty or must bear excise duty marks, as well as items defined in the laws on weapons and ammunition, and also those defined in the laws on explosives, in the laws on the protection of cultural resources, on national archives, on counteracting drug abuse and on the registration of the population and personal identity documents.

63. Another criminal justice authority that may conduct preliminary proceedings is the *Internal Security Agency* (*Agencja Bezpieczeństwa Wewnętrznego*), which operates under the Act on the Internal Security Agency and the Foreign Intelligence Agency (AISA) of 24 May 2002 (consolidated text, J.L. 2015, item 1929, as amended). The Internal Security Agency is responsible for matters concerning the protection of the internal security of Poland and its constitutional system (Article 1 AISA). The tasks of the ISA include the identification, prevention and detection of the following types of offences: a) espionage, terrorism, the unlawful disclosure or use of classified information and other offences against state security; b) offences against the economic foundations of the state; c) corruption among public officials, whenever such corruption may be detrimental to state security; d) offences related to the production of and trade in goods, technologies and services of strategic importance for Poland's security; e) the illegal manufacture and possession of, and international trade in weapons, ammunition and explosives, weapons of mass destruction, and narcotic drugs and psychotropic substances, and the prosecution of perpetrators of such offences (Article 5 paragraph 1 subpara. 2 AISA).

64. The Central Anticorruption Bureau (CAB, Polish: *Centralne Biuro Antykorupcyjne*) is a specialised law enforcement agency that operates on the basis of the Central Anticorruption Bureau Act of 9 June 2006 (CABA) (consolidated text, J.L. 2014 item 1411, as amended). The CAB was created for the purpose of counteracting corruption in the public and business sectors, and in particular in state and local government institutions, and also for the purpose of preventing activities detrimental to the economic interests of the state (Article 1 paragraph 1 CABA). Pursuant to Article 2 paragraph 1 subpara. 1 CABA, the Bureau's anticorruption tasks performed as part of criminal process include identification, prevention and detection of a large number of criminal offences designated in this provision. These are: offences related to the functioning of state or local government institutions (Articles 228–231 CC), offences against the justice system (Article 233 CC), offences against elections and referenda (Article 250a CC), offences against public order (Article 258 CC), offences against the credibility of documents (Articles 270–273 CC), offences against property (Article 286 CC), offences against business operations (Articles 296–297, 299 and 305 CC), offences against monetary and security transactions (Article 310 CC), and also offences related to the financing of political parties (Articles 49d and 49f of the Political Parties Act of 27 June 1997 (J.L. 2011 r. No. 155, item 924), provided that they involve corruption, etc.

65. Fiscal inspection offices (*urzędy kontroli skarbowej*) operate under the Fiscal Inspection Offices and Chambers Act of 21 June 1996 (FIOCA, consolidated text, J.L. 2004, No. 121, item 1267, as amended). Their responsibilities include: 1) conducting inquiries into cases of fiscal offences and fiscal petty offences; 2) performing the role of public prosecutor in cases of fiscal offences and fiscal petty offences; 3) enforcing financial penalties within the scope defined in the Criminal Enforcement Code and Criminal Fiscal Code (Article 5 paragraph 6a TIOCA). The fiscal office conducts preliminary proceedings in cases of fiscal offences and fiscal petty offences, with the exception of cases falling under the jurisdiction of a customs office (Article 133 § 1 paragraph 2 of the Criminal Fiscal Code); these are the offences related to tax law, foreign currency exchange law, customs law and gambling and betting law.

66. Fiscal inspectors conduct preliminary proceedings in cases that involve fiscal inspections, under the procedure of and pursuant to the rules defined in the Code of Criminal Procedure, Code of Petty Offences Procedure and Criminal Fiscal Code, acting on the basis of the Fiscal Inspection Act of 28 September 1991 (consolidated text, J.L. 2015 item 553, as amended). In accordance with Article 133 § 1 paragraph 3 of the Criminal Fiscal Code, in cases revealed through a fiscal inspection carried out by the fiscal inspection office, preliminary proceedings are conducted by fiscal inspectors. Fiscal inspections may include, among other things, reviews of the accuracy of declared taxable bases and the correctness of calculations and payment of taxes, identification and audits of business activities that have not been registered for tax purposes, audits of sources of property and income that do not originate from disclosed sources of income or originate from non-disclosed sources, and a review of statements of financial interests submitted by persons who are obliged to reveal their financial status, for example civilian and uniformed personnel working in customs administration (Article 2 paragraph 1 Fiscal Inspection Act).

67. The Customs Service (*Służba Celna*) operates on the basis of the Customs Service Act of 27 August 2009 (CSA) (consolidated text, J.L. 2015, item 990). The Customs Service is a uniformed formation responsible for enforcing laws that govern the import of goods to, and export of goods from, the customs area of the European Union; it is also responsible for performing duties designated in separate provisions of law, especially with regard to excise duty tax and gambling tax (Article 1 paragraph 1 CSA). Tasks of the Customs Service include the identification, prevention and detection of fiscal offences and fiscal petty offences and also criminal and petty offences related to the import or export of goods; the identification, detection, prevention and counteracting of criminal and petty offences that involve the import and export of goods which are restricted or prohibited because of public safety, public order or international security concerns, in particular: waste, chemicals and mixtures of chemicals, nuclear or radioactive materials, narcotic drugs, psychotropic substances, weapons, ammunition, explosives and goods and technologies of strategic importance (Article 2 paragraph 1 of CSA).

68. The Military Police (*Żandarmeria Wojskowa*) is a uniformed formation responsible for policing the Armed Forces of the Republic of Poland and Polish military personnel (Article 2 of the Police Act). The organisation and jurisdiction, as well as the powers and duties of Military Police personnel are defined in the Act on the Military Police and other military law enforcement authorities of 24 August 2001 (Military Police Act, consolidated text, J.L. 2016, item 96). The Military Police is authorised to detect criminal and petty offences, and also fiscal offences and petty offences committed by military personnel, and to detect and prosecute perpetrators of these offences and identify and secure evidence related to them (Article

4 paragraph 1 subpara. 4 of the Military Police Act). In carrying out these responsibilities, Military Police personnel conduct both operational and intelligence-gathering activities and procedural acts under the CCP.

69. The Trade Inspection Authority (*Inspekcja Handlowa*) is a specialised regulatory body established in order to protect the interests and rights of consumers and the economic interests of the state. It is organised and operates on the basis of the Trade Inspection Authority Act of 15 December 2000 (consolidated text, J.L. 2014, item 148, as amended). Pursuant to the Regulation of the Minister of Justice of 22 September 2015 on non-police bodies authorised to conduct inquiries and bodies authorised to file and prosecute charges before first instance courts in cases in which inquiries have been conducted, and on matters delegated to these bodies (J.L. 2015, item 1725), bodies of the Trade Inspection Authority conduct inquiries and have power to prosecute in cases that involve the offences described in Article 43 paragraphs 1 and 2, and in Article 453 paragraph 1 of the Act on raising minors in sobriety and counteracting alcoholism (J.L. 2015, item 1286) and in Article 38 of the Trade Inspection Authority Act of 15 December 2000 (J.L. 2014, item 148, as amended), which were identified during an audit performed by the Trade Inspection Authority.

70. The State Sanitary Inspection Authority is a body that performs tasks in the area of public health; it was created under the State Sanitary Inspection Authority Act of 14 March 1985 (consolidated text, J.L. 2011, No. 212, item 1263, as amended). Bodies of the State Sanitary Inspection Authority may conduct inquiries into cases concerning the offences described in Article 37b of the State Sanitary Inspection Authority Act (J.L. 2015, item 1412), Articles 96–99 of the Food and Food Safety Act of 25 August 2006 (J.L. 2015, item 594). Article 14 paragraph 3 of the Cosmetics Act of 30 March 2001 (J.L. 2013, item 475), and Articles 31–34, 36–40, 50 and 51 of the Act on chemicals and chemical mixtures of 25 February 2011 (J.L. 2015, item 1203).

71. **The President of the Office of Electronic Communications** (*Prezes Urzędu Komunikacji Elektronicznej*) is a central body of the government administration that operates under the Telecommunications Act of 16 July 2004 (TA) (consolidated text, J.L. 2014, item 243). Pursuant to the Regulation of the Minister of Justice of 22 September 2015 on non-police bodies authorised to conduct inquiries and bodies authorised to file and prosecute charges before first instance courts in cases in which inquiries have been conducted, and on matters delegated to these bodies (J.L. 2015, item 1725), the President of the OEC is authorised to conduct preliminary proceedings (inquiries) in cases of offences under Article 208 paragraph 1 TA, namely using a radio receiver and/or transmitter device without the required permit. The President of the OEC may also support the prosecution's case before the first instance court.

72. **The Forestry Guard** operates under the Forests Act of 28 September 1991 (FA) (consolidated text, J.L. 2015, item 2100). The responsibilities of the Forestry Guard include the counteracting of criminal and petty offences that involve the destruction of forests and other environmental violations (Article 45 paragraph 3 FA). The tasks of the Forestry Guard are performed by officers called 'forest rangers' (*strażnicy leśni*). Forest rangers are authorised to conduct inquiries and submit and support indictments in cases in which the object of an offence is trees or timber originating from state-owned forests, under the procedure and pursuant to the rules determined in the Code of Criminal Procedure (Article 47 paragraph 2 FA).

73. **The Hunting Guard** (*Straż Łowiecka*) is a uniformed and armed formation that use marked, all-terrain means of transport. It is subordinated to a Province Governor and operates under the Hunting Act of 13 October 1995 (HA) (consolidated text, J.L. 2015, item 2168). The State Hunting Guard is tasked with counteracting criminal and petty offences related to hunting (Article 37 paragraph 1 subpara. 3 HA). The Hunting Guard, or, more accurately, their officers – known as 'hunting rangers' - are authorised to conduct inquiries, and to submit and support indictments in cases of offences that involve wild animals, under the procedure and pursuant to the rules determined in the CCP.

B. The Prosecution Service

74. The prosecutor is one the most important actors involved in the course of criminal proceedings, both preliminary and court proceedings. At the stage of preliminary proceedings, the prosecutor performs the role of a criminal justice body that conducts or supervises the conduct of the proceedings. In the course of court proceedings, the prosecutor becomes a party to the proceedings, assuming all the functions of a public prosecution authority.

75. There is no direct constitutional regulation on the public prosecution service. The operations of the public prosecution service are governed by the Code of Criminal Procedure, the Prosecution Service Act of 20 June 1985 (PSA) and the Regulation of the Minister of Justice of 11 September 2014 on the internal rules of official conduct of common organisational units of the prosecution service.

76. Prosecutors are responsible for both the safeguarding of the rule of law, and oversight of the prosecution of crimes (Article 2 PSA). As an organisation, the prosecution service is a legal protection body (Article 1 paragraph 3 PSA). The public prosecution service is currently completely separate from the judiciary and – arguably – is more an element of the executive branch. However, there is some dispute regarding the proper description of the public prosecution service's constitutional position – some are proponents of situating it among the judiciary, and other argue it belongs in the executive. In any case, and notably, the status of the prosecutor is very similar to that of a judge, both in respect of their immunity and the remuneration paid to prosecutors of different levels. This similarity is also visible in the structure of the public prosecution service, which mirrors the multi-tier organisational structure of Polish courts.

77. Pursuant to Article 1 paragraph 1 PSA, the Polish public prosecution service consists of the Prosecutor General and the subordinated prosecutors of common and military organisational units of the public prosecution service (prosecutors' offices), and also the prosecutors of the Institute of National Remembrance – Commission for the Prosecution of Crimes against the Polish Nation. **The Prosecutor General** (*Prokurator Generalny*) is the supreme body of the public prosecution service (Article 1 paragraph 2 PSA).

In accordance with the provisions of the Prosecution Service Act, the public prosecution service is divided into the civilian branch, comprising its common organisational units, and the military branch, which includes its military organisational units. The former comprises four tiers namely:

(1) **Office of the Prosecutor General** (*Prokuratura Generalna*),
(2) **appellate prosecutor's office** (*prokuratury apelacyjne*),
(3) **regional prosecutor's office** (*prokuratury okręgowe*),
(4) **district prosecutor's office** (*prokuratury rejonowe*).

Prosecutors working in these units are known as prosecutors of the Prosecutor General's Office, prosecutors of an appellate prosecutor's office, prosecutors of a regional prosecutor's office and prosecutors of a district prosecutor's office.

The military branch consists of the following:

- **the Supreme Military Prosecutor's Office** (*Naczelna Prokuratura Wojskowa*),
- **military regional prosecutor's offices** (*wojskowe prokuratury okręgowe*),
- **military garrison prosecutor's offices** (*wojskowe prokuratury garnizonowe*).

Finally, the structure of the public prosecution service includes **the Institute of National Remembrance – Commission for the Prosecution of Crimes against the Polish Nation (Instytut Pamięci Narodowej – Komisja Ścigania Zbrodni Przeciwko Narodowi Polskiemu, IPN)**, which is manned by prosecutors of the Central Commission for the Prosecution of Crimes against the Polish Nation. Prosecutors of Local Commissions for the Prosecution of Crimes Against the Polish Nation, prosecutors of the Vetting Bureau and prosecutors of local vetting bureaus. The Institute of National Remembrance was established on 18 December 1998 with a goal to become an apolitical and independent institution to solve the problem of documents left after the Communist State Security bodies dissolved in 1990. It holds functions of state and justice administration, of an archive, an academic institute, an education centre and (since 2007) of a body which conducts vetting proceedings. The latter function is devoted to verification of the past of people who hold public positions.

78. The Polish public prosecution service operates on the basis of a number of principles that govern its structure and activities:

- the principle of centralism,
- the principle of single-person leadership,
- the principle of hierarchical subordination,

– the principle of substitution,
– the principle of devolution,
– the principle of personal disinterest.

79. **The principle of centralism** means that all prosecutors in Poland are subordinated to the central prosecutorial body, namely the Prosecutor General (Article 1 paragraph 2 PSA). The Prosecutor General leads the public prosecution service either personally or through his or her deputies by issuing orders, guidelines and instructions (Article 10 paragraph 1 PSA), which may not concern the content of procedural acts (Article 10 paragraph 2 PSA). The principle of centralism is reinforced by the language of Article 29 paragraph 1 PSA, which provides that guidelines of the Prosecutor General issued in respect of preliminary proceedings are binding on all bodies authorised to conduct such proceedings.

80. **The principle of single-person leadership** means that each organisational unit of the prosecution service (the Prosecutor General's Office, appellate prosecutor's offices, regional prosecutor's offices and district prosecutor's offices) is headed by one person, namely the Prosecutor General, an appellate prosecutor, regional prosecutor and district prosecutor, respectively (Article 17 PSA).

81. **The principle of hierarchical subordination** means that lower-ranking prosecutors are subordinated to higher-ranking prosecutors. For example, the Prosecutor General is the superior prosecutor for prosecutors of common and military organisational units of the public prosecution service, and also for prosecutors of the Institute of National Remembrance – Commission for the Prosecution of Crimes against the Polish Nation (Article 17 paragraph 3 PSA). In turn, an appellate prosecutor is the superior of prosecutors working at a given appellate prosecutor's office, prosecutors of regional prosecutor's offices and prosecutors of district prosecutor's offices located within the jurisdictional area of the appellate prosecutor's office (Article 17 paragraph 5 PSA). Likewise, a regional prosecutor is the superior of prosecutors working at a given regional prosecutor's office, and prosecutors of district prosecutor's offices located within the jurisdictional area of the regional prosecutor's office (Article 17 paragraph 7 PSA), whereas a district prosecutor is the superior of prosecutors who perform actions at his or her district prosecutor's office (Article 17 paragraph 9 PSA).

82. According to the **principle of substitution**, which is closely linked to the principle of hierarchical subordination, a superior prosecutor may appoint subordinate prosecutors to perform actions that fall within the superior prosecutor's authority unless a statute provides that a given action may be performed solely by the superior prosecutor (Article 8b paragraph 1 PSA). The principle of devolution is the reverse of the principle of substitution, which means that a superior prosecutor may take over cases conducted by his or her subordinates and perform actions that were originally supposed to be performed by these subordinates, unless a statute provides for otherwise (Article 8b paragraph 2 PSA).

83. The last of the aforementioned principles is the **principle of personal disinterest**, which means that each prosecutor acts in the name of the entire public prosecution service as a unified body. It is thus irrelevant which particular prosecutor performs a given act in pending proceedings. Such an action is also effective, if is performed, in the course of proceedings led by a prosecutor, by a substituting prosecutor or even if it is continued by another prosecutor.

C. *Trial Courts*

84. In Poland, criminal cases are decided in the first instance by **common courts** *(sądy powszechne)*, namely, **district courts** *(sądy rejonowe)* and **regional courts** (*sądy okręgowe*), and by **military courts** *(sądy wojskowe)* – **military garrison courts** *(wojskowe sądy garnizonowe)* and **military regional courts** *(wojskowe sądy okręgowe)*. Criminal cases are heard by a criminal division (or multiple divisions) of a given court. In accordance with Article 24 § 1 of the Code of Criminal Procedure (CCP), as a rule district courts decide cases in the first instance. Certain cases, prescribed in Article 25 § 1 CCP, are required to be decided by regional courts in the first instance. The classification of cases heard by a regional court is based on the gravity of a given crime and the type of legally protected value violated by the perpetrator of the crime (such as human life) (*infra* paragraph 479).

85. There is no jury in Polish courts similar to the one known in the common law system. However, there are lay judges that participate in panels in criminal cases. As a rule, criminal cases are heard by a one-judge panel in courts. In cases related to felonies, the court adjudicates in a panel composed of one professional judge and two lay judges. In cases concerning criminal offences for which statute provides for the penalty of life imprisonment (e.g., manslaughter), the court adjudicates in a panel of two professional judges and three lay judges.

Due to the particular complexity or importance of a case, a Court of First Instance may decide to examine a case in a panel of three professional judges or one professional judge and two lay judges, instead of sitting in a one-judge panel.

86. Generally the judgments given in the first instance can be challenged by way of appeal to a higher court. The right to appeal against first instance rulings issued in criminal cases is partially regulated in the Constitution of the Republic of Poland. Article 78 of the Constitution provides that each party has the right to appeal against judicial rulings and administrative decisions made in the first instance. Furthermore, Article 176 paragraph 1 of the Constitution states that court proceedings must have at least two stages (*infra* paragraph 762).

87. Criminal cases are adjudicated in the second instance by **regional courts**, which examine appellate measures submitted against the rulings and orders of district courts hearing cases in the first instance (Article 25 § 3 CCP), and by **courts of appeal** (*sądy apelacyjne*), which consider appellate measures submitted against rulings and orders issued by regional courts (Article 26 CCP).

An appellate trial is conducted by a court sitting in a three-judge panel, unless a statute provides for otherwise (Article 29 § 1 CCP). An example of such an exception from the general rule is an appeal against a sentence of life imprisonment; this is heard by a court sitting in a five-judge panel (Article 29 § 2 CCP).

88. In Polish criminal proceedings a ruling of a second instance court may be subject to an appeal in cassation (*kasacja*) (*infra* paragraph 797-804). An appeal in cassation is heard by the Supreme Court (Articles 27 and 525 CCP), which sits in a panel whose composition reflects that of the relevant panel of an appellate court.

D. *Prison System and Probation Service*

89. The **Criminal Enforcement Code** of 1997 (CEC) (J.L. 1997, No. 90, item 557, as amended) is the source of Polish executive criminal law governing all types of criminal penalties. Therefore, Polish law does not follow the example of certain other jurisdictions, and does not separate penitentiary law (*prawo penitencjarne*), which in Poland constitutes merely a part of the broadly understood executive criminal law (*prawo karne wykonawcze*). Discussion on the significance and interrelations between these two notions is presented below (*infra* paragraph 966).

90. The administration of prisons and detention facilities in Poland is vested in the hands of the **Prison Service** (*Służba Więzienna*) that operates on the basis of the Prison Service Act of 9 April 2010 (J.L. 2010, No. 79, item 523, as amended). The structure of the Prison Service, according to Article 8 paragraph 1 of the Prison Service Act includes: the Central Board of the Prison Service (*Centralny Zarząd Służby Więziennej*), Regional Inspectorates of the Prison Service (*okręgowe inspektoraty służby więziennej*), prisons and detention facilities and General Education Centre of the Prison Service and Prison Service education centres and training centres. The above remain under the supervision of the **Director-General of the Prison Service** (*Dyrektor Generalny Służby Więziennej*) who is superior to every **Prison Service officer** (*funkcjonariusz Służby Więziennej*).

91. Generally, the execution of judicial decisions, including those regarding the penalty of imprisonment but also other penalties such as fines and the restriction of liberty, is divided between distinct authorities of judicial and non-judicial character. Among the most important of these are: courts of the first instance or other courts of equal competence, penitentiary courts, the President of the court or authorised judge, a penitentiary judge. For a full discussion on the organisational structure within the prison system, see the last Part of this monograph (*infra* paragraphs 973–979).

E. The Bar

92. In principle, Polish law does not recognise the concept of 'the Bar', or a single common association of lawyers typical for common law jurisdictions. Aspiring **attorneys** (*adwokaci*), **legal advisors** (*radcy prawni*), notaries (*notariusze*), and also judges and prosecutors, must follow separate career and professional education routes before they are admitted to practice; this determines the separate and independent organisation of these professions. Individual professions offer different educational schemes with different professional examinations, and have separate governing bodies. Transferring between the professions is possible, but is clearly governed by stricter rules than in other jurisdictions, and it is thus more problematic.

93. Apart from prosecutors and judges, who obviously take part in criminal proceedings, two other legal professions (attorneys and legal advisors) are also involved. Currently, the division between the two latter professions is only of historical significance as – apart from minor differences resulting from the laws regulating certain aspects of the professions, such as the ability to enter into an employment relationship – both attorneys and legal advisors enjoy the same professional status and have the right to act in criminal or administrative proceedings.

Attorneys are regulated by the Attorney Act of 26 May 1982 (consolidated text, J.L. 2015, item 615). They form a self-governing professional association and are tasked with providing legal assistance and collaborating in the protection of civil rights and liberties and also in the development and application of the law (Article 1 paragraph 1 APA).

Legal advisors practise on the basis of the Legal Advisors Act of 6 July 1982 (LLA) (consolidated text, J.L. 2016, item 233). Legal advisors also have their own professional association; they are tasked with providing legal assistance (Article 4 LAA).

94. As from 1 July 2015, both attorneys and legal advisors can act as defence lawyers (*obrońcy*) in criminal proceedings, which means they can represent defendants and suspects in criminal cases (Article 82 CCP). Notably, under the previously applicable provisions of the CCP, this right was given exclusively to attorneys (see *infra*, paragraphs 552–555, 665–667). Similarly, pursuant to Article 88 CCP, both attorneys and legal advisors are entitled to act as legal representatives (*pełnomocnicy*, singular: *pełnomocnik*) of parties other than defendants in a criminal process (e.g. witnesses) (see *infra*, paragraphs 562–564).

F. Statistical Overview

95. According to data published by the Polish Ministry of Justice, in 2014 the police conducted preliminary proceedings in 828,802 cases; this figure has decreased significantly over the last 10 years (for instance, in 2004 1,296,356 cases were recorded). The figure included 531 cases of manslaughter, 2,444 cases of rape and 17,786 cases of causing bodily harm. The statistics for 2014 also mention

167,390 cases of theft, 87,765 cases of theft with burglary and 9,441 cases of robbery and theft with violence. In 2014 the overall crime detection rate was 65.4%, an increase of 10% in comparison to 2004 (56.2%). The highest detection rate is recorded for manslaughter (95.8%) and the lowest is recorded for theft (28.9%).

96. According to an annual report by the Prosecutor General,[3] 354,885 cases were submitted to courts from the preliminary proceedings conducted in 2014. The above figure includes both the proceedings concluded with an indictment (*akt oskarżenia*) and those resulting in other types of complaints filed with the court, for example a motion for the conditional discontinuation of proceedings or a motion for the discontinuation of the proceedings and application of a protective measure. Among the cases brought to courts upon an indictment, as many as 48.8% included a motion for the delivery of a conviction without trial under Article 335 CCP (see *infra*, paragraphs 633–643). It must be noted, however, that in accordance with the provisions of the CCP in force in 2014, the submission of an indictment to the court together with the above motion was the only existing option for concluding criminal proceedings at this stage in a negotiated form. Since 1 July 2015, additional options have been available in this respect, such as those under the amended Article 335 §§ 1 and 2 CCP or Article 338a CCP. However, there are presently no statistics on the frequency of their use.

97. In 2014, prosecutors submitted to courts a total of 18,835 motions for the application of detention on remand; in 91.5% of cases, these motions were granted. In that year, 3,096 suspects were kept in detention on remand in Poland.

98. In Poland, the acquittal rate is extremely low. In 2014, 7,099 defendants were acquitted in criminal court proceedings; this figure represents 1.94% of all cases.

§3. The Historical Background

I. Historical Criminal Law

99. The history of Polish criminal law dates back to the pre-partition period and can be characterised not only by a lack of unified codification but also by significant distinctions based on a social class. The gentry and other social groups were distinguished in terms of substantive laws but also had separate court systems. Stricter laws were enforced in cities, based on German legislation (*Constitutio Criminalis* Carolina). Slightly more liberal provisions were in force in landed estates, where manslaughter was punished not by death but by the payment of a sum of money known as a 'man price' (*główszczyzna*).

3. *See* the *Sprawozdanie Prokuratora Generalnego z działalności prokuratury w 2014* (Annual Report of the Prosecutor General on the Operations of the Public Prosecution Service in 2014), published on www.pk.gov.pl.

100. Enlightenment thought was introduced into Poland relatively quickly, along with the publication in 1766 of Beccaria's treatise On Crimes and Punishments. The death penalty for witchcraft was abolished and the use of torture during criminal proceedings was prohibited. The first attempts were made at codification. This process resulted in the development of a 'Collection of Court Laws', created under the guidance of Andrzej Zamoyski.

After the implementation of the Constitution of 3 May 1791 (the second oldest constitution in the world after the US Constitution), a codification of the criminal law was prepared. This codification, deeply rooted in Enlightenment thought, foresaw two different versions, one for the Crown and one for Lithuania. The harmonisation of laws and the elimination of class law through the introduction of the principle of equality was proposed. Moreover, the abolition, or significant limitation, of the death penalty was suggested. The three partitions of Poland (1772–1795) between its neighbouring countries: Prussia, Russia and Austria-Hungary meant that innovative ideas concerning reforms of the criminal law and the criminal process could not be implemented. The third partition took place in 1795 and definitively ended the existence of Poland as an independent state. During the next century, the legislation of the occupiers replaced the existing legal system of pre-partition Poland.

II. Interwar Period

101. After Poland regained its independence on 11 November 1918 and, after 123 years, the territories divided into the Russian, Prussian and Austrian partitions were unified, the development of a single legal system was of utmost importance. At that time, four significantly different legal systems were in force on the territory of Poland: Austrian, German, Russian and Hungarian.

As early as 10 November 1919, the Codification Commission started working on new measures which were to be introduced into the territory of the Second Polish Republic. Juliusz Makarewicz was one of the most important experts involved in work on the new codes. His name is frequently used to refer to the first criminal code enacted after the First World War, the so-called Makarewicz Code.

102. In the course of the Commission's work, the concept of developing a single code for the criminal law and criminal procedure was abandoned.

With regard to criminal procedure, the following legal acts regulating the entirety of the shape of the Polish post-war criminal proceedings entered into force as legislative regulations (executive decrees) from the President of Poland:

- Regulation of 19 March 1928 – the Code of Criminal Procedure (J.L. 1928, No. 33, item 313), which entered into force on 1 January 1929;
- Regulation of 6 February 1928 – Common Courts Law (J.L. 1928 No. 12, item 93);
- Regulation of 19 March 1928 on summary proceedings (J.L. 1928, No. 33, item 315).

However, the first post-war act of substantive criminal law was adopted in the regulation from the President of Poland of 11 July 1932 – Criminal Code (J.L. 1932, No. 60, item 571), and entered into force on 1 September 1932.

103. The Code of Criminal Procedure of 1928 introduced three-instance proceedings. In the first instance, cases were heard by the municipal courts (*sądy grodzkie*) (they adjudicate cases concerning offences that carry minor penalties), regional courts (*sądy okręgowe*) (cases not heard in other courts) and regional courts with jury panels (cases concerning offences that carry a penalty of at least ten years of imprisonment, as well as political offences). However, this last type of court operated only on the territory of the former Austrian partition, as they had existed on these lands before Poland regained independence. Regional courts heard appeals against judgments of municipal courts and courts of appeal examined appeals against the first instance judgments of regional courts. The Supreme Court was a third instance court and heard appeals in cassation against judgments of regional courts (and regional courts that adjudicated cases with jurors) issued in the second instance, and also appeals against the judgments of courts of appeal.

Court proceedings were accusatorial in nature, which meant that only a prosecutor could initiate them. However, in some cases an aggrieved person was also entitled to initiate a case.

The office of an investigative judge (*sędzia śledczy*), an official authorised to independently conduct investigations, was introduced to preliminary proceedings. However, the prosecutor maintained material influence over the course of an investigation and could request certain investigative actions to be carried out, with the investigative judge not able oppose such a request. An investigation was similar to court proceedings and was very formalised; records developed during an investigation had the same legal power as court records and could be read out in the course of the court proceedings. This type of preliminary proceedings was conducted for cases heard in regional courts (for courts adjudicating with jurors this was obligatory).

Inquiries conducted by a prosecutor or the police in cases concerning offences subject to lesser penalties were intended to be less formalised. An investigation required only that it be established whether a given act had been committed, who the perpetrator was, and that there existed grounds for an indictment. In principle no records were kept, only so-called notes (*zapiski*). Records were only created if there was a risk of loss of evidence. Unfortunately, the practice of developing time-consuming records was widely and quickly adopted for inquiries, which in practical terms ceased to be different from investigations.

The Code of Criminal Procedure of 1928 was in fact criticised from the very outset, and by 1932 its framework had become significantly modified, for example in the way it limited the rights of accused and aggrieved persons in order to achieve the authoritarian objectives of the then-incumbent authorities.

104. **The Criminal Code of 1932** was an example of a legislative technique that was excellent for its time. Development of Polish language criminal law terminology, non-existent at the time, was one of the achievements of the Codification Commission. This terminology is still used to this day. The standout rules of the criminal process included the principle of legality and the principle of non-retroactivity of the law. This new code provided for the death penalty for the most serious crimes. All of the crimes described in the code were punishable with imprisonment from three months to fifteen years. Some of the most serious crimes were punishable by life imprisonment. There also existed the possibility of imposing a fine on a stand-alone basis, as well as in addition to imprisonment. The code also allowed for the use of protective measures with regard to perpetrators who were legally insane.

It must be stated that the Code of 1932 was incredibly modern and progressive in its nature. In fact, currently applicable substantive criminal laws include numerous solutions which were originally introduced in the pre-war code.

III. Communist Period (1945–1989)

105. A characteristic feature of the post-war period, and especially of its initial stage, was the departure from the model of criminal law and criminal procedure of the interwar period. The end of hostilities did not result in the official reinstatement of pre-war legislation on the territory of Poland. As the country fell under the influence of the Soviet Union, a totalitarian communist system was adopted. The codes of 1928 and 1932 were still applied, but the government introduced additional legislative acts which made criminal law much more repressive. Supplemental legislation either regulated areas that had previously been left outside the scope of the criminal code, in particular by enforcing requirements imposed by the new political system, or introduced new regulations in already legislated areas, thereby informally preventing the application of the code. The prosecution service and the profession of attorney functioned under the same conditions.

106. Between 1949 and 1950, legislative attempts were made to forge the Polish criminal process after the Soviet model. They involved the abandonment of the 'bourgeois' notion of human rights, which was seen as an obstacle preventing law enforcement authorities from effectively dispatching the 'enemies of the communist system'.

Statutes introduced the three-level court structure – county courts (today: district courts), provincial courts (today: regional courts) and the Supreme Court. The public prosecution service was separated from the court system and the role of investigative judge was abolished. Irrespective of the above changes in law, offices of state security (the communist secret police) remained beyond any control of prosecutors. The new legislation also ultimately resolved the issue of the participation of the public in the criminal adjudication process by establishing a multi-judge adjudicating panel in first instance courts; this panel consisted of a professional judge (*sędzia zawodowy*) and two lay judges (*ławnicy*, singular *ławnik*). Finally, the division between an ordinary appeal (*apelacja*) and an appeal in cassation (*kasacja*) was abandoned and replaced with the measure called 'revision' (*rewizja*).

In consequence of the legislative changes and additional powers awarded to state security agencies, alleged perpetrators were arbitrarily detained and interrogated non-stop for hours or even days, as no mechanism for reviewing the reasonableness of detention had been put in place. Often persons were de facto detained on remand without any detention order – this was only issued several days later by the prosecution service. In many cases interrogation involved torture; detainees were not given an official caution or an explanation of the reasons for their detention. A defence lawyer's participation in criminal proceedings was very limited and depended on a prosecutor's consent. Generally speaking, the system of repression against all those who opposed the communist system developed rapidly.

107. The historical conditions resulting from changes at the top of governmental circles in Poland and the victory of a more liberal faction of the ruling party (the events of October 1956) enabled legislative work on a new code of substantive criminal law and code of criminal procedure. The Codification Commission of the day presented several draft versions of these codes in the years 1956–1968, but only the 1968 proposals won at least partial approval of the legal profession. The codes were enacted in 1969 and became effective on 1 January 1970.

108. **The Criminal Code of 1969** adopted some of the solutions contained in the 1932 code though also attempted to avoid replicating some of its errors. In principle, the new code was to adopt a flexible approach to the imposition of sanctions on perpetrators of petty crime but promoted a much stricter policy towards perpetrators of serious offences. For example, it introduced for the first time the measure of conditional discontinuation of proceedings. The objectives guiding the adoption of the new law were never attained. The number of the convicted persons serving the penalty of imprisonment surged. The death penalty was increasingly often applied. The consequences of reoffending were far-reaching, and in certain cases could result in the maximum length of imprisonment imposed as a penalty for a given offence being increased by as much as three times. Also, recidivism excluded the possibility of conditional suspension of proceedings. The level of repressiveness of the new law and its practical application, which resulted in a significant increase in the prison population, brought critical responses that gained momentum over time.

109. **The Code of Criminal Procedure of 1969** was also supposed to humanise the criminal process. The rights of the defence were expanded, as were those of aggrieved persons, the latter with the introduction of the concept of a subsidiary prosecutor which enabled an aggrieved party to join court proceedings as a party. The new code maintained the prosecutor's power to order detention on remand at the stage of preliminary proceedings, but established a mechanism of judicial review over detention rulings. The drafters of the new laws also tried to address the contemporary problem of the justice system (which persists to this day), namely extensively lengthy proceedings. However, measures taken in order to speed up the process led to limitations to the right to defence and the principle of direct examination of evidence. The consequences of these limitations, especially in the context of the right to a defence, are visible even today.

110. Criticism of the system became especially fierce in the final stage of communism in Poland, which was marked by surge of the 'Solidarity' movement. Critics noted the overly repressive nature of criminal law and the incompatibility of national rules of criminal procedure with international conventions, which manifested themselves in insufficient legislative safeguards to the right to defence. An attempt was even made to amend the then-operating laws but it never came to fruition because of the imposition of martial law (on 13 December 1981). No further attempts, intended to develop a new legislative framework of criminal law, were made until Poland overthrew communism, gained total independence from the USSR and opened up to influences from Western Europe.

V. Criminal Law after 1989 and the Codes of 1997

111. Immediately after the change of political system in Poland, the first free parliamentary elections in 1989 and the presidential elections of 1990 (won by Lech Wałęsa), work started to adjust Polish criminal law to international standards, and in particular to the International Covenant on Civil and Political Rights (ICCPR).

112. The first efforts had already been made before the fall of communism. In 1987, the government appointed the Commission for the Reform of Criminal Law, which prepared a number of legislative proposals amending substantive criminal law, criminal procedure and executive criminal law. In 1994, these proposals were brought to public debate. On 18 August 1995, three bills that comprised an entirely new framework of criminal law were lodged with the Sejm. The newly proposed acts were **the Criminal Code, the Code of Criminal Procedure, and the Criminal Enforcement Code**. Ultimately, the codes were enacted on 6 June 1997, and entered into force on 1 September 1998.

113. All three codes have reshaped the system of criminal law in Poland, and show a clear break with the former regulations. However, they also incorporate, be it to a limited extent, the historical achievements of criminal law scholarship. The concepts developed over several decades have been reinforced by standards universally applied across Western countries, especially those of continental Europe. Populists often challenged the new laws, including prior to their enactment, alleging that they were too liberal and would contribute to an increase in crime rates. In subsequent years, these objections served as the basis for many amendments of the codes, both liberal and conservative in their nature (the Criminal Enforcement Code proved to be the least prone to such changes).

VI. Latest Reforms

114. To date, there have been dozens of amendments to the Criminal Code and the Code of Criminal Procedure. Sometimes, and especially in recent years, some experts have argued that these laws should not be further amended, suggesting instead the adoption of brand new codes that would replace the CC and CCP in their entirety. Currently, no new codes are in development, but amendments to the old ones appear constantly and there is no sign that the Parliament intends to curb its inclinations in this respect. The changes of criminal laws were both incidental and fundamental. The former related to adjusting Polish law to EU legislation in connection with Poland's accession to the European Union in 2004 (e.g., the introduction of the European Arrest Warrant (EAW)) or were the consequence of constitutional review decisions of the Constitutional Tribunal, while the latter involved modifications of more general concepts included in the codes.

115. One of the initial fundamental reforms was the major amendment to the Code of Criminal Procedure of 20 July 2000 (J.L. 2000 No. 62, item 717), which quickly proved to have been insufficient. The next amendment, made on 10 January 2003 (J.L. 2003 No. 17, item 155), was guided by the notions of pragmatism and consensualism. More than one-third of the provisions were modified. The main thrust of the amendment was directed at preliminary proceedings (*postępowanie przygotowawcze*). The amendment enabled the police to conduct investigations (*śledztwa,* singular: *śledztwo*), the most advanced form of preliminary proceedings, subject to certain exceptions. The other form of preliminary proceedings, the inquiry (*dochodzenie*), was also simplified. Apart from the above, the amendment expanded the availability of negotiated justice procedures (see *infra*, paragraphs 633–635) and brought additional focus on the use of mediation between the aggrieved person and the defendant in the criminal process.

116. Further amendments of criminal laws, both substantive and procedural, posed additional difficulties in their interpretation and hindered the practical application of criminal provisions, which effectively lowered confidence in the stability of the law. For example, the Code of Criminal Procedure has so far been amended on more than eighty occasions.

117. One of the key amendments to the statutes of criminal law made in recent years was the amendment to the Code of Criminal Procedure, enacted as the Act of 27 September 2013. This amendment was introduced after many years of discussions held both by criminal procedure scholars and within the Ministry of Justice's Criminal Law Codification Commission. The main tenet of the reform was a change in the model of criminal procedure – from inquisitorial to adversarial. According to the former model, the court is obliged to determine the truth and, in practice, steps in to serve the parties' role with regard to the submission and taking of evidence, while under the latter, a trial is about resolving a dispute between the two equal parties to the proceedings (the prosecution and the defence) by a disinterested and impartial court. Apart from this change, which became the core of the amendment, a number of piecemeal modifications of individual provisions attempted at strengthening the adversarial character of the criminal process. Another assumption behind the reform was that criminal proceedings in Poland are excessively lengthy, a phenomenon also observed by the European Court of Human Rights (ECtHR), which flagged this issue as a systemic problem of the Polish justice system. Below are some examples of the changes brought about by the amendment:

- the main trial became more adversarial: the amended provisions obligated parties to take evidence and limit the court's powers to admit and take evidence *ex officio*;

- the contents of an indictment and dossier (materials collected in preliminary proceedings) submitted by a prosecutor to the court were modified in a way that limits the court's access to information about a case prior to the commencement of the judicial stage of the proceedings;
- the court was deprived of the authority to return a case to a prosecutor before or during a trial for the purpose of forcing a prosecutor to supplement evidentiary material;
- the amendment expanded the availability of the so-called negotiated forms of criminal justice by also enabling aggrieved persons to enter into settlements with suspects, and also by adding additional types of cases that can be resolved by a settlement, e.g. felony cases can be resolved this way during a trial;
- the institution of an ex officio defence lawyer was introduced, but only at the judicial stage of criminal proceedings;
- the right of parties to present evidence in appellate proceedings before the second instance court was expanded.

118. The discussed changes are intended to be fundamental, and given the sheer scope of the amendment, the Parliament introduced a *vacatio legis* period of nearly two years, which was designed to enable all interested parties to become familiar with the amended provisions. Before it entered into force, the Parliament made further modifications to the amendment (in the Act of 20 February 2015). The purpose of these modifications was to quickly correct some of the measures introduced by the former amendment and later designated as defective. This endeavour, which in reality modified only the 'obvious' mistakes, ultimately has not affected the overall design of the amended model of criminal procedure. However, it gave rise to far-reaching criticism of the Parliament.

The amendment, which finally entered into force on 1 July 2015, arrived in the middle of a heated public debate and was accompanied by voices of discontent, directly expressed by prosecutors and some judges, and also attempts to revoke or at least suspend its operation. Prosecutors protested against the amendment, arguing that they had been given new responsibilities at the stage of court proceedings but not relieved of any their duties at the pretrial stage of the process (which was partially true). Judges, for their part, opposed the removal of their right to actively participate in a trial, which has historically been a kind of dogma (and also a habit) for the most of them and gave them a sense of control over the proceedings they presided over – a feeling, they feared, soon to be lost forever.

§4. Sources of Criminal Law

I. Introduction

119. According to Article 87 of the Polish Constitution, the universally binding sources of law are the Constitution, statutes, ratified international agreements and regulations (sub-statutory legal acts).

120. **The Constitution** is the supreme law of the Republic of Poland. According to Article 8 of the Constitution, its provisions shall apply directly, unless the Constitution provides otherwise. In practice, however, the direct application of the basic law is rather rare, because of the general nature of constitutional provisions.

121. **A statute** becomes a binding law after being passed by Parliament (*Sejm* and *Senat*), signed by the President and promulgated in the **Journal of Laws of the Republic of Poland** (*Dziennik Ustaw*) (J.L.). The subject matter of statutes is not limited. It is also worth underlining that, according to the principle of proportionality (Article 31 paragraph 3 of the Constitution), any limitation upon the exercise of constitutional freedoms and rights may be imposed only by statute. There is no possibility of restraining rights and freedoms in sub-statutory legislation.

122. **Ratified international agreements**, after promulgation in the J.L., constitute part of the domestic legal order and shall be applied directly, unless their application depends on the enactment of a statute (Article 91 paragraph 1 of the Constitution). The ratification of international treaties, depending on the content of the treaty, is done with prior consent granted by a statute passed by the Parliament, or without it. Prior consent is necessary if an international agreement concerns:

(1) peace, alliances, political or military treaties;
(2) freedoms, rights or obligations of citizens, as specified in the Constitution;
(3) the Republic of Poland's membership in an international organisation;
(4) considerable financial responsibilities imposed on the state;
(5) matters regulated by statute or those in respect of which the Constitution requires the form of a statute (Article 89 of the Constitution).

123. Article 91 paragraph 3 of the Constitution provides that an international agreement ratified upon prior consent granted by statute shall have precedence over statutes if such an agreement cannot be reconciled with the provisions of such statutes. In each case, the primary role of a court or an administrative body is to find a way of interpreting national and international provisions so that possible conflict might be evaded. Only in cases where this is not possible does an international treaty take precedence over a statute.

124. According to the Article 90 paragraph 1 of the Constitution, the Republic of Poland may, by virtue of international agreements, delegate to an international organisation or international institution the competence of organs of state authority in relation to certain matters. This provision enabled, for example, the transfer of powers to the European Union. In case of the above-mentioned delegation, if the international organisation issues legal acts binding on its Member States, they are applied directly and have precedence in the event of a conflict with statute.

125. **Regulations** (sub-statutory legal acts) are issued on the basis of the specific authorisation contained in, and for the purpose of implementation of, statutes by the organs specified in the Constitution (Council of Ministers, prime minister, minister directing a branch of government administration). This authorisation shall specify the appropriate organ to issue a regulation and the scope of matters to be regulated, as well as guidelines concerning the provisions of such an act (Article 92 of the Constitution).

II. International Sources of Criminal Law

126. Although criminal law is often perceived as a key aspect of state sovereignty, its internationalisation is an ongoing process. Therefore, an overview of criminal law sources cannot be made without taking into consideration international treaties and, in the context of cooperation in the EU, legal acts issued by EU institutions.

Since Poland has been a member of the EU its criminal law has been strongly influenced by provisions of EU criminal law. Treaties, framework decisions and directives have an important impact on substantive criminal law (harmonisation of offences and penalties) and judicial cooperation in criminal matters.

127. Ratified international treaties are part of the Polish legal system. They regulate various areas of criminal law. It is impossible to present below the full list of international agreements to which Poland is a party. In general, however, there are five groups of treaties which influence the shape of criminal law regulations.

128. First, Poland is a party to the fundamental human rights conventions, which guarantee, among other things, basic rights and freedoms in the area of criminal law. These are primarily:

(1) The ICCPR (ratified on the 18 March 1977)
(2) The Convention against Torture and Other Cruel, Inhuman or Degrading Treatment or Punishment (ratified on 26 July 1989)
(3) The Convention on the Rights of the Child (ratified on 7 Jun 1991)
(4) The European Convention for the Protection of Human Rights and Fundamental Freedoms (ECHR) (ratified on 19 January 1993)
(5) Protocol No. 7 to the ECHR (ratified on 4 December 2002)

129.

(5) The second important group of conventions ratified by Poland consists of treaties that influence substantive criminal law in the context of criminalisation and punishment. These include:
(1) The Criminal Law Convention on Corruption (ratified on 11 December 2002)
(2) The Convention on Cybercrime (ratified on 20 February 2015)
(3) Additional Protocol to the Convention on Cybercrime, concerning the criminalisation of acts of a racist and xenophobic nature committed through computer systems (ratified on 20 February 2015)
(4) The Council of Europe Convention on preventing and combating violence against women and domestic Violence (ratified on 27 April 2015)

(5) The Council of Europe Convention on the Protection of Children against Sexual Exploitation and Sexual Abuse (ratified on 20 February 2015)
(6) The Council of Europe Convention on Action against Trafficking in Human Beings (ratified on 17 November 2008)
(7) The Council of Europe Convention on the Prevention of Terrorism (ratified on 3 April 2008)
(8) The International Convention Against the Taking of Hostages (ratified on 25 May 2000)
(9) The United Nations Convention Against Corruption (ratified on 15 September 2006)
(10) The United Nations Convention Against Transnational Organized Crime (ratified on 12 November 2001)
(11) The European Convention for the Prevention of Torture and Inhuman or Degrading Treatment or Punishment (ratified on 10 October 1994)
(12) The Convention against Torture and Other Cruel, Inhuman or Degrading Treatment or Punishment (ratified on 26 July 1989)
(13) Protocol No. 6 to the Convention for the Protection of Human Rights and Fundamental Freedoms concerning the Abolition of the Death Penalty (ratified on 30 October 2000)
(14) Protocol No. 13 to the Convention for the Protection of Human Rights and Fundamental Freedoms, concerning the abolition of the death penalty in all circumstances (ratified on 23 May 2014).

130. The third area of criminal law where conventions play an important role concerns procedural aspects of cooperation in criminal matters. Poland is a party to treaties facilitating that cooperation. Among these are:

(1) The European Convention on Extradition (ratified on 15 June 1993)
(2) The European Convention on Mutual Assistance in Criminal Matters (ratified on 19 March 1996)
(3) The European Convention on the Suppression of Terrorism (ratified on 30 January 1996)
(4) Additional Protocol to the European Convention on Information on Foreign Law (ratified on 14 September 1992).

In the above-mentioned group a prominent place is also held by bilateral agreements concerning cooperation in criminal matters, for example on extradition.

131. International treaties ratified by Poland also concern the execution of criminal penalties. Poland is a party to the Convention on the Transfer of Sentenced Persons (ratified on 8 November 1994), and its Additional Protocol (ratified on 1 February 2000), and also to other treaties.

132. Last but not least, Poland is a party to the Rome Statute of the International Criminal Court (ratified on 12 November 2001).

III. National Sources of Criminal Law

A. The Constitution

133. The Constitution is an important source of Polish criminal law. First and foremost among constitutional provisions are the most fundamental principles of criminal law. This is a guarantee, when we consider the restrictions on the amendment of the basic law, that these standards do not depend merely on the political will of the governing majority, and changes in these laws need a wider consensus. Moreover, the constitutionalisation of criminal law enables the Constitutional Tribunal to verify the conformity of penal law statutes with basic law and international treaties. This is an important tool for guaranteeing that the rights and freedoms of individuals in criminal cases are observed. In practice, the Polish Constitutional Tribunal as a 'negative legislator' (it is empowered to declare the non-conformity of statutory provisions with higher rank legal norms, which leads to their being deprived of binding legal force) has an important influence on criminal law. This is especially visible in the context of the Code of Criminal Procedure, which had to be amended more than twenty times after its entry into force in 1998 because of the Constitutional Tribunal's judgments stating the unconstitutionality of its various provisions.

134. Numerous constitutional provisions refer to broadly understood criminal justice system. First, the Polish Constitution guarantees fundamental rights and freedoms to individuals involved in criminal cases. Apart from those also applicable outside of the criminal justice system (e.g., the right to privacy, the right to property), there are a remarkable number of provisions that primarily or exclusively concern matters of criminal law.

135. Article 42 paragraph 1 of the Constitution acknowledges the principles of *nullum crimen sine lege* and *nulla poena sine lege* by stating that only a person who has committed an act prohibited by a statute in force at the moment of the commission thereof, and which is subject to a penalty, shall be held criminally responsible. This principle shall not prevent the punishment of any act which, at the moment of its commission, constituted an offence within the meaning of international law.

136. Article 42 paragraph 2 provides that everyone against whom criminal proceedings have been brought has a right to a defence at all stages of such proceedings. He may, in particular, choose counsel or avail himself – in accordance with principles specified by statute – of counsel appointed by the court. Article 42 paragraph 3 adds that everyone shall be presumed innocent of a charge until such point that guilt is determined by the final judgment of a court.

137. Fundamental procedural rights are guaranteed in Article 45 of the Constitution. It provides that everyone shall have the right to a fair and public hearing of their case (among other criminal cases), without undue delay, before a competent, impartial and independent court. Exceptions to the public nature of hearings may be made for reasons of morality, State security, public order or the protection of the private life of a party, or another important private interest. Judgments must be announced publicly.

138. The Polish Constitution also contains two provisions concerning statutes of limitations. Article 43 stipulates that there shall be no statute of limitation regarding war crimes and crimes against humanity. Article 44 adds that the statute of limitation regarding actions connected with offences committed by, or by order of, public officials which have not been prosecuted for political reasons, must be extended to correspond to the length of the period such reasons exist.

139. Two constitutional provisions refer to criminal penalties. Article 40, in general terms, prohibits subjecting people to torture or cruel, inhuman, or degrading treatment or punishment, as well as the application of corporal punishment. Article 46 states that property may be forfeited only in cases specified by statute, and only by virtue of the final judgment of a court.

B. Statutes

140. The main source of criminal law is statutes (Acts of Parliament). The core regulation of Polish criminal law is included in the following four codes:

(1) The Criminal Code (Act of 6 June 1997);
(2) The Code of Criminal Procedure (Act of 6 June 1997);
(3) The Criminal Enforcement Code (Act of 6 June 1997);
(4) The Criminal Fiscal Code (Act of 10 September 1999).

141. The **Criminal Code** constitutes the primary source of the regulations of substantive criminal law. The Code is divided into three parts. The General Part regulates the general principles that govern the assumption of criminal responsibility; it describes the elements of a criminal offence and the forms of its perpetration, circumstances that exclude criminal responsibility, and defines the types of penalties and other criminal measures and the rules of their application. The Special Part includes over 100 articles that define types of prohibited acts. The Military Part regulates the issues of military criminal law. Prohibited acts are also defined by criminal provisions laid down in a large number of other statutes outside the Criminal Code. Selected statutes of this type have been discussed in (see *infra*, paragraphs 369–373). Pursuant to Article 116 CC, provisions of the General Part of the Criminal Code apply to these statues that are outside the Criminal Code unless the statutes specifically exclude their application.

142. The **Code of Criminal Procedure** regulates the course of proceedings in criminal cases. In principle, this regulation is exhaustive. It is only incidentally that matters of criminal procedure are regulated outside the Code of Criminal Procedure. For example, the provisions concerning state witnesses are included in the State Witness Act of 25 June 1997.

143. The **Criminal Enforcement Code** contains rules governing the enforcement of rulings entered in criminal proceedings or in criminal fiscal proceedings, and also the enforcement of procedural penalties (*kar porządkowych*) and coercive measures that result in depriving persons of liberty and are imposed in criminal cases. The Criminal Enforcement Code governs not only the manner in which penalties are enforced (e.g., types of prisons, the rights and duties of inmates); it also governs adjudication regarding the modification of imposed measures of penal response or coercive measures (such as the change of an imposed penalty, or parole).

144. The Parliament established a separate regulatory framework in the area of criminal fiscal law because of the distinctive nature of this branch of criminal law. Criminal fiscal law deals with the responsibility of natural persons for prohibited acts committed against the financial interests of the state. These are defined as behaviour that negatively affects customs duties, tax obligations or the accounts of grants or subsidies, or violates the rules of international trading in goods and services, foreign exchange transactions or the rules of gambling and betting. The **Criminal Fiscal Code** includes provisions of substantive law, procedural law and executive law. However, these are exclusively regulations specific for the area of criminal fiscal law. In respect of other matters, the Criminal Fiscal Code refers to the provisions of the Criminal Code, the Code of Criminal Procedure and the Criminal Enforcement Code, which are to be applied *mutatis mutandis*.

145. Outside the sphere of the narrowly understood criminal law, there are other areas of repressive law, which are more or less similar to criminal law. An example of such a related area is, first and foremost, the law of petty offences (*prawo wykroczeń*). Under Polish law, petty offences (*wykroczenia*) are distinguished from the category of criminal offences (*przestępstwa*), which comprise only misdemeanours (*występki*) and felonies (*zbrodnie*). However, both the structure and principles of responsibility for petty offences are very similar to the relevant concepts relating to criminal offences. The law of petty offences is regulated in the **Petty Offences Code** (*Kodeks wykroczeń*) of 20 May 1971 and the **Petty Offences Procedure Code** (*Kodeks postępowania w sprawach o wykroczenia*) of 24 August 2001. The liability of juveniles who commit prohibited acts or present signs of antisocial and delinquent behaviour is governed by the Juvenile Justice System Act (*Ustawa o postępowaniu w sprawach nieletnich*) of 26 October 1982. On the contrary, the quasi-criminal responsibility of collective entities (e.g., corporations) for prohibited acts that constitute criminal offences or fiscal offences perpetrated by their officers, appointees or associates are regulated in the Act on the liability of collective entities for acts prohibited under a penalty of 28 October 2002.

C. Regulations

146. In criminal law, regulations issued by the minister (*rozporządzenia*) play only an auxiliary role, supplementing the content of statutory regulations. Since statutes are in principle the only source of criminal law, regulations have a very limited impact on the substantive criminal law. On the contrary, in criminal procedure, regulations provide a more precise explanation of statutory rules. The Minister of Justice has for example issued regulations on mediation proceedings in criminal cases (2015), on subjecting defendants or suspected persons to medical examination and on performing procedural acts with the participation of defendants or suspected persons (2005) and on providing defendants with access to ex officio defence lawyers (2015).

147. Regulations play the same role in the law regulation the execution of criminal sanctions. Statutes contain the authorisation to issue orders (*zarządzenia*). By virtue of an order, the Minister of Justice can establish and close prisons, bearing in mind any relevant needs that may exist. Furthermore, the Director-General of the Prison Service determines the designation of prisons (by way of an order), taking into particular consideration the need for the provision and reasonable use of living quarters for all categories of inmates.

D. *Court Decisions*

148. In Poland, court rulings are not a source of universally applicable law. However, this does not mean that the courts impact is negligible. First of all, one should note the significance of the decisions of the Constitutional Tribunal. The Constitutional Tribunal is often described as the 'negative legislator', as its rulings that declare a provision of criminal law incompatible with a norm of a higher order lead to the elimination of the provision from the law. Sometimes the Constitutional Tribunal also issues 'interpretative judgments', in which it decides what interpretation of a challenged provision conforms to norms of a higher order but does not declare the provision unconstitutional. Since the entry into force of the codes of criminal law (1998), the Constitutional Tribunal has declared the code's provisions unconstitutional on more than ten occasions. It is thus clear that Poland's constitutional court materially affects the shape of Polish criminal law. The jurisprudence of the Supreme Court plays a key role in how the jurisprudential practice of common courts and military courts both develops and becomes more uniform. Apart from deciding appeals in cassation (*infra* paragraphs 797–804), the Supreme Court also has another important power in terms of resolving questions of law referred by criminal courts. A question of law may be presented only by a court of the second instance, in a situation where the examination of an appellate measure reveals a legal issue that requires the clear interpretation of statutory law. Common courts and military courts hearing criminal cases are not legally obliged to follow the arguments presented in decisions of the Supreme Court; however, these decisions have a material impact on the interpretation of laws thanks to the Supreme Court's authority and reputation.

Part I. Criminal Law

Chapter 1. General Principles

§1. Introduction

149. Polish legal scholarship has developed a varied approach to principles of criminal law. This is because individual authors differ in their classifying of particular regulations as principles. However, these differences are only theoretical in their nature because, in general, there are no disputes as to the content of individual provisions, regardless of whether or not they are classified as principles of criminal law. Similarly, the key principles of this branch of law are interpreted in a generally uniform way. The key principles of criminal law will be discussed below.

§2. The *Nullum Crimen Sine Lege* Principle

150. The *nullum crimen sine lege* principle is undoubtedly a crucial tenet of criminal law in a democratic state ruled by law. Its significance is emphasised by the fact that the principle is not only present in domestic legal systems but also has its place in key international human rights conventions – Article 7 of the ECHR and Article 15 of the ICCPR.

151. In Poland, the nullum crimen sine lege principle is enshrined in the Constitution. Article 42 of the Constitution of Poland states that only a person who has committed an act prohibited by a statute in force at the moment of its commission may be held criminally responsible. The above wording is repeated by Article 1 § 1 of the Criminal Code (CC). It is worth noting though that the Polish Constitution also provides that the nullum crimen sine lege principle does not prejudice against holding a person criminally liable for an act which at the time of its commission constituted an offence under international law. Therefore, if domestic norms of criminal law do not criminalise a given behaviour as an offence, this does not mean that a perpetrator cannot be held criminally liable in the case that a given offence is punishable under international treaties or other sources of international law (this rule is known as the 'Nuremberg clause').

152. The scholarship and jurisprudence of the Constitutional Tribunal underscore that the nullum crimen sine lege principle comprises three constituent elements. The first element is the rule, expressed by the Latin maxim nullum crimen sine lege scripta, which states that only written laws – and to be more precise, statutes[4] – can serve as a source of criminal law. The second element is the requirement that provisions of criminal law should be as precise as possible (nullum crimen sine lege certa). The third element prohibits a legal analogy to be applied to the detriment of a perpetrator (nullum crimen sine lege stricta).

153. The principle nullum crimen sine lege scripta deprives the courts of the ability to determine whichat acts are punishable under criminal law by way of judicial decision-making (such an ability has been exercised, for example, by English courts in the case of common law offences), and prevents the creation of offences by custom (which is not a source of universally applicable law). More importantly however, in addition to the above, the principle precludes the imposition of criminal responsibility on the basis of acts of secondary legislation issued by executive bodies. The latter proviso is especially important as it constitutes a guarantee of the strict observance of the principle of division of powers; it guarantees that the authority to regulate issues of criminal responsibility is vested exclusively in the legislative branch (Parliament).

154. According to the case law of the Constitutional Tribunal, a legal provision should *unequivocally designate the recipient of a prohibition, elements of a prohibited act and the type of sanction that may be imposed for the commission of the act in question.*[5] Furthermore, the elements of a prohibited act must be described, to both a recipient of a norm of criminal law and the bodies that apply the law and interpret the norm of criminal law in order to 'decipher' the content of a regulation, in a way that *clearly indicates whether or not given behaviour does, in a specific set of circumstances, satisfy those elements. Since a statute introduces a sanction for prohibited behaviour, it cannot leave individuals unaware of or even unsure as to whether or not certain behaviour constitutes a prohibited act subject to this sanction.*[6]

155. The rule that statutes form the exclusive source of criminal law is not absolute as it is admissible to use so-called blanket provisions, or such provisions that make reference to acts of secondary legislation where elements of a prohibited act are defined in a more detailed manner. The rationale for such measures is pragmatism. Some issues are regulated in acts of secondary legislation because the statutory language must be concise, and, more often than not, due to the requirements of a criminal policy. It must be noted, however, that these acts can only complement the wording of a statutory norm. They may not establish any types or elements of prohibited acts that do not appear in a statutory norm.

---

4. Alternatively, this may also be a norm of international law.
5. Judgment of the Constitutional Tribunal (CT) of 26 Nov. 2003, case no. SK 22/02, OTK ZU vol. 9/A/2003, item 97.
6. *Ibid.*

156. The *nullum crimen sine lege certa* principle means that the language of a provision of a statute of criminal law must be as precise as possible so that its recipients can determine what kind of behaviour constitutes a prohibited act and what does not. This principle is designed, above all, to protect an individual against abuses of power. At the same time, however, a person who is to be held criminally liable must be able to discern between behaviour that is contrary to criminal law and behaviour that is not. This is because such an ability is a necessary condition for both making a conscious choice to behave in a certain way and for ascribing guilt to a perpetrator who has behaved inappropriately.

157. The Constitutional Tribunal emphasises that the pursuit of the full precision of criminal law provisions does not establish a strict prohibition of the use of general, vague or evaluative terms. Therefore, the legislator is not precluded from *defining certain forms of behaviour that constitute a prohibited act in a manner that is general enough to comprise different actions that are prohibited because, for example, of the intended purpose of such actions. In a democratic state ruled by law there is no necessity for the creation of regulations applicable only in a narrowly defined cases (by way of case-based reasoning). This would be impossible for practical reasons. Undoubtedly, one should strive to make criminal provisions as precise as possible. Nevertheless, consideration must be given to the need to maintain the general nature of the law, including criminal law, which means that the courts must be given the opportunity to interpret the law in the process of its application.*[7]

> The Constitutional Tribunal also emphasises that the *nullum crimen sine lege certa* principle *does not require that a legal prohibition or obligation be absolutely clear or communicated in simple terms. (...) The Criminal Code itself uses a large number of vague terms, whose purpose is beyond merely designating the aggravated type of an offence. (...) However, the meaning of such terms is not determined in a legal vacuum (which could lead to uncertainty) but through analysis of the achievements of scholarship, and especially the jurisprudence that authoritatively addresses any existing objective doubts.*[8]

158. The Constitutional Tribunal has formulated requirements that provisions of criminal law must satisfy in order to comply with the *nullum crimen sine lege certa* principle. The Tribunal held as follows:

1) *a provision of criminal law should be precise, clear and legislatively correct;*
2) *a recipient of a norm of criminal law should be able to reconstruct the key elements of a prohibited act solely on the basis of provisions describing the norm and thus with the use of linguistic rules of interpretation;*
3) *an individual should not be uncertain as to whether or not given behaviour constitutes a prohibited act;*

---

7. Decision the CT of 21 Oct. 2009, Case No. P 31/07, OTK ZU vol. 9/A/2009, item 144.
8. Judgment of the CT of 12 Sep. 2005, case no. SK 13/05, OTK ZU vol. 8/A/2005, item 91.

4) *a criminal norm should unequivocally designate the recipient of a prohibition, elements of a prohibited act and the type of sanction that may be imposed for the commission of the act in question;*
5) *any use of terms that are vague or ambiguous in the area of criminal law requires special procedural guarantees that ensure that state bodies provide concrete meaning to a vague expression in a transparent and assessable way.*[9]

159. The criminalisation of 'insults to religious feelings' (Article 196 CC) is an example of the admissible usage of a vague term in the construction of a type of prohibited act. The Constitutional Tribunal found that this usage did not violate the *nullum crimen sine lege certa* principle.[10]

160. The principle of *nullum crimen sine lege stricta* means that analogy-based reasoning that brings about an outcome unfavourable to a perpetrator cannot be used in the course of the interpretation of provisions of criminal law. Therefore, a perpetrator may not be held criminally responsible if a non-prohibited act he or she committed is merely *similar* to an act whose elements have been described in a statute. The prohibition of 'an unfavourable analogy' is closely linked to the necessity to ensure that individuals can foresee the consequences of their actions. One cannot argue with the fact that the above prohibition may sometimes impair the effectiveness of criminal policies. However, here priority is given to the guarantees provided to subjects of criminal law.

161. Given the fact that criminal law relatively often uses terms whose meanings are vague, it is difficult to formulate precise guidelines on how to discern between admissible interpretation and an unfavourable analogy. Unsurprisingly, this issue raises practical concerns. An example here is the body of jurisprudence of Polish courts on the offence of theft with burglary (*kradzież z włamaniem*). Article 279 § 1 of the Criminal Code provides that anyone who commits theft with burglary is subject to a penalty of one to ten years of imprisonment. Without doubt, this provision covers all types of acts that involve the unlawful appropriation of an item of movable property belonging to another person committed after the overcoming of different types of security measures (such as locks, electronic systems, etc.). On the contrary, there is the possibility of an act that involves a perpetrator entering an open room, stealing things and only then overcoming security measures for the purposes of the escape. Courts and some of the scholarship consider such behaviour theft with burglary.[11] However, this position should be assessed critically because the word *włamanie* (breaking and entering, burglary) means the perpetration of an act of overcoming security measures in order to *enter* rather than to *leave* a room. Another example of a determination made in respect of the boundaries of permissible interpretation of the offence of theft with burglary is the Supreme Court's ruling in which

9. Judgment of the CT of 19 Jul. 2011, Case No. K 11/10, OTK ZU vol. 6/A/2011, item 60.
10. Judgment of the CT of 6 Oct. 2015, case no. SK 54/13, OTK ZU vol. 9/A/2015, item 142.
11. Cf. in extenso: L. Wilk [in:] M. Królikowski, R. Zawłocki (Eds.), *Kodeks karny. Część szczególna. Komentarz do art. 222–316*, Vol. II, Warszawa 2013, pp. 554–555.

it was held that a perpetrator who had stolen another person's movable thing by preventing the operation of a security mechanism that protected the object had not committed theft with burglary (in the case in question, the perpetrator had jammed the radio signal of a remote control to a car's door locking system).[12] This position should be regarded as just, even though an act that involves preventing a car lock from engaging is functionally equivalent to actions taken in order to overcome an already engaged lock; from this second perspective it seems reasonable to classify the two types of behaviour in the same way.

§3. The *Nulla Poena Sine Lege* Principle

162. As is the case with the *nullum crimen sine lege* principle, the principle expressed by the Latin maxim *nulla poena sine lege* is regulated principally in Article 42 paragraph 1 of the Polish Constitution. Article 42 provides that a perpetrator may be held responsible only for a prohibited act that is subject to a penalty. The principle means that a perpetrator may only be given a penalty that is prescribed for a given offence in a statute and which has a precisely defined character and features. Furthermore, only a measure (length or value) of a penalty that a statute describes for a given offence can be imposed.

163. The statutory measure of a penalty need not be determined exclusively by a provision that criminalises certain behaviour. It can also be determined by other statutory provisions, for example general provisions that express the sentencing principles included in Chapter VI of the Criminal Code. Such provisions can also be found in other laws outside of the Criminal Code.

164. Pursuant to the *nulla poena sine lege principle,* the legislators are permitted to use 'relatively determined sanctions', or the provisions that authorise a court to decide on the severity of a penalty (e.g., to determine the actual length of a prison term within a certain range – for example, between one year and ten years) or to choose the type of penalty imposed (e.g., a fine, restriction of liberty or a term of imprisonment of up to two years). However, such discretionary authority must not be unlimited, and it would therefore be contrary to the *nulla poena sine lege* principle if a judge had unrestricted authority as to the type and nature of an applied criminal sanction.

165. The *nulla poena sine lege principle* extends not only to penalties, but also to other methods of penal responsesanctions. This means that methods of penal response, just like penalties, they can be imposed only in situations where a statute provides that they may be used as a sanction for a given offence, and also provided that these methods are they must be described in sufficiently precise and detailed terms.

---

12. Decision of the Supreme Court (SC) of 29 Oct. 2012, case no. I KZP 11/12, Biuletyn Prawa Karnego 2012, vol. 10, Item 1.1.4

§4. THE *LEX SEVERIOR RETRO NON AGIT* PRINCIPLE

166. The principle of *lex severior retro non agit* prohibits the retroactive application of norms of criminal law that would be detrimental to a defendant. This principle results from Article 42 paragraph 1 of the Constitution of Poland, which states that only a person who has committed an act prohibited by a statute in force at the moment of its commission may be held criminally responsible. It is worth noting, however, that the Polish Constitution also provides that the principle does not prejudice against the imposition of a penalty for an act which at the time of its commission constituted an offence under international law. Therefore, if domestic norms of criminal law did not criminalise a given behaviour as an offence at the time of its commission, this does not mean that a perpetrator cannot be held criminally liable in a situation in which a given offence was an offence under international treaties or other sources of international law.

167. In Polish criminal law, the *lex severior retro non agit* principle is supplemented by the *lex mitior agit* principle. In accordance with Article 4 § 1 CC, if, between the time when an offence is committed and the time when a case is decided, there has been a change in an applicable statute, the previous law should be applied each time it is more favourable for a perpetrator (Article 4 § 1 CC).

168. The Constitutional Tribunal ruled that the *lex retro non agit* principle does not prevent the legislator from extending the statute of limitations for an offence provided that the offence in question has not become time-barred before the extension becomes effective. The Tribunal justified the above conclusion by holding that regulations on the expiry of the statute of limitations for offences should primarily be linked to *criminal policies that form a part of criminal law rather than to axiological foundations expressed in Article 42 paragraph 1 of the Constitution.*[13]

§5. THE PRINCIPLE OF INDIVIDUAL AND PERSONAL CRIMINAL RESPONSIBILITY

169. Criminal responsibility is individual, which means that only a perpetrator of a prohibited act can be held criminally liable and criminal responsibility cannot be attributed to anyone else, say members of the perpetrator's family or other persons involved in different types of relationships with the perpetrator, as was sometimes historically the case.

Article 21 § 1 CC provides a more detailed definition of individual criminal responsibility: it states that the personal circumstances that exclude, mitigate or aggravate criminal responsibility may be taken into account exclusively in respect of the specific person concerned. An identical principle was established in Article 55 CC, which reads that circumstances that affect the actual measure of a penalty may be taken into account exclusively in respect of the person concerned.

---

13. Judgment of the Constitutional Tribunal of 25 May 2004, case no. SK 44/03, OTK ZU vol. 5/A/2004, item 46.

Criminal responsibility is also personal, which means that a perpetrator may not legally cause responsibility to be transferred to another person who would be held liable in his or her place. Consequently, Article 239 § 1 CC states that is it a criminal offence to serve a sentence for a convicted person while Article 57 of the Petty Offences Code (*Kodeks wykroczeń*) prohibits the organisation or conduct of a public collection of contributions with the purpose of paying a fine imposed as a sanction for an offence. This provision also prohibits persons who are not members of a convicted person's next of kin from paying a fine or offering money to the convicted person or his or her next of kin for this purpose.

§6. The Principle of Guilt

170. Generally speaking, the legislator may freely shape principles of attributing criminal responsibility for legally prohibited acts. However, this freedom is limited by the key principle of criminal law, according to which a perpetrator may be held liable only if he or she is found guilty of having committed an offence. This is because Article 1 § 1 CC clearly states that a perpetrator of a prohibited act does not commit an offence if guilt cannot be attributed to him or her at the time of the act's commission. Criminal responsibility can therefore not be objective or risk-based. In consequence of the above, strict liability offences, which are creations of Anglo-Saxon legal systems, would be contrary to Polish law. Notwithstanding the above, Polish law introduces certain rules of responsibility that are similar to those applicable in cases of strict liability offences. Such rules guide, for example, responsibility for various types of administrative torts (such as violations of competition laws). On the contrary, the latter are not a part of criminal law, although they are treated as an element of the broadly defined 'repressive law' (for discussion on guilt as an element of the offence see *infra*, paragraphs 207–208).

§7. The Principle of Humanitarianism

171. According to the principle of humanitarianism, all human beings should be treated with the respect they rightfully deserve. The principle also prohibits objectification of persons and protects them against being used as instruments of current criminal policies.

The principle of humanitarianism is closely interconnected with respect for human dignity, which – in accordance with Article 30 of Polish Constitution – is inherent and inalienable and constitutes the source of an individual's rights and freedoms. Dignity is inviolable and public authorities are obliged to respect and protect it.

In the context of criminal law, the principle of humanitarianism is expressed in Article 3 of the Criminal Code, which reads that the penalties and other measures provided for in this Code must be applied with consideration for the principles of humanitarianism, and especially with respect for human dignity. This means that all the means of penal response listed in the Criminal Code should be imposed in accordance with the principle of humanitarianism, that is, in a way that prevents a penalty from being inhuman or degrading (inhuman or degrading penalties are also prohibited by Article 40 of the Constitution); moreover, penalties may not be imposed in a way that is disproportionate to the degree of guilt or to the purpose of attaining the objectives of a given penalty.

The principle of humanitarianism applies not only during the sentencing phase, but also during the execution of criminal sanctions. This is because Article 4 of the Criminal Enforcement Code provides that penalties, penal measures, compensatory measures, forfeiture and also protective measures must be applied in a humanitarian manner, with respect for human dignity. The use of torture, or inhuman or degrading treatment or punishment of a convicted person is prohibited. A convicted person retains his or her civil rights and freedoms. Any limitation of such rights and freedoms may only result from a statute or a final ruling issued on the basis of a statute.

Chapter 2. Scope of Application of Criminal Statutes

§1. Principles Concerning the Applicability of Criminal Statutes with Respect to Time

I. Principle of Non-retroactivity

172. Polish criminal law is guided by the binding rule of non-retroactivity of criminal liability. Article 1 § 1 CC provides that only a person who commits an act punishable under the law in force at the time the act is committed bears criminal liability. Therefore, the fundamental principle of criminal law *lex retro non agit* is an essential element of the Polish system of criminal law. This principle also has a constitutional status (Article 42 paragraph 1 of the Constitution of the Republic of Poland).

II. Retroactivity of a 'Milder' Statute

173. Even though the *lex retro non agit* principle applies to Polish criminal law, one can find a notable exception from that rule, which works in favour of the offender (the rule of more lenient (milder) statute). Article 4 § 1 CC provides that *if the law in force during sentencing is different to the law in force when the offence was committed, the new law will apply. However, the former law applies if it is more lenient for the offender.* Therefore, **the new law favourable to the defendant will have a retroactive effect**, even if it came into force after the offence was committed. At the same time, if the former law provides a rule that puts an offender in a more favourable situation (e.g., introduces a lesser sentence for an offence) the former law will apply.

The 'former law' means not only the law that was binding at the time an offence was committed or at the time of sentencing – it may also mean the law that was binding in between the time when an offence was committed and the time when sentencing takes place.

174. In some cases it is not easy to decide which statute is more favourable to a defendant. Polish legal scholarship has developed rules that help in outlining the most lenient rule out of those available:

- the law that is more lenient to a particular defendant, and not in general, should be taken into consideration;
- what must be taken into account is not only the type and degree of the penalty that applies to the case of a particular defendant but also elements that add to passing sentence i.e. possibility of extraordinary mitigation of a sentence (Article 60 CC) or rules applicable to the suspension of a sentence (Article 69 CC);
- it is not possible to apply at the same time rules from two different statutes – only one statute, which in general is more lenient for the defendant in a particular case, can be used (See Resolution of a seven-judge panel of the Supreme Court of 13 January 1970, V KRN 402/69, OSNKW No. 4–5/1970 Item 37).

Polish criminal law establishes additional provisions that apply to legislative changes and operate in situations in which a judgment is final but a sentence has not been yet executed. Therefore, if a sentence concerns an act which carries a penalty which has a lower upper limit under the new law than the penalty imposed, then the measure of penalty will be lowered to the upper limit of the statutory penalty provided for the act under the new law (Article 4 § 2 CC).

Similarly, if according to the new law the offence for which a defendant has been found guilty and sentenced to imprisonment is no longer punishable by imprisonment, an enforceable penalty should be commuted to a fine or the restriction of liberty (Article 4 § 3 CC). In such cases one month of imprisonment is equal to two months of restriction of liberty and sixty daily rates of a fine.

Finally, if an act for which a defendant has been found guilty is no longer punishable, the conviction is *ex lege* expunged. The sentence is no longer enforced and the offence is erased from the criminal record of the originally 'convicted' person.

III. Time of Commitment of an Offence

175. Establishing the time when an offence was committed is essential in criminal law. It allows the determination of whether a committed act was prohibited by the law at the time of an offence, and also which statute is applicable if the law has changed since the commitment of an offence. It is also crucial in determining whether an offender may be held liable with regard to the age at which he or she committed the offence. According to Article 10 § 1 CC, in the provisions of the Code only a person who is 17 years old may be held liable. In case of some offences (e.g., an attempt on the life of the President of Poland, aggravated intentional homicide, causing of grievous bodily harm, causing a life-threatening event) the code provides liability for 15 year-olds (see Article 10 § 2 CC). Establishment of the time when a offence was committed also allows the determination of whether the person was capable of recognising the significance of the prohibited act or of controlling his or her actions due to mental illness, mental deficiency or other mental disturbance (Article 31 CC).

176. The general rule provides that *a prohibited act is deemed to have been committed at the time that the offender acts, or fails to perform an action that they are obliged to perform* (Article 6 § 1 CC). This makes it clear that the time of the commitment perpetration of an offence has to be understood as an act or omission of an act and not the result (effect) of an act (see *supra* paragraphs 190–196).

This is particularly important in case of offences that do require a particular result (in Polish law these are offences of result (*przestępstwa materialne* or *skutkowe*) (see *infra*, paragraph 194)). In such cases, the offence is committed only when a result is achieved (death as a result of murder, damage to property, etc.). The unambigous provision of Article 6 § 1 CC indicates that even though the result of an offence could be achieved later, the actual commitment perpetration of that offence took place when an act, or omission of an act, took place.

This, however, does not help in the case of so-called 'continuous offences' (*przestępstwa ciągłe*) (e.g., illegal possession of a firearm) which are committed during a longer period of time. Therefore, in such cases it is accepted that the time at which a 'continuous offence' is committed is the last act of this kind, or the last moment in which that act occurred. The same interpretation applies to so-called 'offences of multiple acts' (*przestępstwa wieloczynowe*) (e.g., mistreatment) which are usually committed not through a single act but by a repetition of acts, and to offences committed by omission.

§2. Principles Concerning the Territorial Applicability of Criminal Statutes

I. The Territorial Principle

177. The second crucial element in determining the applicability of Polish criminal law is the territorial principle. This ruleIt provides that *Polish criminal law applies to an offender who commits a prohibited act in the Republic of Poland, or on a Polish vessel or aircraft, unless the Republic of Poland is party to an international agreement stating otherwise* (provided in Article 5 CC). That means that **regardless of the nationality of the offender, Polish criminal law will apply to all offences committed on the territory designated as belonging to the Republic of Poland**. Of course, there are notable exceptions to this rule, derived from international law, and in particular from international agreements. One such exception is diplomatic immunity that forbids Poland from investigating and prosecuting offenders who exercise this immunity (see *infra*, paragraph 187).

178. Polish jurisdiction covers the territory of Poland, which is defined under the provisions of The Protection of National Border Act of 12 October 1990 (J.L. No. 1990, No 78, item 461). According to Article 1 of that act, the territory of Poland is delimited by national borders, and includes the airspace above the Polish territory, water reservoirs and interior of the earth. The water borders extend 12 nautical miles from the basic line (Article 3) and the boundaries of Polish airspace are established at around 90 km above ground level. Poland also has jurisdiction over vessels and aircraft that are registered under the Polish flag, however they are not considered Polish territory.

179. To establish the jurisdiction of Polish courts it is necessary to define the place in which an offence has been committed. Article 6 § 2 CC provides guidance in this matter, stating that a prohibited act is deemed to have been committed at the place:

– where the offender acts, or fails to perform an action that the offender is obliged to perform (omission); or
– where the effects of the prohibited act take place (in the case of 'substantive offences'); or
– where the results of the prohibited act are intended by the offender to take place.

This means that a single act may simultaneously be committed in different places (the **principle of ubiquity**). Since this is possible under Polish law, additional rules for the establishment of the jurisdiction of Polish courts are provided in Articles 31–32 CCP. Usually, if an offence has been committed in the judicial circuit of more than one court, the case will be tried before the court in whose judicial circuit investigation was first instituted (Article 31 § 3 CCP). In cases of concurrence of Polish and foreign jurisdictions, international agreements between Poland and a foreign state will decide on the issue.

II. Extraterritorial Criminal Jurisdiction

180. According to the Criminal Code, Poland, in addition to the above rules, reserves the right to investigate and prosecute offences not committed on the territory of Poland. The **principle of active nationality** (*zasada narodowości podmiotowej*) prescribed in Article 109 CC provides that *Polish criminal law applies to Polish citizens who have committed an offence abroad.* In cases an offence being committed outside of Poland, a Polish citizen must expect that the case will be investigated in Poland upon his return.

However, for an act committed by a Polish citizen abroad to be investigated in Poland, it must be considered an offence by the law in force in the state where the offence was committed (Article 111 § 1 CC).

This condition does not apply to a Polish public official who, while performing his or her duties abroad, has committed an offence there in connection with the performance of his duties, or to a person who commits an offence in a place not under the jurisdiction of any state authority (Article 111 § 3 CC).

It should be noted that if an offence has been committed outside of Poland and foreign law is more favourable to the offender, the Polish court when applying Polish law may take these differences into account in favour of the defendant (Article 111 § 2 CC).

181. Offences committed outside of the territory of Poland by foreigners (or stateless people without any nationality) may be investigated and prosecuted on the basis of Polish law in compliance with the **principle of limited objective nationality** (*zasada narodowości przedmiotowej ograniczona*) provided in Article 110 CC. However, in this case one of three conditions has to be met:

(1) an act must be aimed against the interests of the Republic of Poland, a Polish citizen, a Polish legal entity or a Polish organisation that does not have the status of a legal entity; or
(2) an act must be considered terrorism; or
(3) a prohibited act, under Polish criminal law, is subject to a penalty exceeding two years of imprisonment, and the offender must be present in the Republic of Poland while no decision on his or her extradition has been taken.

In this case such an act must also be considered an offence by the law in force in the state where the offence was committed (Article 111 § 1 CC). The exceptions provided in Article 111 § 2 and 3 CC apply accordingly.

182. Polish criminal law also accepts the so-called **royal principle** or **principle of protection of interests** (*zasada narodowości przedmiotowej ochronna nieograniczona*) which applies to a Polish national or foreigner who, regardless of the provisions in force in the place where the offence is committed, commits an offence:

- against the internal or external security of the Republic of Poland;
- against Polish offices or public officials;
- against Poland's material economic interests;
- of false testimony made before a Polish office;
- from which a material benefit was gained, even if indirectly, in the Republic of Poland (Article 112 CC).

183. In Polish criminal law the **principle of universal jurisdiction** (*zasada represji wszechświatowej*), which allows Poland to prosecute certain offences that are considered to be offensive to humanity as a whole, irrespective of who and where the offence was committed, is also observed. According to Article 113 '*regardless of regulations in force in the place where the offence was committed, Polish criminal law applies to a Polish national, or to a foreigner for whom no decision on extradition has been taken, in respect of an offence committed abroad, which the Republic of Poland is obliged to prosecute under international agreements, or in respect of offences prescribed in the Rome Statute of the International Criminal Court*'.

Poland has ratified several international instruments that obligate it to act according to the principle of universal jurisdiction. Some of these are:

- Convention on the Prevention and Punishment the Crime of Genocide (UN Convention of 9 December 1948);
- Geneva Convention for the Amelioration of the Condition of the Wounded and Sick in Armed Forces in the Field (12 August 1949 – the First Geneva Convention);
- Geneva Convention for the Amelioration of the Condition of the Wounded, Sick and Shipwrecked Members of the Armed Forces (12 August 1949 – the Second Geneva Convention);
- Geneva Convention Relative to the Treatment of Prisoners of War (12 August 1949 – the Third Geneva Convention);
- Geneva Convention Relative to the Protection of Civilian Persons in Time of War (12 August 1949 – the Fourth Geneva Convention);
- Convention to Suppress the Slave Trade and Slavery (UN Convention of 25 September 1926);
- Single Convention on Narcotic Drugs (UN Convention of 30 March 1961).

184. Additionally, the Polish Criminal Code contains provisions that penalise offences prescribed in international conventions. Therefore, Poland is obliged to prosecute certain offences not only because these conventions are binding on the territory of Poland but also because they are included in the Polish Criminal Code. These offences include:

- a crime of aggression (Article 117 CC)
- genocide (Article 118 CC)
- crimes against humanity (Article 119 CC)
- war crimes (Articles 122–126 CC)
- piracy (Article 166 CC)
- taking a hostage (Article 252 CC)
- participation in an organised criminal group (Article 258 CC)
- money laundering (Article 299 CC).

§3. Principles Concerning the Personal Applicability of Criminal Statutes

185. Generally, criminal law is applied in an equal way to all offenders if they are old enough to be held criminally liable. According to Article 10 § 1 CC the provisions of this Code apply to anyone aged 17 or older who commits a prohibited act. However, the provisions of this the Criminal Code may apply to minors aged 15 or older who commit a prohibited act enlisted in Article 10 § 2 CC (e.g., murder, aggravated rape or armed robbery), if it is appropriate given the circumstances of the case and the level of mental development of the offender, the characteristics and personal situation, and especially if previously attempts at educational or correctional measures have been ineffective. In such cases the sentence imposed may not exceed two-thirds of the statutory maximum sentence for the offence attributed to the offender; the court may also apply an extraordinary mitigation of punishment. Apart from the above-mentioned, there are further exceptions to the rule that only persons aged 17 or older can be held criminally liable. The application of criminal law to certain persons can be modified for various reasons. In some cases, the applicability of criminal law can be temporarily waived and in some others it can be excluded. This is called immunity. Usually immunity is granted to certain groups of people i.e. high-ranking officials, members of Parliament, judges, diplomats, etc. to allow them to conduct their official functions.

186. In Polish law two types of immunity can be found. The first one, namely **substantive immunity** (*immunitet materialny*), is a permanent exclusion of criminal liability. This means that a person granted such immunity cannot be held responsible for the committed offences, and this also applies to the future. Substantive immunity is quite rare. For example, it is granted to an **attorney** (*adwokat*) in cases when he or she abused the freedom of expression in the course of performing his or her professional duties, in situations where such an abuse would otherwise constitute an insult directed at a party, a party's legal representative or defence lawyer, probation officer, witness, expert witness or translator, which is an offence prosecuted by private accusation, (Article 8 paragraph 2 of the Attorney Act of 26 May 1982 - consolidated text J.L. 2015, Item 615). For such behaviour the responsibility remains only at a disciplinary level. Similar provisions are provided for **legal advisors** (*radcy prawni*) and **public prosecutors** (*prokuratorzy*). Also, **members of both chambers of Parliament** (*posłowie, senatorowie*) enjoy substantive immunity for activities related to their exercise of the office of deputy of the Sejm or senator both during their term of office and afterwards, unless such activities violate third party rights (Article 105 paragraph 1 of the Constitution).

187. The second type of immunity is **procedural immunity** (*immunitet formalny*), which allows for a temporary exclusion of criminal liability. In this case criminal proceedings against a person granted with procedural immunity cannot be initiated or conducted and if they are pending, they must be terminated immediately. The immunity may, however, be waived by the competent authority or when a particular person stops working in her official capacity. Some examples are: President of the Republic of Poland, members of Parliament, ombudsmen, judges, prosecutors and employees of the Supreme Audit Office.

The **immunity of the President of the Republic of Poland** is of a specific character and is regulated in the Constitution of the Republic of Poland (Article 145). For a violation of the Constitution, a statute as well as for the commitment of any offence, the president may be held responsible only before the Tribunal of State. The decision to prosecute the president before the Tribunal of State is vested in the hands of the National Assembly (both chambers of the Parliament sitting together). The position of the Tribunal of State has been discussed in General Introduction (see *supra*, paragraphs 43–44) and in Part II (see *infra* paragraph 478).

Members of Parliament (both of *Sejm* and *Senat*) are granted immunity from the day they are elected in a general election until the date when their term is over. The chamber in which they sit can give permission to charge a member of Parliament with an offence or the member of Parliament himself can waive his or her immunity and agree to be held criminally responsible (Article 105 of the Constitution of the Republic of Poland).

Members of Parliament cannot be arrested or detained on remand without the permission of the relevant chamber of the Parliament. The only exception to this rule is the apprehension in the act and when the arrest is necessary to maintain the proper conduct of criminal proceedings.

Procedural immunity also covers all **judges**. The rule applies to all judges including those sitting at common courts, military courts, administrative courts, judges of the Supreme Court, judges of the Constitutional Tribunal and Tribunal of State. A judge cannot be held criminally liable or deprived of liberty without the permission of the appropriate court determined by law (Article 181 of the Constitution). Similar to members of Parliament, judges cannot be arrested or detained on remand without the permission of the relevant court. Similar provisions apply to **prosecutors**.

A separate type of procedural immunity is **consular and diplomatic immunity** (*immunitet dyplomatyczno-konsularny*). The scope of this immunity is established in Articles 578–584 CCP and in international agreements as well as in international customary law. The basis is provided in Article 31 of the Vienna Convention on Diplomatic Relations of April 1961 and the Article

43 of the Vienna Convention on Consular Relations of 24 April 1963. However, it is the right of the state or an international organisation to waive immunity for a particular person. In such cases the jurisdiction of Polish courts will apply.

Chapter 3. General Principles of Criminal Liability

§1. The Notion of an Offence: Types of Offences

188. The scholarship of Polish criminal law defines an offence as behaviour characterised by the following features:

(1) it is an act committed by a human being;
(2) it is an unlawful act;
(3) it is a punishable act;
(4) it presents a higher than negligible degree of social harm; and
(5) it is a culpable act.

The above approach differs from the method of presenting the structure of an offence in common law countries, where most frequently *mens rea* and *actus reus* are designated as the two constituent elements of an offence. This does not mean that matters considered in the process of establishing criminal responsibility in civil law countries are radically different from those taken into account in common law jurisdictions. The difference is the way in which such concepts are defined in theory. Indeed, the elements listed in paragraphs 1–4 above can be roughly considered as an equivalent of *actus reus,* while the concept of culpability (*zawinienie*) expressed in paragraph 5 can be viewed as corresponding to *mens rea.*

189. Offences are divided into felonies (*zbrodnie*) and misdemeanours (*wyste pki*). A felony is a prohibited act punishable by imprisonment for at least three years, or a more severe penalty. A misdemeanour is a prohibited act punishable by a fine of above 30 daily rates or PLN 5,000 (ca. EUR 1,150), the restriction of liberty for a term longer than a month or a term of imprisonment of longer than a month. The division of offences into felonies and misdemeanours signifies the difference in the gravity of a given prohibited act.

Apart from war crimes and crimes against humanity, the Criminal Code defines fewer than twenty prohibited acts as felonies. The most significant examples of these are voluntary manslaughter and the aggravated forms of rape and robbery. In criminal laws outside the Criminal Code, felonies appear very rarely. The key examples of such felonies are certain offences defined in the Drug Abuse Prevention Act (*Ustawa o przeciwdziałaniu narkomanii*), namely the illegal manufacture, handling, processing of and trading in narcotic drugs or psychotropic substances in a situation where the act in question concerns a significant amount of intoxicating or psychotropic substances, or when the act has been committed for the purpose of obtaining a financial or personal advantage, and the provision of an intoxicating or psychotropic substance to a minor for the purpose of obtaining a financial or personal advantage.

§2. The Material or Physical Element (*Actus Reus*)

I. An Act Committed by a Human Being

190. Under Polish criminal law only a human being may be the perpetrator of an offence. There are two types of offences: those that may be committed by anybody (known as 'common offences', e.g. manslaughter, theft) and those that may be committed only by persons with certain characteristics or in certain circumstances (so-called individual offences, e.g. bribery can be committed only by a public official, desertion can be committed only by military personnel).

Only a person who is able to comprehend the meaning of his or her actions and who is able to control his or her behaviour is capable of committing an offence. For this reason, the legislator limits the extent of responsibility of minors who present a level of intellectual and social development that is insufficient for their understanding of what an offence is. Equally, criminal law prevents the attribution of criminal responsibility to persons who are unable to comprehend the meaning of their actions and control their behaviour due to different kinds of mental disturbances or conditions.

As is quite obvious in present times, in Polish law, criminal responsibility cannot be attributed to animals. Much less obvious and more controversial is the rule that criminal responsibility cannot be attributed to legal persons and other organisational units. However, it must be noted that the above two categories of entities may be held liable under administrative law (e.g., become the subject of sanctions imposed by the President of the Office of Competition and Consumer Protection) and are covered by the special system of liability imposed on collective entities under the Act on the liability of collective entities for acts prohibited under a penalty of 28 October 2002 (J.L. 2002, No. 197, item 1661 as amended). This act enables the imposition of penalties on collective entities in connection with offences committed by representatives of such entities. However, none of the above types of liability constitute criminal responsibility per se.

191. A human act must consist of behaviour that is socially significant; in other words, its consequences must at least be capable of negatively affecting (directly or indirectly) the sphere of social life. This is because there is no rationale for the criminalisation of conduct that may be assessed as wrong but does not adversely affect the life of society.

192. Behaviour may be considered 'an act' (as understood in criminal law) if the perpetrator is psychologically capable of controlling his or her actions. In consequence of the above, an unconditioned reflex, or behaviour resulting from physical duress or a medical condition (e.g., an epileptic seizure or a heart attack) is not an act within the meaning of criminal law. Hence, if in such circumstances a person commits a prohibited act regulated in provisions of a statute of criminal law, then even though the person has behaved in a way described as criminal in the statute, he or she will not be held criminally responsible for his or her actions. Notably, even if the above determination is made, it does not mean that a perpetrator cannot be held criminally responsible for another offence. For example, a person who conceals his or her medical condition and obtains a licence to operate a vehicle and later causes a traffic accident may be held criminally liable for exposing other road users to danger.

193. Each act consists of an observable element (visible conduct) and a psychological element (e.g., a perpetrator's motive). Both are material for the legal assessment of the criminality of a given act.

194. In determining what kind of behaviour constitutes a prohibited act, the legislator may prohibit only a certain type of behaviour (e.g., an insult to a person) or prohibit the causing of a certain result, regardless of the manner in which this result is achieved (e.g., manslaughter). If the case of the former, this pertains to what is known as 'offences of no result' (*przestępstwa bezskutkowe, formalne*), whereas the latter applies to 'offences of result' (*przestępstwa skutkowe, materialne*).

195. A crucial aspect of offences of result is a causal relationship. The notion of a causal relationship is a complex one which raises much controversy, both in criminal law scholarship and in jurisprudence. In short, in criminal law the decisive value is attributed not to the ontological cause-and-effect relation but rather to the designation of how important causal relationships of an ontological nature are for determining criminal responsibility. This is the consequence of the obvious conclusion that not everybody who contributes to the causing of a certain result may, and should, be held criminally liable (e.g., the manufacturer of a firearm that is used to kill a person). According to the concept that should be considered the predominant argument of Polish legal scholarship, the key factor determining the normative attribution of criminal responsibility is a violation of rules of caution in one's conduct which affects a given legal interest, and which creates an extensive and socially unacceptable risk to this interest.[14] The Criminal Code does not define criteria that could be used to assess whether or not the above situation has taken place and the scholarship has not developed a uniform position on this issue. Ultimately, the matter is left for the courts to decide on, on case-by-case basis.

196. An act committed by a human being can take the form of action or omission (inaction). Depending on the type of a given prohibited act, an act may be committed only through action (e.g., theft), only through omission (e.g., a failure to assist a person in a life-threatening situation) or either through action or omission (e.g., voluntary manslaughter, which can be committed by the use of a firearm or as the result of intentionally leaving a wounded person so that he or she bleeds to death).

With regard the responsibility for offences resulting from a failure to act, it must be noted that Article 2 CC provides that criminal responsibility for offences of result resulting from a failure to act may be attributed only to persons who had a specific legal obligation to prevent a result from occurring. This means that the criminal

14. Cf. J. Giezek [in:] M. Bojarski, *Prawo karne materialne. Część ogólna i szczególna*, Warszawa 2010, pp. 113–117.

liability of a gatekeeper who causes a catastrophe by failing to close a gate at a railway crossing is a consequence of the gatekeeper's specific obligation to ensure safety at the crossing, an obligation that results from the nature of his or her work.

In extreme rare cases, the legislator has resolved that criminal responsibility for an offence resulting from a failure to act can be attributed to anybody. An example of such a rule of universal responsibility is Article 162 CC, which provides that any person who fails to assist another person in a situation that involves a direct threat to the aggrieved person's life or the risk of this person sustaining grievous bodily harm will be criminally liable for not assisting, provided that the perpetrator could provide such assistance without exposing himself or herself (or another, third person) to a threat to life or of sustaining grievous bodily harm.

In criminalising certain human behaviour, the legislator is not limited to prohibiting behaviour that involves actions or omissions. Polish law also criminalises the possession of various objects or substances (e.g., narcotic drugs).

II. The Unlawfulness of an Act

197. An act committed by a human being may be considered an offence if, above all, it constitutes a prohibited act. Under Article 115 § 1 CC, a prohibited act constitutes behaviour whose elements are defined in a statute of criminal law. It is the legislator who decides what behaviour constitutes a prohibited act. However, the legislator does not have unlimited discretion in this respect. This is because the only forms of such behaviour that should be prohibited are those that violate or threaten legally protected interests, provided that the degree of such a violation is so serious that it justifies the imposition of a sanction of criminal law rather than the application of other, less severe, measures (e.g., civil law or administrative remedies).

A statute of criminal law must describe in detail all prohibited acts that constitute offences. For practical reasons, the legislator strives to define a given type of prohibited act in the most general manner possible (e.g., 'any person who kills a human being..'). However, more often than not it is reasonable to create a number of different prohibited acts for similar, albeit different types of behaviour, which present various degrees of social harm. Here, the scholarship of criminal law has developed the following classification of prohibited acts:

a) the basic type – based on the general characteristics of a given prohibited act; this type refers to the 'standard' degree of social harm the act presents;
b) the privileged type – in comparison to the basic type, it contains additional elements within a prohibited act's description that result in a more lenient assessment of the social harm the act presents;
c) the aggravated type – in comparison to the basic type, it contains additional elements of a prohibited act's description that result in a more severe assessment of the social harm the act presents.

By way of example, let us consider the offence of voluntary manslaughter: its basic type involves the intentional killing of a human being and is punishable by imprisonment for a term of at least eight years, or the penalty of twenty-five years of imprisonment, or the penalty of life imprisonment (Article 148 § 1 CC). The privileged type of manslaughter is the killing of a human being by a perpetrator in a state of strong mental agitation that may be considered reasonable given the circumstances. In this case, the offence carries the penalty of imprisonment for a term of one to ten years. Conversely, the aggravated type of manslaughter, which is punishable by imprisonment for a term of at least twelve years, the penalty of twenty-five years of imprisonment, or the penalty of life imprisonment, is manslaughter committed with particular atrocity, in connection with hostage-taking, rape or robbery, resulting from particularly reprehensible motives, or committed with the use of explosives.

198. The legislator describes the behaviour that constitutes prohibited acts mainly in the Special Part of the Criminal Code (Articles 117–363 CC). Prohibited acts are also described in other statutes (such as the Drug Abuse Prevention Act or the Mass Events Safety Act).

199. In extraordinary circumstances, it may be the case that a perpetrator will not be held criminally liable even if his or her behaviour meets the statutory description of a prohibited act. This is because the perpetrator's behaviour is not considered unlawful. This happens in situations where certain circumstances, defined in the Criminal Code as 'grounds excluding the unlawfulness of a prohibited act' (Polish: *kontratypy,* defences), appear (see *infra*, paragraphs 219–230).

III. The Punishability of an Act

200. A prohibited act can be considered an offence provided that it carries a criminal penalty (is punishable in criminal law). This is an obvious requirement given the fact that in the case of each offence the legislator designates which means of penal response can be applied to a convicted person. It must be noted, however, that the Criminal Code envisages situations in which the legislator waives punishability due to special circumstances related to a given act's commission. In such cases, the Criminal Code (or another statute of criminal law) uses the phrase 'shall not be subject to a penalty'. Some examples of these situations are given below:

(1) a person who has voluntarily withdrawn from the commission of a prohibited act or prevented a result that constitutes an element of a prohibited act shall not be subject to a penalty;
(2) a person who has voluntarily ceased the preparation of an offence shall not be subject to a penalty for preparation;
(3) a person who exceeds the lawful boundaries of self-defence acting in fear or when agitated shall not be subject to a penalty provided that the fear or agitation may be considered reasonable given the circumstances;
(4) the mother of an unborn baby, who causes bodily harm to the baby or causes a health disorder that poses a threat to the baby's life shall not be subject to a penalty;

(5) a perpetrator who has voluntarily reversed a threat to another person's life or the risk of another person sustaining grievous bodily harm shall not be subject to a penalty for exposing a human being to such a threat or risk.

IV. The Social Harm Presented by an Act

201. A prohibited act can be considered an offence provided that it causes harm to society (is reprehensible and should be punished). This means that a court must determine the degree of social harm presented by a given act on the facts of a particular case. It must be noted, however, that at the general level, the social harm of a prohibited act is also a requisite element for the criminalisation of given behaviour. What follows here is that the legislator should not criminalise acts whose social harm cannot be proved. Moreover, the social harm presented by an act is an important factor affecting the severity of imposed measures of penal response.

Article 115 § 2 CC provides that an assessment of the degree of social harm presented by an offence must consider the following aspects:

a) the type and nature of the violated legal interest;
b) the extent of a loss (caused or threatened);
c) the manner and circumstances in which an act was committed;
d) the significance of obligations breached by a perpetrator;
e) the form of criminal intention;
f) a perpetrator's motives;
g) the type of rules of caution violated and the extent of the violation.

The Criminal Code stipulates that only an act that presents social harm that is not negligible may be classified as an offence (Article 1 § 2 CC). The above means that the legislator law foresees that in practice, in certain situations, a given act that is socially harmful in general may, in a specific case, present negligible social harm because of a perpetrator's personal circumstances or the extraordinary circumstances surrounding its commission. If this happens, it is considered reasonable to avoid holding a perpetrator criminally liable.

The introduction of the requirement that an act must present social harm results in an offence's definition being an offence of result. In consequence of the above, an offence will exist not only if its statutory elements are present, but will also depend on an assessment of the nature of given behaviour and its social significance.

V. The Unity and Multiplicity of Acts

202. A prohibited act is an artificial normative creation, which constitutes a benchmark of human behaviour and which enables the assessment of whether or not given behaviour is legal from the criminal law perspective. However, in practice various practical problems appear in the course of a comparison of a person's behaviour, which is always on a certain continuum, with a behavioural benchmark (the description of a prohibited act) set out in a statute of criminal law. Such a comparison involves the necessity of deciding which part of a person's behaviour is 'an act' in the ontological sense of the word, and whether a number of ontological acts can be considered a single act within the meaning of criminal law. The legislator resolves this issue in statutes of criminal law by creating certain categories of prohibited acts and other special normative structures.

Elements of some prohibited acts will be considered present if the perpetrator exhibits behaviour that consists of multiple acts in the ontological sense. This occurs in the cases of:

(1) double-act offences (Polish: *przestępstwa dwuaktowe*, e.g., theft with burglary under Article 279 § 1 CC, which consists of the overcoming of security measures protecting a given object and then the unlawful appropriation of the object);
(2) lasting offences (*przestępstwa trwałe*, e.g., the offence of unlawfully depriving a person of liberty under Article 189 § 1 CC, which requires the continuous behaviour of a perpetrator);
(3) multiple-act offences (*przestępstwa wieloczynowe*, e.g., abuse of a person under Article 207 § 1 CC, which involves the performance of various actions that cause mental and physical torment to another person);
(4) multiple-type offences (*przestępstwa wieloodmianowe*, e.g., the offence under Article 270 § 1 CC that prohibits *both* the forgery and/or alteration of a document committed for the purpose of using this document as an authentic one *and* then the use of such a document; if a perpetrator forges and later uses a document as an authentic one, he or she will be responsible only for a single offence.

203. There is a special construction, known as the 'continuous act' (*czyn ciągły*), which classifies behaviour that consists of many ontological acts as a single legal act. Under Article 12 CC, if a perpetrator's behaviour consists of two or more actions performed at short intervals in order to achieve a pre-assumed intention, these actions are considered a single prohibited act (Article 12 CC). In the event that a criminal attempt targets a person's personal interests (such as reputation, multiple actions will be considered a single prohibited act if they all affect the same aggrieved person. An example of an situation Article 12 CC situation to which Article 12 CC applies is the systematically recurring theft of cash desk money committed by a cashier.

VI. The Concurrent Application of Provisions of a Criminal Law Statute

204. In the practice of the application of criminal law, a situation often occurs when, a person's behaviour often manifests elements of more than one prohibited act as described in a statute of criminal law. It is worth noting in this context that Polish criminal law has accepted a general rule that one single act may constitute only one offence (Article 11 § 1 CC). Therefore, if an act satisfies the criteria of offences described in two or more provisions of a criminal law statute, the court will sentence the act's perpetrator for only one offence on the basis of all concurrent provisions. Consequently, in such a case the legal classification of an act includes the designation of all provisions that describe the elements of the offence, and the court imposes a penalty under the provision that establishes the most severe penalty, which does not preclude the court from ordering other statutory measures on the basis of all concurrently applied provisions (e.g., the court may apply a penal measure available under a provision that does not set forth the most severe penalty).

A perpetrator may be convicted of a single offence under all the concurrently applicable provisions only when concurrent application is actual (real). This condition results from the concept within scholarship of the so-called apparently **concurrent application** (*zbieg pozorny*). This application occurs in cases where an act establishes basic, aggravated and privileged types of an offence (see *supra*, paragraph 206). In such a situation, an act only apparently manifests the elements of the basic type and the modified (aggravated or privileged) type. In fact, however, the only full and adequate description of a given act is that which appears in the modified type (e.g., manslaughter that occurs 'in the heat of the passion').

205. Even if provisions actually apply in a concurrent manner, this does not mean that the legal classification of an act covers all the provisions violated by a perpetrator's behaviour. This is because the actual concurrence can be either specific (*właściwy*) or non-specific (*niewłaściwy*). The specific concurrence occurs in situations where the actual nature of the act committed can only be conveyed by invoking all the provisions violated by a perpetrator.

An example of **specific concurrence** is the situation in which a perpetrator is charged with taking part in a brawl (Article 158 § 1 CC: *A person who participates in a fight or the beating of another person, in which the victim is exposed to the direct risk of death or the emergence of the result of grievous or moderate bodily harm*), and it has been determined that the perpetrator has caused e.g. moderate bodily harm to another person involved in the fight. In such a case, the accurate legal classification of the act must take into account both Article 158 § 1 CC and Article 157 § 1 CC (the latter provision criminalises the causing of moderate bodily harm).

Conversely, in the case of non-specific concurrence, this nature will be sufficiently conveyed even if some of the applicable provisions are disregarded. In general, **non-specific concurrence** appears in two types of situations. First, it occurs where the 'subsidiarity principle' comes into play, i.e. when a provision of a statute of criminal law can be applied only if there is no other provision that would criminalise given behaviour. An example of this is Article 231 § 4 CC, which reads that Article 231 § 2 CC (*A public official who, by abusing his or her powers or failing to discharge his or her duties, acts to the detriment of a public or private interest in order to obtain a financial or personal advantage*) does not apply in situations that involve the offence of taking a financial advantage regulated in Article 228 CC. If a public official takes a bribe in exchange of an illegal act, his or her behaviour will, as a rule, present the elements of the offences covered under Article 228 § 1 CC and 231 § 2 CC. However, Article 231 § 4 CC classifies the public official's conduct as a prohibited act under Article 228 § 1 CC. Secondly, there is the principle of consumption. This applies to situations in which (for many different reasons) it has been resolved that there is no need for multiple applicable provisions and that it is sufficient to apply only one such provision to address the entirety of the unlawfulness caused by a perpetrator. For instance, a perpetrator of the offence abuse of a person will be responsible for an act under Article 207 CC, but the legal qualification of his or her act will not designate e.g. offences under Article 216 CC (insult to a person) or Article 217 CC (battery) even though the perpetrator's behaviour is likely to manifest elements of these offences as well. The legal classification under Article 207 CC is thus considered (also in respect of the statutory measure of penalty) an adequate response to the nature of the perpetrator's behaviour. If, however, at some point the perpetrator's violence causes moderate bodily harm to the victim of abuse of a person, then the cumulative classification under Articles 217 and 157 CC will apply.

206. The notion of the concurrent application of statutory provisions raises much controversy in practice. This is a consequence of the fact that it is impossible to develop a universally applicable test that can be used to determine the type of concurrence appearing in a given case. This means that in practical terms classifying which kind of concurrence exists in the case of particular behaviour is, to a significant extent, clearly an evaluative exercise.

§3. The Moral or Mental Element (*Mens Rea*)

I. Guilt

207. According to the predominant concept in Polish criminal law, the question of whether a perpetrator can be attributed guilt (culpability) should be dealt with separately from the question regarding the intentional or unintentional nature of the perpetrator's conduct (intentionality). The latter is perceived as a feature of a prohibited act, which consists of not only observable human behaviour but also the sphere of a perpetrator's psychological experiences. Guilt, for its part, is considered a separate element of the structure of an offence. This approach differs from the one characteristic to *common law* countries where both guilt and intention (or absence of intention) are treated as component parts of the concept of *mens rea*. Since the authors have decided to follow the *common law* approach to the matter, culpability and intentionality will be discussed jointly.

208. Pursuant to Article 1 § 3 CC, a **perpetrator of a prohibited act does not commit an offence if guilt cannot be attributed to him or her at the time of the act's commission** (Article 1 § 3 CC). There is a substantial dispute in criminal law scholarship as to the manner in which guilt should be defined. Notwithstanding the doctrinal controversies, nowadays guilt is no longer considered in psychological terms, i.e., the way a perpetrator approaches the prohibited act they he or she commits. Obviously, a perpetrator's approach is significant for the purposes of the determination of the facts of a given case, but it cannot be assumed that it will always have a decisive impact on the process of establishing criminal responsibility. In particular, the psychological theory of guilt fails in the case of offences resulting from a perpetrator's negligence. Here, it is difficult to identify *any* approach on the part of a perpetrator to the act committed: a perpetrator is simply unaware of having violated rules of caution in his or her dealings with a particular legal interest. However, a perpetrator should still be held criminally liable for his or her negligence. For this reason, the normative understanding of guilt is the predominant position of the scholarship of criminal law. Setting aside the various types of normative theories of guilt, it must be noted that guilt involves nothing other than the ability to impute to a perpetrator a defectiveness of his or her motivational process: a perpetrator decides to perform a given act whereas in accordance with socially acceptable rules of conduct, he or she should have behaved differently. Conceived this way, guilt represents a relation between a perpetrator's conduct and model conduct expected from a certain person in a certain situation.[15]

Guilt, as understood in the way described above, performs **two functions**. The first function is **legitimisation**. If a perpetrator is considered not guilty and therefore cannot be imputed with conduct that is contrary to socially acceptable rules governing the treatment of legally protected interests, then this means that even where the perpetrator's behaviour presents elements of a prohibited act, it cannot be considered an offence. The other function of guilt is **limitation**. The limitation function means that the severity of imposed criminal sanctions may not be higher than the degree of guilt.[16]

The assumption that guilt means the ability to impute to a perpetrator a defectiveness of his or her motivational process leads to the conclusion that not everybody is capable of being guilty. Age and mental condition affect this capability. Moreover, in practice, it is possible that in some extraordinary circumstances (related to a perpetrator or an act) guilt cannot be attributed to a perpetrator, even if the perpetrator's conduct manifests the elements of a given type of prohibited act. These are known as excuses, or grounds excluding a perpetrator's culpability (see *infra*, paragraphs 231–238).

II. The Intentional or Unintentional Nature of a Prohibited Act

A. The Intentional Nature of a Prohibited Act

209. Article 9 § 1 CC stipulates that a prohibited act is committed intentionally if a perpetrator has the intention to commit the act, namely if he or she wants to commit it or anticipates a possibility that the act may be committed, and accepts this fact (Article 9 § 1 CC). Thus the essence of intentionality is the existence of an intention to commit a prohibited act. An intention is defined as either the willingness to commit an offence – this is known as a '**direct intention**' (*zamiar bezpośredni*), or the anticipation of the possibility of committing an offence coupled with the acceptance of the realisation of this possibility – referred to as an '**oblique intention**' (*zamiar ewentualny*).

15. For a more extensive discussion, *see* e.g. W. Wróbel, A. Zoll, *Polskie prawo karne. Część ogólna*, Kraków 2010, pp. 314–321.
16. W. Wróbel, A. Zoll, *Polskie prawo karne. Część ogólna*, Kraków 2010, pp. 324–325.

210. The scholarship also includes other classifications of intention. In particular, there is a distinction between sudden and deliberate types of intention (*zamiar nagły* and *zamiar przemyślany*). In the case of the former (known also as 'affective intention', in Polish: *zamiar afektywny*), a perpetrator takes a snap decision to commit an offence, and is often influenced by potent stimuli such as strong mental agitation, while the latter involves a situation in which a decision to commit an offence 'matures' in a perpetrator's mind for a longer period, and is frequently accompanied by time-consuming preparation for the commission of a prohibited act.

Oblique intention is located between direct intention and recklessness (*świadoma nieumyślność*). In practice, it is difficult to establish oblique intention, since the difference between a perpetrator who accepts that an offence will be committed and a perpetrator who has no intention to commit an offence but anticipates that the offence *may* be committed (and attempts to avoid the commission) is quite subtle. In order to identify oblique intention, most frequently an in-depth analysis of the circumstances of a given act is required. For example, the oblique intention to commit manslaughter will be established in a situation where a perpetrator has dealt blows to a victim with such intensity and violence that suggest that the perpetrator must have known that the blows could be fatal for the victim. However, distinguishing the above situation from an instance where a perpetrator is responsible only for a beating of another person that results in the victim's death (not intended by the perpetrator), presents certain evidentiary problems.

211. The form of intention has a material impact of an imposed penalty. In general, direct intention calls for a more severe penalty than oblique intention, and deliberate intention is considered more reprehensible than sudden intention. However, in practice the severity of a penalty depends on the circumstances of a given case and it cannot be excluded that an instance of sudden intention results in the imposition of a penalty as severe as that handed down for an offence committed with deliberate intention, especially when a perpetrator suddenly decides to commit a serious offence (e.g., voluntary manslaughter).

212. Intentionality is closely related to the division of offences into felonies and misdemeanours. Under Article 8 CC a felony can only be committed intentionally, while a misdemeanour can also be committed unintentionally if a statute so provides.

213. The description of a type of a prohibited act does not always expressly designate that a perpetrator's intentional conduct (e.g., the illegal possession of narcotic drugs or firearms) is a condition for the act's commission. However, this does not change the fact that intentionality is always a condition of criminal responsibility unless a statute expressly provides that a prohibited act may be committed unintentionally.

B. The Unintentional Nature of a Prohibited Act

214. **Unintentionality** is, in essence, the **absence of intention**. This concept is explained in greater detail in Article 9 § 2 CC, which stipulates that a prohibited act is committed unintentionally if a perpetrator has no intention to commit the act, but commits it anyway due to his or her failure to exercise the caution required in given circumstances, even though the perpetrator has anticipated or should have anticipated that the act may be committed. It follows from the above that apart from the absence of intention, a material factor here is behaviour that causes an extensive risk to a given legal interest as a consequence of a perpetrator's failure to exercise the caution required in a given situation.

Unintentionality can take one of **two forms**. The first one is **recklessness**. Recklessness exists in a situation where a perpetrator is aware that he or she exposes a given legal interest to an excessive and unacceptable risk and anticipates that a criminal effect (an offence) may result, but thinks he or she is able to avoid it. An example of an offence committed recklessly is a traffic accident resulting from a risky overtaking manoeuvre of another vehicle on a section of a road with an obscured view. The other type of unintentionality is **negligence**. Negligence occurs in a situation in which a perpetrator commits a prohibited act due to his or her failure to exercise the caution required in given circumstances, even though the perpetrator could have anticipated that the act may be committed. In this case, different from recklessness, a perpetrator is not aware that he or she poses a risk to a legally protected interest. Because of this, a perpetrator cannot be punished for taking a wrong decision regarding his or her behaviour, as at the moment this decision was taken he or she was unaware that there was a possibility to have behaved differently and therefore to have obeyed the law. However, a perpetrator may be held criminally responsible for negligent acts because he or she has chosen to act in a way that may objectively be foreseen as inappropriate. This objective foreseeability is assessed from the perspective of a notional reasonable person. This means that the legislator imposes criminal liability as the result of the conclusion that a perpetrator can be expected to have known that he or she was committing a prohibited act.

215. In addition to unintentional offences, Polish criminal law identifies many **intentional offences that contain the additional element of an unintentional consequence**. In accordance with Article 9 § 3 CC, in such a situation a perpetrator assumes more severe liability, which a statute makes contingent on a certain consequence of a prohibited act, if he or she has foreseen or could have foreseen such a consequence. An example of this is an offence described in Article 163 § 3 CC, which establishes criminal responsibility for (intentionally) causing an event that poses a threat to the life or the health of many persons, or to property of a large size (for instance, fire) in a situation in which an *unintentional* consequence of such an event is death or grievous bodily harm suffered by many people.

Chapter 4. Justification, Excuse and Other Grounds of Impunity

§1. General Principles

216. Chapter III of the Polish CC entitled 'Circumstances Excluding Criminal Liability' contains provisions regulating a large group of grounds of impunity (defences). These grounds are not homogeneous in their nature since they include **justifications – grounds excluding the unlawfulness of a prohibited act** (*okoliczności wyłączające bezprawność czynu*) and **excuses – grounds excluding culpability of the perpetrator** (*okoliczności wyłączające winę*).

The grounds of impunity listed in Chapter III of Criminal Code should not be considered as an exhaustive list of circumstances excluding criminal liability. For example, the consent of the victim (see *infra*, paragraph 229) is outside of the scope of the Criminal Code provisions.

217. The definition of an offence in Polish criminal law provides that that an offence is **an act of a human being prohibited under the threat of a penalty by a statute in force at the time of its commission which specifies elements of an offence, which is culpable and from which the resulting social harm is higher than negligible**. The prohibition of an act under the threat of a penalty by a statue in force constitutes the notion of the unlawfulness of an act. Only an act that is wrongful (unjustified) can be considered an offence. Therefore, whenever a person commits an offence that is prohibited under the norms of criminal law (not necessarily provided in the Criminal Code, but also in other statutes) the act should be considered unlawful. However, if an act can be justified in one of the provided ways, the unlawfulness of the act is excluded. These ways are generally called justifications or, even more accurately in Polish law, as 'grounds excluding the unlawfulness of a prohibited act'.

The incorporation of justifications into Polish criminal law is, according to some legal scholars, related to the German concept of 'the negative elements of the offence' (*znamiona negatywne przestępstwa, kontratypy*). In this concept each offence is constructed of positive elements that describe actions (or omissions) undertaken by the offender, and by a lack of negative elements. Therefore, an act should only be considered unlawful if it contains all positive elements of an offence and lacks any of the possible negative elements. If one of the negative elements occurs, one can no longer talk about an unlawful act.

One has to distinguish between the justifications and the notion of negligible social harm (Article 1 § 2 CC). Even though, identically to the case of justifications, an act, which causes negligible social harm, does not constitute an offence, this is not the result of a lack of the unlawfulness of that act, but arises from the absence of the 'substantive element' of an offence.

218. Among the most important **grounds of justification** in Polish criminal law, both codified and non-statutory, one can identify:

- **self-defence** (*obrona konieczna*) – Article 25 § 1 CC;
- **necessity** (*stan wyższej konieczności*) – Article 26 § 1 CC;

- **acting within one's authority or fulfilling one's duties** (*działanie w ramach uprawnienia lub obowiązków*);
- **consent of the victim** (*zgoda pokrzywdzonego*);
- **justified risk** (*uzasadnione ryzyko*) – Article 27 CC.

In case of **excuses**, the act remains unlawful, however cannot be considered as an offence due to the fact that because the culpability of the perpetrator must be excluded. The list of codified excuses includes:

- **insanity** (*niepoczytalność*) – Article 31 § 1 CC;
- **diminished responsibility** (*ograniczona poczytalność*) – Article 31 § 2 CC;
- **insobriety** (*stan nietrzeźwości*) or **intoxication** (*odurzenie innym środkiem*) – Article 31 § 3 CC;
- **error of fact** (*błąd co do faktu*) – Article 28 CC;
- **error of law** (*błąd co do prawa*) Article 30 CC;
- **error relating to grounds of justification or excuse** (*błąd co do okoliczności wyłączających bezprawność czynu lub winę*) – Article 29 CC;
- **following a superior's order** (*rozkaz przełożonego*) – Article 318 CC (see *infra*, paragraph 359).

It must be noted, however, that necessity is sometimes considered as grounds for justification and sometimes as grounds of an excuse, depending on the value of an interest protected by an act. If the interest sought to be protected is of a higher value than the interest sacrificed, it is recognised as justification. However, if the protected interest had an equal or lower value than the sacrificed interest, the necessity will be considered to be one of the grounds of excuse (*infra* paragraph 224).

§2. Grounds of Justification

I. Self-Defence

A. Notion of Self-Defence

219. Article 25 § 1 CC provides that '**anyone Anyone who, acting in necessary defence, repels a direct and unlawful attack on any interest protected by law, shall not be deemed to have committed an offence**'(. Article 25 § 1 CC). The law uses the expression '**necessary defence**' (*obrona konieczna*) and even though traditionally the use the term 'self-defence' is accepted for this justification in criminal law, the code does not limit this justification only to situations in which an attacked interest belongs to the person that repels an attack. Therefore, the interest may be one's own or that of another person. However, because the term 'self-defence' is widely accepted and used in legal scholarship, this term will be also used throughout this monograph.

Self-defence is historically considered a natural right of every human being. It is expressed by Cicero in the Latin phrase *Est enim ea non scripta, sed nata lex, quod vim vi repellere licet* ('For it is not the written but natural law, that it is lawful to repel force with force'). In the Polish literature the acceptance of this right has been justified through different means. One theory provides that self-defence is a form of replacement of the state in its obligation to defend citizens from unlawful acts (theory of replacement). In the socialist doctrine of law, self-defence has even been seen as the obligation of a citizen, being one of the mechanisms for combatting crime. However, it seems that the right to self-defence must, rather, be seen as a human right and this approach is nowadays widely accepted in the literature of Polish criminal law. The Supreme Court, in a dated but still valid judgment, provided that self-defence has as a purpose not only the protection of an interest directly and unlawfully attacked, but also provides the formulation of a principle that the law should not give way to unlawfulness (judgment of the Supreme Court of 27 July 1973, IV KRN 153/73, OSNKW 1974, No 1, Item 5).

B. Requirements

220. Self-defence may be justified only when the following two conditions are met: there must be an attack and the self-defence used must be proportional. These conditions will be discussed below.

Self-defense can be used only when an attack takes place, or at least when an attack threatens a certain interest that must be protected by law. An attack does not necessarily have to take the form of an act, and can also constitute the omission of an act. It must be pointed out again that an attack might be aimed not only at a person who reacts or her interests (self-defence), but also at a third party who is in danger. Article 25 § 1 CC provides for the protection of 'any interest protected by law' and not of any particular interest. Defence against an attack is justified only when the attack meets certain requirements. The attack must be **real, immediate and unlawful**.

The right to self-defence may be exercised only if an attack is **real**. This simply means that if the attack does not exist there is nothing to defend against. Nevertheless, the impression that an attack takes place can be interpreted as an error of fact (see *infra*, paragraph 236) and criminal liability can be excluded anyway by way of the exclusion of an offender's culpability, though only if the error is justifiable.

The **immediacy** of an attack is another element that justifies a defence against aggression. Only current or imminent aggression permits a reaction. As the Supreme Court stated '*the immediacy of the threat comes into play when there is a high degree of probability that the interest at risk will be attacked immediately*' (judgment of the Supreme Court of 11 December 1978, II KR 266/78, OSNKW 1979, No 6, Item 65). Undoubtedly, taking measures against future attacks that have not yet commenced (e.g., the installation of an electric fence around property to repel future possible acts of burglary) cannot be considered self-defence. The moment that is understood to justify the repellence can sometimes be identified with attempts to commit an offence, but not with the preparation to commit an offence, since the latter cannot be understood as putting an interest at immediate risk. However, this immediacy is in its nature open to distinct interpretations and therefore it is almost impossible to provide a clear definition of it.

The attack must be also **unlawful**. This determines that an attack must be committed by a human being, since only a person can act unlawfully. However, this does not mean that an attack constitutes an offence. It is acceptable that an unlawful attack may be committed by a person not criminally liable because of a lack of culpability (e.g., on the grounds of being a minor or insane) or that a person acted outside the limits of the powers granted to them (e.g., beyond the limits of necessity). The unlawfulness of an attack is associated with the problem of permissibility of self-defence against the actions of a public official. It is commonly accepted that the right to self-defence cannot be invoked if the actions of the public official are based on law and carried out in compliance with legal norms (e.g., search and seizure under the Articles 217 and 219 CCP). However, if the actions of a public official consist of the abuse of their rights, it is permissible to react in the form of self-defence. A widely cited example of such behaviour would be stealing goods or the excessive damage to goods during a lawful search.

Self-defense must be also necessary (appropriate). This means that the defence must be proportional and adequate to repel the danger. If the defence goes beyond what is necessary to achieve the goal, which is protecting an interest (i.e., it is excessive), the exclusion of the unlawfulness of committed act would be impossible. Nevertheless, Article 25 § 2 CC provides for some protection (see *infra*, paragraphs 223).

A person defending an interest must be also **aware** that he or she is acting with the aim to repel an attack and with an intent to protect the interest. Unintentional defence is impermissible. A person that attacks a person attempting to attack a protected interest, but who is unaware of the danger of the attack would simply commit an offence (e.g., cause grievous bodily harm) and will not be protected by Article 25 § 1 CC.

The proportionality of a defence must be looked upon in the light of an attack at the moment when the attack took place. In the view of the Supreme Court, the results of a defence are irrelevant if at the time of the attack the form of defence seemed proportionate, since it is the attacker who should be held responsible for the possible results of the defence, not the defender (judgment of the Supreme Court of 31 October 1973, II KR 266/78, OSNKW No 4, Item 61).

C. Exceeding the Limits of Self-Defence

221. Unlike in the case of necessity (Article 26 §§ 1 and 2 CC), the law does not provide explicitly for any precise proportionality requirements between the caused harm and the harm that was prevented. The proportionality of defence arises from regulations that establish the consequences of exceeding its limits when the manner of defence is disproportionate to the danger resulting from the attack (Article 25 § 2 CC).

222. The law provides for two distinct types of excess: intensive and extensive.

Intensive excess means the deliberate use of excessive means or methods of defence in a situation where a person repelling an attack could repel the attack using equally effective but less dangerous means or methods (e.g., instead of shooting an attacker in the head the defender could have repelled the attack by shooting the attacker in a leg, unless the attacker was using a gun or other weapon); however Article 2 (2) (a) of the European Convention of Human Rights, which provides that *deprivation of life shall not be regarded as inflicted in contravention of this article when it results from the use of force which is not more than absolutely necessary in defence of any person from unlawful violence* must be taken into consideration here. This should be interpreted to mean that the death of a person (an attacker) can be justified by the self-defence argument when it remains in relation to the protection of 'any person's' life or personal liberty or integrity. Protection of material interests remain out of the scope of the self-defence argument.

On the contrary, **extensive excess** applies to a defensive action that is undertaken when an attack is not yet at the stage of immediate threat or when a danger has already subsided; therefore, attacking a person who is suspected of plans to attack in the future (but not a person who is approaching with a gun), or attacking a person who has already been disabled, is prohibited.

223. Article 25 § 2 CC provides that committing an offence while exceeding the limits of self-defence in prescribed forms should nevertheless result in a more lenient penalty than would be typically given to a person committing the same offence without invoking excessive self-defence (Article 25 § 2 CC). Therefore, in such cases a court may apply extraordinary mitigation of a penalty or convict a person but refrain from imposing a penalty. Moreover, the court will discontinue the proceedings if the limits of necessary self-defence were exceeded as a result of fear or emotional distress which was justified by the circumstances of the attack (Article 25 § 3 CC).

II. Necessity

A. *The Notion of Necessity*

224. Necessity (sometimes called 'a state of need' or 'protective force') can be defined as a situation in which a protected interest is in immediate danger that can only be averted by sacrificing other protected interests when the danger could not be otherwise avoided (Article 26 § 1 CC).

B. *Conditions of Necessity*

225. Necessity may be justified only if such conditions as the **presence of danger**, the **principle of subsidiarity** and the **principle of proportionality** are met. All of these will be discussed below.

A danger does not have to be caused by a human being, which is the case in justification through self-defence. A danger can **result from any source** that is the result of an action of a human (fire caused by a person), though not necessarily (this can be fire resulting from natural disaster). Nevertheless, a danger must be **real** and if a person sacrifices an interest while mistakenly believing that danger exists, the excuse of error can be invoked (Article 29 CC). Similar to self-defence, only the prevention from **immediate** danger will be accepted. And only an action that is aimed at the prevention of such a danger can be justified by necessity.

The **principle of subsidiarity** with regard to necessity as one of the grounds excluding criminal liability means that only the prevention of a danger that could not be avoided by any other means will be considered as justifiable. Necessity would be rejected when a danger could have been prevented by other conduct, especially such conduct that cannot be described as an unlawful act. Moreover, if fewer interests or those of lower value could have been sacrificed while averting a danger the question might be raised as to whether the reaction was as necessary as it was claimed to have been.

226. Necessity as the grounds for excluding criminal responsibility has two sides. The first one assigns necessity to the group of justifications that exclude the unlawfulness of an act when sacrificed interests are of lower value than interests that have been saved. On the contrary, the sacrifice of interests of the same or higher value than saved interests should be included within the group of excuses excluding only the culpability of an act (Article 26 § 2 CC). However, the provisions regarding necessity as an excuse do not apply where an offender sacrifices an interest that he or she has a special duty to protect, even if it involves exposure to personal danger (Article 26 § 4 CC). It must be noted that the same requirements apply to necessity as a justification and as an excuse.

C. Exceeding the Limits of Necessity

227. Article 26 § 3 CC provides that if the limits of necessity have been exceeded, a court may apply extraordinary mitigation of the penalty, or even refrain from imposing a penalty on the defendant (Article 26 § 3 CC). The law does not provide examples of such exceedance. However, it is clear that the behaviour must go beyond Article 26 § 2 CC, which means that the sacrificed interests must be of a significantly greater value than interests that have been saved.

III. Actions Taken Within One's Authority or in Fulfilment of One's Duties

228. The notion of acting within one's authority or fulfilling one's duties (*działanie w ramach uprawnień lub obowiązków*) is a consequence of the assumption that if one branch of law permits certain behaviour, another branch cannot simultaneously prohibit (let alone punish for) such behaviour. This applies equally to public officials and private individuals. The aforementioned actions relate, for instance, to the authority to detain a person. In the case of public officials, e.g. police officers, such authority may result from the provisions that enable the arrest of a suspected person (Article 244 CCP) while in the case of private individuals, the law provides for the so-called citizen's arrest (*ujęcie obywatelskie*, Article 243 CCP). It must be remembered, though, that the latter authority can only be exercised if a person is detained in the act of committing an offence or in pursuit commenced immediately afterwards, and that detention may only last until the detained person's custody is assumed by competent authorities, who should be informed of the apprehension immediately. If a member of the public apprehending a perpetrator fails to meet any of the above conditions, he or she will be criminally liable.

Authority that excludes the criminality of an act must result from a legal provision of the statutory level. The above-described negative element of an offence (a defence) is not regulated in criminal law but, as was mentioned above, results from the authority to act given by other statutes

IV. The Consent of the Victim

229. A legal interest cannot be considered violated or threatened if a victim has consented to such a violation or being threatened. This defence is known as the consent of the victim (aggrieved person) (Polish: *zgoda pokrzywdzonego*). If consent is given, there is actually *no* victim at all, and the scholarship generally uses the term 'interest holder' (*dysponent dobra*) instead. On the contrary, the consent itself will be legally effective only if it concerns an interest that may be freely disposed by the person granting consent and is given voluntarily and at the moment when the act is committed.

The first condition, namely that **consent must be given in respect of an interest that may be freely disposed by the consenting person**, significantly reduces the applicability of the discussed ground of justification. This is because the majority of legally protected interests may not be violated even with the consent of their holders. The most obvious example of this is causing the death of another human being. In accordance with Polish criminal law, a victim cannot agree to be killed. At the same time, some cases for causing grievous bodily harm may be justified. This can be true in respect of a transplant from a living donor (e.g., a kidney transplant). In such a case, a physician removing the organ obviously does not assume criminal liability, which is excluded by the donor's consent.

The consent given by an interest holder must be **voluntary**. Therefore, a perpetrator's criminal responsibility will not be waived if a perpetrator (or another person) obtains consent from a victim through threat or fraud. Moreover, a victim must be aware that he or she grants consent to certain behaviour on the part of a perpetrator (which is the behaviour that would typically be considered a criminal act in a given situation), but also must know the specific consequences of this behaviour.

Finally, **consent must be given at the moment when the act is committed,** or prior to the commission. Post-facto consent does not exclude a perpetrator's criminal responsibility.

V. Justified Risk

230. Taking justified risk (*uzasadnione ryzyko*), especially that related to scientific experiments, may not give rise to criminal responsibility. Assuming the contrary would thwart scientific progress since the testing of new devices or operation methods would result in liability for any unexpected incidents that may arise.

Article 27 CC permits actions that involve risky behaviour, but only when the following conditions are met:

(1) the purpose of the person taking the risk is to conduct a cognitive, medical, technical or economic experiment;
(2) the anticipated benefit to be obtained from the experiment has cognitive, medical or economic significance,
(3) the benefit can be reasonably anticipated in light of the present state of knowledge;
(4) the purposefulness and manner in which the experiment is conducted are reasonable in light of the present state of knowledge.

If a person is engaged as the subject of an experiment, this person must give his or her consent to participate in the experiment.

Medical experiments are governed by separate provisions of law referred to in Article 27 § 3 CC, namely Articles 21–29 of the Medical and Dental Professions Act of 5 December 1996 (consolidated text, J.L. 2015, item 464).

§3. Grounds of Excuse

I. Insanity

231. According to Article 31 § 1 CC *No offence is committed by anyone who performs a prohibited act while incapable of recognising its significance or of controlling his or her actions due to a mental disease, mental deficiency or other mental disturbance*. This provides the definition of **insanity** (*niepoczytalność*) in Polish criminal law.

The Code provides for three **causes of insanity**:

(1) Mental illnesses

Mental ilnesses are of a progressive character and their origins are organic. In contrast to mental deficiency they do not cause a global reduction of human functioning but rather interfere with some of those aspects (e.g., thinking, perception). The most recognisable mental diseases are: paranoia, cyclophrenia or psychosis.

(2) Mental deficiency (impairment)

Mental deficiency arises in childhood and is not of a progressive character. It takes the form of reduction in overall intellectual ability and features the existence of significant difficulties in learning and social adaptation. Psychiatry uses special tests (e.g., Wechsler-Bellevue test) to determine the intelligence and social functioning of the individual.

(3) Other mental disturbance

Other mental disturbances are a group of causes that are not homogeneous in nature and consist of distinct mental dysfunctions that cannot be included in any of the above groups. Usually pathological intoxication, meningitis and hypnosis are considered other mental disturbances.

232. For the exemption of criminal liability in the case of insanity not only the cause of this state is required, but also a certain **result**, which is either **incapability of recognising the significance of one's actions** or **incapability of controlling one's actions**. Therefore, if one of those results occurred at the time of the commitment of an offence, the culpability of the offender has to be excluded and he would not be held responsible for his actions. This simply means that the offender would not be subjected to any penalty, though the code provides for the possibility of imposing protective measures (e.g., the placement of an offender in a mental facility) to protect society (and sometimes also the offender) from committing any prohibited act again (Article 93 CC et seq).

II. Diminished Sanity

233. The Polish Criminal Code also provides for so-called **diminished sanity** (*poczytalność ograniczona*), also known as a temporary mental disorder. Therefore, Article 31 § 2 CC states: *if an offence was committed while the offender's ability to recognise the significance of the act or to control his or her actions was significantly diminished, the court may apply extraordinary mitigation of the penalty.*

The keyword in this definition is '**significantly** diminished ability', because only this can justify limited culpability. An offender for whom it is established that a prohibited act was committed in a state of diminished sanity is in fact criminally responsible. The only effect that establishing such a state has is the level of culpability that can be assigned to the offender. And it is within the court's discretion as to whether extraordinary mitigation of a penalty is applied.

III. Insobriety and Intoxication

234. Not only mental disorders prescribed in Article 31 § 1 CC may result in the incapability of recognising or controlling actions on the part of the offender. From the practical perspective such incapability is often caused by **insobriety** (*stan nietrzeźwości*) or **intoxication** (*odurzenie innym środkiem*). The excessive use of alcohol, medicines and psychotropic drugs may result in behaviour that falls under the scope of at least Article 31 § 2 CC. However, it would be unreasonable to consider mental disorders and overdoses of drugs or alcohol to be equal, and they definitely should not result in the same consequences for an offender.

For this reason, Article 31 § 3 CC provides that *the provisions of §§ 1 and 2 do not apply where an offender has caused his or her insobriety or intoxication, which leads to an exclusion or limitation of sanity that was or could have anticipated.*

235. In the Polish legal literature one can find distinct justifications for making people responsible for their actions conducted under the influence of alcohol or drugs even when their sanity was diminished. One of them is the doctrine of *actio libera in causa* (freedom of action in due or an act with an illegal cause), which excludes the possibility of determining an offender insane if he or she willingly overdoses on alcohol (or drugs) to commit an offence. The socialist doctrine promoted the concept of responsibility being increased by the fact that an offender acted under the influence of alcohol or drugs. And in Germany the doctrine of so-called *Rauschdelikt* exists, which creates legal fiction that an offender is not responsible for his criminal behaviour, but that he or she is responsible for overdosing on alcohol and breaching the law in such a state of mind.

Under Article 31 § 3 CC the requirement for finding an offender guilty is the offender's anticipation (or the reasonable expectation of this anticipation) that after taking such an amount of alcohol or drugs his or her sanity will be diminished, either wholly or in part. It is clear that taking drugs or drinking alcohol must be conducted voluntarily by the offender and that there is no threat or coercion to do so from other people. Outside of the scope of Article 31 § 3 CC is also pathological intoxication, which may cause diminished sanity and therefore falls under Article 31 § 2 CC.

IV. Error of Fact

236. Polish law also permits a situation in which a perpetrator's culpability is excluded due to the fact that he or she has made an **error of fact** (*błąd co do faktu*). The above rule is based on the assumption that if a perpetrator is unaware of a certain factual element of a given act, he or she cannot be held responsible for this act. Article 28 § 1 CC emphasises that this particular excuse does not extend to any error, but only to **an error as to the circumstances that constitute an element of a prohibited act**. Such an error must also be justified.

A commonly cited example of an error of fact is the case of a person having been fatally shot during a hunt by a hunter who was mistakenly convinced that he or she was shooting at an animal rather than at a human. In such a case, a defendant cannot be found culpable of intentional manslaughter but may be held liable for involuntary manslaughter. If an offence is of an unintentional type only, a perpetrator may assume no criminal responsibility whatsoever.

On the contrary, Article 28 § 2 CC stipulates that a perpetrator who commits an act while reasonably (but mistakenly) convinced that a circumstance that constitutes an element of a prohibited act and carries a more lenient penalty is in place, will be charged under a provision that carries a more lenient penalty. For example, a person who commits voluntary manslaughter (offence under Article 148 § 1 CC) while mistakenly convinced that the victim demanded assistance in causing his or her death because of a serious and incurable medical condition, will be responsible for euthanasia (offence under Article 150 CC).

V. Error of Law

237. Theoretically, everybody should know the law and ignorance of the law is generally not an excuse. According to the famous Latin sentence, 'ignorance of the law harms' (*ignorantia iuris nocet*). Nevertheless, with the amount of law that is produced every day by Parliament, it would be unreasonable to expect that citizens be aware of at least some offences newly introduced into law or rarely used. Typically, offences such as killing another person, robbery or fraud are widely known and no one can hide behind the excuse of a lack of knowledge of their existence. However, on the contrary, the fact that a failure to report the commitment of certain offences to authorities (Article 240 CC) or a breach of voting secrecy (Article 251 CC) constitute offences punishable by law is not general knowledge.

Therefore, Article 30 CC provides that a person does not commit an offence if he or she commits a prohibited act in the justifiable unawareness of the act's illegality. However, if the perpetrator's error is not justified, a court may apply extraordinary mitigation of penalty. It is crucial that a person is *mistaken* about the law that is binding, and not *disagreeing* with it.

VI. Error Relating to Grounds of Justification or Excuse

238. **An error relating to the grounds of justification or excuse** (*błąd co do kontratypu lub okoliczności wyłączającej winę*) also results in the exclusion of culpability. According to Article 29 CC, no offence is committed by anyone who performs a prohibited act while **justifiably** mistaken that grounds of justification or excuse exists (Article 29 CC). If the mistake cannot be justified the person that committed an act is fully criminally responsible, however the extraordinary mitigation of the penalty is possible.

Chapter 5. Forms of Criminal Offence

§1. General Principles

239. Chapter II of the Polish CC entitled 'Forms of commitment of an offence' contains provisions regulating a large and incoherent group of **forms in which an offence can be committed. Two separate subgroups can be singled out: inchoate offences** (typically criminal attempt but also some forms of conspiracy) and **complicity in commitment of an offence** (in some works within this series called 'parties to criminal offences'). These are not treated as separate offences, but as special forms of liability for the commitment (intended) perpetration of the main offence.

In the foreign literature the term "forms" to describe all forms of attempt and complicity is rarely used and it might appear a little misleading. However, since the structure of Polish law refers directly to this term, it will be used throughout this monograph.

§2. Inchoate Offences

I. Overview

240. The concept of **inchoate offences** (*formy stadialne*) is bound up with the idea of the 'march of an offencepath towards perpetration of the offence' (*iter delicti*). The idea of committing an offence is born in the mind of the future potential perpetrator. However, the law does not recognise consider mere thinking about the commitment perpetration of an offence as punishable. Psychologically internal acts remain outside of the scope of criminal law.

The list of acts punishable by under criminal law begins with **preparation** (*przygotowanie*) to commit an offence e.g. acquiring or preparing tools or conspiring. Generally, the criminalisation of preparation is not a rule but, rather, an the exception. Committing an offence in the form of punishable preparation is punishable only with respect to some offences and only when a law specifically provides for it (see *infra*, paragraphs 241–244).

After the stage of mere preparation of an offence, the actual **attempt** (*usiłowanie*) to commit an offence it may be visible. An attempt basically means that a perpetrator with the intent to commit a prohibited act directly aims to commit that act, but it is subsequently not committed. The reasons why the commitment did not occur may be intentional or unintentional. The difference between these two scenarios and their consequences will be discussed below (see *infra*, paragraphs 245–248).

Finally, the actual **commitment perpetration** of an offence takes place. Everything that happened before falls in the category of inchoate offences.

II. Preparation

241. **Preparation** (*przygotowanie*) is punishable only when the law establishes so (Article 16 § 2 CC). Therefore, as a rule the preparation to commit an offence is not punishable by Polish law. The justification to punish some offences for their preparation is dictated by the weight of legal interests protected by law. However, this is not the only factor, since e.g. the simple preparation of manslaughter is not punishable.

242. In the Polish CC, the preparation to commit the following offences is punishable:

- crime of aggression (Article 117 § 2 CC);
- genocide (Article 118 § 3 CC);
- coup d'etat (Article 127 § 2 CC);
- violent assault on a military unit (Article 140 § 3 CC);
- some offences against public safety, such as causing a life-threatening event or piracy (Article 168 CC);
- causing a disaster in land, water or air traffic (Article 175 CC);
- forgery, counterfeiting or altering documents (Article 270 § 3 CC);
- counterfeiting or altering currency or securities (Article 310 § 4 CC);
- desertion (Article 339 § 4 CC).

243. Preparation to commit an offence in Polish criminal law may take **two forms** (see Article 16 § 1 CC). The first form is described as taking actions that are intended to create conditions for the undertaking of an act directly leading to the commitment of a prohibited act, and in particular to obtain or use means, collect information or prepare an action plan. The second form of preparation is **conspiracy**, i.e. the agreement between two or more people to commit an offence. Some countries, though not Poland, recognise conspiracy as a separate inchoate form of committing an offence. In the case of Poland, conspiracy is by law and by interpretation a part of the broader form, which is preparation (it is sometimes called 'the preparation to commit an offence in a personal form').

The actions that may be undertaken in the course of the preparation of an offence are not limited in any way to those mentioned in Article 16 § 1 CC. The imagination of the person preparing an offence might be broader than that of the legislator. However, to hold a person criminally responsible for the commitment of the preparation of an offence these acts must be conducted with the **aim of committing an offence**. If someone, as a hobby or as a part of his work, gathers information on security features that prevent forgery, counterfeiting or altering documents, this will not be considered as the preparation of an offence. However, if it can be proven that the real aim of gathering such information was to alter documents in an illegal way, criminal responsibility may be attributed to such a person.

244. The law enables a perpetrator to avoid criminal responsibility or, to be more exact, a penalty, for criminal preparation, provided that the perpetrator behaves in way described in the legal term of **'active repentance'** (*czynny żal*), namely when he or she has voluntarily withdrawn from an attempt to commit a prohibited act, and in particular destroyed prepared resources or prevented future use of such resources, and, if the perpetrator has conspired with another person in order to commit a prohibited act, has made material attempts aimed at preventing the commission of a prohibited act (Article 17 § 1 CC). However, the Criminal Code establishes stricter requirements for the invoking of active repentance in respect of criminal preparation of certain offences described in the Special Part of the CC. For example, in order to show active repentance for the preparation of an attack against a constitutional body of the Republic of Poland (offence under Article 128 § 2 CC) a perpetrator must disclose to a law enforcement authority all material circumstances of the committed act (Article 131 § 2 CC).

III. Attempt

245. Under Polish law, criminal responsibility is attributed also attributed to a person who attempts to commit an offence. **An attempt** (*usiłowanie*) is something more than preparation. It is defined as the action (or inaction) of a person who, acting with the intention to commit a prohibited act, envisages the commission of this act directly through his or her behaviour, though the actual commission does not occur (Article 13 § 1 CC). An attempt to commit an offence is subject to the same criminal sanction as that applicable to the actual commission (Article 14 § 1 CC). In practice, however, due to the fact that in the sentencing phase the court also takes into consideration 'the type and measure of negative consequences of an offence' (Article 53 § 2 CC), the penalty imposed on a perpetrator of an attempted offence is usually more lenient because this type of offence most frequently has no negative consequences.

It may be inferred from the fact that an **intention** (*zamiar*) is a necessary feature of an attempt that it is impossible to attempt to commit an unintentional offence. Conversely, an attempt may well be discerned in the case of perpetrators acting with either a direct or an oblique intention, as the Criminal Code does not limit the liability for an attempt to offences that may be committed only with direct intention.

246. A perpetrator's behaviour may be considered to constitute a punishable attempt if it **could lead directly to the perpetration of a prohibited act**. Behaviour that *indirectly* leads to the commission of a prohibited act may merely constitute preparation. Obviously, determining when an action (or inaction) of a perpetrator leads directly to the commission of an act is a matter of discretionary evaluation and, to a large extent, depends on the act and the circumstances of its commission. However, this determination is of fundamental significance because preparation, as a rule, is not punishable while an attempt is *always* punishable. This question remains controversial and the jurisprudence of the Polish Supreme Court offers no categorical resolution to the problem.

A necessary requirement for an attempt is also **the absence of the commission of an act**. This requirement is self-explanatory: if an act were committed, a perpetrator would be charged with commission and not attempt.

247. As in the case of preparation, active repentance shown by a perpetrator of an attempted offence (withdrawal from commission or prevention of a result that constitutes an element of a prohibited act) will result in no penalty being imposed on this perpetrator (Article 15 § 1 CC). This is a consequence of the assumption that persuading would-be perpetrators to withdraw from their criminal attempts brings benefits to society even if the cost is a waiver of a penalty. Moreover, the motives guiding a perpetrator who expresses active repentance are immaterial. A penalty will be waived even if the only factor affecting a perpetrator's behaviour is the fear of criminal liability. A 'repentant' perpetrator will also not be held criminally liable for preparation – this is a direct consequence of the language of Article 17 § 2 CC. On the contrary, if the action taken in order to withdraw from commission or prevent a result that constitutes an element of a prohibited act proves to be ineffective (ineffective active repentance), a perpetrator will be charged with an attempt, although they may hope for extraordinary mitigation of a penalty (Article 15 § 2 CC).

IV. Attempting the Impossible

248. The Criminal Code establishes criminal responsibility for behaviour that leads directly to the commission of an act where the actual commission does not happen not because of a perpetrator's active repentance but rather due to the perpetrator being unaware of the fact that it is impossible to commit the offence. Such behaviour is referred to as an **impossible attempt** (*usiłowanie nieudolne*). However, an impossible attempt will be punishable only if a perpetrator is unaware that commission is impossible due to **the absence of an object on which a prohibited act may be committed or because of the use of means unsuitable for the commission of a prohibited act** (Article 13 § 2 CC).

The rationale behind making such behaviour punishable is not to address a violation of or even a threat to any legal interest, but rather to respond to the danger that may result from the future actions of a perpetrator. This is because one can hypothetically assume that in light of a certain failure in the present, a perpetrator attempting the impossible may make another (successful) attempt at committing the act in the future.

The penalty for an impossible attempt is, as a rule, equal to the penalty imposed for an attempt proper, since the Criminal Code does not differentiate the measure of such penalties depending on whether an attempt is possible or impossible, and employs only the term 'attempt' (Article 14 § 1 CC). However, Article 14 § 2 CC stipulates that in the case of an impossible attempt a penalty may be extraordinarily mitigated or even waived altogether.

§3. Parties to Criminal Offences

I. Overview

249. Polish criminal law distinguishes between **forms of perpetration** (*formy sprawstwa*) and **accessorial liability** (*odpowiedzialność akcesoryjna*). In the first group one can find such forms of commitment of an offence as:

(1) **direct (principal) perpetration** (*sprawstwo*)
(2) **complicity** (*współsprawstwo*)
(3) **directing the commission of an offence** (*sprawstwo kierownicze*).

The law regulates this by simply stating that *not only is the offender of a prohibited act liable, whether alone or together with an accomplice, but also anyone who organises a prohibited act to be carried out by another person, or who, taking advantage of the dependency of another person on him or her, orders that person to commit the prohibited act* (Article 18 § 1 CC).

The second group is limited to two forms, which are **instigation** or inducement (*podżeganie*) and **aiding** the commitment of an offence (*pomocnictwo*) (Article 18 § 2–3 CC). It must be noted however, that in many states instigation and aiding are treated as forms of participation in someone else's offence. As a consequence, if a perpetrator's liability is excluded, the liability of the instigator or of the aider is also excluded accordingly. Obviously, this strict theory has many exceptions and currently the liability of instigator and aider is treated independent from the liability of the perpetrator. But in Polish criminal law, instigation and aiding, since the Criminal Code of 1932, are understood as separate forms of commitment perpetration of an offence and not forms of participation in someone else's offence. Therefore, naturally the liability of the aider and instigator is fully independent from the liability of the principal perpetrator.

250. The liability of all perpetrators for an offence, regardless of the form in which they committed the offence, is of an **individual** character in Polish criminal law. According to Article 20 CC, *everyone participating in carrying out a prohibited act is liable within the limits of his or her intent, or lack thereof, irrespective of the liability of other participant*s. This means that the exclusion of liability of one of the perpetrators has no effect on the criminal liability of other perpetrators. Moreover, the liability of perpetrators is limited to their intent. This can mean that one perpetrator will be liable for an intentional offence while another individual will be liable for an unintentional offence. Therefore, all excesses of co-perpetrators remain outside of the scope of liability of other perpetrators.

Article 21 § 1 CC also confirms the **principle of the independent individual criminal liability of all participants in the commitment of an offence**. It provides that *personal circumstances excluding, mitigating or aggravating an individual's criminal liability are only considered for the person they relate to*. These circumstances cannot be elements of an offence and are not circumstances affecting the sentence (*a contrario* Article 55 CC). These are, for example, circumstances excluding or limiting criminal liability or guilt, e.g. insanity (Article 31 § 1 CC), as well as extraordinary mitigation or the aggravation of a penalty.

Regulations relating to a perpetrator's voluntary withdrawal from an attempt to commit a prohibited act or an attempt to prevent consequences of a prohibited act (which is known as 'active repentance', or *czynny żal* in Polish) apply to all perpetrators of an offence prescribed in Article 18 CC (including aider and instigator). According to Article 23 § 1 CC, the perpetrator will be not held responsible if he or she voluntarily prevented the commitment of an act. If the coperpetrator took efforts but was not successful in his actions the court may extraordinarily mitigate the penalty (Article 23 § 2 CC).

II. Forms of Perpetration

A. Direct Perpetration

251. The most common form of commitment of an offence is **direct perpetration** (*sprawstwo*). This means that one person by his or her own actions, or by the omission of an act, has fulfilled all necessary elements of an offence.

B. Complicity

252. The second form of perpetration is **complicity** (*współsprawstwo*), which means that two or more persons commit an offence jointly. Co-perpetrators (accomplices) must, before or during the perpetration of an offence, achieve an agreement. This agreement does not necessarily have to be made explicitly. Implied forms of agreement are also considered as adding to the joint commission of an offence.

The liability for the commitment of an offence in complicity concerns not only actions undertaken by each co-perpetrator individually but also for actions undertaken by other co-perpetrators. Therefore, the range of the agreement is crucial in attributing to an accomplice the commitment of an offence. However, if the accomplice joined the action when the commitment of the offence had already commenced, he or she will be responsible only for the part of criminal activity in which he or she took part. Unless an agreement made before the commencement of an act involved joining the action at a later stage and it was discussed and accepted before by the accomplice. Similarly, if one of the co-perpetrators acted beyond the agreement, others will not be liable for his or her excess. This can be illustrated through a situation in which an accomplice agreed to commit only a theft and burglary in a house but in the course of events one of the perpetrators killed the owner of the house. Only the actual perpetrator of that act will be responsible for the killing. The rest of the accomplices would be held liable for theft and burglary only.

253. The simultaneous commitment of an act by two individuals but without any previous agreement cannot be considered complicity. For example, when two perpetrators decide to steal something from the same shop and conduct this offence at the same time by chance. Each of them will be held liable for their his or her actions independently.

The most problematic situation remains that in which co-perpetrators agree to commit an offence together but only certain elements of an offence are fulfilled by actions of all co-perpetrators while some of them perform actions that fulfil other elements of the same offence. Such conduct of a perpetrator can easily be confused with aiding in the commitment of an offence since the perpetrator's involvement in the commitment of an offence is only a limited one. Therefore, it is crucial to establish a clear distinction between aiding and complicity. According to the current theory of liability of accomplices in Polish law, what matters is **the significance of the role of the individual in the commitment of an offence**. If, without actions undertaken by the individual, an offence would not be achieved or very would be hard to achieve, it means that the role that the individual played in the commitment of an offence would definitely be the role of an accomplice.

254. Polish criminal law also establishes so-called **necessary cooperation** (*uczestnictwo konieczne*). This can be found in different articles of the Special Part of the Criminal Code: for example, committing rape in concert with another person (Article 197 § 3 CC) or participation in an organised group or association whose purpose is to carry out a criminal offence (Article 258 CC). Necessary cooperation is different from complicity because it is an element of a legal definition of the offence. The offence cannot be carried out without the participation of the other person.

C. Directing the Commission of an Offence

255. Committing an offence **through another person,** seen as leadership in the commitment of an offence and **ordering** the commitment of an offence, is are defined in Polish law as **directing the commission of an offence** (*sprawstwo kierownicze*)

256. **Committing an act through another person** was introduced in the Polish Criminal Code to establish the criminal liability of a person that takes leadership uses others to in the commitment of the offence. However, it is essential that the leader former person never directly commits the act. It is possible to attribute an offence to the leader only if he or she retained actual control over the commitment of a prohibited act. The power to decide on the commencement of an act, as well as changes in the conduct and continuation of that act, must remain in the hands of the leader. According to some legal scholars, this form of commitment of a prohibited act is similar to the instigation or aid in commitment of an offence and does not constitute a separate form. Despite these views, the Polish CC clearly provides for committing an act through another person as a separate form of perpetration of an offence.

257. The second form of directing the commission of an offence is **ordering the commitment of an offence**. In this case the person that orders the commitment of an offence does not lead control the individual perpetrator, leaving all decisions to this individual besides the direct order to commence it. To commit an offence in this form the person that gives the order must **take advantage of the dependency of the individual perpetrator**. This differentiates this form of commitment of an offence from instigation. If there is no dependency between the person that orders the commitment of an offence and the individual perpetrator, one can only talk about instigation. Usually this form of commitment of ordering an offence is attributed to bosses of groups of organised crime, where details of an offence are decided by subordinates but the ultimate decision to commit it remains in hands of one person – the boss.

III. Instigation and Aiding

A. Instigation

258. **Instigation** (*podżeganie*) means the inducement of another person to commit a prohibited act (Article 18 § 2 CC). Such conduct does not have to take a verbal form; a person may be induced by, e.g., a gesture.

Instigation requires direct intention, which means that an instigator must want to induce a perpetrator to commit a prohibited act and must want to have this act committed rather than merely accept the possibility that his or her actions may lead to its commission. Given the above, instigation cannot be unintentional.

The act described as incitement of the commission of an offence (Article 255 CC, *nawoływanie do popełnienia przestępstwa*) is an offence separate from instigation. The difference is that instigation affects an individual person or a specified group of persons, whereas incitement (which may be communicated through mass media) is directed at a generally undefined group of persons, including random recipients.

A penalty for instigation is imposed within the statutory limits stipulated for direct (principal) perpetration (Article 19 § 1 CC). In this case, the Criminal Code does not provide any grounds for the extraordinary mitigation of a penalty.

B. Aiding

259. **Aiding** (*pomocnictwo*) is defined in Polish law as the mode of liability in which a perpetrator (aider), acting with the intention to have another person commit a prohibited act, behaves in a way that facilitates the commitment of an offence, and in particular delivers tools, means of transport, offers advice or information; it also covers situations when an aider who, having assumed a specific obligation to prevent the commitment of a prohibited act, facilitates the commitment of the act by another person through his or her inaction the commission of the act by another person.

Thise above definition serves as the basis for distinguishing two distinct types of aiding: **physical** (e.g., delivery of tools) and **psychological** (e.g., offering advice).

The timing of an aider's actions is crucial for determining whether he or she is criminally responsible for aiding the commission of an offence. This is because aiding involves only those actions that precede or accompany the commission of a prohibited act. If an action is taken after an offence has been committed, e.g. a person harbours the perpetrator of an act, such action may present the elements of the offence of being accessory after the fact (*poplecznictwo* – Article 239 CC). In such a case, and in the case of certain offences, persons aiding a perpetrator post-factum may be held criminally liable for the offence of handling stolen goods (but not as aiders – Article 291–292 CC).

260. There are some problems involved in distinguishing between complicity and aiding is not easy. Notwithstanding multiple theories on this issue developed by the scholarship and in the absence of a uniform jurisprudential position of the Supreme Court, it should be assumed that the relevant differentiating criteria are, first and foremost, the elements of an offence, and then the perpetrator's intention (has a given person acted with an intention characteristic of an accomplice or instead with that typical for an aider).

261. It is accepted that, unlike with aiding differs from instigation in that, a perpetrator acting with an oblique intention may also be charged with aiding. However, aiding cannot be unintentional. The scholarship also dismisses the notion of liability for aiding (as well as for instigation) in the case of unintentional offences. On the contrary, an attempt to instigate or aid is possible and punishable.

At the same time, for individual offences, or offences that may be committed only by perpetrators with certain characteristics (e.g., only a member of the military may commit the offence of desertion), it is sufficient that an aider (and also an instigator) is aware of the presence of such a characteristic in the perpetrator (Article 21 § 2 CC). The above means that a civilian may instigate a member of military personnel to commit desertion or assist the latter in committing this offence.

Similar to instigation, a penalty for aiding is imposed within the statutory limits margins stipulated for direct (principal) perpetration (Article 19 § 1 CC). On the contrary, the court imposing a penalty for aiding may apply extraordinary mitigation of a penalty (Article 19 § 2 CC).

Chapter 6. Classification and Survey of Criminal Offences

§1. General Classification of Criminal Offences

I. Statutory Dichotomy of Criminal Offences

262. The main criterion that allows for the classification of **criminal offences** (*przestępstw*) is the **gravity of an offence** (*waga przestępstwa*). According to Article 7 CC, offences Offences in Polish criminal law can be divided into **felonies** (*zbrodnie*) and **misdemeanours** (*występki*). (Article 7 CC).

Felony can be defined as ais the prohibited act punishable by a penalty of not lower than three years of imprisonment (Article 7 § 2 CC). What matters here is the lower end of the statutory penalty range. By way of example, a felony will carry a sentence of three to fifteen years of imprisonment, while an offence carrying a sentence of two to ten years is classified as a misdemeanour. An example of a felony is voluntary manslaughter (Article 148 § 1 CC) and an aggravated type of rape, e.g. committed together with another person (Article 197 § 3 CC).

A **misdemeanour** is a prohibited act punishable by a fine of above 30 daily rates or above 5,000 PLN, a restriction of liberty of not lower than one month and a penalty of imprisonment of not lower than one month (Article 7 § 3 CCP). The number of misdemeanours in Polish criminal law is much higher than the number of felonies. For example, rape in its basic type (Article 198 § 1 CC) and theft (278 § 1 CC) are classified as misdemeanours.

263. The consequence of differentiating between felonies and misdemeanours is in general of procedural character. For instance, preliminary proceedings in the case of felonies will be undertaken in the form of an investigation (*śledztwo*) and in case of misdemeanours, generally, in the form of an inquiry (*dochodzenie*). The formality of proceedings and the engagement of the prosecutor in the case of investigations will be higher than in the case of inquiries (see *infra*, paragraphs 568–569). The other procedural consequence is that, only in the case of misdemeanours, the prosecutor will have the right to conduct negotiated justice proceedings, according to Article 335 CCP, and file a motion to sentence a defendant without holding a trial (with or without indictment). This is forbidden in the case of felonies (see *infra*, paragraph 53).

264. Apart from criminal offences, the law has created the category of **petty offences** (*wykroczenia*), or acts that are subject to a penalty no harsher than that imposable for misdemeanours. It must be remembered, however, that the Criminal Code exclusively describes felonies and misdemeanours while petty offences are regulated in the Petty Offences Code (*Kodeks wykroczeń*). Notwithstanding the above, all types of prohibited acts can also be regulated in laws other than the aforementioned codes, which means that the list of criminal offences presented in the Criminal Code is by no means exhaustive. All offences regulated outside the Criminal Code are subject to the provisions of its General Part.

II. Intentional and Unintentional Offences

265. The second classification of offences is based on the criterion of culpability and allows the differentiation between **intentional offences** (*przestępstwa umyślne*) and **unintentional offences** (*przestępstwa nieumyślne*). Article 8 CC states that **a felony can be committed only intentionally, while a misdemeanour may also be committed unintentionally but only if the law provides so**. There are no exceptions from the rule of felonies being only intentional offences.

However, even in the case of misdemeanours, unintentional misdemeanours are much rarer than intentional ones. When the provisions of law are silent on the form of guilt, the presumption should be that a misdemeanour is of an intentional character (e.g., theft – Article 278 CC, or fraud – Article 286 CC). Some examples of unintentional misdemeanours are involuntary manslaughter (*nieumyślne spowodowanie śmierci*) (Article 155 CC) or causing a traffic accident (Article 177 CC). However, in such cases the law explicitly provides that both offences are unintentional.

The issues of guilt (*wina*) and intentionality have been discussed in detailed in Chapter 3. General Principles of Criminal Liability (see *supra*, paragraphs 207–215).

III. Offences Involving a Commission of an Act or Resulting from a Failure to Act

266. Another classification of offences is based on differentiating between **offences involving a commission of an act** (*przestępstwo z działania*) or **offences resulting from a failure to act** (*przestępstwo z zaniechania*).

Some offences are considered solely as those that can be committed in the form of an act (e.g., rape – Article 197 CC). Others belong to the second group of offences committed in the form of the omission of an act (e.g., a failure to provide assistance – Article 162 CC). However, some may belong to both groups and only the behaviour of the perpetrator will allow the determination of how in fact an offence has been committed (voluntary manslaughter – Article 148 CC).

The issue of acts and omissions which constitute offences, has been discussed in detail in Chapter 3. General Principles of Criminal Liability (see *supra*, paragraph 196).

IV. Offences of Result and Offences of No Result

267. The fourth criterion upon which offences can be divided is the result of an offence. Polish criminal law recognises **offences of result,** (*przestępstwa skutkowe, materialne*), and **offences of no result** (prze*stępstwa bezskutkowe, formalne*).

Offences of no result are those that can be committed even if no actual result comes from them. It is enough that an offender behaves in a certain way for the offence to occur. For example, a failure to provide assistance (Article 162 CC) or giving false testimony (Article 233 CC).

Offences of result are those that can be committed only if a result occurs and, in fact, the result is one of the elements of such an offence. Example of such an offence are criminal damage (Article 288 CC) or depriving a person of liberty (Article 189 CC).

V. Offences Subjected to Public or Private Prosecution

268. Another useful criterion allowing for the differentiation between offences is the criterion of the public or private interest that an offence attacked affected or threatened. The first group is larger and is called **offences subject to public prosecution, public offences** (*przestępstwa ścigane z oskarżenia publicznego, przestępstwa publicznoskargowe*). The second group of offences is called **offences subject to private prosecution, private offences** (*przestępstwa ścigane z oskarżenia prywatnego, przestępstwa prywatnoskargowe*).

The group of **offences subject to private prosecution** is rather small. It consists of four offences only, namely: causing a minor bodily injury or a minor impairment to health (Article 157 § 2 and 3 CC), defamation (Article 212 CC), insult (Article 216 CC) and breach of personal inviolability (Article 217 CC). It is solely the aggrieved party's responsibility to investigate and prosecute these offences. The common element here is the assumed lack of public interest in investigating and prosecuting these offences (see *infra*, paragraphs 659–663, 751–761).

Offences subject to the public prosecution can be further divided into two subgroups: the group of **offences prosecuted ex officio** (*przestępstwa ścigane z urzędu*) and **offences that are prosecuted upon complaint** (*przestępstwa ścigane na wniosek*). According to Article 9 § 1 CCP, criminal justice bodies carry out proceedings and undertake actions ex officio, unless, by virtue of the law, a complaint from a specified person, institution, or authority, or permission from an authority is required. Therefore, commencing preliminary proceedings in the case of offences investigated upon complaint is possible only if the aggrieved person files an official complaint. Examples of offences prosecuted upon complaint are: criminal threat (Article 190 CC) and theft committed to the detriment of next of kin (Article 278 § 4 CC). Therefore, they may appear similar to offences subject to the private prosecution, since the public interest is low. They are, however, investigated by the police and the prosecutor for the simple fact that it would be too difficult for the aggrieved party to gather enough evidence independently to prove the case in court. Offences prosecuted upon complaint and the procedure regarding taking a complaint have been discussed in detail in Part II (see *infra*, paragraphs 589–590).

§2. Survey of Criminal Offences

269. The nature of this monograph does not allow a comprehensive study of all distinct offences that are a part of Polish criminal law. The number of offences is massive and they are not even regulated in a clear manner, which makes a discussion of them even more complicated. In general, offences can be divided into two distinct groups, i.e. those that are provided in the Criminal Code and those that are regulated outside of the scope of the code in separate statutes. Both groups of offences will be discussed below accordingly.

I. Offences of the Criminal Code

A. General Introduction

270. The Polish Criminal Code contains three distinct parts: (I) The General Part, (II) The Special Part and (III) The Military Part. The contents of the first part have been discussed above. The contents of the second and third parts are solely limited to the definitions of offences and penalties provided separately for each offence. Both of these remaining parts are furthermore divided into chapters that refer to certain groups of offences, e.g. Chapter XIX Offences Against Life and Health or Chapter XXXV Offences Against Property. The Military Part however also contains some general provisions when it comes to offences committed by soldiers (Chapter XXXVIII).

271. The criterion on which the systematic order of offences in the Special Part is based is the protected legal interest (*dobro prawne*) attacked by the offence. The type of legal interest attacked can be derived from the title of each chapter. Nevertheless, there are some doubts when it comes to certain offences as to whether they should be assigned to a particular group. For example, fraud (*oszustwo*) has been included in the Chapter XXXV Offences against property but the right place for that offence could also be Chapter XXXVI Offences against commercial operations.

272. The Special Part of the Criminal Code starts with chapters containing offences that violate the legal interests of society as a whole (against peace, against the Republic of Poland, etc.), followed by offences violating the most basic rights of the individual (the life and health). After that, offences against other legal interests are described in a sometimes contested order. Below, the groups of offences will be discussed in accordance with the structure adopted in the CC.

B. Offences in the Special Part of the Criminal Code

273. Chapter XVI – **Crimes against peace, crimes against humanity and war crimes** (*Przestępstwa przeciwko pokojowi, ludzkości i przestępstwa wojenne*) (Articles 117–126 CC). For many years Polish law lacked a comprehensive regulation of crimes against peace, crimes against humanity and of war crimes. One of the best known (and piecemeal) norm-setting attempts in this area was the Decree of 31 August 1944 on the imposition of penalties on Fascist and Nazi criminals guilty of murder and abuse of a person of the civilian population and prisoners of war and on traitors to the Polish nation (consolidated text J.L. 1946, No. 69, item 377, as amended). This decree, however, applied to a narrowly defined category of offences. Another law, the Peace Defence Act of 29 December 1950 (J.L. 1950, No. 58, item 521) exclusively regulated war propaganda as a crime against peace.

Despite relevant attempts having been taken at the legislative stage, the new Criminal Code of 1969 did not regulate crimes against peace, humanity and war crimes.

274. A new chapter devoted to these offences was only added in 1997 to the Criminal Code. To underline the chapter's significance, drafters of the code decided to make it the first chapter of the code's Special Part.

275. Offences described in Chapter XVI can be divided into four groups: crimes against peace, the crime of genocide, crimes against humanity and war crimes. Definitions of these offences are similar to (albeit not the same as) their counterparts present in international conventions such as the Rome Statute of the International Criminal Court.

276. The category of **crimes against peace** (*przestępstwa przeciwko pokojowi*) includes the offences of initiating or waging a war of aggression (Article 117 § 1 CC), which may be commenced as inchoate offences by preparation (Article 117 § 2 CC) and the offence of publicly inciting a war of aggression (Article 117 § 3 CC).

277. Article 118 CC defines **genocide** (*ludobójstwo*) more broadly than the 1948 Convention on the Prevention and Punishment of the Crime of Genocide (J.L. 1952 No. 2, item 9, as corrected). This article describes the crime of genocide as, among other things, manslaughter or inflicting grievous bodily harm *with the intent to destroy, in full or in part, any ethnic, racial, political or religious group, or a group with a certain world-view.* Preparation to commit genocide is also punishable.

278. **Crimes against humanity** (*przestępstwa przeciwko ludzkości*) include a massive or systematic attack against a civilian population undertaken with the intent to implement or support a policy of a state or an organisation, which can take the form of one of the serious prohibited acts (offences) enumerated in the provision regulating this offence, for example manslaughter, rape, imprisonment or the use of torture (Article 118a CC).

The use of violence against a person because of the person's national, ethnic, political or religious affiliation, or because of the absence of religious beliefs also constitutes a crime against humanity (Article 119 CC).

279. All **war crimes** (*przestępstwa wojenne*) are punishable only if they are committed "contrary to a prohibition established in international law' or 'in violation of international law', which is a clear reference to the subject matter of Geneva and Hague Conventions, and of customary international law.

The Criminal Code provisions on war crimes criminalise violations of international law norms governing, e.g. the admissibility of certain methods of warfare and types of weaponry, the treatment of prisoners of war and civilians, etc. (Articles 120–126 CC). Public incitement to commit crimes against humanity or war crimes and publicly expressing approval for such offences are also punishable by criminal law (Article 126a CC). Furthermore, a superior who, failing to exercise a duty of reasonable control, permits the commission of any acts described in Articles 118-126a CC is criminally liable, including if he or she commits this act unintentionally (Article 126b CC).

280. Chapter XVII – **Offences against the Republic of Poland** (*Przestępstwa przeciwko Rzeczypospolitej Polskiej*) (Articles 127–139 CC)

281. Offences against the Republic of Poland are the most serious offences committed against the state and some of its institutions. The purpose of defining these offences is to protect the state and its constitutional system.

282. The offences in this category include **high treason** (*zdrada główna*), which involves actions taken in collaboration with other persons that directly lead to depriving Poland of its independence, detaching a portion of its territory, or overthrowing by force its constitutional system (Article 127 CC). This offence may be committed only by a group of at least three persons.

High treason should be distinguished from a **coup d'etat,** which consists in taking actions that lead to the forceful removal of a constitutional body of the Republic of Poland, and also preparations for such actions (Article 128 §§ 1 and 2 CC). In this case, there is no requirement for at least three perpetrators for the offence to be committed; their actions do not need to be taken with the purpose of depriving Poland of its independence, etc. Another punishable act from this category is affecting by force or by unlawful threat the official activities of a constitutional body of the Republic of Poland (Article 128 § 3 CC).

283. **Diplomatic treason** (*zdrada dyplomatyczna*) defined in Article 129 CC, involves actions taken to the detriment of the Republic of Poland; however, this offence may only be committed by a person who is authorised to act in the name of the Republic of Poland in relations with the government of a foreign state or a foreign organisation (e.g., an ambassador or an official of the Ministry of Foreign Affairs).

284. The offence of **espionage** (*szpiegostwo*) may be committed by a person who is engaged in the activities against the Republic of Poland of a foreign intelligence service against the Republic of Poland, or a person who, while engaged in the activities of a foreign intelligence service or acting for the benefit of such a service, furnishes a foreign intelligence service with information, the transmission of which may be detrimental to the Republic of Poland, or by a person who organises or directs the activities of a foreign intelligence service, and also by a person who collects or stores information, or connects to a computer network with the purpose of obtaining such information (Article 130 CC).

Furthermore, an operative of a Polish intelligence service can commit the offence of providing intelligence disinformation, for example deceiving a Polish intelligence service by furnishing counterfeit or altered documents or by concealing true information of material importance to the Republic of Poland (Article 132 CC).

285. The discussed category of offences also includes public **insult to the**

Nation or the Republic of Poland (*znieważanie Narodu lub Rzeczypospolitej Polskiej* – Article 133 CC), **assault against the President of Poland** (*zamach na Prezydenta RP*), which may take the form of an attempt on the President's life (Article 134 CC) or a physical assault (Article 135 § 1 CC), **insult to the President of Poland** (*zniewaga Prezydenta RP* – Article 135 § 2 CC), and also **insult to state symbols** (*znieważanie symboli państwowych*), which may involve behaviour such as destroying or damaging emblems, banners, flags or other state symbols, both Polish (Article 137 § 1 CC) and those of a foreign state (Article 137 § 2 CC). Other offences that may be committed against foreign public officials are regulated in Article 136 CC with the proviso that such offences are punishable only if a foreign state enforces similar regulations according to the principle of reciprocity.

286. Certain offences against the Republic of Poland regulated in Articles 127–128 and 130–131 (high treason, coup d'etat and espionage) are also prosecuted by the Polish state if they are committed against an allied state that ensures reciprocity in this respect (Article 138 § 2 CC).

Chapter XVIII – **Offences against national defence capability** (*Przestępstwa przeciwko obronności*) (Articles 140–147 CC)

287. The diverse category of offences against defence capability includes, first and foremost, the offence of **subversion** (*dywersja* – Article 140 CC). Subversion may take the form of a violent assault on a unit of the armed forces, or destroying or damaging a defence facility or equipment, provided that the purpose of these actions is to undermine the defensive power of the Republic of Poland. Commission of the same act but with a different purpose may only lead to a perpetrator being responsible for destruction of property (Article 288 CC).

288. Polish law criminalises service in a foreign military force (*służba w obcym wojsku* – Article 141 § 1 CC) but this prohibition does not apply to Polish nationals who are also nationals of, and reside in, another state (Article 141 § 3 CC). On the contrary, criminal law establishes an absolute prohibition of mercenary military service, which is also prohibited by international law (Article 141 § 3 CC). Another punishable offence is **organising recruitment to a foreign military** (or to mercenary service) (*organizowanie zaciągu do obcego wojska* – Article 142 CC).

289. There is also a separate offence of **avoiding military service** (*uchylanie sie od służby wojskowej*), which may be committed by a person who inflicts, or enables another person to inflict, grievous bodily harm or other material disruption of bodily functions or a health disorder on himself with the intention of obtaining exception from compulsory military service or a postponement of such service (Article 143 § 1 CC); this offence also includes doing the same for another person (Article 143 § 2 CC). Other provisions of Chapter XVIII (Articles 144–147 CC) criminalise other forms of avoiding military service.

290. Chapter XIX – **Offences against life and health** (*Przestępstwa przeciwko z˙yciu i zdrowiu*) (Articles 148–162 CC)

291. The first of the offences defined in Chapter XIX is **voluntary manslaughter** (*zabójstwo*) defined as the intentional killing of another human being (Article 148 § 1 CC).

Next, the Criminal Code defines the offence of **murder** (*morderstwo*), which is the aggravated type of manslaughter and involves the intentional killing of another human being but also requires that a perpetrator's act satisfies any of the following conditions of murder:

(1) the killing is committed with particular atrocity;
(2) the killing is connected with the taking of a hostage, rape or robbery;
(3) the killing is caused by particularly reprehensible motives;
(4) the killing is committed with the use of a firearm or explosives (Article 148 § 2 CC).

The penalties for murder are imprisonment for a term of at least twelve years, the penalty of twenty-five years of imprisonment or the penalty of life imprisonment. The same penalties may be imposed for the manslaughter of a public official committed in the course of (or in connection with) the official's discharge of his or her professional duties relating to the protection of people's safety, or the protection of public safety or order (Article 148 § 3 CC).

On the contrary, a privileged type of manslaughter, usually termed '**voluntary manslaughter in the heat of passion**' (*zabójstwo w afekcie*), involves the killing of another human being by a perpetrator in a state of strong mental agitation that may be considered reasonable given the circumstances (Article 148 § 4 CC). 'Strong mental agitation' is understood as a non-abnormal mental state in which emotions take superiority over the intellect, and which causes a limitation of the mind's controlling ability. As a rule, such agitation is deemed 'reasonable' in certain circumstances, when strong mental agitation is a response to behaviour of the soon-to-be victim such as abuse of a person, marital infidelity, grave insult – in other words, in a situation where the manslaughter was, to some extent, provoked by the victim.

Another privileged type of manslaughter is **infanticide** (*dzieciobójstwo*), which may be committed only by a mother and involves the killing of her own child in the course of birth while influenced by the experience of the birth (Article 149 CC). The penalty for infanticide is imprisonment for a term from three months to five years.

The last privileged type of voluntary manslaughter is **euthanasia** (*zabójstwo eutanatyczne*), which is the killing of another human that is driven by compassion for the victim and committed at the victim's request (Article 150 § 1 CC). The Criminal Code provides that a perpetrator of euthanasia may benefit from extraordinary mitigation of a penalty; in exceptional cases, the court may choose not to impose a penalty on the perpetrator (Article 150 § 2 CC).

292. Under Polish law, it is a criminal offence to **persuade another person to commit suicide or assist another person in committing suicide**, regardless of whether the suicide attempt proves to be successful (Article 151 CC).

293. **Abortion** (*aborcja*), understood as termination of a woman's pregnancy, is punishable by Polish law under certain conditions. Termination of a pregnancy, even with a woman's consent, is subject to the penalty of imprisonment of up to three years, unless it is performed in accordance with a statutory provision (Article 152 § 1 CC). The provision in question is Article 4a of the Act on family planning, protection of a human foetus and conditions of admissibility of the termination of pregnancy, which enables abortion in the following situations:

(1) if a pregnancy poses a threat to the life or health of the pregnant woman;
(2) if prenatal test and other medical indications suggest a substantial probability of a severe and irrevocable defect of the foetus or an incurable condition that threatens the foetus' life;
(3) if there is a reasonable suspicion that a pregnancy is the result of a prohibited act (e.g., rape).

It is also a criminal offence to assist a pregnant woman in the termination of a pregnancy and to persuade a woman to perform an abortion, though here the woman herself will not be held criminally liable for the offence (Article 152 § 2 CC). The aggravated type of this offence is the termination of a pregnancy that results from the use of violence against a pregnant woman or otherwise terminating a pregnancy without her consent, and also causing the termination of a pregnancy in a pregnant woman by force, unlawful threat or under false pretences. These forms of the offence of abortion are punishable under Polish law, provided that certain conditions are met (Article 153 § 1 CC). An abortion that results in the death of the pregnant woman carries a more severe penalty (Article 154 CC).

294. The Criminal Code further regulates the offence of **inflicting bodily harm** (*spowodowanie uszczerbku na zdrowiu*), which may involve either a disruption of bodily functions (e.g., bone fracture) or inflicting a health disorder, that is, causing pathological abnormalities (e.g., HIV infection). Inflicted bodily harm can be grievous (e.g., when a person is blinded or suffers another form of severe disability – Article 156 CC), moderate (this category includes all the remaining cases of inflicting bodily harm provided that a disruption of bodily functions or a health disorder lasts for a period longer than seven days – Article 157 § 1 CC), or light (a disruption or disorder lasting for a period shorter than seven days – Article 157 § 2 CC). The latter category is an offence prosecuted by private accusation (see *infra*, paragraphs 659–663, 751–761).

295. Other offences against life and health that are criminalised by Polish criminal law are, among others, brawl (*bójka*), defined as a struggle between at least three persons where each person involved assumes simultaneously the role of an attacker and the attacked; **beating** (*pobicie*), which is where at least two persons attack at least one person (Article 158 CC); **exposing a human being to a direct threat of death or of sustaining grievous bodily harm** (Article 160 CC); **failing to assist another person at risk** of death or of sustaining grievous bodily harm (Article 162 CC). In the case of the latter offence, criminal responsibility is waived if providing assistance to another person would result in the person providing assistance being exposed to the same risk as that to which the potential recipient of assistance is subjected.

296. Chapter XX – **Offences against public safety** (*Przestępstwa przeciwko bezpieczeństwu powszechnemu*) (Articles 163–172 CC). The main type of offence against public safety is the offence of **causing an incident that poses a threat to the general public** (*sprowadzenie zdarzenia powszechnie niebezpiecznego*), described in Article 163 CC. An incident that poses a threat to the general public is every incident that endangers the life and health of multiple persons. The above provision applies only to this specific situation, whereas the safety of individual persons is protected under Article 160 CC. A threat to the general public is considered to include a threat to property of a large size. The financial value of the property is irrelevant for the purposes of determining its size, which is understood as relating to physical dimensions.

An incident that poses a threat to the general public may take any of the following forms:

(1) a fire;
(2) the collapse of a structure, flooding, landslide or rockslide, or avalanche;
(3) the detonation of explosives or flammables or other rapid releases of energy; the dissemination of poisonous, suffocating or skin-irritating substances;
(4) a rapid release of nuclear energy or a release of ionising radiation.

Bringing about the direct risk of an incident that poses a threat to the general public (*sprowadzenie bezpośredniego niebezpieczeństwa zdarzenia powszechnie niebezpiecznego*) is also a criminal offence (Article 164 CC). Both offences can also be committed unintentionally.

Moreover, Article 165 CC criminalises the **causing of an incident that poses a public threat of a different type** (*sprowadzenie niebezpieczeństwa powszechnego w innej postaci*), which may involve the causing of an epidemiological risk, the manufacturing of or trading in medically hazardous substances in foodstuffs, damaging or disabling public utility facilities (e.g., gas or water delivery systems), interfering with processing, or the collection or communication of computer data.

297. The discussed category of offences also includes the offence of hijacking a sea or an inland vessel or an aircraft by a perpetrator who uses deceit or violence against a person or who threatens the use of such violence (Article 166 CC). Arming or modifying a sea vessel designed for piracy is also a criminal offence (Article 170 CC).

A new type of offence is **financing terrorism** (*finansowanie terroryzmu*), which may involve collecting, transferring or offering money, financial instruments, securities, foreign currencies, property rights, or movable or immovable property for the purposes of financing a terrorist offence (Article 166a CC).

298. It is worth noting that for some of the offences described in Chapter XX, the mere preparation may also be committed through preparationan offence (Article 168 CC). Article 169 CC stipulates that perpetrators of some of the abovementioned offences may avoid penalty on condition that they voluntarily reverse a threat (show active repentance).

Chapter XXI – **Offences against traffic safety** (*Przestępstwa przeciwko bezpieczeństwu w komunikacji*) (Articles 173–180 CC)

299. The first offence among offences against traffic safety is the offence of **causing a traffic catastrophe** (*spowodowania katastrofy komunikacyjnej* – Article 173 CC). A catastrophe must affect land, water or air traffic and threaten the life and health of multiple persons or property of a large size. This means that the definition of the offence in question includes an element of threat to the public. The aggravated type of this offence is causing a traffic catastrophe that results in the death of a human being or grievous bodily harm suffered by multiple persons (Article 173 § 3 CC).

Bringing about the direct risk of a traffic catastrophe is also a criminal offence (Article 174 CC); the same is true of the preparation to cause such a catastrophe (Article 175 CC). However, if a perpetrator reverses an impending risk, he or she will not receive a penalty (Article 176 § 1 CC). It is also possible to grant extraordinary mitigation of a penalty to a perpetrator who has committed the act but has nevertheless voluntarily reversed the threat to the life or health of the persons affected (Article 176 § 2 CC).

300. Another offence against the safety of traffic is the causing of a traffic accident (*spowodowanie wypadku komunikacyjnego* – Article 177 CC). Similar to a traffic catastrophe, a traffic accident may occur in concern land, water or air traffic. The offence may be perpetrated by either a person operating a vehicle or by a pedestrian. This offence is unintentional, as an accident is frequently linked to negligent behaviour of the perpetrator who commits this offence, as the relevant provision reads, '*by violating, even unintentionally, the safety rules for land ..traffic*'. An accident is criminally punishable only if it results in moderate bodily harm (as indicated in Article 157 § 1 CC). Conversely, Article 177 § 2 CC defines the aggravated type of this offence, the classifying criterion of which is a result caused by an accident, namely the death of another person or grievous bodily harm.

301. The Criminal Code provides for more severe penalties for the commission of offences against traffic safety where the acts described in Articles 173, 174 and 177 CC are committed in a state of intoxication or under the influence of a narcotic drug, or if a perpetrator flees from the scene of an accident (Article 178 CC).

Operating a vehicle while being intoxicated or under the influence of a narcotic drug (*prowadzenie pojazdu w stanie nietrzeźwości lub pod wpływem środka odurzającego*) is also a stand-alone criminal offence (Article 178a CC). Repeat offenders of this offence are subject to harsher penalties (Article 178a § 4 CC).

The Criminal Code defines the state of intoxication as the situation where a perpetrator's blood alcohol content is, or leads to a concentration of, higher than 0.5 per mille, or when the alcohol content in 1 sq. dm of breathing air is, or leads to a concentration of, higher than 0.25 mg (Article 115 § 16 CC). Vehicle operators with alcohol content levels lower than those mentioned above will be charged with committing a petty offence.

302. In addition to the above, Chapter XXI criminalises the offence of **permitting the operation of a motor vehicle or other vehicle when it is in a condition that is immediately threatening to the safety of land, water or air traffic, or permitting the operation of a motor vehicle or other vehicle on a public highway, in a residential area or in a traffic area by an intoxicated person, a person under the influence of a narcotic drug or by a person who does not possess the required licence** (Article 179 CC); and the offence of **performing, in a state of intoxication, duties directly related to the maintenance of the safety of vehicles** (Article 180 CC).

Chapter XXII – **Offences against the environment** (*Przestępstwa przeciwko środowisku naturalnemu)* (Articles 181–188 CC)

303. This category of offences include the offence of **destroying plant or animal life** (*niszczenie świata roślinnego lub zwierzęcego* – Article 181 CC). Here, criminal responsibility is assumed by perpetrators who cause destruction of considerable scale (Article 181 § 1 CC) or destruction that results in material losses in protected areas (i.e., national wildlife or scenic reserves) (Article 181 § 2 CC), and also – irrespective of the place where destruction is inflicted – it is assumed by perpetrators who destroy or damage protected species of plants or animals. This offence can be committed either intentionally or unintentionally.

304. Another kind of offence against the environment is **environmental pollution** (*zanieczyszczenie środowiska* – Article 182 CC). As a criminal offence, environmental pollution involves the contamination of water, air or soil with either a substance or with ionising radiation of such a volume or in such a form that it may pose a threat to human life or health or cause material deterioration of the quality of water, air or the surface of the earth, or substantial contamination of plant or animal life. An aggravated type of this offence is the commission of the aforementioned act in connection with the operation of a system which is operated as part of an establishment and involves the use of environmental resources that requires a licence.

Additional provisions criminalise causing environmental pollution related to the illegal handling of waste, primarily violations of waste management rules stipulated in the Waste Management Act of 14 December 2012 (consolidated text J.L. 2013, item. 21), and also environmental pollution caused by nuclear materials or other sources of ionising radiation (Articles 183–184 CC).

305. The legislator further criminalises **failures to discharge existing obligations regarding the upkeep and maintenance of (and failure to use) devices that protect water, air or the earth's surface against contamination** or devices that protect against radioactive contamination or ionising radiation, and also instances of constructing or making available for use or occupancy building structures that lack such protective devices (Article 186 CC). **Destroying, seriously damaging or materially diminishing the natural value of a legally protected area or facility, which results in a considerable loss,** is also a criminal offence (Article 187 CC).

306. Chapter XXIII – **Offences against liberty** (*Przestępstwa przeciwko wolności*) (Articles 189–193 CC). The basic offence defined within the category of offences against liberty is the offence of **unlawfully depriving a person of his or her liberty** (**unlawful detention,** *pozbawienie człowieka wolności* – Article 189 § 1 CC). Obviously, this offence involves the deprivation of liberty in the physical sense of the word, and may take various forms of actually depriving a victim of the ability to leave a space established by a perpetrator. If unlawful detention lasts longer than seven days, it is subject to a more severe penalty (Article 189 § 2 CC). The same is true of unlawful detention coupled with exceptional torment (Article 189 § 3 CC).

307. Another offence against liberty is a **criminal threat** (*groźba karalna* – Article 190 CC). Here, the thereat affects liberty understood as freedom from anxiety and fear for one's well-being. This offence involves threatening to commit an offence against another person or against persons close to him or her. A criminal threat is present each time a specific consequence is achieved, namely when the threat's recipient experiences reasonable fear that the threat will materialise. This does not mean, however, that the threat must be real. It is sufficient that the recipient of the threat believes that it is real.

308. **Stalking,** or **persistent harassment** (*uporczywe nękanie* – Article 190a § 1 CC), is an offence previously unknown to Polish criminal law, and which was added to the Criminal Code relatively recently (in 2011). It involves the persistent harassment of another person or of this person's next of kin, which causes in the victim a sense of danger, which is reasonable in the given circumstances, or materially violates the victim's privacy.

A variety of this offence is impersonating another person by using this person's likeness or other personal data in order to cause a loss to property or personal injury to this person (Article 190a § 2 CC).

The aggravated type of the offence of stalking is the commission of either of the above acts that results in the victim attempting to take his or her own life (Article 190a § 3 CC). If this happens, a stalker may be sentenced to imprisonment for a term of up to ten years.

309. Other offences against liberty are, for example, **trafficking in human beings** (*handel ludźmi* – Article 189a CC), **duress** (*zmuszanie*), or using violence or an unlawful threat in order to force another person to perform or refrain from a certain action or to submit himself or herself to certain conduct (Article 191 § 1 CC); the **forceful collection of debts** (*wymuszanie zwrotu wierzytelności* – Article 191 § 2 CC), the **performance of a medical procedure without a patient's consent** (*wykonanie zabiegu leczniczego bez zgody pacjenta* – Article 192 CC) and **breach of domestic peace** (*naruszenie miru domowego*) understood as the freedom of undisturbed occupation and use of one's home or apartment, but also of a premises, room or a fenced area (Article 193 CC).

310. Chapter XXIV – **Offences against freedom of conscience and religion** (*Przestępstwa przeciwko wolności sumienia i wyznania*) (Articles 194–196 CC). The narrow category of offences against freedom of conscience and religion includes such offences as **discrimination on the grounds of religious affiliation**

or the absence of religious affiliation (*dyskryminacja na tle przynależności wyznaniowej lub bezwyznaniowości*), which means restricting a person's human rights on the above grounds, for instance by refusing to employ the person or refusing to provide a service for this person (Article 194 CC). Other types of conduct that violates the freedom of religion include: **malicious interference with the public performance of a religious ceremony** (*złośliwe przeszkadzanie publicznemu wykonywaniu aktu religijnego*) of a church or other religious association with a regulated legal status (Article 195 § 1 CC); **malicious interference with a funeral** (*złośliwe przeszkadzanie pogrzebowi*), mourning ceremonies or rites, or showing disrespect to a corpse, human ashes or a person's place of burial (Article 195 § 2 CC); or **insulting the religious feelings of other persons** (*obrażanie uczuć religijnych innych osób*) by way of the public abuse of an object of religious worship or place dedicated to the public celebration of religious rites (Article 196 CC).

311. Chapter XXV – **Offences against sexual liberty and decency** (*Przeste pstwa przeciwko wolności seksualnej i obyczajności*) (Articles 197–205 CC). The most important offence against sexual liberty and decency is **rape** (*zgwałcenie* – Article 197 §§ 1 and 2 CC). Rape means subjecting another person to sexual intercourse (§ 1) or submitting another person to, or forcing another person to perform, other sexual acts (§ 2) through the use of force, unlawful threat or deceit. There is no requirement that the actual act must be carried out between the victim *and* the perpetrator, although this is most frequently the case; rape may also take the form of a perpetrator forcing a victim to have sex with a third party. Obviously, the offence of rape may can also be committed by a perpetrator who is the spouse of a victim.

The Criminal Code describes four aggravated types of rape: rape that is committed by the perpetrator along with another person (gang rape); rape of a minor under 15 years of age; rape of an ascendant, descendant, adopted child, adoptive parent, or a sibling; and rape committed with particular atrocity (Article 197 §§ 3 and 4 CC).

Another sexual offence is causing the same result as that of rape, but by way of **taking advantage of the vulnerability or insanity of another person** (*wykorzystanie bezradności innej osoby lub jej niepoczytalności* – Article 198 CC). The above behaviour exhibited towards a vulnerable or insane person will not be deemed a criminal offence if the person's consent to a sexual act may be presumed.

The offence described in Article 199 CC also causes a result identical to that of rape; here, the difference is that a perpetrator **abuses a relationship in which the victim is dependent or takes advantage of his or her critically difficult situation**.

312. Article 200 § 1 CC criminalises the offence defined as an '**indecent act**' (*czyn lubieżny*). This involves sexual intercourse with a minor under the age of 17 or submitting such a person to, or forcing another person to perform, other sexual acts.

The subsequent sections of Article 200 CC establish penalties for, among other things, presenting a minor under the age of 15 with pornographic content or providing a minor with objects of pornographic nature or disseminating pornographic content in a manner that enables such a minor to access such content (§ 3), and for presenting a minor under the age of 15 with a performance of a sexual act with the intention of achieving one's sexual satisfaction or the sexual satisfaction of another person (§ 4), and also for the advertising or promoting of activities consisting in the dissemination of pornographic content in a manner that enables a minor under the age of 15 to access such content (§ 5).

Since 2009, criminal sanctions have been imposed for a number of new sexual offences such as **grooming**, or establishing, through an information technology and communication system or a telecommunication network, contact with a minor under the age of 15 and attempting to hold a meeting with such a minor by misleading the minor, exploiting the minor's error of judgment or inability to exercise reasonable judgment or by way of an unlawful threat, or for using the above systems for the proposal of sexual intercourse (Article 200a CC) and for **promoting or approving paedophile behaviour** (*propagowanie lub pochwalanie zachowań o charakterze pedofilskim* – Article 200b CC).

313. Criminal penalties are also imposed for **incest** (*kazirodztwo* – Article 201 CC); the **dissemination of pornography** (*rozpowszechnianie pornografii* – Article 202 CC); forcing another person into prostitution (*zmuszanie do prostytucji* – Article 203 CC), and also persuading another person to work as a prostitute, or **procuring** (*stręczycielstwo* – Article 204 § 1 CC); facilitating another person's work as a prostitute for the purpose of obtaining a financial advantage, or **facilitating prostitution** (*kuplerstwo* – Article 204 § 2 CC); and obtaining a financial advantage from another person's work as a prostitute, or **pimping** (*sutenerstwo* – Article 204 § 3 CC).

314. Chapter XXVI – **Offences against the family and guardianship** (*Przestepstwa przeciwko rodzice i opiece*) (Articles 206–211 CC). The offences described in Chapter XXVI were established in order to protect the family and guardianship as legal institutions. This category of offences is far from uniform and includes such different offences as bigamy (*bigamia* – Article 206 CC); the **abuse of a person** (*znecanie się* – Article 207 CC); **inducing a minor to become an inveterate drinker** (*rozpijanie małoletniego* – Article 208 CC); **avoiding to pay spousal or child maintenance** (*uchylanie się od alimentacji* – Article 209 CC); **abandoning a child or a vulnerable person** (*porzucenie dziecka lub osoby nieporadnej* – Article 210 CC) or **kidnapping such persons** (Article 211 CC); and also **illegal adoption** (*nielegalna adopcja* – Article 211a CC).

315. In the group of the aforementioned offences, special emphasis should be put on the **offence of abuse of a person** (Article 207 § 1 CC), due to the fact that this offence is relatively frequently prosecuted in Poland. The abuse of a person may take the form of physical or psychological abuse, and affect a perpetrator's next of kin or another person who is in a permanent or temporary relationship of dependency with a perpetrator, or a minor or a person who is vulnerable due to their physical or mental state. This offence may be committed only intentionally, either with a direct or oblique intention.

There are also aggravated types of abuse of a person. The first one is abuse of a person with particular atrocity (Article 207 § 2 CC). The second type is abuse of a person that results in a victim attempting to take his or her own life (Article 207 § 3 CC). In the case of the latter type, a perpetrator of abuse of a person may cause the result of the act (the suicide or attempted suicide) only unintentionally.

316. Under Polish law, a perpetrator who commits the offence of **avoiding to pay spousal or child maintenance**, which involves exposing a person entitled to receive spousal or child maintenance (*alimenty*) from the perpetrator to the risk of being unable to satisfy this person's basic living needs by way of persistent avoidance of the relevant obligation to pay the maintenance, which has arisen under a statute or a court ruling, is subject to a criminal penalty (Article 209 CC). A crucial element of this offence is the persistence of a perpetrator's conduct: in order to be held liable for the offence, a perpetrator has to be objectively capable of performing the obligation to pay maintenance but maliciously fail to do so, and this failure must be persistent and stubborn.

317. Chapter XVII – **Offences against dignity and personal inviolability** (*Przestępstwa przeciwko czci i nietykalności cielesnej*) (Articles 212–217 CC). An important subcategory of offences against dignity and personal inviolability is the offences prosecuted by private accusation (see *infra*, paragraphs 751–761). The first one is **defamation** (*zniesławienie* – Article 212 CC) which involves slander or libel against another person, a group of persons, an institution, legal person or an organisational unit without legal personality which is accused of such conduct or characteristics that may degrade it in the eyes of the public or put it at risk of losing the trust required for a given position, profession or type of activity. The aggravated form of defamation occurs when the aforementioned act is performed through means of mass communication (Article 212 § 2 CC). Only a factual statement, as opposed to a statement expressing the subjective assessment of facts, may be defamatory.

Statements that fall into the realm of 'the right to criticism' described in Article 213 CC are not defamatory under law. The Criminal Code stipulates that there is no defamation when a privately made accusation is *true*. Exceptionally, in the case of this offence, the burden of proving that a defamatory accusation is true lies with a defendant charged with defamation. On the contrary, when a defamatory accusation has been made publicly, liability for defamation will be waived if a defendant proves that the accusation is true and serves a socially justified interest; however, if the accusation is made against a person serving in public office, the above onus to prove the existence of a socially justified interest is not required.

318. The second offence against dignity and personal inviolability prosecuted by private accusation is an **insult to a person** (*zniewaga* – Article 216 CC). The Criminal Code does not describe any elements of an insult to a person. It is accepted that an insult is a demonstrative gesture or a word expressing contempt for another person. Such conduct will constitute the offence of insult provided that it is committed in the presence of an insulted person, in public, or with the intention of insulting. The aggravated form of this offence is insult committed through means of mass communication (Article 216 § 2 CC).

319. The last offence in this subcategory is the **offence of battery**, or as the Criminal Code calls it, 'a violation of bodily inviolability' (*naruszenie nietykalności cielesnej* – Article 217 CC). This Article enigmatically reads that battery may involve hitting a human being or otherwise violating his or her bodily inviolability. Such violations may include spitting at somebody, slapping somebody's face, pulling a person's hair, knocking off somebody's cap, punching or kicking somebody, etc.

320. Chapter XXVIII – **Offences against the rights of persons in gainful employment** (*Przestępstwa przeciwko prawom osób wykonujących pracę zarobkową*) (Articles 218–221 CC). Offences against rights of persons in gainful employment are a narrow category: there are only four such offences. The first one is **violating employee rights** (*naruszanie uprawnień pracowniczych* – Article 218 CC) and involves malicious or persistent violations of the rights of an employee under an employment relationship or social security laws. This may be, e.g., a refusal to pay a salary or issue a certificate of employment. The Criminal Code also criminalises such violations of social security laws that may involve a failure to register required data or the registration of untrue data that affect a person's right to benefits or the value of such benefits (Article 219 CC). It is, however, immaterial whether or not an insured person has agreed to these actions of his or her employer.

321. The remaining offences in this category are **exposing an employee to a direct risk** (*narażenie pracownika na bezpośrednie niebezpieczeństwo*) to life or a direct risk of grievous bodily harm through the action of a person responsible for occupational health and safety that consists of a failure to discharge a relevant obligation (also an unintentional failure) (Article 220 CC); and a **failure to report an occupational injury** (*niezawiadomienie o wypadku przy pracy*) or occupational disease, or a failure to present relevant documentation (Article 221 CC).

322. Chapter XXIX – **Offences against the activities of state and local government institutions** (*Przestępstwa przeciwko działalności instytucji państwowych oraz samorządu terytorialnego*) (Articles 222–231 CC). In practice, offences against the activities of state and local government institutions can be divided into two subcategories. The first one is offences that may be committed by persons from outside these institutions; these offences usually involve aggressive behaviour that interferes with the operations of state or local government institutions. The other subcategory includes so-called administration offences (*przestępstwa urzędnicze*) committed by persons working at these institutions, including offences committed by public officials. The latter term is defined in Article 115 § 13 CC by the enumeration of individual positions served by public officials, including the President of Poland, a deputy to the Sejm, senator, councillor, judge, lay judge, prosecutor, staff of the government and local government administration, etc.

323. The first subcategory includes, *inter alia*, offences of **battery against an official** (*naruszenie nietykalności cielesnej funkcjonariusza*) or a person appointed to act as an official's deputy which occurs in the course of or in connection with performance of their official duties (Article 222 § 1 CC); physical assault against a public official (*czynna napaść na funkcjonariusza publicznego*), which may take the form of an attack on an official perpetrated jointly with another person, with the use of a firearm, knife, etc. (Article 223 CC); **influencing official acts of state or local government bodies or personally conducted by officials** (*wywieranie wpływu na czynności urzędowe organów państwowych lub samorządowych lub samych funkcjonariuszy*) by violence or an unlawful threat (Article 224 § 1 i 2 CC); and **preventing or hindering the conduct of official duties** (*udaremnianie lub utrudnianie wykonywania czynności służbowych* – Article 225 CC). It is also a criminal offence to **insult an official** (or a person appointed to act as an official's deputy) in the course of or in connection with performance of their official duties (Article 226 § 1 CC).

The same subcategory includes the offence of **impersonating an official**, known as the 'appropriation of a function' (*przywłaszczenie funkcji*), which may involve conducting an act related to the powers of a public official by a person falsely acting as a public official or inducing another person to believe that the perpetrator is a public official (Article 227 CC); and the offence of **paid protection** (*płatna protekcja*), or undertaking to act as an intermediary in achieving a favourable outcome in return for a financial advantage or a promise of a financial advantage; here, a perpetrator's conduct must involve invoking influence in an institution (Article 230 CC). This offence of **paid protection** may be committed only intentionally, and only with a direct intention.

324. A public official may commence the offence of corruption, or **passive bribery** (*łapownictwo bierne* – Article 228 CC). This offence includes the acceptance of a financial or personal advantage (or a promise of such) that must be linked to an official's public function. Notably, the above means that accepting a bribe that is unrelated to a corrupted official's function is not passive bribery. The offence of passive bribery has its aggravated types, in particular conditioning the performance of an official act on receipt of an advantage (or demanding such advantage) (Article 228 § 4 CC); or accepting an advantage of a substantial value (Article 228 § 5 CC).

On the contrary, **active bribery** (*łapownictwo czynne* – Article 229 CC) is a common offence, which means that it may be committed by anybody. Active bribery involves giving an advantage or offering a promise of an advantage to a person performing a public function in connection with such a function. This offence has aggravated types similar to those of corruption. However, it also has a privileged type, which applies when bribery affects a matter of a minor significance or when a perpetrator commits the act while forced to do so by his or her living situation. Interestingly, a person giving a bribe assumes no criminal responsibility if a financial or personal advantage has been given and accepted and the person that gave the bribe (active briber) has reported this to a law enforcement authority and disclosed all information before the offence has come to the attention of the law enforcement authority (Article 229 § 6 CC).

325. Furthermore, Article 231 CC defines the offence of **abuse of power** (*nadużycie władzy*), which consists of exceeding one's authority or failing to perform duties which results in an action detrimental to a public or private interest. This offence may only be committed by a public official, whose authority and duties are defined by normative acts and internal regulations applicable to a given position and a function. The act may, but does not have to, be committed with the purpose of obtaining a financial or personal advantage; however, if this is the case, the offence carries a more severe penalty.

326. Chapter XXX – **Offences against the justice system** (*Przestępstwa przeciwko wymiarowi sprawiedliwości*) (Articles 232–247 CC). The first offence from this category is influencing a court's official actions (*wywieranie wpływu na czynności urzędowe sądu* – Article 232 CC). However, in practical terms, the most important offence in this group is **giving false testimony** (*składanie fałszywych zeznań*) defined in Article 233 CC. The act in question involves testifying an untruth or concealing the truth in one's testimony that is to be used as proof in court proceedings or in other proceedings conducted under a statute. A testifying person will assume criminal responsibility for giving false testimony if he or she receives an official caution for this liability under Article 233 CC from an official taking testimony. The same result will be achieved if an official accepts solemn affirmation from a testifying person.

Criminal sanctions are also imposed for falsely accusing another person of the commission of a criminal offence (including a fiscal offence), a petty offence, a fiscal petty offence or a disciplinary violation (Article 234 CC). In order to be held criminally liable, the false accuser must be aware of the fact that the accusation is false and must submit the accusation to a law enforcement or judicial body (the police, a prosecutor, court), and not to simply any person. Another criminal offence is **reporting to a law enforcement body a criminal or fiscal offence which has not in fact been committed to a law enforcement body** (*zawiadomienie organu powołanego do ścigania o niepopełnionym przestępstwie lub przestępstwie skarbowym* – Article 238 CC). In this case also, a perpetrator must be aware that the reported incident has not actually taken place.

A penalty is also imposed on a perpetrator who **conceals evidence exonerating a defendant accused of committing an offence** (Article 236 § 1 CC) – in this case, a perpetrator's act may consist of both intentionally concealing behaviour and ordinary inaction. A criminal penalty will not be imposed on a perpetrator who commits the offence in question in fear of criminal responsibility that may be imposed on the perpetrator personally or on the perpetrator's next of kin (Article 236 § 2 CC).

327. An offence similar to those described above is the **creation of false evidence** (*tworzenie fałszywych dowodów*) or the taking of other deceptive measures intended to subject another person to prosecution for a criminal offence, fiscal offence, petty offence, fiscal petty offence or disciplinary violation (Article 235 CC). Such actions are subject to a penalty regardless of whether they have been taken before the initiation of legal proceedings or are carried out in the course of proceedings.

Article 239 § 1 CC also imposes criminal liability on a person that provides help to perpetrator of an offence after a crime has already been committed. An accessory is responsible for the offence of **assisting a principal perpetrator** (*poplecznictwo*), which consists of hindering or preventing criminal proceedings by helping the perpetrator of an offence (also a fiscal offence) to avoid criminal responsibility. The actions of an accessory after the fact may take the form of harbouring a perpetrator, covering up traces of an offence or serving a penalty for a convicted person; here, the legislator only gives examples of an accessory's conduct anticipating a highly creative approach on the part of perpetrators. It must be noted that covering up traces of one's own offence does not constitute the discussed offence.

328. In Polish criminal law, the rule is that reporting an offence is merely a social obligation rather than a legal one. Exceptions from this rule are the offences enumerated in Article 240 CC: a failure to report any of them results in the assumption of criminal responsibility. The offences in question are: genocide (Article 118 CC), a massive or systematic attack against a civilian population (Article 118a CC), war crimes (Article 120–124 CC), high treason (Article 127 CC), coup d'etat (Article 128 CC), espionage (Article 130 CC), an attempt on the life of the President of Poland (Article 134 CC), attack against a military unit (Article 140 CC), voluntary manslaughter (Article 148 CC), causing a public threat (Article 163 CC), hijacking of an aircraft or vessel (Article 166 CC), unlawful detention (Article 189 CC), trafficking in human beings (Article 189a CC), hostage-taking and keeping (Article 252 CC) and terrorist offences. Obviously, criminal responsibility will not be assumed by a perpetrator who has refrained from reporting an offence in fear of criminal responsibility that may be imposed on him or her personally or on his or her next of kin.

329. Among the remaining offences against the justice system, the following should be noted: the **offence of unlawfully influencing participants in proceedings** (*przestępstwo bezprawnego nacisku na uczestników postępowania*), that is using violence or unlawful threats in order to exert influence on the actions of a witness, expert witness, translator, prosecutor or defendant (Article 245 CC); the **offence of coercing a person to give testimony** (*przestępstwo wymuszania zeznań*) with violence, unlawful threats or physical or psychological abuse (Article 246 CC); and the offence of **breaching the secrecy of criminal proceedings** (*naruszanie tajemnicy postępowania karnego*) that applies to preliminary proceedings and certain forms of court proceedings (Article 241 CC). Also, **escape from custody**, termed 'unlawful self-liberation' (*bezprawne samouwolnienie się* – Article 242 CC), the unlawful **liberation of a prisoner** (*uwolnienie więźnia* – Article 243 CC), and the abuse of a temporary leave from prison (Article 242 CC) are criminal offences. Finally, a penalty is imposed on a person who **does not comply with a prohibition imposed on him or her by a court** (Article 244 CC), e.g. a prohibition from occupying a certain post, operating vehicles, contacting specified individuals, etc.

330. Chapter XXXI – **Offences against elections and referenda** (*Przestępstwa przeciwko wyborom i referendum* – Articles 248–251 CC). A **criminal violation of election laws** (*przestępne naruszenie prawa wyborczego*), governed by Article 248

CC, constitutes a multiple-variant offence that disrupts the proper course of an election to the Sejm or the Senate, presidential election, European Parliament election, local government election or a referendum, as described in the of Election Code. Criminal acts designated in this article may take the form of counterfeiting lists of candidates, destroying records, committing abuses during vote-counting procedures, etc.

331 *331.* This category of offences also includes the offence of **disrupting elections,** which may be committed by disrupting election meetings, hindering the free exercise of the right to vote or the right to be elected, disrupting the voting or vote-counting process, and also through disrupting the preparation of records or other election (referendum) documents, provided that such a disruption is committed with the use of violence, unlawful threats or deceit (Article 249 CC); **exerting unlawful influence on elections** (*bezprawny wpływ na wybory*) by using the above methods in order to influence the way a person votes (Article 250 CC); **bribery during elections** (*łapownictwo wyborcze* – Article 250a CC); and a **breach of voting secrecy** (*naruszenie tajności głosowania*) by obtaining knowledge of a voter's preferences, expressed while voting, against a voter's will (Article 251 CC).

332. Chapter XXXII – **Offences against public order** (*Przestępstwa przeciwko porządkowi publicznemu*) (Articles 252-264a CC). As its name suggests, all offences described in Chapter XXXII should be designed to protect the same object, namely public order. However, this is only partially true, as – for example – the rationale behind establishing the first offence defined in the chapter, hostage-taking (Article 252 CC), is to protect, among other things, the safety (or liberty) of citizens rather than public order per se. Regardless of this, it should be assumed that in the case of offences described in the discussed chapter, a perpetrator's conduct may be noticed by an undefined number of persons (or by a defined, though large, number of persons). Therefore, such offences may be deemed 'public' in their nature.

333. As was already mentioned, the first offence in this category is **hostage-taking** (*przestępstwo wzięcia zakładnika* – Article 252 CC). This offence consists in the taking or keeping a person for the purpose of forcing a state or local government body, an institution, organisation, natural person or a group of persons to act in a certain way. The act itself involves deprivation of a person's liberty, which is accompanied by a threat of causing bodily harm to the hostage or even killing the hostage in the event that a perpetrator's demands (which usually, though not always, concern a financial payment) are not met. This offence has an aggravated type that applies whenever a hostage is subjected to exceptional torment. Preparation for hostage-taking is also a criminal offence. A perpetrator who expresses active repentance is eligible for extraordinary mitigation of a penalty.

334. Another offence against public order is the **participation in a mob** (*udział w zbiegowisku publicznym* – Article 254 CC). This offence consists in the participation in such a mob, or in the spontaneous gathering of a significant number of people in a public place, whose participants jointly commit a violent attack on a person or property. Such participation must be active (e.g., a perpetrator chants abuse at somebody or throw stones) rather than passive (a passer-by accidentally walks through the place where a mob has gathered). Considering the above, participation in a mob must clearly be intentional. On the contrary, certain consequences of such participation, such as the death of a human being or inflicting grievous bodily harm (elements of the aggravated type of the offence in question), do not need to be (and usually are not) intended by a perpetrator.

Article 260 CC defines another offence similar to participation in a mob, namely **violating the freedom of assembly** (*naruszanie wolności zgromadzeń*). This offence consists of preventing, by violence or unlawful threats, the lawful organisation of a gathering, assembly or a march, and also dispersing such events.

335. Another offence against public order is **abusing freedom of speech** (*nadużywanie wolności wypowiedzi* – Article 255 CC). The basic type of this offence involves public incitement of an offence or publicly expressing approval for an offence (Article 255 § 1 CC). If the incited offence is a felony, the penalty carried by this offence is appropriately higher (three instead of two years of imprisonment). Notably, if such incitement is directed at individually identified persons, the act will also present elements of the offence of instigation (Article 18 § 2 CC).

A relatively new and severely punishable offence is **facilitating terrorism** (*ułatwianie terroryzmu* – Article 255a CC), which involves the dissemination or public presentation of content that may facilitate the commission of terrorist offences with the intention of causing the commission of a terrorist offence.

Also, public **propagation of a fascist or other totalitarian regime** (*propagowanie faszystowskiego lub innego totalitarnego ustroju państwa*) or incitement of hatred on grounds of nationality, ethnicity, race, religion or the absence of a religion (Article 256 § 1 CC) is subject to a penalty. The same penalty, namely a fine, the penalty of restriction of liberty or the penalty of imprisonment of up to two years, applies in the case of disseminating, manufacturing, recording or importing, purchasing, storing, possessing, presenting, transferring or transporting a printed document, record or other item that includes the content described in § 1 of Article 256 or carries fascist, communist or totalitarian symbols (Article 256 § 2 CC). The above acts are not criminal offences if they are carried out as part of artistic, educational, collector's or scientific activities (Article 256 § 3 CC).

For similar reasons, criminal penalties are imposed for **publicly insulting a group within a population or individual persons because of their national, ethnic, racial or religious affiliation (or the lack of a religious affiliation)** and also for battery of a person resulting from such motives (Article 257 CC); **disrespecting a monument or other public location** (*znieważanie pomnika lub innego miejsca publicznego*) designed to commemorate a historic event or a person (Article 261 CC); and **disrespecting a grave** (*znieważenie grobu*), which in practice consists of showing disrespect of a corpse, human ashes or a person's place of burial, or ransacking such a place (Article 262 §§ 1–2 CC).

336. One of the most important offences described in this chapter is the offence of **participating in an organised criminal group or an organised criminal association created with the intent of committing a criminal or fiscal offence** (*udział w zorganizowanej grupie albo związku mającym na celu popełnienie przestępstwa* *lub przestępstwa skarbowego* – Article 258 CC). For the purposes of this offence, a criminal association must include a permanent and organised team of at least three people, which means that such an association has clearly defined recruitment procedures and internal rules of authority and discipline. A group also includes at least three people, but is more loosely organised. Still, members of a criminal group are involved in more complex activities than the joint and collaborative actions described in Article 16 § 1 CC.

A defendant accused of the aforementioned offence may receive a harsher treatment depending on the nature of a criminal group or an association. If an organisation is armed or has been created in order to commit a terrorist offence (Article 258 § 2 CC), the Criminal Code stipulates harsher penalties. This is also true in respect of a defendant who has established or leads such an organisation (Article 258 §§ 3–4 CC). Conversely, if a defendant withdraws from a criminal group or an association and discloses its operations, or prevents the commission of a planned offence, he or she may avoid a penalty (Article 259 CC).

337. The remaining offences defined in the category of offences against public order are, among others, **manufacturing firearms or ammunition or trading in firearms or ammunition** (*wyrabianie broni palnej, amunicji lub handel nią* – Article 263 § 1 CC), and also the simple **possession of firearms or ammunition without a proper licence** (*posiadanie broni palnej lub amunicji bez wymaganego zezwolenia* – Article 263 § 2 CC). Moreover, losing firearms or ammunition, unintentional in its essence, is also a punishable act (Article 263 § 4 CC).

Another criminal offence from this category is **illegally crossing the Polish state border** (*nielegalne przekroczenie polskiej granicy państwowej* – Article 264 § 2 CC). However, crossing the Polish border will only be a criminal offence if committed with the use of violence, threat, deceit or in collaboration with other persons. An ordinary illegal crossing of the border is merely a petty offence (Article 49a POC). Separate offences are **organising an illegal crossing of a border** (*organizowanie nielegalnego przekraczania granicy* – Article 264 § 3 CC), and enabling or facilitating another person's stay in the territory of Poland in contravention of the law, provided that this is done with the intent of obtaining a benefit (Article 264a CC).

338. Chapter XXXIII – **Offences against the safety of information** (*Przeste pstwa przeciwko ochronie informacji* – Articles 265-269b CC). The first of the offences against the safety of classified information is the **offence of disclosing state secrets** (*przestępstwo przeciwko ochronie infomacji niejawnych*), namely disclosing classified information marked as 'secret' or 'top secret' or using this information in contravention of the law (Article 265 § 1 CC). The aggravated type of this offence is disclosing a secret to a person acting in the name of or on behalf of a foreign entity (Article 265 § 2 CC).

Criminal sanctions are also applied in the case of a **breach of professional or official secrecy** (*naruszenie tajemnicy zawodowej i służbowej* – Article 266 CC). A professional secret is confidential information that has been obtained in connection with the performance of one's function, the practice of one's profession or the carrying out of public, social, business or scientific activities. An official secret is information that has been obtained in connection with the performance of one's official duties, which – if disclosed – may pose a risk to a legally protected interest.

339. The **secrecy of correspondence** is also protected. An action that involves unauthorised access to information that is not intended for a perpetrator, obtained by way of opening a closed letter, connecting to a telecommunication network, or overcoming or circumventing a security feature, is criminalised in Article 267 § 1 CC.

Similarly, it is a criminal offence to violate the sphere of a person's private life by way of placing or using an eavesdropping or video device or other device or software in order to obtain information which a perpetrator is not authorised to receive (Article 267 § 2 CC).

340. Further provisions of Chapter XXXIII criminalise the **prevention or hindering of access to information** (*uniemożliwianie lub utrudnianie dostępu do informacji*). This behaviour may take various forms, such as destroying, damaging, deleting or modifying a record of important information, or it may consist in employing other means that prevent or hinder an authorised person from accessing a relevant piece of information (Article 268 § CC), but may also involve destroying, damaging, deleting, modifying or hindering access to computer data (Article 268a CC), including data of special importance for national defence, safety in communication, the operation of government administration, another state body or institution or local government (Article 269 CC).

341. Chapter XXXI – **Offences against the credibility of documents** (*Przeste ̧pstwa przeciwko wiarygodności dokumentów* – Articles 270–277 CC). Within the category of offences against the credibility of documents, particular emphasis should be put on the offence of **falsifying a document** (*sfałszowanie dokumentu*), regulated in Article 270 CC. According to the definition laid down in Article 115 § 14 CC, a document is any object or other information carrier, to which a specific right relates or which, due to its content, constitutes the proof of a right, legal relationship or a legally significant circumstance.

Falsification of a document means forging or altering a document with the intent of using it as an authentic one. Using a document altered in this way is subject to the same penalty as that applicable in the case of falsification. Also, preparation for the falsification of a document is punishable under criminal law (Article 270 § 3 CC).

A separate type of offence is the so-called **intellectual falsification of a document** (*fałsz intelektualny dokumentu*), defined in Article 271 CC as an introduction of untrue content to a document (as opposed to the physical alteration of a document). Another criminal offence is **fraudulently obtaining certification of false information** (*wyłudzenie poświadczenia nieprawdy*) by deceptively misleading the issuer of a document (Article 272 CC).

342. Under Polish law, penalties are also imposed for **theft or appropriation of**

a personal identity document (*kradzież lub przywłaszczenie dokumentu tożsamości*) or the use of a document confirming the identity of another person (Article 275 § 1 CC); **unlawful transportation, carrying or sending of a document abroad** (*bezprawne przewożenie, przenoszenie lub przesyłanie za granicę dokumentu* – Article 275 § 2 CC); **and disposal of one's own or another person's personal identity document** (*zbywanie własnego lub cudzego dokumentu tożsamości* – Article 274 CC); and also **destruction of documents or border signs** (*niszczenie dokumentów lub znaków granicznych* – Article 276 CC).

343. Chapter XXXV – **Offences against property** (*Przestępstwa przeciwko mieniu*) (Articles 278–295 CC). A notable offence against property is **theft** (*kradzież*), defined in Article 278 § 1 CC as '*taking an item of movable property belonging to another person with the purpose of appropriation*'. Here, protection is given not only to items that a given person owns but also to movable property that remains in this person's possession.

The act of **obtaining another person's software without the consent of an authorised person** (*uzyskaniu cudzego programu komputerowego*) is subject to the same penalties as theft, provided that a perpetrator has acted with the intent of achieving financial advantage (Article 278 § 2 CC).

The offence known as **theft with burglary** (*kradzież z włamaniem*) is defined as an act by a perpetrator that involves overcoming a security feature by way of damaging this feature (e.g., breaking a door, cutting a padlock) in order to commit theft (Article 279 CC).

Appropriation (*przywłaszczenie*) is an offence similar to theft and involves the identical behaviour but affects property rights in and not a tangible item of property (Article 284 CC). **Dishonestly obtaining telephone services**, a separate offence in this category, described in the Criminal Code as 'theft of telephone pulses' (*kradzież impulsów telefonicznych* – Article 285 CC), involves accessing a telecommunication device for the purpose of using telephone services at the expense of another person.

344. Article 280 CC regulates another offence against property: **robbery** (*rozbój*). Robbery is defined as the taking of another person's item of movable property with the purpose of appropriation (theft) through any of the three methods designated in this article, namely with the use of violence against a person, or with a threat of immediate use of violence, or by inducing a state of unconsciousness or helplessness in a person.

If the above outcome is achieved with the use of a firearm, a knife or other similar dangerous item or incapacitating agent, or by an action that otherwise presents a direct threat to life, or together with another person who uses such a weapon, item, agent or method, it will constitute the aggravated type of robbery.

Theft with violence (*kradzież rozbójnicza*) is an offence separate from robbery: it involves the use of the same methods as in robbery, but only for the purpose of retaining the possession of an item that has already previously been taken (Article 281 CC). Another offence in this category is forcing another person to dispose of property with violence, the threat of an attempt at a person's life or health or of a violent attack on property (Article 282 CC).

345. **Fraud** (*oszustwo*) (regulated in Article 286 CC), is another offence of practical importance. Fraud consists in causing another person to dispose of property in a way that is unfavourable to this person by misleading the person, or by exploiting the person's error of judgment or inability to properly understand undertaken actions. This offence may be committed only intentionally, with the direct intention of obtaining a financial advantage. The criminal responsibility for fraud is immaterial as regards whether or not such financial advantage has actually been obtained.

Another offence, **computer fraud** (*oszustwo komputerowe*), occurs when a perpetrator affects, in an unauthorised way, automatic processing, the collection or transmission of computer data, or modifies, deletes or enters new computer data (Article 287 CC). Here, a perpetrator must act with the intent of obtaining a financial advantage or causing loss to another person.

346. The remaining offences against property are: **destroying or damaging an item of property** (*niszczenie lub uszkodzenie rzeczy*) or rendering it unfit for use (Article 288 CC); **appropriation of a motor vehicle with the intent of using it for a short period of time**, sometimes named 'joyriding' (*zabór pojazdu mechanicznego w celu krótkotrwałego użycia* – Article 289 CC); and forestry theft, or cutting down trees in a forest with the intent of appropriation (Article 290 CC). The offence of **handling stolen goods** (*paserstwo*) is defined in Article 291 CC as purchasing or assisting in selling an item of property obtained through a prohibited act or accepting such an item or assisting in hiding such an item. This offence may also be committed unintentionally (Article 292 CC).

347. If an offence against property affects property of a substantial value, that is property whose the value of which, as of the moment when the act was committed, exceeded PLN 200,000, or property with a special cultural significance, a stricter penalty may be applied (Article 294 CC).

348. Chapter XXXV – **Offences against business operations** (*Przestępstwa przeciwko obrotowi gospodarczemu*) (Articles 296–309 CC). The category of offences against business operations is particularly wide. The key offences in this group are **abuse of trust** (*nadużycie zaufania* – Article 296 §§ 1–3 CC) and **mismanagement** (*niegospodarność* – Article 296 § 4 CC). The former consists in causing a substantial loss to property by way of abusing the authority awarded to a person who is obliged to manage the financial affairs or commercial operations of a natural person, legal person or an organisational entity without legal personality under a statutory provision, the decision of a competent body or under a contract. Also covered here is the failure of a person to discharge such imposed duties. The aggravated form of abuse of trust appears when the commission of this offence results in a direct threat of causing a substantial loss to property being brought about, when the offence is committed with the intent of obtaining a financial advantage, or when a large loss to property is caused, regardless of the form in which the offence is committed.

Mismanagement occurs when the offence of abuse of trust is committed unintentionally.

349. Other offences from this category are **commercial bribery** (*łapownictwo gospodarcze* – Article 296a CC) and **sports bribery** (*łapownictwo sportowe* – Article 296b CC). Both offences may be committed in either an active form (giving an advantage or a promise of advantage) or a passive form (accepting an advantage).

350. The offence described in Article 297 CC, sometimes referred to as **credit fraud or subsidy fraud** (*oszustwo kredytowe lub subwencyjne*) consist in submitting a document that is forged, altered or certifies an untruth or in submitting an inaccurate document, or an inaccurate written statement regarding circumstances material for obtaining credit, a loan, surety, guarantee, letter of credit, grant, subsidy, a bank's confirmation of an obligation, electronic payment instrument or a public tender contract. This action needs to be taken for the purpose of obtaining the aforementioned benefits or contract from a bank or an organisation carrying out a similar activity, or from a body or institution that administers public funds related to the aforementioned benefits or contract.

351. **Insurance fraud** (*oszustwo ubezpieczeniowe*) (an offence regulated in Article 298 CC), consists in causing an event that serves as the basis for the payment of an indemnity for the purpose of obtaining this indemnity under an insurance contract. Here, a perpetrator must act intentionally, but active repentance results in impunity.

352. Article 299 CC contains an extensive regulation of the offence of **money laundering** (*pranie brudnych pieniędzy*), which, apart from money itself, may also involve securities, rights in property, and immovable or movable property obtained as proceeds of a prohibited act. The article presents very specific examples of actions affecting money and other assets mentioned above (e.g., accepting, transferring, moving abroad) that trigger criminal responsibility for money laundering. The purpose of these actions must prevent or significantly reduce the risk of the identification of criminal origins or the location of 'laundered' property, and also the risk of its detection, seizure or forfeiture.

353. Other offences included in Chapter XXXVI are **offences committed to the detriment of creditors** (*przestępstwa dokonywane na szkodę wierzycieli*), such as intentional insolvency or bribery of a creditor (Articles 300–302 CC), **inaccurate or dishonest maintenance of commercial accounts** (*nierzetelne lub niezgodne z prawdą prowadzenie dokumentacji działalności gospodarczej* – Article 303 CC); the **offence of usury** (*lichwa*) understood as the exploitation of a difficult situation involuntarily assumed by another natural or legal person, or an organisational unit without legal personality by way of conclusion of a contract that imposes on that person or entity the obligation to render performance which is obviously incommensurate with the mutual performance of the other party to this contract (Article 304 CC); **preventing a tender** (*udaremnianie przetargu* – Article 305 CC); and removing or forging identification marks of merchandise (*usuwanie lub fałszowanie oznaczeń towaru* – Article 306 CC)

354. Chapter XXXVII – **Offences against monetary and security transactions** (*Przestępstwa przeciwko obrotowi pieniędzmi i papierami wartościowymi*) (Articles 310–316 CC). The most important offence in this category is **money forgery** (*fałszowanie pieniędzy* – Article 310 CC). Here, a perpetrator's conduct may involve falsifying, i.e. creating counterfeit money, provided that this was done for the purpose of introducing counterfeit money into circulation, or altering, i.e. making changes to genuine banknotes or coins generally for the purpose of increasing their face value. Money forgery is a felony which may be committed only intentionally (direct intention is required). Also, preparation for the commission of this offence is punishable by criminal law (Article 310 § 4 CC).

For the purposes of criminal responsibility, forgery of other non-cash payment instruments – documents that authorise the receipt of a sum of money, or express a duty to pay the principal, interest, a share in profits, or confirm one's membership in a company – are treated in the same way as forgery of money.

Criminal sanctions are also imposed for **entering counterfeit money** or documents **into circulation** (*puszczenie w obieg fałszywego pieniądza*) and for accepting such money or documents for the purpose of entering them into circulation, and also for storing, moving, carrying or dispatching them, or assisting in selling or concealing them (Article 310 § 2 CC). The privileged type of this offence is entering into circulation counterfeit money that a perpetrator has received as genuine (Article 312 CC).

355. Another offence from this category is the **forgery of value or official marks** (*fałszowanie znaków wartościowych lub urzędowych*), e.g. post marks, or the removal of indications of their redemption, and also dispatching, purchasing, using or storing such marks provided that this is done for the purpose of using counterfeit marks or putting them into circulation (Article 313 § 1 i 2 CC).

Also, the **forgery of official marks** (such as a seal of an office) **that confirm an authorisation or a result of a test** constitutes a criminal offence, provided that the forgery is committed for the purpose of using such marks in public circulation. Using items that bear forged marks is also punishable by law (Article 314 CC).

356. The remaining offences from the category of offences against monetary and security transactions are **falsifying a certified measuring or testing device** (e.g., scales) with the intent of using it in commercial transactions (*fałszowanie zalegalizowanego narzędzia pomiarowego lub probierczego* – Article 315 CC); and **disseminating untrue information in documentation related to security transactions** (*rozpowszechnianie w dokumentacji związanej z obrotem papierami wartościowymi nieprawdziwych informacji*) or concealing information about the financial status of an offeror provided that such information materially affects a purchase or sale of securities or may result in an increase or decrease of a contribution (Article 311 CC).

C. Military Offences

357. As discussed above, military offences are included in the Polish Criminal Code and placed in its separate Third Part entitled 'Military Part'. It contains a preliminary chapter on general issues regarding offences committed by military personnel followed by 10 chapters referring to distinct group of offences.

358. The first chapter of the Military Part (Chapter XXXVIII) contains general provisions on military personnel and governs basic issues relating to the specific treatment given to offenders from this group by Polish criminal law. It stipulates that the General and Special Parts of the Criminal Code apply to military personnel unless the Military Part provides for the contrary (Article 317 § 1 CC). Some of the provisions of the Military Part also apply to civilians working for the military and other persons, if a statute so declares (Article 317 §§ 2–3 CC).

359. Among the **clauses excluding criminal responsibility of military personnel**, one should note Article 318 CC, which stipulates that a member of military personnel does not commit a criminal offence if he or she commits a prohibited act while obeying an order, unless by obeying an order he or she intentionally commits an offence. Another instance of waving the criminal responsibility of a member of military personnel is the situation known as the 'limits of ultimate need' (*granice ostatecznej potrzeby*), namely where a member of military personnel responds to a case of disobedience or resistance in respect of an order that he or she was authorised to issue by employing measures necessary to enforce the order, provided that circumstances require immediate reaction and the order cannot be enforced in any other way (Article 319 CC).

360. Apart from the penalties described in the General Part of the Criminal Code, military personnel can be subject to a **specific penalty of military confinement** (*areszt wojskowy*), which is regulated by provisions on imprisonment and may last for a period between a month and two years (Article 322 §§ 1–2 CC). The penalty of military confinement is served at a designated prison. During the term of his or her confinement, a convicted member of military personnel undergoes military training. When compared to civilian convicts, military personnel also receive somewhat different conditions for serving the penalty of restriction of liberty: this penalty is served, *inter alia*, in a specifically designated military unit (Article 323 CC).

361. Additional, **military-specific penal measures** are a dishonourable discharge from professional military service (*wydalenie z zawodowej służby wojskowej*) and a reduction in rank (*degradacja*) (Article 324 § 1 CC). However, the penal measure of pecuniary payment (408–409)may not be imposed on a member of military personnel (Article 324 § 2 CC).

362. Also, **probation measures applied against military personnel** are subject to modifications. While ordering the conditional discontinuation of criminal proceedings, the court may request a relevant commanding officer to impose a military disciplinary penalty (Article 333 § 1 CC). The court may appoint a military probation officer, a superior or another member of military personnel designated by a superior to exercise probate supervision of a convicted member of military personnel (Article 334 § 2 CC). Article 336 § 1 CC stipulates that a penalty of imprisonment imposed on a member of military personnel in compulsory service may be deferred for six months from the final date of such service.

363. The offences described in the Military Part are included in six chapters. Chapter XXXIX regulates **offences against the duty to perform military service** (*przestępstwa przeciwko obowiązkowi pełnienia służby wojskowej* – Articles 338–342 CC), such as unauthorised absence from barracks or a designated location, desertion (understood as permanent avoidance of military service), refusal to serve in the military or perform a duty resulting from military service, or self-mutilation performed by a member of military personnel in order to avoid service or the execution of an order.

364. Chapter XL describes **offences against the rules of military discipline** (*przestępstwa przeciwko zasadom dyscypliny wojskowej* – Articles 343–349 CC), including the failure to execute an order, the refusal to execute an order or the improper execution of an order, physical assault on a superior, preventing a superior's performance of an official act by the use of violence or unlawful threats, insulting a superior or another member of military personnel in connection with their performance of official duties. Regulations governing these offences are applied *mutatis mutandis* to prohibited acts committed against military personnel of an allied state, provided this state ensures reciprocity.

365. Chapter XLI regulates **offences against the rules governing the treatment of subordinates** (*przestępstwa przeciwko zasadom postępowania z podwładnymi* – Articles 350–353 CC), which include degrading or insulting a subordinate, hitting a subordinate or exposing him or her to another kind of battery, and physical or psychological abuse of a subordinate. These provisions are also applied to a member of military personnel who commits any of the above prohibited acts against a serviceman or servicewoman of a lower rank, and also against a serviceman or a servicewoman with a rank equal to that of the perpetrator but with a shorter term in service.

366. Another category of prohibited acts is included in Chapter XLII, which regulates **offences against the rules of handling weaponry and armed military equipment** (*przestępstwa przeciwko zasadom obchodzenia się z uzbrojeniem i uzbrojonym sprzętem wojskowym* – Articles 354–355 CC). Criminal responsibility is imposed on a member of military personnel who fails to exercise caution when handling or using military weapons, ammunition, explosives or other means of warfare and thereby unintentionally causes a disruption of bodily functions or a health disorder in another person. Criminal responsibility will also be assumed by a member of military personnel who, while operating an armed motor vehicle, violates, even unintentionally, the safety rules for land, water or air traffic unintentionally causing an accident that results in a health disorder or a disruption of bodily functions for a period of longer than seven days or in a substantial loss to property. In both the cases mentioned above, a more severe penalty applies if the acts result in the death of another person or grievous bodily harm in another person.

367. **Offences against the rules of service** (*Przestępstwa przeciwko zasadom pełnienia służby*) are regulated in Chapter XLIII (Articles 356–357 CC). The first offence is a violation of obligations resulting from a provision or an instruction that governs the course of service, provided that such a violation presents a direct risk of a loss that the service sought to prevent. The other offence is committed by a member of military personnel who has been assigned to a service or is on duty and who induces himself or herself into a state of intoxication (with the use of alcohol or another substance). These two offences are prosecuted upon complaint, which may be submitted only by the commanding officer of a military unit.

368. The last category of military offences is **offences against military property** (*przestępstwa przeciwko mieniu wojskowemu*) regulated in Chapter XLIV (Articles 358–363 CC). They include, among other things, the unauthorised disposal of weapons or other means of warfare, the failure to perform duties or the abuse of authority resulting in a loss of weapons or other means of warfare, destroying weapons or other means of warfare, the unauthorised use of military aircraft or a sea or an inland vessel, the unauthorised use of a military motor vehicle and the unauthorised use of military equipment.

II. Criminal Offences in Special Criminal Laws

A. Drug Offences

369. In Polish criminal law **drug offences** (*przestępstwa związane z problemami narkomanii*) are regulated outside the Criminal Code in the 2005 Drug Abuse Prevention Act (DAPA). This act primarily contains provisions on the manufacturing, possession and trading in narcotic and psychotropic drugs and penal provisions that govern the criminal liability for violations of the rules set out in the DAPA. An appendix to the act includes a list of narcotic and psychotropic drugs. Due to its practical significance, the regulations of the DAPA should be discussed in greater detail.

370. Articles 53–64 DAPA regulate offences of manufacturing, processing or modifying narcotic or psychotropic drugs and entering them into circulation, participating in dealing in such drugs, providing them to another person, and also possessing drugs.

371. The DAPA also provides the option to apply a specific probation measure against an addicted person who has been charged with an offence that carries the penalty of imprisonment for the maximum term of five years (Article 72). This measure is ordered by a prosecutor and may involve suspension of proceedings conducted against a perpetrator who agrees to undergo treatment, rehabilitation or join other educational and prevention programmes. Upon the expiration of such a programme, a prosecutor decides whether the proceedings should be continued or applies to the court for its conditional discontinuation.

372. Another interesting regulation contained in the DAPA is the possibility of waiving the prosecution of an offence that involves only the possession of a narcotic or psychotropic drug (Article 62a). This article stipulates that proceedings may be discontinued even before they are officially launched provided that all the following conditions are satisfied: the amount of possessed drugs is insignificant, they are for the personal use of a perpetrator, and the imposition of a penalty on a perpetrator would be unreasonable in light of the circumstances in which an act was committed and the degree of social harm presented by an act.

B. *Other Offences in Special Criminal Laws*

373. Offences described in the Criminal Code are merely a part of the criminal law in Poland. Many prohibited acts are defined in separate statutes and some of them are extremely rarely applied in practice. A list of some of the key statutes that describe additional criminal offences is presented below:

- Criminal Fiscal Code of 10 September 1999 (consolidated text, J.L. 2013, Item 186, as amended);
- Weapons and Ammunition Act of 21 May 1999 (consolidated text, J.L. 2012, Item 576, as amended);
- Civilian Use of Explosives Act of 21 June 2002 (consolidated text, J.L. 2012, Item 1329, as amended);
- Aviation Act of 3 July 2002 (consolidated text, J.L. 2012, item 933, as amended);
- Commercial Partnerships and Companies Code of 15 September 2000 (J.L. No. 94, Item 1037, as amended);
- Insolvency and Reorganisation Act of 28 February 2003 (J.L. No. 60, item 535, as amended);
- Act on the combating of unfair competition of 16 April 1993 (consolidated text, J.L. 2003 No. 153, Item 1503, as amended);
- Electronic Services Act of 18 July 2002 (J.L. No. 144, Item 1204);
- Banking Law Act of 29 August 1997 (consolidated text, J.L. 2012, item 1376, as amended);
- Articles 178–183 of the Financial Instruments Transactions Act of 29 July 2005 (J.L. No. 183, Item 1538, as amended);
- Tax Procedure Code of 29 August 1997 (consolidated text, J.L. 2005 No. 8, Item 60, as amended).
- Electronic Signature Act of 18 September 2001 (J.L. No. 131, Item 1450);

- Act on the prevention of entering into financial circulation of financial values originating from illegal or undisclosed sources and on the prevention of the financing of terrorism of 16 November 2000 (consolidated text, J.L. 2003 No. 153, Item 1505, as amended);
- Public Statistics Act of 29 June 1995 (J.L. No. 88, Item 439, as amended);
- Compliance Assessment System Act of 30 August 2002 (consolidated text, J.L. 2004 No. 204, Item 2087, as amended);
- Act on the limitation on public officials' ability to carry out business activities of 21 August 1997 (consolidated text, J.L. 2006 No. 216, Item 1584);
- Accounting Act of 29 September 1994 (consolidated text, J.L. 2002 No. 76, Item 694, as amended);
- Industrial Property Law Act of 30 June 2000 (J.L. 2013, Item 1410).

Chapter 7. The Sanctioning System

§1. General Overview

374. The subject of the imposition of criminal penalties is governed not only in the Criminal Code and other statutes with penal provisions, but also – partially – in the Constitution of the Republic of Poland. First and foremost, Article 40 of the Constitution follows international human rights treaties and prohibits the imposition of cruel, inhuman or degrading penalties. The same article also prohibits corporal punishment. Article 46 is another constitutional provision that is significant from the perspective of the application of criminal sanctions: it stipulates that an item of property may be subject to forfeiture only in cases specified by statute, and only by virtue of the final ruling of a court.

The Criminal Code designates types of sanctions that may be imposed in criminal cases and establishes rules governing their imposition. The Criminal Fiscal Code contains an equivalent regulation applicable to fiscal offences. Sometimes, special rules in this area also appear in other statutes. For example, the Drug Abuse Prevention Act of 29 July 2005 contains regulations that lay down specific sanctions that may be imposed against persons addicted to narcotic or psychotropic drugs.

375. The system of measures of penal response is a complex one. The principal method of responding to an offence is to impose a penalty. However, apart from penalties, the Criminal Code enables the imposition of:

(1) penal measures;
(2) compensatory measures;
(3) forfeiture;
(4) measures related to putting a perpetrator to the test of good behaviour (known as probation measures).

A separate category of measures of penal response is that of protective measures, which are imposed on legally insane perpetrators, perpetrators with personality disorders or sexual preference disorders and also addicted perpetrators (see *infra*, paragraphs 448–455).

376. Different from many European jurisdictions, Polish criminal law generally does not allow an opportunistic discontinuation of proceedings which is accompanied by the imposition of certain obligations on a perpetrator (e.g., remedying a loss, paying a sum of money, taking on educational courses). An exception to this rule is Article 59a CC, which stipulates that if an aggrieved person (victim) so requests, criminal proceedings (both preliminary and court proceedings) may be discontinued in the situation where:

(1) proceedings apply to a misdemeanour punishable with imprisonment for a term of less than three years or a misdemeanour against property punishable

with imprisonment for a term of less than five years or a misdemeanour under Article 157 § 1 CC (causing light or moderate bodily harm);
(2) a the perpetrator has reconciled with a victim, in particular as the consequence of mediation, and redressed a loss or compensated a victim for an inflicted moral loss;
(3) it has been determined that a perpetrator has not been convicted for an intentional offence committed with the use of violence.

If the act has affected more than one victim, in order to be eligible for discontinuation a perpetrator must reconcile with all victims, redress the loss sustained by all victims and compensate all victims for any moral loss inflicted. However, proceedings will not be discontinued if there is a special circumstance which indicates that discontinuation would be contrary to the need to achieve the objectives of a penalty.

§2. PENALTIES

I. The Nature and Catalogue of Penalties

377. Penalties constitute the key measure of responding to the commission of an offence. This means that, as a rule, if criminal responsibility for an offence is attributed to a perpetrator, he or she will receive one of the penalties listed below. As an exception to this rule, a court may refrain from imposing a penalty or order a penal measure, compensatory measure or forfeiture instead of a penalty (see *infra*, paragraph 468).

Article 32 CC provides for the following types of criminal penalties:

(1) a fine;
(2) restriction of liberty;
(3) imprisonment (officially termed 'deprivation of liberty');
(4) twenty-five years of imprisonment;
(5) life imprisonment.

The above list of penalties is generally exhaustive: there is only one additional penalty that is not listed above, namely military confinement (as defined in Article 332 § 1 CC). The latter penalty, however, may only be imposed on military personnel.

The order in which Article 32 enumerates penalties is significant. While compiling this list, the legislator started with non-custodial penalties and only afterwards moved to the penalty of imprisonment. The above suggests that, as far as the rules of judicial determination of a sentence are concerned, the legislator gives priority to non-custodial penalties.

II. The Penalty of a Fine

378. In accordance with Article 33 § 1 CC a fine is measured and imposed in daily rates (*stawki dzienne*). The Polish system of judicial imposition of fines, similar to its German counterpart, departs from a simple designation of an amount to be paid by a convicted person in a criminal judgment. Instead, the court imposing the penalty of a fine on a defendant first determines the number of daily rates, and later designates the amount of a single rate. The sum payable by a defendant to the State Treasury is the mathematical product of both figures.

The system of daily rates adopted in the Criminal Code is not universally applied in Polish criminal law as many statutes define offences punishable by fines with predetermined values. For instance, Article 107 paragraph 1 of the Banking Law Act establishes the prohibition from performing banking transactions without an appropriate permit and makes violations of this prohibition punishable by a fine of the maximum amount of PLN 10,000,000 and the penalty of imprisonment for a term of up to five years.

In determining the number of daily rates, the court considers the circumstances of an offence committed by a convicted person, and in particular its gravity, nature of the violated legal interests and consequences caused. On the contrary, while determining the value of a daily rate, the court takes into consideration a perpetrator's income, personal and family conditions, financial situation and income perspectives. This enables the fair and equal treatment of accomplices to an offence in a situation where the financial status of one accomplice, and in consequence, his or her ability to pay a fine, materially differs from that of the other accomplice. This is because in such a case the court orders the same number of daily rates and only differentiates the rate amount only in respect of one accomplice.

As a rule, the lowest number of daily rates is 10 and the highest is 540. However, special provisions may modify the number of imposed rates. For example, Article 38 § 2 CC reads that a fine that is extraordinarily increased may consist of up to 810 daily rates, and Article 309 CC enables the imposition of a fine in the amount of up to 3,000 daily rates in the case of convictions for certain economic offences.

Pursuant to Article 33 § 3 CC a single daily rate of a fine may not be lower than 10 zloty (ca. 2.20 euro) and higher than 2,000 zloty (ca. 444 euro).

379. The penalty of a fine may be imposed as the only penalty for a committed offence (a 'stand-alone fine'). Under Article 33 § 2 CC, a fine may be imposed in addition to the penalty of imprisonment (but not the penalty of twenty-five years of imprisonment or life imprisonment), if a perpetrator has committed an act with the intent of obtaining a financial advantage or if a perpetrator has actually obtained a financial advantage (a 'cumulative fine'). In this case, there are no specific requirements as to the nature of a given act. It is only relevant that a perpetrator has obtained a financial advantage or acted with such an intent in mind, even if no actual advantage is obtained. Therefore, this does not necessarily need to be an economic offence or an offence against property. A fine may also be imposed as an additional sanction under Article 71 § 1 CC, namely in a situation where a court suspends the execution of a penalty of imprisonment and it is impossible to impose a fine together with imprisonment on any other basis (e.g., under Article 33 § 2 CC).

If a provision that criminalises given behaviour contains the expression 'shall be subject to a fine', then the measure of a fine is defined by the aforementioned general rules governing this penalty's application. However, sometimes the legislator limits this freedom. An example of such a situation is Article 221 CC, which stipulates an offence punishable by a fine of up to 180 daily rates.

III. The Penalty of the Restriction of Liberty

380. The penalty of the restriction of liberty can take a number of different forms. Pursuant to Article 34 § 1a CC, this penalty may involve:

(1) obligation to perform free and supervised community service;
(2) obligation to remain at a specified place of permanent residence or at another designated location, enforced with the use of an electronic monitoring system;
(3) obligations referred to in Article 72 § 1 items 4-7a CC, namely:
  (a) obligation to perform remunerated work, pursue a course of study or vocational training;
  (b) obligation to refrain from excessive use of alcohol or any use of a narcotic drugs;
  (c) obligation to undergo therapy for addiction;
  (d) obligation to undergo another type of therapy, specifically psychotherapy or psychoeducation therapy;
  (e) obligation to take part in correctional and educational activities;
  (f) obligation to refrain from associating with specified social groups or frequenting specified kinds of places;
  (g) obligation to refrain from making contact with an aggrieved person or other persons in a specified manner, or from approaching an aggrieved person or other persons;
(4) deduction of 10% to 25% of a person's monthly pay for work for a good cause specified by the court.

Pursuant to Article 34 § 1b CC, the above obligations and deduction can be imposed jointly or separately. This means that courts may freely determine the nature of the imposed penalties of restriction of liberty, join elements of this penalty and determine how long they should apply. A court may impose an obligation for only a part of the term of a penalty.

381. If a court obliges a defendant to perform free and supervised community service, this service may be performed for 20 to 40 hours in a month (Article 35 § 1 CC).

Deduction from pay for work may be imposed only against a person who is employed. Within the period of a measure's application, a convicted person may not terminate his or her employment relationship without the court's approval (Article 35 § 2 CC).

Imposition of the obligation to remain at a specified place of permanent residence or at another designated location, which is enforced with the use of an electronic monitoring system, is associated with equipping a convicted person with a transmitter and other devices that enable the monitoring of his or her place of stay. In determining the period of electronic monitoring, a court must give consideration to a convicted person's conditions of employment and other obligations imposed on the convicted person; in any case, the duration of monitoring cannot be longer than 12 months, and 70 hours per week, and 12 hours per day (Article 35 § 3 CC).

382. A person sentenced to the penalty of the restriction of liberty must always comply with the following obligations, regardless of the type of the imposed restriction:

(1) he or she may not change their place of permanent residence without the court's consent; and
(2) he or she must provide explanations to competent supervisory authorities through the course of the penalty.

While imposing the penalty of the restriction of liberty, a court may additionally impose the pecuniary payment mentioned in Article 39 item 7 CC (see *infra*, paragraphs 408-409) or obligations referred to in Article 72 § 1 items 2 and 3 CC, namely the obligation to apologise to an aggrieved person and the obligation for a convicted person's to perform the duty to provide maintenance for another person (e.g., a child).

Pursuant to Article 34 § 1 CC, unless a statute provides for otherwise, the penalty of the restriction of liberty may be applied for a period of at least a month but not longer than two years. There is no provision in the Criminal Code that would allow a penalty of the restriction of liberty to be applied for a term exceeding two years.

The penalty of the restriction of liberty is imposed in months and years.

383. The present form of the penalty of the restriction of liberty is a consequence of the amendment to the Criminal Code that entered into force on 1 July 2015. This amendment introduced a number of changes to this penalty, making it more flexible and allowing the imposition of its new types. The purpose of the amendment was to enable courts to more frequently apply the discussed penalty more frequently instead of the conditionally suspended penalty of imprisonment, which had been considered an insufficiently severe and ineffective means of penal policy.

A penalty of the restriction of liberty may not be joined with other penalties. Article 37b CC provides for an exception to this rule: it stipulates that in cases of misdemeanours punishable by the penalty of imprisonment, the court – irrespective of the lowest statutory penalty for a given offence – may concurrently impose a penalty of imprisonment for the maximum term of three months (and if the lowest statutory penalty for a given offence is at least ten years – six months) *and* a penalty of the restriction of liberty for a term of up to two years. Here, the penalty of imprisonment is served first unless a statute provides for otherwise.

The court may discharge a person sentenced to a penalty of the restriction of liberty from the remainder of this penalty, deeming it completed, provided that a person has served at least half of the imposed penalty, respected the legal order and also complied with the imposed obligations, penal measures, compensatory measures and forfeiture.

IV. Penalties Involving Imprisonment

384. The Polish Criminal Code defines three separate penalties that involve the deprivation of a convicted person's liberty (imprisonment). These are:

(1) the penalty of imprisonment (*pozbawienie wolności*);
(2) the penalty of 25 years of imprisonment (*25 lat pozbawienia wolności*),
(3) the penalty of life imprisonment (*dożywotnie pozbawienie wolności*).

385. The penalty of imprisonment (a term in prison) lasts for at least a month and for no longer than fifteen years. This penalty is imposed in months and years (Article 37 CC). In exceptional cases, the court may impose a term of imprisonment that is longer than fifteen years. First, this is admissible whenever a statute stipulates a possibility of an extraordinary increase (aggravation) of a penalty imposed. In accordance with Article 38 § 2 CC, the extraordinarily aggravated penalty must not exceed twenty years of imprisonment. This type of penalty is also imposed in months and years. Second, the imposition of a penalty harsher than fifteen years of imprisonment is possible in a situation where a perpetrator commits several offences and an aggregate penalty is imposed (see *infra*, paragraphs 472–476). The court imposes such a penalty by adding a term of imprisonment to the highest of the penalties imposed for the concurring offences. However, the aggregate term of imprisonment so calculated may not exceed twenty years (Article 86 § 1 CC). Third, a penalty of up to twenty years of imprisonment may also be imposed in a situation where a statute allows for the decrease of an upper limit of a penalty that may be imposed for an offence that normally is subject to the penalty of twenty-five years of imprisonment.

Article 32 et seq. CC are general provisions. The statutory measure of a penalty for a defined offence is determined by the provision that criminalises given behaviour. The Criminal Code uses the following, fixed formulas defining a term of imprisonment:

(1) from one month to three years;
(2) from three months to five years;
(3) from six months to eight years;
(4) from one to ten years;
(5) from two to twelve years;
(6) from three to fifteen years.

The Criminal Code also makes offences punishable by a fine, the restriction of liberty or imprisonment (up to one or two years).

386. The penalties of twenty-five **years of imprisonment** and **life imprisonment** are in principle custodial penalties, which should be applied only where, irrespective of an assessment of an offence committed, circumstances of the case indicate that the prospects of a perpetrator's rehabilitation are small while society must be protected against the perpetrator.

387. Pursuant to Article 37a CC, if a given prohibited act is punishable under a statute of criminal law by the penalty of imprisonment for a term of up to eight years, a fine or a penalty of restriction of liberty may be imposed instead of imprisonment; however, the latter penalty may not involve exclusively the obligations referred to in Article 34 § 1a item 3 CC (*supra* paragraph 380).

§3. Penal Measures

I. The Nature and Catalogue of Penal Measures

388. Penal measures are measures of penal responsecriminal sanctions whose the aim of which is to complement the effect of the penalty imposed on a convicted person. It is obvious that the penalties (discussed *supra* § 2) are not able to meet all repressive and preventive objectives which are set for criminal law.

Before the 1997 Criminal Code entered into force, penal measures were described as 'additional penalties' (*kary dodatkowe*). This term, however, does not adequately describe their nature and the way in which they are imposed. It is worth noting that these measures can frequently be as onerous as penalties (e.g., deprivation of public rights). Moreover, Article 59 CC provides for the possibility of imposing a penal measure instead of a penalty. In such cases, its nature is not at all additional.

389. The catalogue of penal measures has been standardised by Article 39 CC. These are:

(1) deprivation of public rights;
(2) prohibition from engaging in a specified occupation, profession or business;
(3) prohibition from engaging in a business relating to nurturing, treating or educating minors, or from taking care of them;
(4) prohibition of associating with specific social groups or frequenting specified kinds of places, prohibition from making contact with specified individuals, prohibition from approaching specified individuals, prohibition from leaving a specified place of stay without the court's consent;
(5) prohibition from entering a mass event;
(6) prohibition from entering gambling facilities and engaging in gambling games;
(7) obligation to temporarily leave the premises occupied together with the aggrieved person;
(8) prohibition from operating vehicles;
(9) pecuniary payment;
(10) publication of the sentence.

II. Deprivation of Public Rights

390. Deprivation of public rights is a penal measure of a predominantly repressive nature. According to Article 40 § 1 CC, deprivation of public rights covers the loss of the right to vote, actively or passively, in public authority elections (e.g., for the Sejm and the Senate), in professional or economic bodies elections (e.g., for a bar association), the loss of the right to participate in the administration of justice (prohibition from being a professional or a lay judge), and loss of the right to perform a function in public and local and professional self-government authorities and institutions, as well as the loss of military rank and reverting to the rank of private. The deprivation of public rights also includes the loss of medals, decorations and honorary titles and the loss of the capacity to acquire them during the period of the deprivation of rights.

Because of the far-reaching implications of ruling for the deprivation of liberty, such a ruling is only possible in the case of sentencing a person to imprisonment for a period of no less than three years. Moreover, Article 40 § 2 CC states that this sentencing must be for the commission of an offence driven by particularly reprehensible motives. This kind of offence is, for example, manslaughter committed 'just for fun', or without any specified motive, or in order for the perpetrator to gain some professional benefit.

Deprivation of public rights is imposed for a period of one to ten years. The measure is effective from the moment the ruling becomes final and binding. However, the period the deprivation of public rights is imposed for does not run concurrently with the penalty of imprisonment served for an offence. The period in which the measure is in force is often de facto longer than implied solely from the period for which the deprivation of public rights is ruled.

III. Prohibition from Engaging in a Specified Occupation, Profession or Business

391. Prohibition from engaging in a specified occupation, profession or business has been designed to be a precautionary measure and to protect society from persons who fail to perform their professional duties in an appropriate way. This measure is also designed to have a preventive effect and to develop the awareness of people who engage in a specified occupation, profession or business. From the perspective of a convicted person this measure also has a repressive nature, as it prevents him or her from performing activities which, more often than not, are his source of income.

Pursuant to Article 41 § 1 CC, it is possible for the court to impose the prohibition from engaging in a specified occupation or profession if, when committing an offence, the perpetrator has abused his position or profession, or has shown that his further occupation of such a position or further practising of such a profession poses a threat to substantive, legally protected interests (pursuant to Article 41 § 1 CC). A public official accepting a financial advantage, or a medical doctor or attorney committing a violation of their professional duties in a way that results in a patient or client suffering damage, are examples of such situations.

Pursuant to Article 41 § 2 CC the court may impose the prohibition from engaging in a specified business during the process of sentencing for an offence committed in relation to operating such business activity – if its further operation poses a threat to substantive, legally protected interests. An example of this could be running a waste treatment business, where the treatment is performed in a way that poses a risk to the natural environment and human life and health.

In each case the Criminal Code leaves it to the court to choose the prohibitions discussed above. Consequently, the court decides on the measures on the basis of the circumstances of each case.

Prohibition from engaging in a specified occupation, profession or business can be imposed for a period of one to fifteen years. The measure is effective from the moment the ruling becomes final and binding. However, the period during which it should apply does not run currently with the penalty of imprisonment served by a perpetrator, even if the latter penalty is for another offence.

IV. Prohibition from Engaging in a Business Relating to Nurturing, Treating or Educating Minors, or from Taking Care of Them

392. Prohibition from engaging in a business relating to nurturing, treating or educating minors, or taking care of them, has been designed to, first and foremost, protect children from persons who use the activities they engage in to commit offences to the detriment of children (especially violent or sexual offences). The prohibition applies to any form of activity, not only commercial activity. Consequently, the prohibition can also apply to charitable activities.

Pursuant to Article 41 § 1a CC, the court may impose the lifetime prohibition from engaging in all or specified occupations, professions or businesses relating to nurturing, treating or educating minors, or taking care of them, while sentencing to a penalty of deprivation of liberty for an offence against sexual liberty or decency committed against a minor, and while sentencing to a penalty of imprisonment for an intentional offence against life and health to the detriment of a minor.

A court can impose the prohibition from engaging in a business relating to nurturing, treating or educating minors, or taking care of them, for a designated period (one to fifteen years), or indefinitely. This is decided on the basis of the circumstances in which a particular offence is committed, relating to both the offence and the perpetrator.

In Article 41 § 1b, the Criminal Code provides for a single basis on which to use the discussed measure obligatorily. The obligation to apply this measure indefinitely becomes binding if the perpetrator is sentenced again under the circumstances indicated on Article 41 § 1a CC.

The measure is effective from the moment the ruling becomes final and binding. However, the period during which it should apply (ordered by the court) does not start to run while the person is serving prison time, even if the person was sentenced to prison for another offence.

V. Prohibition from Associating with Specific Social Groups or Frequenting Specified Kinds of Places, Prohibition from Making Contact with or Approaching Specified Individuals, Prohibition from Leaving a Specified Place of Stay Without the Court's Consent

393. Prohibition from associating with specific social groups or frequenting specified kinds of places, prohibition from making contact with specified individuals, prohibition from approaching specified individuals, prohibition from leaving a specified place of stay without the court's consent is undoubtedly repressive in its nature and is connected to limiting a perpetrator's freedom to move around and to contact other persons. At the same time, it functions as an important preventive measure – that is, it protects persons at risk of contact with a convicted person, or isolates a convicted person from places in which he or she could pose a threat and commit further offences.

394. The discussed measure can have four types:

(1) an order to refrain from associating with specified social groups or frequenting specified kinds of places (e.g., schools, nursery schools, football hooligan groups);
(2) an order to refrain from contacting specified persons (e.g., the aggrieved person and related persons, children; the prohibited contact could be personal, or have any other form, e.g., telephone contact);
(3) an order to refrain from approaching specified persons (e.g., the aggrieved person, at a distance specified by the court);
(4) an order to refrain from leaving a specified place of stay without the court's consent.

A court may impose one or more of the above prohibitions.

The prohibition may be linked with the obligation to report to the police or any other designated authority within specified periods of time, and the prohibition from approaching specified persons can also be controlled through electronic monitoring.

395. A court may impose the discussed prohibition if any of the following grounds is satisfied:

(a) sentencing for an offence against sexual liberty or decency committed against a minor;
(b) sentencing for a different offence against liberty, or an intentional violent offence, especially against a next of kin.

In cases discussed in point (b), this prohibition may also be imposed in situations when the offence was committed against an adult.

Whether the use of a particular prohibition is justified is decided in each instance by a court, taking the circumstances of a particular case into consideration. However, it is generally not obligatory.

396. Article 41a § 2 CC determines the obligatory basis for imposing the prohibition from associating with specific social groups or frequenting specified kinds of places, the prohibition from making contact with specified individuals, the prohibition from approaching specified individuals, and the prohibition from leaving a specified place of stay without the court's consent – this is sentencing to imprisonment without conditionally suspending the sentence for an offence against sexual liberty or decency committed against a minor.

The prohibition from associating with specific social groups or frequenting specified kinds of places, the prohibition from making contact with specified individuals, the prohibition from approaching specified individuals, and the prohibition from leaving a specified place of stay without the court's consent can be imposed for a period between one and fifteen years.

Article 41a § 3 CC provides for the possibility of indefinitely imposing the prohibition from associating with specific social groups or frequenting specified kinds of places, the prohibition from making contact with specified individuals, the prohibition from approaching specified individuals, and the prohibition from leaving a specified place of stay without the court's consent. This is permissible if a perpetrator receives another sentence under the circumstances indicated in article 41a § 2 CC.

Article 41a § 3a CC provides for a special basis for the obligatory imposition of the prohibition discussed in the form of the prohibition to approach the aggrieved person. This is the case in a situation when the obligation to leave the premises occupied jointly with an aggrieved person (this penal measure is discussed in more detail in *infra* paragraph 404) is imposed for offences defined in chapters XXV and XXVI CC, that is, for offences against sexual liberty and decency, and against the family and care.

397. The prohibition from associating with specific social groups or frequenting specified kinds of places, the prohibition from making contact with specified individuals, the prohibition from approaching specified individuals and the prohibition from leaving a specified place of stay without the court's consent is effective from the moment the ruling becomes final and binding. However, the period during which it should apply does not run while the person is serving prison time, even if the person was sentenced to imprisonment for another offence.

VI. Prohibition from Entering a Mass Event

398. Prohibition from entering a mass event is a penal measure used in relation to perpetrators of offences committed in relation to such events. On the one hand, this measure is intended to have a preventive effect on these persons, and, on the other, it is intended to secure the safety at such events.

Despite the fact that, pursuant to Mass Events Safety Act of 20 March 2009 (J.L. of 2009, no. 62, Item 504, as amended), a mass event can either be an artistic and entertainment-type event or a sports event, the discussed penal measure is practically only used in relation to sports events, which are almost exclusively football matches.

Qualifying a particular event as a mass event predominantly depends on its size. In the case of a sports event, an event with a capacity of no fewer than 300 people (indoor venues) and a capacity of no fewer than 1,000 people (open-air venues) is regarded as a mass event.

An optional basis on which a court can impose the prohibition from entering a mass event is the previous commission of an offence in relation to such an event or a perpetrator having been previously sentenced for a misdemeanour involving anti-social behaviour (for the definition of the term cf. *infra* paragraph 464), if the perpetrator's participation in mass events poses a threat to the legally protected interests. Examples of such interests are the life and health of other participants of the mass event, or public order.

399. Committing an offence in relation to a mass event does not necessarily mean it is committed it during the actual event. A perpetrator can commit an offence before or after the event. This can include various offences: not only participating in a brawl, or disrupting an event, but also making punishable threats on internet forums in relation to a mass event.

Specific offences and petty offences against the security of mass events are specified in Articles 54–61 of the Mass Events Safety Act of 20 March 2009.

400. The Criminal Code provides for two obligatory bases for imposing the prohibition from entering a mass event. First, it can be imposed if it is stipulated by a special provision. An example of this is Article 66 of the Mass Events Safety Act of 20 March 2009, which obliges the court to impose prohibition from entering a mass event in the case of a perpetrator having previously committed offences against life and health, offences against general safety, and offences related to the violation of the integrity of the human body, or a physical assault on a public official committed in relation to a mass sports event. The prohibition is also obligatorily imposed in the case of a person having previously committed the offence of bringing to and possessing at a mass event weapons, pyrotechnic articles or other dangerous items or explosives, and of having previously entered the field of play or other area where a sports tournament was taking place during a mass sports event. Second, the obligation to impose the discussed penal measure becomes binding if a perpetrator receives another sentence for an offence committed in relation to a mass event.

401. The prohibition from entering a mass event takes two forms. First, it includes the prohibition from entering any mass event taking place in Poland, as well as football matches played by the Polish national team or a Polish sports club outside of Poland. Second, this prohibition may be combined with the obligation for a convicted person to remain at a specified place of permanent residence during certain mass events which the convicted person is prohibited to attend; this may be ensured with the use of the electronic monitoring system. In a situation in which imposing the above obligations would be impossible or pointless, it is possible to impose the obligation for the convicted person to appear at an organisational unit of the police or at a place specified by an appropriate police commissioner during specified mass events which the sentenced person is prohibited from attending.

In the case of imposing any of the above obligations, the court determines the mass events during which the given obligation is to be fulfilled. The court names the sporting disciplines, sports clubs and the territorial scope of the events covered by the obligation.

402. The prohibition from entering a mass event is imposed for a period from two to six years.

The obligation for a convicted person to remain at a specified place of permanent residence during certain mass events which the convicted person is prohibited from attending is imposed for a period from six to twelve months. The obligation for the convicted person to appear at an organisational unit of the police or at a place specified by an appropriate police commissioner during specified mass events which the sentenced person is prohibited from attending is imposed for a period of six months to six years. However, this period may not exceed the period for which the prohibition from entering a mass event is imposed.

In justified cases the court may impose that once the period for which the obligation for the sentenced person to remain at a specified place of permanent residence during certain mass events which the sentenced person is prohibited from attending is imposed has elapsed, the convicted person will be obliged to appear at an organisational unit of the police or at a place specified by an appropriate police commissioner during specified mass events. The period of application of this additional measure, calculated together with the period of fulfilling this obligation within the duration of the prohibition, may not exceed the period for which the prohibition is imposed, *supra* paragraph 408.

The prohibition from entering a mass event is effective from the moment the ruling becomes final and binding. However, the period during which it should apply does not run while the person is serving prison time, even if the person was sentenced to imprisonment for another offence.

VII. Prohibition from Entering Gambling Facilities and Engaging in Gambling Games

403. The prohibition from entering gambling facilities and engaging in gambling games has been designed to eliminate persons who have committed an offence in relation to organising or participating in gambling games from participating in what are widely understood as gambling games. Consequently, this applies to both organisers of gambling games and players. However, it should be pointed out that the prohibition is ineffective towards persons who organise gambling games. It applies exclusively to entering gambling facilities (e.g., casinos), and this is not a necessary prerequisite for running gambling games.

The condition for imposing the prohibition from entering gambling facilities and from engaging in gambling games is that a convicted person has been previously sentenced for an offence committed in relation to the organising of or participating in gambling games. In practice, this can include various situations. Apart from offences committed in relation to organising gambling games, the theft of money for the purposes of gambling games may also be taken into consideration. A court is under no obligation to impose this measure.

Prohibition from entering gambling facilities and engaging in gambling games is imposed for a period from one to ten years.

Prohibition from entering gambling facilities and engaging in gambling games is effective from the moment the ruling becomes final and binding. However, the period during which it should apply does not run while the person is serving prison time, even if the person was sentenced to imprisonment for another offence.

VIII. The Obligation to Temporarily Leave Premises Occupied Together with an Aggrieved Person

404. The obligation to temporarily leave premises occupied together with an aggrieved person is a criminal reaction measure aimed at tackling domestic violence. Its purpose is to provide adequate protection to victims of domestic violence, and, at the same time, to enable the use of penalty other than imprisonment against a perpetrator.

A court may impose the obligation to temporarily leave premises occupied together with an aggrieved person, in the case of sentencing for the following offences:

(1) an offence against sexual liberty or decency committed against a minor,
(2) another offence against liberty,
(3) an intentional violent offence, especially against a next of kin.

A court is obliged to impose the obligation to temporarily leave premises occupied together with an aggrieved person when sentencing to a penalty of unconditional imprisonment for an offence against sexual liberty or decency committed against a minor.

This order may be linked with the obligation to report to the police or any other designated authority within specified periods of time.

The obligation to leave premises may relate to any premises which the perpetrator occupies together with an aggrieved person, regardless of the convicted person's rights to the premises (e.g., ownership, tenancy).

When imposing the obligation to temporarily leave premises occupied together with an aggrieved person, the court specifies the deadline for the performance of the order.

The obligation to temporarily leave premises occupied together with an aggrieved person is imposed for a period from one to ten years.

IX. Prohibition from Operating Vehicles

405. Prohibition from operating vehicles is a basic instrument of criminal policy in relation to perpetrators of driving offences. Its main aim is to ensure road safety by temporarily preventing persons who pose a threat to other road users through their behaviour from using roads.

A court may impose the prohibition from operating vehicles of a specified kind while sentencing a road user for an offence against traffic safety, especially if the circumstances of the offence in question show that the operation of vehicles by this person poses a threat to the safety of traffic. A road user is not always a driver. For example, they could also be a pedestrian. The court determines the type of vehicles (e.g., passenger cars, motorcycles, etc.) covered by the prohibition in the ruling.

The court is under an obligation to impose the prohibition from operating vehicles if a perpetrator has committed an offence against traffic safety while intoxicated or under the influence of a narcotic drug, or has fled from the scene of an incident or catastrophe in land, water or air traffic. In such cases, the prohibition is imposed for a period of no less than three years and applies to all motor vehicles or to specified motor vehicles.

406. Article 42 §§ 3 and 4 CC provides for two bases for the obligatory imposition of the prohibition from operating all motor vehicles indefinitely. The obligation becomes binding in the following cases:

(1) committing the offence of operating a motor vehicle on land, water or in air traffic while intoxicated or under the influence of a narcotic drug if the perpetrator had previously been lawfully sentenced for operating a motor vehicle or causing an accident or a catastrophe in land, water or air traffic when intoxicated or under the influence of a narcotic drug;
(2) committing the offence of operating a motor vehicle in land, water or air traffic while intoxicated or under the influence of a narcotic drug if the perpetrator committed the offence while banned from operating motor vehicles, because of previously being sentenced for an offence;
(3) committing the offence of causing a catastrophe in land, water or air traffic which resulted in death or the grievous bodily harm of another person if the perpetrator was intoxicated or under the influence of a narcotic drug, or fled from the scene of the incident.

Only in exceptional cases justified by extraordinary circumstances, may the court depart from imposing the prohibition from operating vehicles in the above situations.

Imposing the prohibition from operating all motor vehicles indefinitely is obligatory if the perpetrator receives another sentence in the circumstances discussed in 1–3.

407. Prohibition from operating vehicles is imposed for a period from one to fifteen years, or indefinitely. By imposing the prohibition, the court imposes an obligation on the sentenced person to return a document authorising him or her to operate a vehicle. The period for which the prohibition is imposed does not begin until this obligation has been fulfilled.

X. Pecuniary Payment

408. Pecuniary payment means paying a sum of money, of the amount specified by the court, to a good cause. This measure is a form of compensation for a committed offence which is directed at society as a whole.

According to Article 43a CC, imposing a penal measure in the form of pecuniary payment is permissible under three situations:

(1) when the court refrains from imposing a penalty (see *infra*, paragraph 468);
(2) where a statute so provides:
   (a) in the case of the conditional discontinuation of proceedings (see *infra*, paragraphs 425–429);
   (b) in the case of the conditional suspension of the enforcement of a sentence (see *infra*, paragraph 430–439);
(3) in the case of sentencing a perpetrator for an offence:
   (a) of operating a vehicle while intoxicated or under the influence of a narcotic drug,
   (b) permitting, against a particular obligation (e.g., imposed on a traffic controller), the operation of a motor vehicle or other vehicle that is in a condition immediately threatening to safety in land, water or air traffic, or permitting the operation of a motor vehicle or other vehicle by an intoxicated person, a person under the influence of a narcotic drug or by a person not in possession of the required licence,
   (c) performing activities directly related to ensuring the safety of motor vehicle traffic while intoxicated or under the influence of a narcotic drug (e.g., railway watchman, traffic warden).

In the above cases, pecuniary payment is either an alternative to a penalty (if, or course, it can fulfil the aim of the penalty), or is an additional criminal penalty imposed on the perpetrator.

409. Pecuniary payment in the cases mentioned in paragragh 414 (Items 1 and 2) may amount to up to PLN 60,000 (ca. EUR 13,640). However, in the case of Item 3, the court is obliged to impose pecuniary payment of at least PLN 5,000 (approx. EUR 1,140). The pecuniary payment amounts to at least PLN 10,000 in the case of sentencing a perpetrator for the offence of operating a vehicle while intoxicated or under the influence of a narcotic drug if this offence was committed while the perpetrator was banned from operating motor vehicles if he had previously been lawfully sentenced for operating a motor vehicle or causing an accident or a catastrophe in land, water or air traffic when intoxicated or under the influence of a narcotic drug. The maximum amount of the imposed punitive damages may not exceed PLN 60,000.

The Criminal Code provides that the court imposes pecuniary payment to be made to the Fund for Victim and Post-Penitentiary Support. This is a special-purpose state fund managed by the Minister of Justice. The fund's assets finance ventures whose purpose is to assist persons released from prisons and remand centres, as well as victims of crimes, witnesses and their next of kin.

XI. The Publication of a Sentence

410. Pursuant to Article 43b CC, the court may order the publication of a sentence in a particular manner if it is expedient, especially due to the social impact of the sentence, unless it infringes an aggrieved person's interests (Article 43b CC).

The court decides on the expediency of the publication of a sentence. Such a step is justified, especially due to the social impact of a sentence. The publication of a sentence has therefore been designed to have a preventive impact on both the perpetrator and, importantly in this context, society as a whole (general prevention). However, the purpose of the discussed penal measure is not to publicly discredit or compromise a perpetrator. Therefore, the court should consider the potential effects of the publication of a sentence and its influence on the achievement of preventive aims. At the same time, it should not allow for the information from a published sentence to be used against the objectives that had driven the publication of the sentence, e.g. a given person being lynched in the media.

The infringing of an aggrieved person's interests due to the publication of a sentence can occur, for example, in the case of a sexual offence (e.g., rape). It must be stressed, however, that the publication of a sentence does not depend on an aggrieved person's consent, or the lack of it. The court is only obliged to analyse an aggrieved person's interests vis a vis the publication of the contents of a sentence. However, the decision in this matter is made independently by the court.

In has been indicated in case law that *he publication of a sentence should only take place in such cases that have raised particular social interest, caused outrage or concern. It is also expedient to use this measure in the case of offences frequently committed in a given area, or within a given milieu* (cf. Judgment of the Court of Appeal in Katowice of 28 June 2007, II AKa 190/07, *Orzecznictwo SA w Katowicach* 2007, vol. 4, Item 6).

411. The method of the publication of a sentence is determined by the court. A sentence can be published in the press, released through the mass media, or on the court's website.

There are specific norms regarding the publication of a sentence in Article 215 CC, which indicates that the court may impose the publication of a sentence for defamation at the request of an aggrieved person. Consequently, an aggrieved person's decision is, in this case, of crucial importance.

XII. Fulfilment of a Penal Measure

412. The fulfilment of a penal measure generally occurs once the obligation imposed on a convicted person is completed (e.g., a pecuniary payment is made), or after the expiry of the period for which the measure was imposed (e.g., prohibition from operating vehicles). Article 84 CC provides for the possibility for the court to decide that a penal measure has been fulfilled before the expiry of the period for which it had been imposed. After the expiry of half of the period for which the penal measure was imposed, the court may decide that it has been fulfilled if the convicted person has respected the legal order and the penal measure has been fulfilled for at least one year.

The above rule does not apply to the following penal measures:

(1) the prohibition from engaging in a specified occupation, profession or business;
(2) prohibition from engaging in a business relating to nurturing, treating or educating minors, or from taking care of them, in the case of a perpetrator sentenced to a penalty of imprisonment for an offence against sexual liberty or decency committed against a minor, and in the case of a perpetrator sentenced to a penalty of imprisonment for an intentional offence against life and health to the detriment of a minor;
(3) the prohibition from operating vehicles, if a perpetrator has committed an offence against traffic safety while intoxicated or under the influence of a narcotic drug, or has fled from the scene of an incident or a catastrophe in land, water or air traffic.

If a penal measure has been imposed indefinitely, the court may regard it as fulfilled if the convicted person has respected the legal order and there is no threat of him or her committing an offence similar to the one for which the penal measure was imposed, and the penal measure has been fulfilled for at least fifteen years.

§4. Compensatory Measures

413. Up until 1 July 2015, the measures aimed at redressing the damage inflicted on an aggrieved person as a result of an offence were included as part of the penal measures. However, bearing in mind that they are of a different nature to the penal measures and that they have a specific (compensatory) objective to achieve, the legislator decided to single them out as a separate category of penal sanctions. This step was also dictated by the fact that damages are remedied pursuant to the rules of the civil law (the law of tort) and not according to the rules set out in the regulations concerning the measure of a penalty and other penal measures defined in the Criminal Code.

The Criminal Code provides for two compensatory measures – the obligation to remedy damage, and punitive damages.

414. As a compensatory measure, **the obligation to remedy damage** means that a convicted person may be required to redress the damage that was the result of an offence (in the case of loss to property) or compensate an aggrieved person for an injury suffered (in the case of non-pecuniary, or moral, loss).

In general terms, the existence of a loss (injury), the causal effect between the offence committed by a perpetrator and a loss (injury) suffered, as well as the amount of the damages (compensation) are determined pursuant to the rules provided for in the civil law (the law of tort). Article 46 § 1 CC reads, however, that the civil law regulations concerning the possibility of awarding a disability pension do not apply.

The court does not need to wait until all material circumstances relating to the amount of damages or compensation (such as those concerning the medical condition of an aggrieved person) have been established to adjudicate a criminal case. The court may award damages or compensation to the extent permitted by the findings made in the course of the proceedings. Article 46 § 3 CC reads explicitly that the award of damages or compensation does not preclude the ability to assert the unsatisfied part of the claim in civil proceedings. This solution is meant to accelerate criminal proceedings and at the same time enable an aggrieved person to assert full amount of compensation before a civil court.

The amount of the damages or compensation is determined by the size of the loss or injury caused.

415. **Punitive damages** (*nawiązka*), the second compensatory measure, take two forms:

(1) punitive damages awarded to an aggrieved person; or
(2) punitive damages awarded for a good cause.

Punitive damages are a form of lump sum compensation for a financial loss or for moral injury.

If there are considerable difficulties imposing an obligation to remedy damage or compensate an injury (this refers primarily to problems determining the amount of the damages or compensation), the court may impose punitive damages (rather than impose that obligation) of up to PLN 200,000 (approx. EUR 45,450), payable to an aggrieved person. If an aggrieved person dies as a result of an offence committed by a convicted person, the court may award punitive damages to a next of kin whose circumstances have deteriorated significantly as a result of the aggrieved person's death. If there are several next of kin, punitive damages is awarded to each of them.

The court awards punitive damages to an aggrieved person, and if the aggrieved person dies as a result of an offence committed by a convicted person, the court awards punitive damages to next of kin whose circumstances have deteriorated significantly as a result of the aggrieved person's death, if the perpetrator is convicted for causing a road accident or a catastrophe in road, sea or air traffic, if the perpetrator was intoxicated or under the influence of a narcotic drug, or fled from the scene of the incident. The court awards punitive damages amounting to at least PLN 10,000 (approx. EUR 2,273) but no more than PLN 100,000 (approx. EUR 22,730).

Punitive damages for an aggrieved person may be awarded pursuant to the general regulations set out in Articles 46 and 47 CC, as well as pursuant to other provisions of the CC. The following cases may be listed at this point:

(1) conviction for a misdemeanour involving antisocial behaviour, unless the court has imposed the obligation to remedy the damage or to compensate for the injury suffered;
(2) a ruling for the conditional discontinuation of the proceedings unless the court has imposed the obligation to remedy the damage or to compensate for the injury suffered; or
(3) a conviction for defamation, insulting another person through means of mass communication.

416. Punitive damages for a good cause can take various forms. Pursuant to the Criminal Code:

(1) when sentencing a perpetrator for an intentional offence against life or health, or for another intentional offence resulting in the death of a human being, grievous bodily harm, the disruption of bodily functions or a health disorder, the court may rule for punitive damages to be paid to the Fund for Victim and Post-Penitentiary Support,
(2) in the case of sentencing a perpetrator for an offence against the environment, the court may rule for punitive damages to be paid to the National Fund for Environmental Protection and Water Management; or
(3) when sentencing the perpetrator for causing a road accident or a catastrophe in road, sea or air traffic, if the perpetrator was intoxicated or under the influence of a narcotic drug, or fled from the scene of the incident, when it is impossible to award punitive damages to an aggrieved person because the aggrieved person has not been identified, the court will award punitive damages to the Fund for Victim and Post-Penitentiary Support.

The aforementioned punitive damages for a good cause may be awarded in the amount of up to PLN 100,000. The punitive damages referred to in Item 3 above amounts to at least PLN 10,000, unless there are special circumstances that justify awarding it at a lower amount.

417. Punitive damages may also be awarded pursuant to special regulations contained in legal statutes other than the Criminal Code. For example, if a perpetrator commits an offence consisting in the intentional destruction of or damage to a historic monument subject to the Historic Monument Protection Act, the court is obliged to award punitive damages, in the amount between three times and thirty times the minimum wage, to be paid to a good cause relating to the protection of historic monuments.

Punitive damages awarded to the State Treasury is a special form of punitive damages. In such a case, punitive damages is awarded instead of forfeiture of items that had been used for committing an offence or were meant for that purpose, if the imposition of forfeiture would be incommensurate with the gravity of the offence committed.

§5. Forfeiture

418. As in the case of punitive damages and the obligation to remedy damage, up until 1 July 2015 forfeiture had been considered a penal measure. However, because of its specific nature, the legislator decided to single it out as a separate type of penal sanction.

Forfeiture is decreed in order to deprive a perpetrator (and in some cases other people as well) of the tools required for the commission of offence, proceeds of offence, as well as items whose possession and trading are forbidden.

Forfeited property becomes the property of the State Treasury.

419. In the case of items that were used for the commission of an offence or that were meant for that purpose, the court may impose their forfeiture, if required, under a special provision. If the imposition of forfeiture is incommensurate with the gravity of a committed offence, the court may impose punitive damages for the benefit of the State Treasury rather than forfeiture. The court is required to impose forfeiture of property that derives directly from offence.

420. In the event that the imposition of forfeiture referred to in paragraph 425 is impossible, the court may impose forfeiture of items which are equivalent in value to the items that were used to commit an offence or were intended to serve in the commission of an offence.

Forfeiture, as referred to in paragraph 425 is not imposed if property is to be returned to an aggrieved person or another eligible entity.

421. While sentencing a person for an offence consisting in the violation of prohibition from the production, possession, distribution, transferring, carrying or transportation of specific items (e.g., narcotic or psychotropic drugs), the court may impose their forfeiture, and in situations prescribed by a statute, the court is obliged to impose their forfeiture.

422. The Criminal Code provides not only for the possibility of ordering the forfeiture of items derived directly from offence but also the forfeiture of the benefits gained as a result of offence. Pursuant to Article 45 § 1 CC, if a perpetrator has gained a financial advantage, even indirectly, from the commission of an offence, and if this advantage is not subject to forfeiture, the court will impose the forfeiture of such advantage or of an advantage that is equivalent in value. Forfeiture is not imposed in full or in part, if an advantage (or an advantage that is equivalent in value) is to be returned to an aggrieved person or another entity.

Forfeiture of a financial advantage gained as a result of offence is linked with specific presumptions of the law, the intention of which is to reverse the burden of proof relating to the legal or illegal origin of a given financial advantage. Pursuant to

Article 45 § 2 CC, while sentencing for an offence from whose commission a perpetrator has gained a financial advantage (even indirectly) of substantial value (i.e., in excess of PLN 200,000, or around EUR 45,000), it is deemed that the property which the perpetrator has taken possession of, or has acquired entitlement to, while committing the offence or afterwards, constitutes a benefit derived from the commission of the offence until the moment of a sentence is passed (even if it is not final), unless the perpetrator or another person concerned proves otherwise. The second presumption concerns property which had been transferred to a private individual, a legal entity or an organisational unit without legal personality in fact or under any other legal title. In such a case, it is believed that items remaining in the autonomous possession of that person or organisational entity, and other property rights that person is entitled to, belong to the perpetrator, unless it is impossible to believe, considering the circumstances in which the property was acquired, that it originated from a prohibited act (even indirectly).

423. Forfeiture is generally imposed if a perpetrator is convicted. However, pursuant to Article 45a CC it is sometimes possible to impose forfeiture even when there is no conviction (Article 45a CC). This option is permitted under the following circumstances:

(1) when proceedings are discontinued because the social harm presented by the act is negligible;
(2) when proceedings are conditionally discontinued (*infra* paragraph 425–429);
(3) when proceedings are discontinued because it is found that a perpetrator committed a prohibited act in a state of insanity;
(4) or when there are circumstances excluding the punishment of a perpetrator of a prohibited act (such as defences, or a circumstance excluding guilt).

The above solution is necessary because, for example, the imposition of forfeiture of a narcotic drug is reasonable not only when a perpetrator is convicted for having such a drug but also in cases when a perpetrator is insane, etc., and proceedings are subject to discontinuation or when proceedings have been discontinued because an act presented negligible social harm.

§6. Probation Measures

I. General Overview

424. Measures related to putting a perpetrator to a test of good behaviour (probation measures) make up a group of criminal response measures that have a broad range of application and that can be used at different stages of criminal proceedings. The trait they have in common, however, is the fact that they are linked to the legislator's decision to refrain from sentencing a defendant or enforcing a defendant's penalty due to the fact that the defendant (convicted person) displays a positive change in behaviour and presents a low likelihood of reoffending (a positive criminological prognosis). They are also linked to the designation of a time frame in which defined duties are imposed on a defendant (convicted person) and it depends on whether these duties are fulfilled or not as to whether a potential penalty is sentenced or enforced.

The Polish Criminal Code provides for three measures related to putting a perpetrator to the test of good behaviour:

(1) conditional discontinuation of proceedings;
(2) conditional suspension of a sentence;
(3) parole.

II. Conditional Discontinuation of Proceedings

425. Conditional discontinuation of proceedings is covered by Articles 66–68 CC. This is imposed by a court in a form of a judgment which means attributing fault for the committed offence to the perpetrator and is a specific type of criminal law sanction. Discontinuation of proceedings is conditional because throughout the course of a probation period, as well as six months after it has come to an end, it is possible to resume proceedings and impose criminal sanctions on a perpetrator, as applicable for the offence committed by him.

426. Conditional discontinuation of proceedings can only be imposed by a court. This is possible once the following conditions are met:

(1) the offence is punishable by imprisonment of up to five years;
(2) the perpetrator has not been previously convicted of an intentional offence;
(3) the fault and social harm are minor;
(4) circumstances in which the offence was committed raise no doubts (consequently, a trial is not required), *infra* paragraphs 698–700;
(5) the demeanour of a perpetrator, his or her characteristics, personal circumstances and previous way of life make it reasonable to expect that, in spite of the discontinuation of the proceedings, he or she will respect the legal order, especially by not committing an offence (this expectation is called a 'positive criminological prognosis').

427. Conditional discontinuation of proceedings is a sanction used predominantly in the case of light and medium-gravity offences and for perpetrators who have not previously committed an intentional offence. This measure is therefore a chance for a perpetrator to avoid penaltiesy and is used to motivate them to respect the legal order. Despite the fact that conditional discontinuation of proceedings is recorded in the National Criminal Register, the person in relation to whom this measure was imposed cannot be recognised as a convicted person.

Criminal proceedings are conditionally discontinued for a probation period that lasts from one year to three years and runs from the moment the ruling becomes final and binding.

428. Along with conditional discontinuation of proceedings, if damage was done, a court imposes on the perpetrator the obligation to repair the damage in part or in full, and, if feasible, it also imposes the obligation to provide compensation for a moral injury suffered by a victim, or it imposes punitive damages instead of these obligations.

Additionally, the court can impose the following obligations on a perpetrator:

(1) the obligation to inform the court or a probation officer about the progress of a probation period;
(2) obligation to apologise to an aggrieved person;
(3) obligation to carry out the incumbent obligation to provide maintenance for another person;
(4) obligation to refrain from excessive use of alcohol or any use of a narcotic drugs;
(5) obligation to undergo therapy for addiction;
(6) obligation to undergo another type of therapy, specifically psychotherapy or psychoeducation therapy;
(7) obligation to take part in correctional and educational activities;
(8) the obligation to refrain from making contact with an aggrieved person or other persons in a specified manner, or from approaching an aggrieved person or other persons;
(9) the obligation to leave premises occupied together with an aggrieved person,

The court can also impose a pecuniary payment (see *supra*, paragraph 408-409) or prohibition from operating vehicles for up to two years.

During a probation period the court may place a perpetrator under the supervision of a probation officer or a trustworthy person, an association, institution or social organisation responsible for education, preventing antisocial and delinquent behaviour, or for providing assistance to convicted persons.

429. Over the course of a probation period, a perpetrator is obliged to fulfil the imposed obligations and respect the legal order. Should he or she violate the above requirements, it is permissible, or even obligatory, to resume the discontinued proceedings.

The obligatory basis for resumption of conditionally discontinued proceedings is the commission by the perpetrator of an intentional offence during a probation period., for which he or she is finally convicted. It must be stressed that simply committing an offence is not enough: there must be a final judgment passed in relation to that offence.

The court may resume criminal proceedings if a perpetrator has flagrantly violated the legal order during a probation period, including once the ruling on the conditional discontinuation of proceedings has been passed, but before its validation, especially if the perpetrator has committed an offence unintentionally, if he or she evades supervision, carrying out an imposed obligation or the imposed penal measure, compensatory measure, or forfeiture, or fails to fulfil a settlement with an aggrieved person. The decision to resume conditionally discontinued proceedings is dependent upon the circumstances of a given case and a perpetrator's explanations.

The court is obliged to resume criminal proceedings if the circumstances discussed above have occurred after a perpetrator had been given a written caution by a professional court-appointed probation officer, unless there are exceptional reasons not to do so.

Conditionally discontinued proceedings cannot be resumed later than six months from the moment of the completion of a probation period. The six months of additional time, which is provided for in the Criminal Code, is linked to the obligation to determine whether an offence has been committed during a probation period through a final judgment. Due to the fact that criminal proceedings often last a few months, the introduction of the above-mentioned period into the Criminal Code was made on pragmatic grounds. It is necessary to make a provision that committing an offence, which may result in resuming conditionally discontinued proceedings, must take place within a probation period. In the six months after the completion of a probation period, only a final judgment in the case of this offence can be passed.

III. Conditional Suspension of the Enforcement of a Sentence

430. Conditional suspension of the enforcement of a sentence means that a sentence is ordered in a judgment, and, at the same time, it is decided that the sentence will not be carried out during the probation period. This is to enable a defendant to show that despite the fact that the sentence will not be carried out, he or she will change his or her behaviour and respect the legal order.

Conditional suspension of the enforcement of a sentence is covered by Articles 69–76 CC.

Due to the fact that in recent years suspended imprisonment has been the most widely applied criminal penalty in Poland (in over half of all judgments), the legislator, by amending the Criminal Code on 1 July 2015, decided to limit the possibilities for imposing this sentence in order for the courts to more frequently draw on fines or, most of all, to rule for the restriction of liberty. These sentences are regarded as the more effective instruments of penal policy. The basic change as regards the possibility for imposing a conditional suspension of the enforcement of a sentence is linked to limiting the maximum sentence that can be suspended. As of 1 July 2015, this is a maximum of one year of imprisonment, whereas before the change it was possible to suspend a sentence of up to two years of imprisonment.

431. The court is able to conditionally suspend the enforcement of a sentence of imprisonment not exceeding one year if the following conditions are met:

(1) a perpetrator was not sentenced to imprisonment when committing the offence; and
(2) it is sufficient to achieve the purposes of the penalty with regard to a perpetrator, especially to prevent his or her relapse to offence.

While suspending the enforcement of a penalty, the court shall primarily consider a perpetrator's conduct, his or her characteristics, personal circumstances, previous way of life, and behaviour after committing an offence.

The probation period for which a court can suspend the enforcement of a sentence lasts from one year to three years and runs from the moment the verdict becomes final and binding. However, in the case of the suspension of the enforcement of a penalty imposed on a young offender (a perpetrator is under 21 years of age at the time of committing a prohibited act, and under 24 years at the time of the first instance ruling), or a perpetrator who committed an offence involving violence to the detriment of a person who lives with him, the probation period will last from two to five years.

The legislator provided for a special basis of suspending the enforcement of a penalty if a perpetrator decides to cooperate with law enforcement agencies and reveals information concerning the offences committed (*infra* paragraph 466). In this case, the penalty of imprisonment up to five years might be conditionally suspended for a trial period of up to 10 years.

In two cases, there are far-reaching restrictions on the ability to suspend the enforcement of imprisonment, notably:

(1) to a perpetrator of a misdemeanour involving antisocial behaviour;
(2) to a perpetrator of an offence referred to in Article 178a § 4 CC, that is an offender who operated a motor vehicle while intoxicated or under the influence of a narcotic drug if the person committed that offence while being banned from operating motor vehicles or if that person had been previously lawfully sentenced for operating a motor vehicle or causing an accident or a catastrophe in land, water or air traffic when intoxicated or under the influence of a narcotic drug.

In the situations referred to above, the court may conditionally suspend the enforcement of a penalty only in particularly justified cases. Such cases must be indicated in the statement of reasons of the final ruling.

432. To make the suspended imprisonment actually cumbersome for a perpetrator, the legislator decided to combine that penalty with other means of affecting a perpetrator.

While suspending the enforcement of a sentence, the court may impose a fine if its imposition in addition to imprisonment is not possible on any other basis (this is known as an 'additional fine'). However, the fine will not be collected (unless it had been collected previously) if the court orders the enforcement of the sentence of imprisonment. If the fine has been paid, the sentence of imprisonment will be reduced by a period corresponding to a half of the number of daily rates paid, rounded up to a full day.

When suspending the enforcement of a sentence, the court imposes on a convicted person one of the obligations mentioned in para. 428 or obligation to carry out the incumbent obligation to provide maintenance for another person, or the obligation to behave in any other appropriate manner during a probation period which may prevent relapse into offence.

If, however, the court imposes a penal measure in addition to suspended imprisonment, the above obligations do not need to be imposed.

The court may also impose one of the following obligations:

(1) making a pecuniary payment (see *supra*, paragraph 408-409);
(2) remedying the damage caused by the offence, in whole or in part (unless the court imposed a compensatory measure in addition to the suspended imprisonment).

In its judgment, the court may decide to place a perpetrator under the supervision of a probation officer or a trustworthy person, an association, institution or social organisation responsible for education, preventing antisocial and delinquent behaviour, or for providing assistance to convicted persons.

433. The supervision is mandatory in respect of:

(1) a minor who has perpetrated an intentional offence;
(2) an perpetrator who is an habitual offender (*infra* paragraph 461–462);
(3) a perpetrator of an offence committed in relation to an aberration of sexual preferences (e.g., a paedophile);
(4) a perpetrator who has committed an offence involving violence to the detriment of a person who resides with him.

434. The obligations relating to a suspended sentence are imposed after a convicted person had been heard. However, where a convicted person is required to undergo a therapy for addiction, his or her consent must be obtained first. This is because the legislator rightly assumed that such treatment only makes sense if a convicted person actually wants to undergo it.

435. During a probation period, the court may modify the obligations it has previously imposed. In justified cases, the court may also release a perpetrator from the performance of a previously imposed obligation. The same applies to the supervision.

The penalty of imprisonment must be enforced if:

(1) a person has committed a similar intentional offence during his or her probation period, for which he or she has been sentenced to unconditional imprisonment by a final and binding verdict;
(2) the definition of 'a similar offence' is given in Article 115 § 3 CC, which reads that similar offences are offences of the same type (such as sexual offences, offences against traffic safety). Likewise, nonhomogeneous offences involving the use or threat of violence or offences committed with a view to gaining a financial advantage are also considered similar offences.
(3) in the case of a person convicted of an offence involving the use of violence or unlawful threats towards a next of kin or a minor sharing the same residence, if that person has flagrantly violated the legal order during the probation period by again using force or unlawful threat towards a next of kin or a minor sharing the same residence.

The court may decree the enforcement of the penalty if the convicted person:

(1) has flagrantly violated the legal order during their probation period, especially if that person has committed an offence other than an intentional offence for which he has been sentenced to unconditional imprisonment by a final and binding verdict;

(2) is evading payment of a fine, supervision, carrying out of imposed obligations or imposed penal measures, compensatory measures or forfeiture (the court is obliged to order the enforcement of a sentence if the circumstances discussed above have occurred after a perpetrator has been given a written caution by a court-appointed probation officer, unless there are exceptional reasons not to do so).

(3) has flagrantly violated the legal order, especially by committing an offence after a sentence had been passed but before it has become final and binding.

Ordering the enforcement of a sentence generally means that any penalty imposed will be executed in full. However, the court may reduce a sentence by not more than half, upon taking account of the progress of the probation to date, and in particular when considering the execution of the obligations imposed.

As in the case of resuming proceedings that have been conditionally discontinued, the enforcement of a sentence may not be ordered after the lapse of six months from the completion of a probation period, see *supra*, paragraph 435.

436. The court decrees the enforcement of a penalty if a person has committed a similar intentional offence during a probation term, for which he has been sentenced to unconditional imprisonment by a final and binding verdict. In all other cases, rather than order the enforcement of a sentence, the court may – if the Criminal Code permits such an order to enforce the sentence – change the prison term to the restriction of liberty in the form of free supervised community service. In such a case, one day in prison is equal to two days of restriction of liberty. The court may also impose a fine (rather than order the enforcement of a prison sentence), assuming that one day in prison is equal to two daily rates of fine. Such a decision is taken upon considering the gravity and the type of a prohibited act imputed to a convicted person, provided that the court concludes that changing a prison term to the restriction of liberty or a fine will meet the objectives of the penalty. The penalty of the restriction of liberty must not be longer than 2 years, and the fine must not be higher than 810 daily rates.

437. If a convicted person is evading the penalty of restriction of liberty (community service), the payment of a fine, carrying out the obligations or penal measures imposed on him or her, or forfeiture or compensatory measures, the court will repeal the change and decree that a sentence of imprisonment be enforced. If the court repeals the change and orders the enforcement of a sentence of imprisonment, the court will count the fine paid or the community service performed to that date towards the prison term, assuming that one day in prison is equal to two daily rates of a fine or two days of restriction of liberty.

438. Where a person has been sentenced to suspended imprisonment, the sentence will be erased, by the operation of law, six months after the end of a probation period. If the court has ordered a fine or restriction of liberty in a place of imprisonment, the general rules relating to erasure of criminal record of the former penalties as set out in Article 107 CC will apply accordingly (*infra* paragraph 1039).

439. If the court has imposed a fine, a penal measure, forfeiture or a compensatory measure on a convicted person, the sentence will not be deleted until those measures have been completed, pardoned or expired under the rules of the statute of limitations.

IV. Parole

440. Unlike conditional discontinuation of proceedings or conditional suspension of the enforcement of a sentence, parole (*warunkowe przedterminowe zwolnienie*) is applicable to persons who have already commenced the serving of their term of imprisonment. It may be applied to any sentence involving a prison term, including twenty-five years' imprisonment and life imprisonment.

Parole is covered by Articles 77–82 CC and Articles 159–163 of the CEC.

441. Parole may be granted if the attitude of a convicted person, his or her characteristics and personal circumstances, the circumstances of the offence and his or her behaviour after committing the offence and while serving a penalty make it reasonable to expect that the person will respect the legal order after their release, especially by not committing another offence, and that the person will comply with the penal measure or preventive measure imposed by the court.

As a rule, a convicted person may be provisionally released after serving at least a half of their sentence. However, repeat offenders (see *infra*, paragraph 461) who are sentenced to imprisonment (Article 64 § 1 CC are eligible for parole after serving two-thirds of their sentence. Habitual offenders (see *infra*, paragraph 461) who are sentenced to prison (Article 64 § 2 CC) may be paroled after serving three quarters of their sentence.

A person who has been sentenced to twenty-five years in prison is eligible for parole upon serving fifteen years in prison. A person sentenced to life imprisonment may be paroled upon serving twenty-five years in prison.

These rules are also applied to the sum of two or more prison sentences that may not be combined and that run consecutively. However, under those circumstances a convicted person is eligible for parole after serving fifteen years in prison, unless he or she has also been sentenced to life imprisonment. In such a case, he or she may be provisionally released after serving twenty-five years in prison.

442. In exceptional situations (e.g., due to the modus operandi of a perpetrator, his or her motivation and the gravity of the offence), the court imposing a penalty involving imprisonment may impose more severe eligibility criteria for the provisional release of the convicted person (e.g., in the case of life imprisonment, the court may rule that parole may be granted not earlier than after thirty years in prison).

443. If a person is paroled, the remainder of his or sentence becomes a probation period. However, this probation may not be shorter than two years and may not be longer than five years. For habitual offenders (see *infra*, paragraph 461), a probation period must not be shorter than three years.

In the case of persons who have been granted parole after being sentenced to twenty-five years in prison or to life imprisonment, the probation period is ten years.

444. Parole is granted by a penitentiary court. Within regional courts, there is a penitentiary division and the judges in that division take decisions as the penitentiary court (the penitentiary court).

A parole application may be filed by a convicted person, as well as by the head of a correctional facility or by a court-appointed probation officer.

During a probation period, the penitentiary court may place a parolee under the supervision of a court-appointed probation officer or a trustworthy person, an association, organisation or institution responsible for education, preventing antisocial and delinquent behaviour, or for providing assistance to convicted persons. The court may also impose obligations on a convicted person similar to those imposed in the case of the conditional suspension of the enforcement of a sentence (*supra* paragraphs 430–439).

445. A parolee is always placed under supervision if the parolee is:

(1) a person convicted for sexual offences (under Articles 197–203 CC) committed in relation to an aberration of sexual preferences;
(2) a minor who has perpetrated an intentional offence;
(3) a perpetrator who is a repeat offender (see *infra*, paragraph 461); or
(4) a person convicted to life imprisonment.

446. A penitentiary court may change a probation period, impose, enlarge or modify certain obligations imposed on a parolee, place a convicted person under supervision or discharge him or her from supervision.

A parolee is recalled, or his parole is cancelled, if he or she has committed an intentional offence during his or her probation period for which he has been sentenced to unconditional imprisonment by a final and binding verdict. A parolee who has previously been sentenced for an offence involving the use of violence or unlawful threats towards a next of kin or a minor sharing the same residence must also be recalled if he or she has flagrantly violated the legal order during a probation period by again using violence or unlawful threats towards a next of kin or a minor sharing the same residence.

The penitentiary court may cancel parole if a convicted person has flagrantly violated the legal order during their probation period, especially by committing another offence or if the parolee has been sentenced to a penalty other than unconditional imprisonment, or if a parolee is evading supervision, carrying out imposed obligations or penal measures, forfeiture or compensatory measures. The recall from parole is mandatory if the circumstances discussed above have occurred after a convicted person had been given a written caution by a court-appointed probation officer, unless there are exceptional reasons not to do so.

If a person is recalled from parole, the period they he or she hasve lived in freedom is not credited towards the term of a sentence.
A person recalled from parole who has been reincarcerated becomes eligible for parole only after serving at least one year of the penalty of imprisonment. Persons sentenced to twenty-five years in prison or to life imprisonment and recalled from parole may reapply for parole after serving at least five years in prison.

447. If parole is granted, a sentence is considered to have been completed upon the granting of parole, unless a parolee has been recalled during their probation period and within six months thereafter.

§7. Protective Measures

448. Protective measures, as the name implies, are intended to ensure the safety of society and respect for the legal order. They are not a homogeneous group. A catalogue of protective measures is defined in Article 93a CC. These are:

(1) electronic monitoring of a person's place of stay;
(2) therapy;
(3) therapy for addiction; and
(4) placement in a psychiatric facility.

Furthermore, in certain situations described by statute (e.g., Article 99 CC), the obligation to temporarily leave the premises occupied together with the aggrieved person, following obligations and prohibitions may be imposed by way of protective measures as well as the following prohibitions:

(1) the prohibition from engaging in a specified occupation, profession or business;
(2) the prohibition from engaging in a business relating to nurturing, treating or educating minors, or taking care of them;
(3) the prohibition from associating with specific social groups or frequenting specified kinds of places, prohibition from making contact with specified individuals, prohibition from approaching specified individuals, prohibition from leaving a specified place of stay without the court's consent;
(4) the prohibition from entering a mass event;
(5) prohibition from entering gambling facilities and engaging in gambling games;
(6) the obligation to temporarily leave the premises occupied together with the aggrieved person; and
(7) the prohibition from operating vehicles.

449. Protective measures may be imposed on a perpetrator:

(1) if the proceedings concern a prohibited act he or she committed in a state of insanity (see *supra*, paragraphs 231–232);
(2) who has been sentenced for an offence committed in a state of diminished responsibility (see *supra*, paragraph 233);
(3) who has been sentenced for manslaughter, causing grievous bodily harm, forcing sexual intercourse on a vulnerable person, forcing intercourse on a minor by abusing a relationship of subordination, having sexual intercourse with a person under 15 years of age, or in relation to an aberration of sexual preferences;
(4) who has been sentenced to unconditional imprisonment for an intentional offence against life and health, against freedom, against sexual liberty and decency, against the family and care, committed in relation to a personality disorder of such nature or severity that it is at least highly likely that a prohibited act involving the use or threat of violence will be committed;
(5) who has been convicted of an offence committed in relation to the addiction to alcohol, a narcotic drug or any other similar substance.

The court may order a protective measure, if necessary, in order to prevent a perpetrator from repeating a prohibited act, and it may order other legal measures set forth in the Criminal Code or ordered pursuant to other statutes are insufficient.

The court may impose one or more protective measure on the perpetrator.

A protective measure in the form of placement in a psychiatric facility may only be ordered in order to prevent a perpetrator from repeating a prohibited act presenting significant social harm.

450. Pursuant to Article 93b § 3 CC, protective measures and the manner of its execution should be appropriate to the degree of social harm caused by the prohibited act that a perpetrator may commit, and its likelihood; it should also take account of the needs and the progress of any therapy or therapy for addiction (Article 93b § 3 CC).

Unlike in the case of penalties, the term of a protective measure is not defined upfront. While a measure is being applied, the court reviews whether it is necessary to extend it and repeals a protective measure if it is no longer required.

The court may change a protective measure imposed on a perpetrator or the manner in which it is executed if a previously imposed measure has become inadequate or impossible to implement. In the event that a protective measure in the form of commitment to a psychiatric facility is repealed, the court may order one or several non-custodial protective measures.

451. In the case of an insane person who is incapable of forming the relevant fault (guilt) required for criminal liability, a protective measure (or measures) applied is the only penal response to the prohibited act he or she has committed. As for people with diminished responsibility and people with personality disorders or an aberration of sexual preferences, a protective measure may be ordered in addition to a sentence of imprisonment. In the discussed case, the court may also decree a protective measure (except for commitment to a psychiatric facility) during a period until such a perpetrator has completed his sentence.

452. A protective measure may be executed while a person is serving his or her sentence, and thereafter. As a rule, a protective measure is applied after a person has completed his or her sentence or has been released on parole, if a perpetrator had been sentenced to a penalty of unconditional imprisonment, twenty-five years of imprisonment or life imprisonment.

A protective measure can also be reordered after the repealing of a previous one. This option is available if a perpetrator's conduct after the repealing of a protective measure implies the need for the reapplying of a protective measure. In such a case, the court may decree the same or a different protective measure (except for commitment to a psychiatric facility). However, this decision may not be taken later than within three years from the repealing of the original measure.

453. Electronic monitoring of a person's place of stay (electronic tagging) involves continuous monitoring of a perpetrator's movements with the aid of technological devices, including a personal transmitter.

454. The obligation to undergo therapy is linked with the obligation on a perpetrator to appear at a facility designated by the court at dates given by a psychiatrist, sexologist or a therapist, as well as to undergo pharmacotherapy in order to reduce sexual urges, or psychotherapy or psychoeducation in order to improve their functioning in society.

A perpetrator ordered to undergo therapy for addiction is required to appear at a facility designated by the court at dates given by a doctor and to undergo treatment for addiction to alcohol, a narcotic drug or any other similar substance.

455. The court orders a perpetrator who is insane to a psychiatric facility if there is a high likelihood that he will repeat a prohibited act presenting significant social harm in relation to his mental illness or mental impairment.

The order on the commitment to a psychiatric facility is also mandatory in the case of a perpetrator who has committed an offence in a state of diminished responsibility, if he or she has been sentenced to a penalty of unconditional imprisonment for a term of twenty-five years or for a term of life imprisonment and there is a high likelihood that he or she will commit a prohibited act presenting significant social harm in relation to his or her mental illness or mental impairment.

As for the perpetrator referred to in paragraph 456 items 2 and 3, the order on the commitment to a psychiatric facility is mandatory if he or she has been sentenced to a penalty of unconditional imprisonment, for a term of twenty-five years or a term of life imprisonment and there is a high likelihood that he will commit an offence against life, health or sexual liberty in relation to an aberration of sexual preferences.

§8. SENTENCES AND OTHER MEASURES OF PENAL RESPONSE

I. The Principles and Directives of Sentencing in Criminal Cases: General Background

456. The principles and directives of sentencing in criminal cases under Polish law are regulated in the Criminal Code. They are usually quite general guidelines although they are more specific in respect to specific offenders or offences. Unlike in some common law countries, there are no sentencing guidelines binding on the courts in Poland.

The issues concerning sentencing in criminal cases and other measures under criminal law are regulated in Articles 53–63 CC. However, the provisions concerning recidivism and 'professional crime' (Articles 64 and 65 CC) are also important in this context.

457. As a general rule, the court will determine penalty at its discretion within boundaries prescribed by statute. Therefore, an adjudicating court is given some leeway when determining a sentence. However, that freedom is not unlimited. It is within the frames imposed by the statutory regulations. The limits of statutory penalty for a given offence are of paramount importance. The court will also consider other regulations that allow it to modify the limits of the statutory penalty. This modification can lead to the pronouncement of a sentence being abandoned (e.g., when the statute stipulates that a perpetrator is not subject to a penalty under special circumstances), extraordinary mitigation or the aggravation of a penalty.

It is a fundamental rule of sentencing that a penalty must not exceed the degree of a perpetrator's guilt. Therefore, the law does not permit a situation where a perpetrator would be punished only or predominantly for purposes other than individual prevention. For example, it is impermissible to impose a very severe penalty for actions which present minor social harm only to achieve a deterrent effect, etc. By combining the measure of a penalty with the degree of a perpetrator's guilt, the legislator prevents its objectification and the its treatment as a tool for reaching the objectives of penal policy.

Article 55 CC provides for the principle that penalties must be specific to an offender. It reads that circumstances that affect the actual measure of a penalty may be taken into account exclusively in respect of the person concerned. Consequently, if there are multiple participants in an offence, participation in the commission of an offence does not mean that all participants are automatically liable for the consequences of the offence. Each perpetrator is liable only to the extent of his or her own participation in the criminal activity.

458. When imposing a penalty in a given case, the court is required to take into account certain factors, most notably:

(1) the degree of a perpetrator's guilt;
(2) the degree of social harm presented by an act (*supra* paragraph 201);
(3) preventive and educational objectives that a penalty is to achieve in respect of a convicted person (the directive of individual prevention);

(4) the need to raise the legal awareness of society (the directive of general prevention).

Article 53 §§ 2 and 3 CC list more detailed issues that the court must consider whenever determining a sentence. Those are:

(1) the motivation and the behaviour of a perpetrator;
(2) the fact that an offence is committed together with a minor;
(3) the manner and degree in which the obligations imposed on a perpetrator have been violated;
(4) the type and scope of the negative consequences of an offence;
(5) the characteristics and personal circumstances of a perpetrator;
(6) a perpetrator's way of life before committing the offence and his or her behaviour after the offence was committed, and in particular any efforts to remedy damage or otherwise fulfil the sense of justice in the society;
(7) the behaviour of an aggrieved person;
(8) positive results of mediation between an aggrieved person and a perpetrator or a settlement they have reached during proceedings held before a court or a public prosecutor.

459. Article 58 § 1 CC formulates the 'directive of preference for non-custodial penalties'. Pursuant to that article, if statute provides for the ability to select the type of a penalty, and an offence punishable by imprisonment for a term of up to five years, the court decrees a prison term only when another penalty or penal measure cannot serve the purpose thereof.

Apart from general directives applicable to all penalties, the Criminal Code also contains special directives applicable to the imposition of specific penalties or the imposition of penalties on specific types of perpetrators. In this context, it should be pointed out that:

(1) the penalty of restriction of liberty involving the obligation to perform free supervised community service is not imposed if a convicted person's health or his or her characteristics and personal circumstances make it reasonable to assume that he will not fulfil that duty;
(2) while imposing a penalty on a juvenile or young offender, the court aims primarily at educating the perpetrator;
(3) the penalty of life imprisonment must not be imposed on a perpetrator who has not attained 18 years of age while committing an offence.

The principles and directives of sentencing discussed above apply respectively to other measures of penal response, except for the obligation to redress the damage caused by an offence or to compensate for the harm suffered.

II. Extraordinary Aggravation of a Penalty

460. Extraordinary aggravation of a penalty occurs in situations where the legislator law has modified the standard statutory measure of a penalty for a given offence. The modification can involve either raising the minimum or the maximum limits of the statutory penalty for a given offence, or ordering obligatory sentences above the minimum statutory threat of penalty (thus excluding the ability to mitigate the punishment pursuant to the regulations on the extraordinary mitigation of a penalty or refraining from the imposition of a penalty).

The decision on extraordinary aggravation of a penalty is taken if:

(1) an offence is committed by a **repeat offender** (Article 64 CC);
(2) an offence is committed by a perpetrator who has made commission of offences his regular source of income (a '**habitual offender**') or who has committed offences acting in an organised criminal group or an organised criminal association, and also a perpetrator who has committed an offence of terrorist nature;
(3) a **perpetrator has committed continuing offences** (Article 91 CC);
(4) a **perpetrator has committed a misdemeanour involving antisocial behaviour** (Article 57a CC).

When an offence is committed by a repeat offender the court may decide to apply extraordinary aggravation of the penalty. It should be underlined, however, that this applies only to a situation described in Article 64 CC. Consequently, when a perpetrator commits another offence, Article 64 CC will serve as the basis for applying extraordinary aggravation of the penalty. Even if that is not the case, relapse into offence is an aggravating circumstance and is always taken into consideration when determining the sentence.

461. Article 64 §§ 1 and 2 CC set out the conditions that must be fulfilled in order to impose an extraordinarily aggravated penalty. The first case ('simple recidivism') concerns a perpetrator (a '**repeat offender**') who has been sentenced to imprisonment for an intentional offence and who commits an intentional offence similar to the first offence for which he was sentenced previously within the period of five years from serving at least six months of the penalty. Under these circumstances, the extraordinary aggravation of the penalty involves the ability to impose a penalty up to the upper limit of the statutory penalty plus an additional half. Article 64 § 2 CC ('multi-recidivism') deals with a perpetrator, who has been previously sentenced under circumstances described above (a 'habitual offender') and who has in total served at least one year in prison, and who commits another intentional offence against life or health, rape, robbery, theft with burglary or any other offence against property involving the use of or threat of violence again within a period of five years from fully or partially serving the last penalty. In such a case, the court will impose a prison term that exceeds the lowest statutory penalty provided for the offence attributed to the perpetrator (therefore, the court may not mitigate the penalty), up to the upper limit on the statutory penalty plus an additional half. In both cases described above, the increase of the upper limit on the statutory penalty does not apply to a felony, hence the penalty must not exceed fifteen years of imprisonment. As regards misdemeanours, the extraordinarily aggravated penalty must not exceed twenty years of imprisonment, in accordance with Article 38 § 2 CC. Bearing in mind that a felony is graver than a misdemeanour, the legislator has not been too consistent when formulating the rules of aggravating penalty.

462. The court may apply extraordinary aggravation of the penalty of imprisonment in the same manner as in the case of habitual offenders if a perpetrator:

(1) has made commission of offences his regular source of income;
(2) commits offences acting in an organised criminal group or an organised criminal association;
(3) has committed an offence of a terrorist nature.

Pursuant to Article 115 § 20 CC, an offence of a terrorist nature is a prohibited act subject to imprisonment with an upper limit of at least five years which is committed with the purpose of:

(1) seriously terrorising a large number of people;
(2) compelling a public authority of the Republic of Poland, another state or an international organisation to perform or to omit to perform certain actions;
(3) causing a serious disruption of the political system or economy of the Republic of Poland, of another state or an international organisation,

as well as a threat to commit such an act.

463. Committing **continuing offences** is the basis for extraordinary aggravation of a penalty. Continuing offences are defined in Article 91 CC, which reads that continuing offences take place when a perpetrator has committed, at short time intervals, two or more offences in a similar manner before a first sentence, even a non-final one, regarding any of these offences has been issued. Under such circumstances, the court imposes one penalty (even though the perpetrator has committed several offences), pursuant to the provision which is the basis for the penalty for each of these offences, up to the upper limit of the statutory penalty plus an additional half.

464. Committing a **misdemeanour involving antisocial behaviour** is the basis for extraordinary aggravation of a penalty. It is defined in Article 115 § 21 CC, which reads that a misdemeanour of a hooligan nature involves an intentional attack on health, liberty, honour or personal inviolability, public safety, the functioning of the state and local government institutions, public order, or the intentional destruction, damaging or rendering useless someone else's item of property, if a perpetrator acts publicly and for no reason or for a manifestly trifling reason, thus demonstrating a flagrant disregard for the legal order. While sentencing for such a misdemeanour, the court imposes a penalty to the extent of no less than the lowest statutory penalty provided for an offence attributed to the perpetrator increased by an additional half.

465. In the case of the concurrence of several independent grounds for extraordinary aggravation of a penalty, the court may apply extraordinary aggravation of a penalty only once, by collectively taking into consideration the grounds for extraordinary aggravation. In the case of the concurrence of grounds for extraordinary mitigation and aggravation of a penalty, the court may apply either extraordinary mitigation or aggravation of a penalty.

III. Extraordinary Mitigation of a Penalty

466. The application of extraordinary mitigation of a penalty means the imposition of a penalty below the statutory minimum for a given offence or the imposition of a more lenient penalty. Under the Criminal Code, extraordinary mitigation of a penalty may be applied:

(1) in cases provided for in statute (therefore, there must be a special legal basis, such as when determining a penalty for aiding, when exceeding the limits of necessary defence or necessity, when imposing a penalty on a minor);
(2) with respect to a young offender (an offender under 21 at the moment of commission of the offence and under 24 at the moment of sentencing in the first instance court) if justified for educational reasons;
(3) in particularly justified cases when even the lowest penalty stipulated for the offence in question would be incommensurate, and particularly:
    (a) if an aggrieved person and a perpetrator have reconciled, the damage has been repaired, or an aggrieved person and a perpetrator have agreed as to the manner of reparation for the damage;
    (b) taking into consideration the attitude of a perpetrator, especially if he or she has attempted to repair the damage or prevent the damage from occurring;
    (c) if a perpetrator of an unintentional offence or someone close to him or her has suffered a major detriment in connection with the offence committed.
(4) with regard to a perpetrator who has committed an offence in complicity with other persons, if he or she has disclosed information concerning the individuals participating in the offence and the material circumstances of its commission to a law enforcement authority responsible for prosecuting crime (mandatory extraordinary mitigation of a penalty);
(5) with regard to a perpetrator who has, apart from giving explanations in his own case, revealed and presented material circumstances of an offence subject to a penalty exceeding five years in prison to a law enforcement authority that had no prior knowledge of these facts (upon the motion of the prosecutor);
(6) when the court admits the motion for conviction without trial or voluntary assumption of criminal liability, hence a sentence under negotiated procedures (see *infra*, paragraphs 633–635).

467. The application of extraordinary mitigation of a penalty means the imposition of a penalty below the statutory minimum or a more lenient penalty according to the following rules:

(1) if the act is a felony subject to at least twenty-five years in prison, the court will impose imprisonment for at least eight years;
(2) if the act is any other felony, the court will impose imprisonment not lower than one-third of the minimum statutory penalty;
(3) if the act is a misdemeanour and the minimum statutory penalty is a prison term above one year, the court will impose a fine, restriction of liberty or imprisonment;
(4) if the act is a misdemeanour and the minimum statutory penalty is imprisonment for less than one year, the court will impose a fine or restriction of liberty;
(5) if the act carries a fine and a restriction of liberty or those penalties and imprisonment, then extraordinary mitigation of a penalty involves refraining from the imposition of the penalty and ordering a penal measure, compensatory measure or forfeiture.

In the event of the concurrence of the grounds for extraordinary mitigation of a penalty, the rules discussed above apply accordingly.

IV. Refraining from the Imposition of a Penalty

468. The Criminal Code describes special situations where it is possible to refrain from imposing a penalty. If the court decides to do so, a defendant will be sentenced for an offence committed but no penalty will be imposed.

The court may refrain from the imposition of penalty:

(1) in cases provided for in statute (such as exceeding the limits of necessary defence or necessity, if there are special circumstances in favour in a case of euthanasia manslaughter);
(2) with regard to a perpetrator who has committed an offence in complicity with other persons, if he or she has disclosed information concerning the individuals participating in the offence and the material circumstances of its commission to a law enforcement authority responsible for prosecuting offences, especially if his or her role in the commission of the offence was minor, and the information he or she provide helps prevent another offence;
(3) if an offence is punishable with imprisonment for up to three years or a more lenient penalty, and the social harm presented by a prohibited act is negligible and the objectives of the penalty will be fulfilled in that way (however, it is necessary here to impose a penal measure, forfeiture or compensatory measure at the same time);
(4) when the court admits a motion for conviction without trial or voluntary assumption of criminal liability, hence a sentence under consensual procedures, and the misdemeanour imputed to an accused carries a penalty of not more than five years of imprisonment (however, it is necessary here to impose a penal measure, forfeiture or compensatory measure at the same time).

V. Not Being Subject to a Penalty

469. In addition to various possibilities of modifying the statutory measure of a penalty by the court and the ability to refrain from the imposition of penalty, there is also the possibility of not being subject to a penalty. If the Criminal Code reads that a perpetrator is not subject to a penalty, the criminal proceedings against that person are discontinued. Thus, this is not about waiving a penalty after attributing criminal liability for a committed offence (as in the case with refraining from the imposition of a penalty) but rather about withdrawing completely from holding a person liable for a criminal offence due to special circumstances under which the prohibited act was committed.

For example situations where a perpetrator is not subject to a penalty, see *supra* paragraph 200.

VI. Crediting a Period of Application of Coercive Measures Towards a Penalty and Other Measures of Penal Response Imposed

470. The period of actual deprivation of liberty (detention) is credited towards the custodial sentence imposed in a case. The measure on the basis of which a defendant was deprived of liberty is irrelevant. This may be detention, detention on remand, a placement in a youth detention centre, etc. If necessary, a period of imprisonment is rounded up to a full day. One day of actual deprivation of liberty is equal to one day of imprisonment, two days of restriction of liberty (community service) or two daily rates of a fine. When crediting a period of actual deprivation of liberty towards a specific amount of fine, it is assumed that one day of imprisonment is equal to double the amount of the daily rate determined by the court. A day is equivalent to a period of 24 hours counted as of the moment of actual imprisonment.

471. As regards the penal measures imposed on a convicted person, such as obligation to temporarily leave the premises occupied together with the aggrieved person and the prohibitions mentioned above (see *supra* para. 389) the following preventive measures are included:

(1) police supervision combined with obligations corresponding to the obligations arising from penal measures imposed on a person as referred to above in items 3 to 5;
(2) obligation to temporarily leave the premises occupied together with the aggrieved person; and
(3) the suspension of a person's right to perform official duties or practise a trade or profession or the order to refrain from performing a certain activity or operating certain types of vehicles;
(4) obligation to refrain from driving certain types of vehicles;
(5) prohibition from leaving the country.

The period of confiscation of a person's driving licence or any other relevant document is credited towards a penal measure in the form of a prohibition from operating vehicles.

§9. AGGREGATE PENALTY

472. Where a perpetrator has committed two or more offences and the court has imposed penalties of the same type or different penalties subject to aggregation, the court will rule for an 'aggregate penalty'. Such a penalty is imposed if a perpetrator's actions are reviewed during the same proceedings. There is in addition the possibility of combining the penalties decreed in separate judgments of the criminal courts. This is known as an 'aggregate sentence' (*wyrok łączny*) and has been regulated in Articles 568a-577 of the Code of Criminal Procedure (CCP).

An aggregate penalty is imposed in order to make a penalty reasonable in a situation where a perpetrator would need to serve several penalties (including in particular the penalty of imprisonment). Were it not for regulations on the aggregate penalty, the perpetrator would have to spend decades in prison.

473. The procedure for determining an aggregate penalty is rather complex. However, there are several basic principles.

Aggregation applies primarily to penalties of the same type. Hence, it is possible to aggregate fines, penalties of the restriction of liberty or, in the most frequent case, imprisonment.

The penalty of imprisonment and the penalty of the restriction of liberty can also be aggregated. In such a case, the court imposes an aggregate penalty of imprisonment, assuming that one month of restriction of liberty equals fifteen days in prison.

If the penalty of imprisonment for twenty-five years or the penalty of life imprisonment is the strictest of the penalties imposed for concurring offences, this penalty is imposed as the aggregate penalty.

In case of the concurrence of two or more penalties of imprisonment for twenty-five years, the court may impose a penalty of life imprisonment or a penalty of twenty-five years in prison as the aggregate penalty.

When imposing an aggregate penalty, the court will primarily consider the preventive and educational objectives that the penalty is to achieve in respect of the convicted person, as well as the need to raise the legal awareness of society.

474. The court imposes an aggregate penalty amounting to no less than the highest of the penalties imposed for the concurring offences and no more than the total sum of the penalties imposed for the concurring offences, but not exceeding 810 daily rates of a fine, two years of restriction of liberty or 20 years of imprisonment. The penalty of imprisonment is imposed in months and years. However, the court may impose an aggregate penalty of twenty-five years in prison if the total of imposed penalties of imprisonment amounts to twenty-five years or more, and at least one of the penalties subject to aggregation amounts to ten years or more.

When imposing an aggregate penalty of a fine, the court determines the amount of the daily rate once again. However, the amount of the daily rate must not be higher than the highest daily rate determined previously.

When imposing an aggregate penalty of the restriction of liberty, the court will determine once again the obligations or the level of deductions from remuneration; the court may also require a perpetrator to apologise to an aggrieved person, and to carry out the incumbent obligation to provide maintenance for another person, as well as award a pecuniary payment.

475. If a convicted person is sentenced to suspended imprisonment and to unconditional imprisonment, the court may conditionally suspend the enforcement of the imposed aggregate penalty not exceeding one year if a perpetrator has not been sentenced to prison when committing the offence, and if it is sufficient to achieve the objectives of the penalty with regard to the perpetrator, especially to prevent his or her relapse to offence.

When imposing an aggregate penalty of suspended imprisonment, the court may order an additional fine (*supra* paragraph 432), even if such a fine has not been imposed under any penalty subject to aggregation.

In the case of sentencing to penalties of suspended imprisonment, the court may issue an aggregate sentence and impose an aggregate penalty of unconditional imprisonment. In such a case, one month of suspended imprisonment is equal to fifteen days of the penalty of unconditional imprisonment.

476. The regulations concerning the aggregate penalty apply accordingly to more than one penal measure involving the deprivation of public rights imposed by the court and penal measures imposing prohibitions or obligations of the same type (e.g., prohibition from operating vehicles, the obligation to undergo therapy).

Part II. Criminal Procedure

Chapter 1. Principles, Institutions and Stages

§1. THE JUDICIAL ORGANISATION

477. The structure of the judicial system was partially discussed in the General Introduction (see *supra*, paragraphs 28–46). The following provides a more detailed presentation of the criminal justice bodies that have jurisdiction over court proceedings as well as the bodies responsible for the preliminary investigations.

I. Trial Courts

A. *Jurisdiction of Criminal Courts*

478. Criminal cases are decided in the first instance by the common courts *(sądy powszechne),* namely district courts *(sądy rejonowe)* and regional courts (*sądy okręgowe*), and by military courts *(sądy wojskowe)*: military garrison courts *(wojskowe sądy garnizonowe)* and military regional courts *(wojskowe sądy okręgowe).* Criminal cases are heard by a criminal division (or multiple divisions) of a given court. A case involving an offence may also be heard by the Tribunal of State *(Trybunał Stanu).* However, the Tribunal has jurisdiction only over the criminal responsibility of:

(1) the President of the Republic for criminal and fiscal offences (Article 145 paragraph 1 of the Constitution and Article 2 paragraph 1 of the Tribunal of State Act of 26 March 1982[17]);
(2) the Speaker of the Sejm or the Speaker of the Senate, if temporarily performing the duties of the President, for criminal and fiscal offences (Article 2 paragraph 3 read in conjunction with Article 2 paragraph 1 of the Tribunal of State Act of 26 March 1982);
(3) a member of the Council of Ministers for criminal and fiscal offences committed in relation to their post (Article 156 paragraph 1 of the Constitution of Poland and Article 2 paragraph 4 of the Tribunal of State Act of 26 March 1982).

17. J.L. 1982 No. 11, Item 84, as amended.

The overwhelming majority of criminal cases are heard by common courts.

479. As a rule district courts decide cases in the first instance (Article 24 § 1 CCP). There are more than 300 such courts across Poland. Under Article 25 § 1 CCP, regional courts (forty-eight in Poland) hear cases that involve:

(1) certain felonies defined in the Criminal Code (such as manslaughter, trafficking in human beings, gang rape or rape committed with particular atrocity) and in special laws (e.g., trafficking in large quantities of narcotic substances);
(2) a series of explicitly mentioned misdemeanours in the CC (e.g., crimes against peace and humanity or war crimes, crimes against the Republic of Poland, certain crimes against property, money laundering, acting in an organised criminal group or association, causing impairment to health that results in a person's death, participation in a fight that results in a person's death);
(3) other misdemeanours that are within the jurisdiction of regional courts under specific provisions of law (Articles 43–44 of the Press Law Act of 26 January 1984:[18] the use of violence or unlawful threats in order to force a journalist to publish or refrain from publishing a press article or make or refrain from making a journalistic intervention, the hindering or suppressing of press criticism, or abusing a position or function to the detriment of another person due to journalistic criticism published in a socially justified interest).

The classification of cases heard by a regional court is based on the gravity of a given offence and the type of legally protected interest violated by the perpetrator of the offence (such as human life).

480. Military courts decide cases of military personnel in active duty (also foreign military personnel present on the territory of Poland) and civilians employed by the military, provided that the offence they are charged with is linked to their professional status. Exceptionally, military courts also have jurisdiction over cases in which defendants are civilians who conspire to commit offences that violate the legally protected interests of the Polish armed forces.

481. There are two factors that determine which of the courts has territorial jurisdiction to hear a case. First, each court exercises jurisdiction over a certain area. This jurisdiction is defined in the Regulation of the Minister of Justice of 7 October 2014 on the determination of locations and jurisdiction areas of courts of appeal, regional courts and district courts and that of the Minister of National Defence of 9 May 2014 on the determination of locations and jurisdiction areas of military courts.

Second, territorial jurisdiction over an offence is exercised by the court in whose circuit the offence has been committed (Article 31 § 1 CCP). If an offence has been committed on board a Polish naval vessel or aircraft located abroad, jurisdiction is exercised by the court of the vessel or aircraft's home port. If an offence has been

18. J.L. 1984 No. 5, Item 24, as amended.

committed in several judicial circuits, jurisdiction is with the court in whose circuit the preliminary proceedings were first initiated.

482. If it is impossible to determine the place where an offence was committed, jurisdiction is exercised by the court in whose circuit:

(1) the offence has been revealed;
(2) the defendant has been seized;
(3) the defendant had a permanent place of residence or was staying temporarily;

– depending on where the preliminary proceedings have been initiated (Article 32 § 1 CCP).

The above criteria are applied *mutatis mutandis* if an offence has been committed abroad.

483. If it is impossible to determine the territorial jurisdiction of a court pursuant to the above rules, the case will be heard by the District Court for Warszawa-Śródmieście or the Regional Court of Warsaw, depending on the type of the offence imputed to the defendant.

484. If a person is charged with several offences and the cases fall under the jurisdiction of different courts of the same level, the jurisdiction will be exercised by the court in whose circuit preliminary proceedings were first initiated. On the contrary, if cases are within the jurisdictions of courts of different levels, the case will be heard by the higher court (Article 33 CCP).

In the event that more than one person is charged with an offence or some offences closely linked to each other, such persons will be tried in the same proceedings, if such proceedings are pending against them simultaneously (Article 34 §§ 1–2 CCP). A part of a case may be severed to be tried separately if law enforcement authorities or a court signify a need to do so (e.g., if one of the perpetrators has gone into hiding).

485. Exceptionally, a court exercising jurisdiction may transfer a case to another court due to special circumstances designated in the CCP. There are four situations in which this may happen:

(1) at the request of a district court, a Court of Appeal can transfer a case that involves any offence, for reasons of its particular importance or complexity, to a regional court (Article 25 § 2 CCP);
(2) a court superior to a court with the jurisdiction to hear the case (the 'competent court') may transfer a case to another court of the equal rank, if the majority of the persons who need to be summoned to appear during the trial live close to the latter court but away from the competent court (Article 36 CCP);
(3) the Supreme Court may transfer a case for the consideration of another court of the equal rank if this serves the best interests of the justice system (Article 37 CCP);

(4) a court of higher rank will transfer a case to another court of equal rank if, due to the reason of the disqualification of judges, the case cannot be tried in the former.

486. After a case is filed, a court is obliged to examine its jurisdiction ex officio (Article 35 § 1 CCP). The assessment of jurisdiction is a duty of the adjudicating panel appointed to hear a given case. If the panel decides that the case is covered by the jurisdiction of another court or a non-judicial body, it issues a decision in which it determines that it has no jurisdiction and designates a body to whom the case is transferred. Such a decision is subject to a party's appeal (Article 35 § 3 CCP).

The court is obliged to examine its jurisdiction not only after the case is filed, but also in the course of the entire case. If a court of a lower level determines that a court of the higher level is competent to hear a case or if a common court finds that a military court has jurisdiction to hear the case (or vice versa), it is always necessary to adjourn the trial and refer the case to a competent court. However, if a court finds that it does not have territorial jurisdiction or that a lower court is competent to hear the case during a trial, the court may refer the case to another court only if it is necessary to adjourn the trial (for instance, when it is necessary to wait for an expert witness' opinion or in the case of a defendant's illness). Therefore, under these circumstances the court is not obliged to refer the case; it does so only and solely if it is forced to adjourn the case for another reason. This rule clearly shows that the legislator gives priority to the expedience of the proceedings.

B. Composition of the Adjudicating Panel

487. As a rule criminal cases are heard by a one-judge panel in courts (Article 28 § 1 CCP). In cases related to felonies, the court adjudicates in a panel composed of one professional judge and two lay judges (Article 28 § 2 CCP). In cases concerning criminal offences for which statute provides for the penalty of life imprisonment (e.g., manslaughter), the court adjudicates in a panel of two professional judges and three lay judges (Article 28 § 4 CCP).

488. Due to the particular complexity or importance of a case, the Court of First Instance may decide to examine the case in a panel of three professional judges or one professional judge and two lay judges, instead of sitting in a one-judge panel (Article 28 § 3 CCP).

489. If a court decides on a matter other than the criminal responsibility of a defendant, it issues a ruling at a hearing, in a one-judge panel, unless statute provides for otherwise or the President of the court *(prezes sądu)* orders that the case should be heard by a panel of three judges due to the particular complexity or importance of the case (Article 30 § 1 CCP).

490. In order to guarantee judicial impartiality, a judge or judges called on to adjudicate in a case are designated according to the order in which cases are filed, and from the alphabetical list of judges of a given court or a division that has been made known to the parties (Article 351 CCP). Exemptions from this rule are admissible only in cases of a judge's illness, or for another important reason, which must be disclosed in the order setting the trial date. Exceptionally, when an indictment includes a felony charge carrying the penalty of twenty-five years of imprisonment or life imprisonment, the adjudication panel is appointed, by the drawing of lots, on a motion of a public prosecutor or defence lawyer.

II. The Prosecutor

491. As a rule, the prosecutor is responsible for prosecuting before the court as well as investigating offences and supervising investigations conducted by other criminal justice bodies. In fact, the involvement of the prosecutor in investigations can be tremendous since he or she, by law, must participate in crime scene investigations in which a suspicious death has occurred (which means almost all deaths besides those in hospitals), as well as in autopsies, and can also take part in searches and the examination of witnesses and the suspect during preliminary proceedings. Therefore, the Polish prosecutor is at the same time a lawyer who prosecutes cases on a daily basis as well as investigative body that actively participates in investigative procedures.

492. The structure of the Prosecution Service and the duties of prosecutors are regulated in the PSA, which has been amended many times (consolidated text J.L. 2011, No 270, Item 1599 with changes). Important changes to those regulations, adopted in 2010, separated the function of the Prosecutor General (*Prokurator Generalny*) from the Ministry of Justice with the aim of providing more political independence to the Prosecution Service. The organization of the Prosecution Service as well as principles governing works of the prosecutor have been discussed in General Introduction (see *supra*, paragraphs 74–83).

493. As a rule, the prosecutor either conducts preliminary proceedings or supervises them if he decides to delegate the proceedings to another agency. The police and other criminal justice bodies responsible for the conduct of preliminary proceedings execute prosecutorial decisions, orders and instructions, but can also undertake their own if there is a need to do so. In practice most preliminary proceedings are only in theory conducted by the prosecutor and most evidentiary procedures are undertaken by the police and other agencies, with the notable exception of those evidentiary procedures that by law (or by decision of the prosecutor) cannot be delegated to a body other than a prosecutor, e.g. appointing two forensic psychiatrists as expert witnesses to give an opinion on the mental health of the suspect (Article 202 § 1 CCP). Nevertheless, the prosecutor supervises proceedings and takes full responsibility for them (see *infra*, paragraphs 574–579).

494. The prosecutor is also responsible for prosecuting cases before the court. As a rule, the prosecutor prosecutes all cases (Article 45 § 1 CCP) but the law gives competence to prosecute certain groups of cases to other agencies, e.g. the Border Guard (*Straż Graniczna*) and a fiscal inspection office (*urząd kontroli skarbowej*).

The cases in which prosecuting remains in the hands of an agency other than the prosecutor are in practice very rare. The agencies that have power to prosecute cases are discussed in Chapter 3 – Court Proceedings and Remedies (see *infra*, paragraphs 657–658).

495. The prosecutor, when prosecuting a case, becomes a party to the court proceedings. However, unlike other parties, the prosecutor is at the same time the representative of the government and works not in his or her own interest (as other parties do), but in the public interest. Therefore, it is expected that, at least to some extent, the prosecutor will behave impartially and act in favour of a defendant whenever the situation during court proceedings demands it (see *infra*, paragraph 510).

§2. The Stages of the Criminal Proceedings

496. The modern Polish criminal procedure can be characterized as adversarial, and this is particularly the case after the amendment of the CCP that came into force on 1 July 2015. Before that date the system could be described as inquisitorial or, at most, quasi-inquisitorial. During a trial the presiding judge was given a leading role and parties only supplemented his or her actions, usually choosing to be passive. That led to strong criticism of the system, as it seemed the burden of proof was in the hands of the court. Now the role of the judge during a criminal trial has been limited and presentation of evidence is vested in the hands of the parties: the prosecutor and the defendant. The court still has some competencies for calling and examining evidence but according to the new provisions this is considered more as the exception than the rule. Although it is still to be seen how the new regulations will work in practice, since its introduction the new resolution has been strongly opposed, especially by prosecutors and some judges.

497. Criminal procedure can be divided into three stages: (1) the preliminary proceedings, (2) the court proceedings and (3) the execution proceedings.

498. Preliminary proceedings are conducted or supervised by the prosecutor. However, in practice, it is the police who undertake the proceedings and the role of the prosecutor is very often limited to accepting an indictment or decision on dismissal of the case, especially in cases of lesser importance – inquiries (*dochodzenia*). Nevertheless, if the prosecutor wants to, he or she can play a very active role during the preliminary proceedings by ordering the collection of certain evidence and even interrogating witnesses and the suspect. This usually happens in more complicated cases – investigations (*śledztwo*). The prosecutor is also obliged in some cases to undertake certain investigatory actions, such as participating in crime scene investigations or autopsies. In all cases, even if the prosecutor remains unengaged in preliminary proceedings, he retains full responsibility for the timely conduct of proceedings and actions undertaken during that stage. As a result of this, prosecutors are obliged to engage in proceedings even when they could easily be left to the sole authority of the police. In preliminary proceedings there is no investigative judge (as in France and Belgium) or judge for preliminary investigations (as in Germany). The role of the court during this stage of proceedings is limited to deciding on matters prescribed by law, e.g. on pretrial detention (Article 250 § 2 CCP) or participating in actions that cannot be repeated, e.g. interrogation of a dying witness (Article 316 § 3 CCP), as well as – in some cases provided by law – deciding on interlocutory appeals filed against decisions taken by a prosecutor. The decisions on conducting search and seizure, which in some countries are vested in the hands of the judge, are a prosecutorial domain in Poland and are only reviewed by the court if questioned.

499. The prosecutor is bound by the principle of legality, which is understood as an obligation to investigate and prosecute all offences (Article 10 CCP). There is little discretion in decisions that the prosecutor can take at the end of preliminary proceedings. In most cases the prosecutor has the final decision about whether to bring a case to a court or to drop it. Only recently have the police been equipped with the competence to decide on the dismissal of the least complicated cases without prosecutorial approval. Preliminary proceedings may end with the dismissal of the case (subject to a review of an interlocutory appeal filed by the parties) or with a case being brought to court.

500. The most typical way to bring a case to court is an indictment supplemented with a dossier containing all the materials gathered in preliminary proceedings with regard to the criminal responsibility of the accused. The indictment, checked by the court only to determine whether it contains all necessary formal requirements, commences the full trial with the presentation of evidence and the hearing of witnesses in open court. However, the prosecutor also has alternatives to sending the indictment to court, and this might result in only holding a hearing (*posiedzenie*) instead of a trial (*rozprawa*). The hearing is usually shorter, less formal and the evidence is not examined, although it may still end with a full judgment. The prosecutor can decide to send a case for a hearing instead of a trial in cases when the suspect admits to having committed an offence (Article 335 § 1 CCP) or when the suspect does not such an admission but agrees to be sentenced without a trial (Article 335 § 2 CCP). In both of these cases the circumstances of the case and the guilt of the defendant must not raise any doubt. The hearing ends with a judgment sentencing the defendant to the penalties and penal measures that were agreed between the suspect and the prosecutor during the preliminary proceedings.

501. The case can also be decided during a hearing in other situations, e.g. when the prosecutor has filed a motion for the conditional discontinuation of proceedings (*wniosek o warunkowe umorzenie postępowania*) according to Article 336 CCP, or when the prosecutor has filed a motion for discontinuation of proceedings and imposition of protective measures (*wniosek o umorzenie postępowania i zastosowanie środków zabezpieczających*) according to Article 324 CCP. The court, in cases in which preliminary proceedings have been conducted in the form of inquiry, and when it finds a trial unnecessary in view of the material gathered in preliminary proceedings, may issue a penal order (*wyrok nakazowy*) only when it is possible to sentence the accused to a penalty of restriction of liberty or to a fine (Article 500 CCP).

502. The proceedings are conducted as a rule in an open court. The judgment may be based solely on circumstances revealed in the course of the main trial (Article 410 CCP). The trial is held before the court that controls the proceedings and calling for and examining evidence remains in hands of the parties. The parties of the trial are the prosecutor and the defence, however, the aggrieved party may, upon its own decision, become an auxiliary prosecutor (*oskarżyciel posiłkowy uboczny*) and act in the court together with the prosecutor. The trial starts with the presentation of the charges contained in indictment, along with the pleadings of the defendant and, usually, his or her explanations (Article 386 CCP). Afterwards the presentation of evidence by the parties commences. The court is responsible for deciding on the admission of all evidence that the parties are willing to examine. The court currently has limited powers to call and examine evidence *proprio motu* (Article 167 § 1 CCP). There is no strict order of presentation of evidence during a trial, however evidence supporting the charges should, if possible, be introduced before evidence supporting the defence (Article 369 CCP). The same applies to the examination of evidence – the party calling a witness should ask questions first (Article 370 § 2 CCP). There is no established right for the defendant to confront a witness and no right to cross-examine a witness called by the other party. Even though during a trial the proceedings are conducted orally, in some cases the previous testimonies of witnesses and explanations of the defendant received during preliminary proceedings as well as other records of testimonies may be read (see Article 389–394 CCP). The proceedings may also be shortened upon an agreement achieved between the defendant and prosecutor in the court (Article 387 CCP) or upon the consent of the attending parties (Article 388 CCP). The trial concludes with closing arguments of the parties and the judgment delivered together with the sentence to the defendant.

503. All judgments are subject to an appeal, decided both upon the facts and law of the case. After a judgment received from the court of second instance the judgment becomes final (*prawomocny*). The final judgment can be changed solely through extraordinary measures of appeal such as cassation (*kasacja*) and the reopening of proceedings (*wznowienie postępowania*).

§3. The Principles Governing Criminal Proceedings

I. General Issues

504. The CCP does not contain a full and systematic list of principles; criminal procedure is governed by the set of fundamental rules developed through tradition. The principles are either directly expressed in the CCP or inferred from other rules. Some of them can be derived directly from the Constitution: presumption of innocence – Article 42 paragraph 3, right to defence – Article 42 paragraph 2.

505. The most important principles governing Polish criminal proceedings are:

(1) the principle of material truth (*zasada prawdy materialnej*);

(2) the principle of impartiality (*zasada obiektywizmu*);
(3) the presumption of innocence principle (*zasada domniemania niewinności*) and *in dubio pro reo* rule (*reguła rozstrzygania wątpliwości na korzyść*);
(4) the principle of the right to defence (*prawo do obrony*);
(5) the principle of free evaluation of evidence (*zasada swobodnej oceny dowodów*);
(6) the principle of conducting proceedings ex officio (*zasada ścigania z urzędu*);
(7) the principle of legality (*zasada legalizmu*);
(8) the principle of accusatorial proceedings (*zasada skargowości*);
(9) the principle of adversarial and inquisitorial proceedings (*zasada kontradyktoryjności i inkwizycyjności*);
(10) the principle of direct examination of evidence (*zasada bezpośredniości*);
(11) the principle of public proceedings (*zasada jawności*).

II. The Principle of Material Truth

506. The principle of material truth (*zasada prawdy materialnej*) is codified in Article 2 § 2 CCP, which states, that *the findings can be based exclusively on accurately determined facts*. It is contested in doctrine whether this rule should be considered as an overriding principle or is equal to all other principles. It is also widely discussed whether the principle of material truth is rooted in the Constitution of the Republic of Poland.

507. The recent amendments to the CCP are seen as changing the position and meaning of the principle of material truth. For many years, the calling for and examining of evidence during a trial by the court have been seen as a safeguard that allows the court to fulfil the obligations imposed on it by Article 2 § 2 CCP. The fundamental change of Article 167, through which calling and examining evidence is vested in the hands of the parties and allows the court to act *proprio motu* only in 'exceptional cases justified by extraordinary circumstances', is considered to be reshaping the principle of material truth. This is the case following the deletion from Article 366 § 1 CCP of the obligation imposed on the presiding judge to make sure that all significant circumstances of the case, as well as circumstances that facilitated the perpetration of the offence, are clarified. Moreover, the current wording of one of the aims of the criminal proceedings provided in Article 2 § 1 CCP must be taken into consideration. According to Article 2 § 1 paragraph 1 CCP, it is not the 'innocent person', as was stated before the 1 July 2015, but the 'person, whose guilt has not been proven' who cannot be held criminally responsible. That modification was designed to clearly establish that it is an obligation of the prosecutor and not the court to overcome the presumption of innocence. The changes in Article 5 § 2 CCP prescribing the *in dubio pro reo* principle also influence the current understanding of the principle of material truth. According to Article 5 § 2 CCP, *doubts, which have not been resolved in evidentiary proceedings, are resolved exclusively in favour of the accused.* The interpretation of that rule implies that the doubts were not resolved during the trial, most likely because of the lack of action on the part of the prosecutor, and not because they cannot be resolved objectively.

508. Sometimes the existence of procedures allowing the court to decide on the merits of a case more quickly and without a full trial being held (see Articles 335, 338a, 343, 343a and 387 CCP) in a form in which negotiations between the prosecutor and the defendant take place, are considered to infringe the principle of material truth. An example of this kind of situation might be when a defendant's guilty plea almost automatically results in a judgment being issued which remains in compliance with the agreement of the prosecutor and defendant. However, in every case, the court is obliged to verify the circumstances of the case and does not have to accept the agreement. Therefore, the negotiated justice forms of concluding the criminal proceedings, if properly conducted, cannot be considered as running against the principle of material truth.

III. The Principle of Impartiality

509. The principle of impartiality (*zasada obiektywizmu*) states that authorities conducting criminal proceedings are obliged to examine and take into consideration the circumstances both for and against the defendant (Article 4 CCP). This principle does not only bind the court while making the final decision with regard to the defendant's guilt and all other decisions in the course of the trial; it also applies to all other authorities conducting criminal proceedings, including the prosecutor and the police, during preliminary proceedings. It should be interpreted as an obligation on the part of the bodies conducting investigations and inquiries to gather both incriminating and exonerating evidence.

510. In 2015, due to changes in legislation, the principle of impartiality has been reinterpreted by some with regard to the role of the prosecutor during a trial. It has been argued that because of the growing adversarial nature of court proceedings in the Polish criminal process, the prosecutor becomes a party during a trial and is not bound at this stage by the principle of impartiality. From the moment when an indictment is sent to the court, the only task of the prosecutor is to provide evidence against the defendant (see P. Hofmański, in: P. Hofmański, J. Śliwa, *Dwugłos w sprawie nowego kształtu postępowania przygotowawczego*, Prok. I Pr. 2015, Nr 1–2, section 79–80).

IV. The Presumption of Innocence Principle and *in dubio pro reo* Rule

511. The presumption of innocence principle (*zasada domniemania niewinności*) is a codified principle provided in Article 5 § 1 CCP, which states that the defendant is presumed to be innocent until guilt is proven and affirmed by the final judgment of a court. It is also rooted in Article 42 paragraph 3 of the Constitution of the Republic of Poland: *everyone shall be presumed innocent of a charge until his guilt is determined by the final judgment of a court.* The principle is binding on all authorities taking a part in criminal proceedings (the court, the prosecutor, the police, etc.) and during every stage of proceedings, i.e. during preliminary proceedings as well as during court proceedings. It is binding until a final judgment finding the defendant guilty or a final judgment to conditionally discontinue proceedings is issued.

512. The *in dubio pro reo* rule (*reguła rozstrzygania wątpliwości na korzyść*) arises as a consequence of the presumption of innocence. This means that doubts which have not been resolved in evidentiary proceedings are resolved exclusively in favour of the defendant (Article 5 § 2 CCP). The new wording of that rule (see *supra*, paragraph 507), discussed above, releases the court from the obligation to resolve doubts by all means. The court may react only in 'exceptional cases justified by extraordinary circumstances' (see Article 167 § 1 CCP) and it is the obligation of the prosecutor to resolve these doubts. Furthermore, from this interpretation one can derive the distribution of the burden of proof (*ciężar dowodu*) in criminal proceedings. The burden of proof can be defined as the duty to demonstrate the legitimacy of a certain claim in the interest of the entity that has issued that claim. In Polish doctrine of criminal procedure the burden of proof is differentiated from the duty to prove (*obowiązek dowodzenia*), which can be defined as the legally imposed obligation to examine evidence or to demand the examination of evidence by another organ. This duty arises not because of self-interest but because of the interest of some other person. Until recently it may not have seemed that obvious that the burden of proof is on the prosecutor, since the court had the responsibility to actively search for evidence and examine it during a trial (under the previous wording of Article 167 CCP and its interpretation). Currently the court, as a rule, remains unengaged in the presentation of evidence and therefore it seems as it is the sole obligation of the prosecutor to prove the guilt of a defendant. At the same time it is not clear whether or not the burden of proof may be switched to the defendant when he raises certain claim (e.g., circumstances excluding criminal responsibility, such as self-defence). Technically it is still the obligation of the prosecutor to prove or disprove certain facts raised during the trial. But in practice the defence will benefit from putting evidence forward to such claim and therefore such behaviour is often seen in the courtroom.

V. The Principle of the Right to Defence

513. The right to defence is expressly stated in the Article 42 paragraph 2 of the Constitution: *anyone against whom criminal proceedings have been brought shall have the right to defence at all stages of such proceedings. He or she may, in particular, choose defence lawyer or avail himself or herself – in accordance with principles specified by statute – of a defence lawyer appointed by the court.* This principle is also enshrined in Article 6 CCP which provides that *the defendant has the right to defend himself or herself, including the use of defence lawyer. The defendant should be informed of this right.*

514. The right to defence is seen in Polish legal scholarship from two perspectives: **the substantive** and **the formal**. The right to defence seen **from the first perspective** (*prawo do obrony w znaczeniu materialnym*) means the right to undertake all possible actions in connection with pending proceedings, which are designed to completely refute the charges or obtain a decision that reflects the degree of guilt of the offender. Therefore, a defendant can undertake, and this must be underlined, all legal actions to find the best solution for himself in the criminal process. For example, a defendant can request the admission of evidence, have witnesses examined and he or she can also comment on all evidentiary procedures and appeal against decisions issued during the course of proceedings. Moreover, the passive behaviour of a defendant and the full exercise of the right to remain silent can also be seen as a form of defence in its substantive aspect. The right to remain silent and the freedom from being forced to incriminate oneself (*nemo se ipsum accusare tenetur*) are inherent to idea of a fair trial (*rzetelny proces*) being one of the most important guarantees to a defendant. A defendant may make use of these rights without any explanation with regard to the reasons for the use and doing so cannot be seen as a circumstance that aggravates the situation of defendant. The right not to be forced to incriminate oneself, seen as passive behaviour on the part of a defendant during proceedings, is limited in some situations. Article 74 § 1 CCP obliges the defendant to submit to:

(1) An external examination of the body and other tests not infringing his or her bodily integrity, in particular fingerprints and photographs of the defendant may be taken to present the defendant to other persons for the purposes of identification.
(2) Psychological and psychiatric tests and bodily examinations involving medical procedures, with the exception of surgical procedures, provided that they are carried out by authorised healthcare personnel in accordance with medical knowledge and without risk to the health of the defendant and providing also that such examinations are necessary; in particular, if the above conditions are fulfilled, the defendant subjects himself or herself to the collection of blood, hair and bodily secretions, subject to point 3.
(3) Collection by a police official of a buccal mucosa smear, if the collection is absolutely necessary and does not pose a threat to the health of the defendant or other people.

515. **As far as its formal aspect is concerned**, the right to defence (*prawo do obrony w znaczeniu formalnym*) is the right to a defence lawyer. There are two forms of the right to a defence lawyer:

(1) **optional defence** (*obrona fakultatywna*) when a defendant can make his own decision whether to choose a defence lawyer or not;
(2) **mandatory defence** (*obrona obligatoryjna*) when by law a defendant must have a defence lawyer during the proceedings (Article 79 § 1 and 2 and Article 80 CCP); in this case, if a defendant has not chosen a defence lawyer on his or her own, the court is obliged to appoint a defence lawyer for the defendant (ex officio defence);

516. Until 2015, the appointment of an ex officio **defence laywer** (*obrońca z urzędu*) was limited to situations in which the mandatory defence was prescribed by law, as well as when the defendant or suspect could prove that he or she was unable to bear the costs of defence without prejudice to his or her necessary maintenance or that of his or her family. Since 2015, Article 80a CCP gives the defendant, only during the court proceedings, the right to request the appointment of an ex officio defence lawyer regardless of his or her financial situation. However, in case of conviction the defendant will be held financially responsible for the costs of the proceedings, including the costs of the defence lawyer. In the case of acquittal or discontinuation of the proceedings, the costs of the process are covered by the State Treasury (see Article 632 paragraph 2 CCP). The right of the suspect to request the appointment of an ex officio defence lawyer during the preliminary proceedings due to his or her poor financial situation was sustained (Article 78 § 1 CCP). An ex officio defence lawyer is always appointed by the President of the court or other authorised judge or court referendary (*referendarz sądowy*) or, during court proceedings, by the court itself. During the preliminary proceedings, the prosecutor may, if it seems necessary according to Article 79 § 1 and 2 and Article 80 CCP, only apply to the court to appoint the lawyer and cannot exercise this power personally.

517. **The mandatory defence** (*obrona obligatoryjna*) is granted to a defendant in Polish criminal proceedings in following situations (Article 79 § 1 and 2 and Article 80 CCP):

(1) the defendant has not attained 18 years of age;
(2) the defendant is deaf, mute or blind;
(3) there is a justified doubt as to whether the defendant's ability to comprehend the meaning of his or her actions or to control his behaviour was not, at the time of committing the offence, significantly reduced, or non-existent;
(4) there is a justified doubt as to whether the condition of the defendant's mental health allows him or her to participate in the proceedings or to conduct his or her defence in an independent and reasonable manner;
(5) if the court deems it necessary due to circumstances impeding the defence (i.e., they are an elderly person or a person who has problems with communication);
(6) in proceedings before the regional court, if being charged with a felony.

In the case of mandatory defence, it is up to the defendant to choose the defence lawyer on his own but if he does not do so, the ex officio defence lawyer will be granted by the court. Some of the above prerequisites are obvious and objective (a person is either 18 or not). However, in the case of doubts regarding the ability of the defendant to comprehend the meaning of the act that he or she is accused of, or in the case of the mental health of the defendant to being sufficient for them to stand a trial, it is necessary to appoint two forensic psychiatrists as expert witnesses (see *infra*, paragraphs 949). The defence lawyer is appointed immediately when doubts arise in the process and expert witnesses are appointed accordingly. Only upon their opinion stating that the criminal responsibility of the defendant was not diminished and that the defendant is able to stand the trial is it possible (although not obligatory) to discharge the defence lawyer from his or her duties (see Article 79 § 4 CCP).

518. If **the defence is optional** it is up to the defendant to choose his or her **defence lawyer**. As a rule, the defendant appoints the defence lawyer personally. However, if the defendant is detained on remand, the defence lawyer may be appointed by another person. The defendant must be informed about this immediately (Article 83 § 1 CCP) to confirm such appointment. Appointment may be done in writing or by a declaration recorded by the authority conducting the criminal proceedings (Article 83 § 2 CCP), e.g. declaration made during hearing on detention on remand.

VI. The Principle of the Free Evaluation of Evidence

519. The evidence in Polish criminal procedure at all stages should be evaluated freely (*swobodna ocena dowodów*). As stated in Article 7 CCP *the criminal justice bodies conducting the proceedings form their convictions on the basis of evidence examined and evaluated freely with due consideration given to the principles of sound reasoning and life experience*. There are no legal rules that bind the court or any other criminal justice body with regard to the evaluation of evidence. The reliability of the evidence and its probative value must be determined solely by the body in charge of the proceedings at the moment of the evaluation of evidence. Therefore, the legal evaluation of evidence, as a feature of the traditionally inquisitorial systems up until eighteenth century, has long been abandoned.

520. According to the established view of the Supreme Court, expressed in its decision of 3 September 1998, V KKN 104/98 (Prokuratura i Prawo Journal 1999 (Prok. i Pr.), insertion to issue 2, item 6), *the conviction of the court of the credibility of some evidence and the lack of credibility of other evidence remains under the protection of Article 7 CCP if:*

1) *it is preceded by a disclosure of all the circumstances of the case during the trial,*
2) *it constitutes a consideration of all factors both in favour of or against the defendant,*
3) *it is consistent with the indications of knowledge and life experience and, moreover, has been substantiated in a justification of the sentence in an exhaustive and logical manner.*

521. The free evaluation of evidence is nevertheless controlled by the common possibility of appealing a decision or a judgment. Therefore, the court of higher instance (or in the case of prosecutorial decisions the court competent to hear the case or in some cases a superior prosecutor) will have the power to review a decision or a judgment and assess the evaluation of the evidence. In particular, it is clearly visible in the case of the possibility to appeal court judgments. The statement of reasons of judgment should contain an indication of which facts the court deemed proven and which not, on what evidence the court based its reasoning and why the court did not acknowledge evidence to the contrary (Article 424 § 1 paragraph 1 CCP). The same content is not necessary in the case of other decisions, but when the decision is to contain the legal justification (which is a rule) and the criminal justice body issuing that decision provides the reasoning, the body adjudicating the interlocutory appeal also needs to assess whether the evaluation of evidence has been conducted correctly.

VII. The Principle of Conducting Proceedings Ex Officio

522. Another codified principle of criminal proceedings is the principle of conducting proceedings ex officio (*zasada ścigania z urzędu*) (Article 9 § 1 CCP). Criminal justice bodies carry out proceedings and undertake actions ex officio, unless, by virtue of the law, a complaint from a specified person, an institution, or an authority, or permission from an authority is required. Therefore, it is not the will of the aggrieved party to conduct the proceedings but the obligation of an organ to trigger the commencement of the proceedings. However, it must be seen more broadly than as just always obliging the prosecutor and the police to initiate investigation when an offence has been committed. The criminal justice bodies are obliged to act ex officio until the termination of criminal proceedings to determine and bring the offender before the court or to discontinue preliminary proceedings. Additionally, Article 9 § 2 CCP provides that the parties, and also other persons directly interested, may request the conducting of actions that the criminal justice bodies are obliged to undertake ex officio.

523. The ex officio principle is limited by the rule that in some cases criminal prosecution may be initiated and conducted solely upon a complaint (*ściganie na wniosek*). As a result, offences have been divided in two groups: **offences that are prosecuted upon complaint** (*przestępstwa ścigane na wniosek*) and **offences that are prosecuted without complaint** (*przestępstwa bezwnioskowe*). A complaint can be filed by an aggrieved party and criminal justice bodies are prohibited from taking any actions until receiving the complaint. Only those actions that are urgent in order to secure forensic traces or material evidence or actions that aim to clarify whether the complaint will be filed or permission obtained are allowed (Article 17 § 2 CCP). If no complaint has been filed, the proceedings must be immediately terminated (see *infra*, paragraph 589).

524. Polish criminal law also provides for a group of **offences prosecuted by private accusation** (*przestępstwa ścigane z oskarżenia prywatnego*), which are also an exception to the ex officio principle. It is the sole responsibility of the aggrieved party to investigate and prosecute such offences. Criminal proceedings with regard to offences subject to private accusation are regulated in Articles 59–61 and 485–499 CCP and discussed in Chapter 3 (see *infra*, paragraphs 751–761).

VIII. The Principle of Legality

525. The prosecutor does not enjoy very much discretion, as he or she is bound by the **principle of legality** (*zasada legalizmu*), sometimes called the **principle of mandatory prosecution:** the obligation of an organ devoted to the investigation of offences to initiate and conduct preliminary proceedings and the prosecutor to prosecute a case (Article 10 § 1 CCP). This principle is valid only with regard to offences investigated ex officio and not those which are prosecuted upon complaint or by private accusation (see *infra*, paragraphs 751–761).

526. In opposition to the principle of legality there remains the **principle of opportunity** or opportunistic principle (*zasada oportunizmu*), sometimes also called the **principle of prosecutorial discretion**. According to this principle this is a right of the prosecutor or other criminal justice body conducting preliminary proceedings to initiate them and subsequently to prosecute a case. The decision not to commence proceedings or to discontinue them can be based on the premise that it not in the public interest or is without merit for other reasons, including for the reason that the offence is of a minor kind.

527. The principle of legality dominates Polish criminal procedure, subject to some opportunistic exceptions. There is no agreement on all such exceptions, however the following can be considered the most important:

(1) discontinuation of preliminary proceedings due to the absorption of an offence by other proceedings (*umorzenie absorpcyjne*) (Article 11 CCP) (see *infra*, paragraph 652);
(2) discontinuation of preliminary proceedings conducted against a state witness (*świadek koronny*) within fourteen days after a judgment against defendants against whom the crown witness has testified has become final. The status of the state witness is granted in exceptional situations according to the State Witness Act of 25 June 1997 (consolidated text J.L. 2014, Item 1801);
(3) discontinuation of preliminary proceedings against a juvenile offender if the circumstances of the case do not give grounds for its initiation or conduct or when the educational and correctional measures are without merit according to Article 21 § 2 Juvenile Justice Act of the 26 October 1982 (J.L. 2014, Item 382).

It is debatable as to whether the discontinuance of preliminary proceedings in the case of restitution by defendant (*umorzenie restytucyjne*) (Article 59a CC), introduced to the Polish legal order in 2015, can also be considered an exception to the legality principle (see *infra*, paragraph 653).

IX. The Principle of Accusatorial Proceedings

528. The ex officio principle refers in particular to preliminary proceedings that oblige criminal justice bodies to initiate and conduct this stage of proceedings. The view of the parties (the accused and the aggrieved party) on whether the proceedings should be conducted is irrelevant. On the contrary, court proceedings can be commenced only at the demand of the prosecutor (acting as a party to the court proceedings and no longer as an authority) or from another authorised entity. This is known as the principle of accusatorial proceedings (*zasada skargowości*) (Article 14 § 1 CCP).

529. The accusation (*skarga*) usually filed by the prosecutor (see below on other entities capable of initiating the court proceedings) has the primary objective of commencing proceedings. Moreover, it also obliges a court to conduct proceedings since there is no judicial review of an indictment or other forms of accusation. If the prosecutor decides to file an accusation a court must accept it, if all required formal elements are present, and decide on its merits. On the contrary, without the accusation of the prosecutor it is forbidden to commence and conduct court proceedings. Lastly, an accusation contains all necessary information on the defendant and offences that he or she is charged with and gives a court and other parties a chance to get acquainted with the view of the prosecutor on the facts of the case and the applicable law in each case.

530. Most typically an accusation is understood as motion to initiate court proceedings after the conclusion of preliminary proceedings. Such an accusation exists in the form of the prosecutor's indictment (Article 332 CCP), a motion for conditional discontinuation of proceedings (Article 336 CCP), a motion for the discontinuation of proceedings and imposition of protective measures (Article 324 CCP) or an independent motion to sentence a defendant without holding a trial (Article 335 § 1 CCP). However, there are also other forms of accusation that can trigger the subsequent stage of the criminal process, such as an appeal (*apelacja*) against a judgment or an interlocutory appeal (*zażalenie*) against decisions removing the possibility of delivering a judgment, as well as cassation (*kasacja*) and a motion to reopen proceedings (*wniosek o wznowienie postępowania*). An interlocutory appeal against other decisions (e.g., a decision imposing detention on remand) is another form of accusation that commences so-called incidental proceedings (*postępowanie incydentalne, wpadkowe*).

531. In most situations court proceedings are commenced with an accusation filed by the prosecutor (Article 45 § 1 CCP). But in some cases, another public agency may act as a public accuser pursuant to the special provisions of the law defining its powers (Article 45 § 2 CCP). An example of such an agency is the fiscal inspection office (*urząd kontroli skarbowej*) that handles cases regarding offences prescribed in Criminal Fiscal Code (*Kodeks karny skarbowy*). Polish criminal proceedings also recognise, on two occasions, the right of a private person to trigger court proceedings. In the first case, if the prosecutor issues for the second time a decision to refuse initiation of criminal proceedings or a decision on the discontinuation of preliminary proceedings, the aggrieved party can prosecute a case with a so-called **subsidiary accusation** (*skarga subsydiarna*). In the second case, offences prosecuted upon private accusation, e.g. slander or insult, can be prosecuted solely by the aggrieved party sending to the court a **private accusation** (*skarga prywatna*). Only rarely will the prosecutor engage in court proceedings triggered by a subsidiary or a private indictment.

532. Until the 2015 amendment of the Polish CCP, after filing an accusation with a court the prosecutor would lose control over the accusation i.e. the withdrawal of the accusation was not binding on the court and the proceedings could continue. The amendments to Article 14 § 2 CCP changed this situation substancially. The prosecutor may withdraw an indictment until the commencement of court proceedings at the first hearing of the main trial. In the course of the evidentiary phase of a trial before a Court of First Instance the withdrawal of an indictment is only allowed upon the consent of a defendant. Submitting an indictment against the same person for the same offence a second time is not permitted.

X. The Principle of Adversarial and Inquisitorial Proceedings

533. The principles of adversarial and inquisitorial proceedings are uncodified principles and they must be derived from the analysis of other rules in the CCP. Proceedings conducted in accordance with the **principle of adversarial proceedings** are conducted in the form of a dispute between two equal parties, which is resolved by the impartial court. This is a feature of court proceedings in which all participants have certain roles that need to be observed by them: the prosecutor accuses bearing the burden of proof, the defendant defends himself and the court resolves the dispute. In preliminary proceedings the **principle of inquisitorial proceedings** prevails, which means that all functions in the course of proceedings are taken by one body – the prosecutor (or the police working under prosecutorial supervision). The prosecutor decides on the initiation of the investigation, gathers evidence for and against the suspect and finally is responsible for deciding how to end the case: to prosecute the case or discontinue it. The parties (the suspect and the aggrieved party) play only supporting roles.

534. For decades the Polish rules of procedure applicable to the judicial phase of criminal proceedings have been more inquisitorial than adversarial. The court, by law and its interpretation, was responsible for calling and examining evidence during a trial regardless of the behaviour of the parties. Subsequently, the parties became more and more passive as their role was always complimentary to the role of the court and shaped by it. This is not to say that proceedings could not be conducted according to the principle of adversariality. However, because a court was bound by the principle of material truth and was personally responsible for establishing the truth during a trial, by habit the parties stepped aside and waited for the mistakes of the court in order to appeal against them. The amendment of Article 167 CCP changed the situation substantially, introducing a new form of presentation of evidence during a trial. Since 1 July 2015 it is the responsibility of the parties, and in particular of the prosecutor, to submit evidence to a court for its admission and subsequently examine it before the court. The court can call and examine evidence *proprio motu* only in *exceptional cases justified by extraordinary circumstances* (Article 167 § 1 CCP), which limits the activity of the court tremendously (see *infra*, paragraphs 917–918).

535. As was stated above, preliminary proceedings are conducted in accordance with the principle of inquisitorial proceedings. However, some exceptions for the adversarial form of the conduct of proceedings are clearly visible. First of all, Article 299 § 1 CCP states that the aggrieved party and the suspect are parties to this stage of proceedings. Both parties have certain rights that allow them to actively participate in preliminary proceedings, thus making them less inquisitorial. For example, they have the right to file evidentiary motions requesting the conduct of certain evidentiary procedures (Article 315 § 1 CCP). They can also participate in the conduct of evidentiary procedures upon their request (Article 316–318 CCP). Moreover, they have the right to get acquainted with the dossier of the case during the disclosure at the conclusion of preliminary proceedings (Article 321 CCP) and even earlier, in order to obtain access to the materials gathered at this stage of proceedings (Article 156 § 5 CCP). This all gives an opportunity to the parties to relax the inquisitorial way of conducting preliminary proceedings.

XI. The Principle of Direct Examination of Evidence

536. The principle of direct examination of evidence (*zasada bezpośredniości*) is not expressly stated in the Code of Criminal Procedure and is inferred from certain rules referring to the presentation of evidence. It refers mostly to the court since the presentation of evidence is conducted in a direct form during court proceedings. However, it cannot be limited to this stage only and is also binding on the criminal justice bodies conducting preliminary proceedings.

537. One of the rules that help form the conviction that evidence should be examined directly at all stages of criminal process is Article 92 CCP, which states that all rulings made in a criminal case must be based on the entirety of circumstances revealed in the course of proceedings and relevant to the case. Moreover, every judgment must be based only on the entirety of circumstances revealed in the course of a trial (Article 410 CCP).

538. However, it seems that even though the principle is clearly understood, there are many exceptions to it and therefore in practice the exceptions are becoming a rule. Courts make frequent use of the possibility:

- to conduct evidentiary proceedings only in part, upon the consent of the parties and if the explanation of the defendant pleading guilty does not raise doubts (Article 388 CCP);
- to issue a judgment without presentation of evidence during a trial in the case of negotiated forms of resolving a dispute between parties (Article 335 § 1, 335 § 2, 338a, 387 CCP);

- of reading records of witness testimonies or explanations of the accused received during preliminary proceedings in certain situations, e.g. when they refuse to testify, testify differently than in earlier statements or declare that they cannot recall certain facts (Articles 389 and 391 CCP);
- of examining evidence by an assigned member of the trial chamber (*sędzia wyznaczony*) or by another trial chamber, known as the 'requested court' (*sąd wezwany*), which can happen when the conduct of certain evidentiary procedures by the trial chamber of the court competent to hear the case causes serious difficulties or when a witness fails to appear in court due to insurmountable obstacles (Article 396 CCP);
- to issue a judgment in the form of a penal order (Article 500 CCP).

XII. The Principle of Transparency of Proceedings

539. The principle of transparency of proceedings (*zasada jawności*) is not codified, but it can be derived from the Constitution of the Republic of Poland, which expressly states in Article 45 paragraph 1, that *everyone shall have the right to a fair and* ***public*** *hearing of his or her case, without undue delay, before a competent, impartial and independent court.*

540. This principle is observed distinctly during preliminary proceedings and during court proceedings. In general, preliminary proceedings are conducted in secret, although there are some exceptions, while court proceedings, especially when held in the form of a trial (this might be different in the case of individual hearings), are, as a rule, public. The transparency of the proceedings can also be understood as the transparency towards the participants to the proceedings (**internal transparency** (*jawność wewnętrzna*)) or as the transparency towards the public and media (**external transparency** (*jawność zewnętrzna*)).

541. **External transparency** is probably the most commonly identified with the principle of public proceedings, even though there is much more to this principle. During preliminary proceedings external transparency is almost totally excluded. Neither the public nor media can obtain access to the materials and actions undertaken by the police and prosecutor at this stage of criminal proceedings. Only in exceptional situations, upon the agreement of the prosecutor conducting or supervising the proceedings, can the materials of the preliminary proceedings be revealed to people other than the participants in the case (Article 156 § 5 CCP). It is also impossible to take part in evidentiary procedures, e.g. the search or interrogation of a witness at this stage of proceedings except for the participants in the case. At the same time, trials (this is not the same for hearings) are open to public and anyone, including the media, can access the proceedings at this stage and observe what happens in the courtroom (Article 355 CCP). Nevertheless, the same rule provides that limitations on transparency can be provided by law. Among the long list of limitations (see Articles 356–363 CCP) one can find the interest of the participant to the proceedings (e.g., the victim of a rape not willing to testify in an open courtroom) or the need to protect the confidentiality of certain information. The file of court proceedings is, without any prerequisites, available to persons other than participants in proceedings only upon the permission of the President of the court (Article 156 § 1 CCP).

542. **Internal transparency**, i.e. access to proceedings by the participants in the case, can be observed during both stages of the criminal process, although it is again much more limited in the case of investigations and inquiries. If there is no need to ensure the correct course of proceedings or to protect important state interest, in the course of preliminary proceedings, parties, defence lawyers and legal counsels are allowed to review case files, make certified copies or photocopies and may obtain certified copies or photocopies of case files (Article 156 § 5 CCP). A meaningful form of obtaining access to the file of materials collected during preliminary proceedings is the disclosure procedure available both to the suspect and the aggrieved party, as well as their defence lawyer and legal counsels at the conclusion of preliminary proceedings, according to Article 321 CCP (see *infra*, paragraphs 621–625) During court proceedings, access to case materials is almost unlimited for the participants in the proceedings (Article 156 § 1 CCP). They do not need to provide any justification, can review the court files upon their request and they are immediately granted that right.

§4. The Legal Position of the Accused (Suspect)

I. The Notion of the Suspect and Accused

543. The CCP provides precise definitions regarding some participants in criminal proceedings. The terms used in Poland may be somewhat problematic and demand further explanation. Article 71 § 1 CCP provides that as a suspect (*podejrzany*) can be defined a person, with regard to whom a decision presenting charges has been issued, or who, without the issuance of such a decision, has been informed about charges in connection with the initiation of the person's interrogation in the capacity of suspect. In the following paragraph the code provides that an **accused** (*oskarżony*) is a person against whom an indictment has been submitted to a court, and also a person with regard to whom a prosecutor has filed a request for a conditional discontinuation of proceedings. Therefore, the suspect is a figure in preliminary proceedings who becomes an accused when a case is moved to a court (usually to be prosecuted, but also when the court decides to resolve a case in a consensual manner).

544. We can observe a formalistic approach to defining the status of the suspect, which means that unless the criminal justice bodies officially decide that a person should be charged with have committed an offence and unless they formally issue such a decision, that person cannot be called the suspect (see *infra*, paragraph 609). What is particularly important here is that from the moment a person becomes a suspect, the whole package of rights, including the right to remain silent and the right to defence lawyer, are granted and subsequently remain with the defendant. Therefore, the protection of a person that is being charged is triggered at the moment the decision on charges is formally issued.

545. Usually, before a person becomes a formal suspect, he or she can be treated in preliminary proceedings as a **suspected person** (*osoba podejrzana*). This figure can be identified as someone on whom the attention of criminal justice bodies is focused, but who has not yet been officially charged with an offence. In other words, this person is just suspected of having committed an offence but there is not enough evidence to substantiate a decision to charge him or her. The suspected person has no rights similar to those granted to the suspect. However, criminal justice bodies are allowed to conduct some activities against suspected persons, e.g. wiretapping can be used (Article 237 § 4 CCP) and a suspected person can be arrested under certain circumstances (Article 244 § 1 and 247 § 1 CCP). Because a suspected person does not enjoy the status of the suspect in criminal proceedings, he is not covered by the same package of rights. This is not to say that a suspected person is not protected at all before charges are laid out. However, the protection is limited solely to situations where the suspected person is being arrested. In such a case, the CCP grants some protection (see Articles 244–246 CCP) but it is definitely not as complex as the protection that the suspect is provided with.

546. Only a natural person can become a suspect (an accused). Polish law provides for corporate criminal liability but these situations are very rare, both in theory and practice, and are regulated by the Act of 28 October 2002 on the Corporate Criminal Liability for Acts Punishable under the Law (J.L. 2002, No 197, Item 1661 as amended). For those reasons the issue of corporate criminal liability remains outside of the scope of this monograph.

II. The Rights of the Accused (Suspect)

547. The accused, and the suspect accordingly, are protected by a wide range of rights. The catalogue of such rights is not provided clearly. Some rights of the accused arise from the Constitution and are supported by the CCP. Some of them are just the creation of the provisions of the CCP. Nevertheless, there is no one spot where all the rights are presented in a full and coherent manner. Even the provisions on the rights that must be presented to the suspect at the time of charging him or her with an offence (Article 300 § 1 CCP) do not serve this purpose fully.

It must be noted that most of the rights provided in the ECHR are observed in criminal proceedings in Poland.

548. One of the most important rights of the accused is **the right to defence**. It is seen twofold, as a **right to use all possible means to defend himself**, i.e. initiating evidentiary procedures and participating in the conduct of such procedures, questioning witnesses and contesting decisions issued against the accused in a form of interlocutory or ordinary appeal, as well as the **right to retain a defence lawyer**.

An inherent element of the first aspect of the right to defence is the **right to remain silent** and **freedom from being forced to incriminate oneself.**

549. The next right available to the accused is the right to information at all of its stages. It is especially crucial to inform the suspect on his or her rights in the course of preliminary proceedings, where he or she is not yet assisted by a defence lawyer. Therefore, Article 300 § 1 CCP provides binding guidelines regarding what the suspect should be informed about. These rights have to be provided for the suspect prior to the first interrogation in preliminary proceedings, in a written document the receipt of which he confirms with a signature.

Therefore, the suspect in preliminary proceedings and the accused during court proceedings accordingly, has the right:

- to give statements and to decline to give statements;
- to decline to answer questions (asked by e.g., interviewing police officers, a prosecutor or a judge during a hearing);
- to information on the content of charges and changes made to them;
- to submit requests for evidentiary procedures to be undertaken during preliminary proceedings;
- to be assisted by the defence lawyer, including the information on the possibility of applying for the granting of defence lawyer ex officio if the suspect can duly prove that he is unable to bear the costs of defence without prejudice to the necessary maintenance of the suspector his or her family (this rule does not apply in court proceedings since, according to Article 80a CCP, every accused at that stage of criminal process will be granted with defence lawyer ex officio upon his or her request);
- to be acquainted with the dossier upon the conclusion of preliminary proceedings;
- to initiate and take part in mediation (Article 23a § 1 CCP);
- to be assisted by an interpreter (Article 72 § 1 CCP),;
- to be interrogated in the presence of their appointed defence lawyer (Article 301 CCP);
- to initiate or agree to the conduct of court proceedings against the defendant without holding a full trial (Articles 335, 338a, 387 CCP).

The suspect must also be informed of his obligations arising from the CCP. These are obligations regarding the passive behaviour of the suspect (accused) during the proceedings, (Article 74 CCP), regarding the presence of the suspect (accused) during the course of proceedings and the consequences of not informing the relevant criminal justice bodies of a change of residence (Articles 75, 133 § 2, 138 and 139 CCP).

The suspect must also be informed of the possibility of the aggrieved party filing a motion to discontinue the proceedings in the case of restitution provided by the suspect (accused) (Article 59a CC) (see *infra*, paragraph 653).

550. The accused (suspect) also has **the right to an interpreter** (*prawo do skorzystania z pomocy tłumacza*). The proper execution of the right to defence relies heavily on the understanding of the charges and the rights and obligations, but also with regard to the whole course of criminal proceedings in which the accused takes part. If one does not understand these because of a language barrier, the right to defence becomes tremendously limited.

Therefore, the law provides that the accused who does not have a sufficient command of Polish is entitled to the assistance of an interpreter (Article 72 § 1 CCP). Such assistance is provided free of charge to the accused.

An interpreter should be summoned to assist in all procedures involving the participation of the defendant. At the request of the accused or his or her defence lawyer, the interpreter should also be summoned when the accused needs to communicate with his lawyer in connection with a procedure in which the accused is entitled to participate (Article 72 § 2 CCP).

Moreover, a decision to charge a suspect with an offence, a decision supplementing or changing the charges, an indictment and also every decision and judgment that can be contested in the form of appeal or interlocutory appeal or that concludes the proceedings (e.g., a judgment or a decision on discontinuation of proceedings) must be served upon the suspect (accused) together with a translation (Article 72 § 3 CCP). If the suspect (accused) so agrees and if the appeal or interlocutory appeal against a decision or the judgment that concludes the proceedings is not admissible, it is sufficient to announce the translated judgment or decision orally.

551. Another important right of the accused is **the right to communicate with the defence lawyer in private**. The accused who is detained on remand may communicate with his lawyer without the presence of other persons, and may also do so by correspondence (Article 73 § 1 CCP).

However, this right is not absolute and can be limited in the course of preliminary proceedings. At that stage of the criminal process, the prosecutor, allowing for communication between the suspect, who is detained on remand, and his or her defence lawyer, may impose the restriction that either the prosecutor or another person authorised by him, will be present at the time of the communication (Article 73 § 2 CCP). These restrictions may be imposed only in particularly justified cases (*szczególnie uzasadnione wypadki*) and not last longer or be imposed later than within fourteen days from the date when the suspect was detained on remand (Article 73 § 2 and 3 CCP).

III. The Defence Lawyer

552. The defence lawyer (*obrońca*) represents the accused (suspect) in the course of criminal proceedings. Only the suspect and the accused, accordingly, may be represented by the defence lawyer. All other participants in criminal proceedings are represented by a legal counsel (*pełnomocnik*).

Only an attorney (*adwokat*) or legal advisor (*radca prawny*) can become a defence lawyer (Article 82 CCP). One defence lawyer may defend more than one accused (suspect), if their interests do not conflict (Article 85 § 1 CCP). Also, an accused (suspect) cannot have more than three defence lawyers at one time (Article 77 CCP).

553. According to Article 86 § 1 CCP a defence lawyer may undertake actions exclusively in favour of the accused (suspect). At the same time, the participation of the defence lawyer in the proceedings does not preclude the personal participation of the accused (suspect) - Article 86 § 2 CCP. Therefore, commonly in the course of a trial both the defence lawyer and the defendant request that certain evidentiary procedures are conducted, ask questions to witnesses under examination and give statements on different occasions.

554. A defence lawyer appointed by the accused (suspect) or established ex officio is authorised to act in the entire proceedings, including in the course of procedures undertaken after the judgment has become final, if no limitations have been introduced (Article 84 § 1 CCP).

A defence lawyer established ex officio is obliged to undertake all actions until the proceedings are concluded with a final decision or judgment concluding the criminal proceedings. However, if the proceedings are to be undertaken outside the defence lawyer's place of business or residence, the President of the court where the proceedings are to be undertaken, and in preliminary proceedings the President of the court of the location of the proceedings, may, at the justified request of the defence lawyer, entrust some of these tasks to a local attorney or legal advisor (Article 84 § 2 CCP).

In cassation proceedings or in proceedings for the reopening of previously conducted proceedings, a defence lawyer established ex officio should draft and sign the complaint in cassation or the motion for reopening the proceedings or inform the court that in his opinion there are no grounds to file any of these submissions (Article 84 § 3 CCP).

555. The provisions regarding optional and mandatory defence as well as the possibility of establishing a defence lawyer ex officio or as appointed by the accused have been presented in Chapter 1 (see *supra*, paragraph 513–518).

§5. The Legal Position of the Aggrieved Party

I. General Issues

556. In Polish criminal proceedings the position of the **aggrieved party** (*pokrzywdzony*) is very strong. It is even mentioned within the aims of the Polish criminal process that the code ensures that in the course of criminal proceedings the legally protected interests of the aggrieved party are taken into consideration (Article 2 § 1 item 3 CCP). Moreover, the aggrieved party – typically for the continental model of criminal procedure – can take an active part in the course of the criminal process.

557. The broad and complicated **definition of the aggrieved party** is provided in Article 49 CCP. In general, it is a natural or a legal person, whose legal interest (*dobro prawne*) has been infringed or threatened by an offence (Article 49 § 1 CCP).

Furthermore, an entity without legal personality such as a state or a self-governmental institution or another organisational entity that has legal capacity by virtue of separate provisions (Article 49 § 2 CCP) may also act in the capacity of an aggrieved party.

An insurance company can also be considered an aggrieved party to the extent that it compensates or is obliged to compensate any damage caused by an offence to the aggrieved party (Article 49 § 3 CCP).

In cases concerning certain offences against employees, bodies of the National Labour Inspectorate (*Państwowa Inspekcja Pracy*) may exercise the rights of an aggrieved party if, within the scope of their activity, they have revealed the offence or requested that proceedings be initiated (Article 49 § 3a CCP).

And finally, in the case of offences, as a result of which an institution or an organisational entity referred to in Article 49 § 2 CCP has suffered damage to property and the bodies of the aggrieved party institution of the organisational entity are not acting on their behalf, the authorities of state control may exercise the rights of an aggrieved party, if within the scope of their activity they have revealed the offence or requested that proceedings be initiated (Article 49 § 4 CCP).

558. It is the choice of the aggrieved party to actively participate during the course of the criminal process. However, by law the aggrieved party is the party in the preliminary proceedings (Article 299 § 1 CCP). The notion of the 'party in the criminal proceedings' has been discussed in Chapter 2 – Preliminary Proceedings (see *infra*, paragraph 587). However, to become a party to the criminal process at the stage of court proceedings the aggrieved party must express an intent to do so. To become the so-called auxiliary prosecutor (*oskarżyciel posiłkowy uboczny*) the aggrieved party must file a statement with the court that he or she wishes to exercise the right to actively participate in the court proceedings. The procedure to become the auxiliary prosecutor as well as the rights of such entity have been discussed in Chapter 3 – Court Proceedings and Remedies (see *infra*, paragraphs 659–660).

559. The aggrieved party in the case of ***offences prosecuted upon private accusation*** (*przestępstwa ścigane z oskarżenia prywatnego*) may also file a private indictment with a court. An example of such an offence is causing a minor bodily injury or a minor health impairment (Article 157 § 2 and 3 CC). The prosecutor would usually not become involved with the investigation and prosecution of these offences, since they do not threaten the public interest. Proceedings in cases brought by private accusation are discussed in Chapter 3 – Court Proceedings and Remedies (see *infra*, paragraphs 751–761).

560. In the case of an aggrieved party that is not a natural person, actions in proceedings are carried out by the body authorised to act on its behalf (Article 51 § 1 CCP). If the aggrieved party is a minor or is fully or partially incapacitated his or her rights are exercised by his or her statutory representative or by a person under whose permanent care the aggrieved party remains (Article 51 § 2 CCP). If the aggrieved party is not legally competent, particularly due to age or health, his or her rights may be exercised by the person under whose permanent care the aggrieved party remains (Article 51 § 3 CCP).

561. In the case of the aggrieved party's death, the rights that would have been vested in him may be executed by his next of kin, and if there are no such persons or they are unknown, by the prosecutor acting ex officio (Article 52 § 1 CCP). If the authority conducting the proceedings has information concerning the aggrieved party's next of kin, it should instruct at least one of them of their rights (Article 52 § 1 CCP).

II. The Legal Counsel of the Aggrieved Party

562. The aggrieved party may appear in person during the course of criminal proceedings. But the aggrieved party also has the right to appoint a legal counsel (Article 87 § 1 CCP). Only an attorney (*adwokat*) or a legal advisor (*radca prawny*) may act as a legal counsel in a criminal case (Article 88 CCP).

563. Appointing a legal counsel is the right of the aggrieved party but an aggrieved party who does not have a legal counsel of his or her own choice may request the appointment of a legal counsel ex officio, if he or she can prove that he or she is unable to bear the costs of legal representation without prejudice to the necessary maintenance of himself or herself or his or her family (Article 78 § 1 CCP, read in connection with Article 88 CCP). This rule applies to preliminary proceedings. During court proceedings the aggrieved party is granted with a legal counsel ex officio upon the aggrieved party's request even without proving the lack of ability to cover the costs of legal representation (Article 87a § 1 CCP). This applies only to an aggrieved party that has decided to stay active during the court proceedings, i.e. by exercising the role of auxiliary prosecutor. The latter provision has been introduced to the CCP with recent amendments to the code enforced on the 1 July 2015 and makes equal the rights of the accused (suspect) and aggrieved party with regard to legal representation during the course of court proceedings.

564. An aggrieved party may not have more than three legal counsels at the same time (Article 77 CCP, read in connection with Article 88 CCP). And in general the same rules that apply to defence lawyers apply also to these legal counsels (Article 88 CCP). However, in the case of matters not provided for in the CCP, the provisions governing the appointment of legal counsel in civil proceedings apply accordingly to legal counsels retained in criminal proceedings (Article 89 CCP).

Chapter 2. Preliminary Proceedings

§1. General Remarks

I. The Notion and Objectives of Preliminary Proceedings

565. Preliminary proceedings are the first stage of criminal proceedings in Poland. The literal translation of the name of this stage into English is 'preparatory proceedings' (*postępowanie przygotowawcze*), which describes the purpose that stage serves in the criminal process. Its aim is the preliminary preparation of the case, which leads to the determination of whether the case should be prosecuted or concluded in some other form. What is particularly important here is that, during preliminary proceedings, evidence is gathered in a very formal way to be later introduced during the trial. It is even fair to say, and accepted in Polish doctrine, that information gathered during preliminary proceedings is considered as evidence, and that this is viewed as equal with evidence that is admitted at trial.

566. Article 297 § 1 CCP provides an exhaustive list of the **objectives of preliminary proceedings**, which correspond with the main objectives of criminal proceedings in Poland (see Article 2 § 1 CCP). These are:

(1) establishing whether a prohibited act was committed and whether it constitutes an offence;
(2) revealing and, if necessary, apprehending the perpetrator;
(3) collecting information pursuant to Articles 213 and 214 (data concerning the personal information and lifestyle of accused);
(4) clarifying the circumstances of the case, including the identity of aggrieved parties and the extent of damage;
(5) collecting, securing and preserving evidence within a scope necessary to verify the grounds for the submission of an indictment or the of concluding proceedings in another way, as well as to file evidentiary motions to admit evidence and to examine evidence during the trial.

567. The main principles that govern the preliminary proceedings are the principle of conducting proceedings ex officio (see *supra*, paragraphs 522–524), the principle of legality (see *supra*, paragraphs 525–527) and the principle of inquisitorial proceedings (see *supra*, paragraphs 533–535).

II. Forms of Preliminary Proceedings

568. Preliminary proceedings can be conducted in two forms: **investigation** (*śledztwo*) or **inquiry** (*dochodzenie*). The main points of difference between them are:

– the type of offences that are a subject of these proceedings;

- the level of involvement of the prosecutor in the conduct of preliminary proceedings;
- the level of formality of investigative actions.

Investigation is usually conducted in more complicated cases. This includes all felonies (offences punishable by imprisonment for at least three years) and some misdemeanours, e.g. those in which a suspect is judge or prosecutor (see Article 309 CCP). The remaining cases are dealt with in the form of an inquiry. The prosecutor is always deeply involved in the conduct of investigations, while the police or another investigative body conducts the inquiry, which in such cases is supervised by the prosecutor. This distinction is in some ways rather superficial, since the prosecutor in most investigations can easily delegate his powers to the police or another investigative body and in practice supervises rather than conducts preliminary proceedings in both forms (see *infra*, paragraphs 577–579). An inquiry, however, demands a lower level of formality in the conduct of proceedings, which means that some of the decisions taken (e.g. the decision to commence an inquiry or the decision to charge the suspect with an offence) do not have to be prepared in a separate document and can be a part of another document (in this case – a record of the interview with the suspect) or even waived (in a decision to close an inquiry).

569. Investigation is treated in the CCP as a basic form of preliminary proceedings. However, it is certainly the case that **more often preliminary proceedings are conducted in the form of an inquiry** (in 2014 81.5% of cases out of 682,113 preliminary proceedings were conducted in this way). Nevertheless, this traditional distinction is fading and suggestions that it should be abolished are being raised.

III. Participants Involved in Preliminary Proceedings

A. *General Issues*

570. The CCP clearly regulates that only some natural persons or legal entities with certain status given by law can play certain roles in criminal proceedings. Generally, all involved in criminal proceedings have the status of **participant in the proceedings** (*uczestnik postępowania*), however only some can be called **a party to the proceedings** (*strona postępowania*) or a **criminal justice body** (*organ procesowy).* The criminal justice bodies are state organs that exercise powerful authority to order and demand whatever is necessary in the course of criminal proceedings.

571. The status of a **party to the proceedings** gives the participant certain powers during the proceedings. For example, only a party can demand to be heard or to participate in evidentiary or other procedures as well as appeal against decisions made by a criminal justice body. The law provides that besides parties and criminal justice bodies there are other participants in criminal proceedings, who can include counsel of the parties: defence lawyer for the accused and suspect (*obrońca*) or legal counsel for other participants in the proceedings (*pełnomocnik*), those who testify in the courtroom (witness, expert witness, as well as accused) and participants that assist judicial authorities in the proper conduct of proceedings (e.g., interpreter, forensic science specialist). The other participants do not have the same powers as the parties.

572. The role played by each participant varies depending on the stage of proceedings. For example, during preliminary proceedings the prosecutor performs the role of judicial body, while during a trial he or she becomes a party. A victim, who is a party during preliminary proceedings, can become a party during the trial stage only when certain requirements are met.

573. **In preliminary proceedings** we can recognise the following **criminal justice bodies**:

(1) prosecutor;
(2) police and other criminal justice bodies responsible for the conduct of pretrial proceedings;
(3) a court that in some situations plays some role in preliminary proceedings.

Additionally, the following **parties to preliminary proceedings** can be identified as:

(1) the suspect;
(2) the aggrieved person.

B. *Criminal Justice Authorities Involved in the Conduct of Preliminary Proceedings*

1. The Prosecutor

574. The **criminal justice body responsible for the conduct of an investigation is the prosecutor** (Article 311 § 1 CCP). However, at the same time the prosecutor can **delegate the competence to conduct proceedings** to the police (or other criminal justice authority competent to conduct the investigation). This is so due to the belief that it would be impossible for the prosecutor to conduct all investigations in person.

The delegation of the conduct of an investigation can take three different forms (Article 311 § 2 CCP):

(1) delegation of the investigation as a whole – the police will be able to undertake all investigative procedures independently, besides those that are by law reserved for the prosecutor or those that the prosecutor retains within the scope of his or her powers;
(2) partial delegation of an investigation – the police will be able to conduct one line of investigation while the others will be conducted by the prosecutor;

(3) delegation of certain investigative procedures – the police will be able to conduct only some investigative procedures (e.g., question a witness, conduct a search) while the conduct of the investigation as such remains in the hands of the prosecutor; the delegation in this form is allowed exclusively in cases in which investigation is conducted against certain suspected persons (e.g., against the prosecutor or a judge).

575. The police are bound by the scope of delegation only to a certain extent. If in the course of investigative procedures additional necessary procedures not enlisted by the prosecutor arise, the conduct of these procedures is even obligatory for the police (Article 311 § 4 CCP). The prosecutor, however, may retain some investigative procedures, e.g. the examination of certain witness or the suspect even if the investigation has been delegated to the police in total (Article 311 § 6 CCP). There are also some investigative procedures reserved solely for the prosecutor, e.g. issuing a decision on the initiation of an investigation (Article 305 § 3 CCP), appointing two forensic psychiatrists as expert witnesses – in order to give an opinion on the mental health of the suspect (Article 202 § 1 CCP) or demanding from the court the detention of the suspect on remand (Article 250 § 2 CCP).

576. In contrast to an investigation, **an inquiry, as a rule, is conducted by the police** or other specialised agencies (Article 325a § 1 CCP). However, similar to an investigation, the prosecutor can decide to take over some investigative procedures. There are also some investigative procedures that are reserved for the prosecutor similar to in the case of an investigation.

577. As a rule, in all preliminary proceedings (even fully delegated ones), it is the **duty of the prosecutor to supervise the preliminary proceedings** at all times (Article 298 § 1 CCP). The prosecutor supervises preliminary proceedings to the extent to which he or she does not conduct them personally (Article 326 § 1 CCP). The purpose of this is to ensure the proper and effective course of the entire proceedings under his or her supervision (Article 326 § 2 CCP). In practice, quite often the supervision of the prosecutor is a fiction since the police conduct most fully delegated investigations without any help or mentoring from the prosecutor. The prosecutor usually simply extends the proceedings when the time comes (see *infra*, paragraphs 604–608), at most pointing out the additional investigative procedures that should be undertaken before the closure of the investigation. Nevertheless, the responsibility for the conduct of investigations is always with the prosecutor and all its shortcomings, including the excessive length of the proceedings, are considered as a failure on the part of the prosecutor. For that reason, and also because of the excessive supervisory competencies that can be enforced whenever the prosecutor feels such a need, the prosecutor is sometimes called a *dominus litis* (master of the proceedings).

578. The scope of the supervisory competencies of the prosecutor during preliminary proceedings is prescribed in detail (Article 326 § 3 CCP). The prosecutor may, in particular:

(1) request to be informed about the intentions and plans of the person conducting preliminary proceedings, indicate the direction that the proceedings should take and issue relevant orders in this regard;
(2) demand to be presented with the materials gathered during the course of the preliminary proceedings;
(3) participate in the procedures performed by the person conducting the proceedings, perform them personally or take over the entire proceedings;
(4) issue decisions, orders or instructions, as well as change or revoke decisions and orders issued by the person conducting preliminary proceedings.

579. Unfortunately, the prosecutor has limited powers over the person conducting preliminary proceedings to have prosecutorial decisions, orders and instructions implemented. If such a person fails to comply with them, the prosecutor supervising the proceedings may only demand from the superior of that person the initiation of disciplinary proceedings, the results of which the prosecutor must be informed of (Article 326 § 4 CCP). In practice, because of the mutual cooperation between prosecutors and the police, as well as other criminal justice bodies responsible for the conduct of preliminary proceedings, the relationship between them usually works smoothly.

2. The Police and Other Criminal Justice Bodies

580. The law provides for the two agencies responsible for the conduct of preliminary proceedings – the prosecution service and the police. However, in fact there are far more agencies that may be involved at this stage of the criminal process. According to Article 312 § 1 CCP, all competencies in the criminal process given to the police can be also exercised by other agencies such as:

(1) Border Guard (*Straż Graniczna*)
(2) Internal Security Agency (*Agencja Bezpieczeństwa Wewnętrznego*)
(3) Customs Service (*Służba Celna*)
(4) CAB (*Centralne Biuro Antykorupcyjne*)
(5) Military Police (*Żandarmeria Wojskowa*)

All the above-mentioned agencies may conduct preliminary proceedings within the limits of their competencies, which are prescribed in detail in laws governing their status and organisation. For example, the Border Guard conducts the preliminary proceedings in matters of recognition, prevention and detection of offences related to the crossing of the state border or those concerning foreigners working (Article 1 paragraph 2 (4) (a) of the Act of 2 October 1990 on the Border Guard (consolidated text: J.L. 2014, item 1402 as amended).

581. Also, other agencies referred to in special provisions may conduct preliminary proceedings. These include the Trade Inspection Authority (*Inspekcja Handlowa*), State Sanitary Inspection Authority (*Państwowa Inspekcja Sanitarna*), fiscal inspection office (*urząd kontroli skarbowej*), Forest Guard (*Straż Leśna*), etc. They are only authorised to conduct inquiries, not investigations, but in some cases they are even allowed to prosecute. These agencies may conduct preliminary proceedings within the limits of their competencies, which are prescribed in detail in laws governing their status and organisation.

3. The Role of the Court

582. **Polish criminal procedure does not recognise the traditional feature of the inquisitorial system, which is the investigative judge.** There is also no judge for a preliminary investigation, as is sometimes the case in other countries with the continental tradition. Nevertheless, it is well understood that during preliminary proceedings, primarily conducted by non-judicial bodies (a prosecutor, the police, etc.) some actions must be vested in the hands of a body much more independent and impartial than agencies commonly involved in the investigation of offences.

583. There are three spheres in the course of preliminary proceedings in which the court intervenes:

(1) evidentiary procedures conducted by the court in the cases described in the CCP;
(2) decisions designated for the court's exclusive competence;
(3) reviewing decisions of the prosecutor in the case of interlocutory appeal.

584. In certain situations, the CCP gives power to the court to **conduct evidentiary procedures during preliminary proceedings**, which ordinarily is a duty of the agencies responsible for the conduct of preliminary proceedings. The court, according to Article 185a-185c CCP is obliged to examine vulnerable witnesses, something which should happen only once during the course of the criminal proceedings. Therefore, the court engages in the examination of a witness at a very early stage of criminal proceedings, even before the trial starts, so the witness will not have to testify again during the trial; this is in order to prevent the witness from being further traumatised or victimised. The vulnerable witnesses granted this dispensation are: children under the age of 15 who are victims or witnesses of sexual offences or offences against the family. It also applies to all victims of rape or other sexual offences regardless of the age of the victim. Moreover, if there is a risk that it will not be possible for a witness to be examined during a trial, a party, the prosecutor or other criminal justice body conducting preliminary proceedings may request that the court examine the witness (Article 316 § 3 CCP). Obviously, the court is not bound by such a request and may refuse to do so.

585. Some **decisions in preliminary proceedings** are considered to be of such importance that only the court, as an independent and impartial body, is able to issue them. In particular, these are decisions that touch upon the rights of the suspect and other participants in the proceedings. The examples of such decisions might be:

(1) to examine the mental health of the suspect combined with their observation in a medical institution (Article 203 § 1 CCP);
(2) to detain the suspect on remand (Article 250 § 2 CCP);
(3) the forfeiture of assets or the collection of the sum of money posted as financial surety (Article 270 § 1 CCP).

It must be noted that **search and seizure warrants**, even though infringing the right to privacy and property, **are not issued by the court during preliminary proceedings**. This is the sole competence and responsibility of the prosecutor; however, a person whose rights have been infringed by the issuance of a prosecutorial warrant may file an interlocutory appeal with the court (see *infra*, paragraph 952).

586. This leads to the third sphere in which the court plays an important role in preliminary proceedings – **reviewing decisions of the prosecutor** in the case of an interlocutory appeal filed by one of the parties to the preliminary proceedings (the suspect or aggrieved party) or other people whose rights have been violated (Article 302 CCP). A general rule provides for the right to an interlocutory appeal (in Article 465 § 2 CCP): prosecutorial decisions can be contested by interlocutory appeal to the court competent to examine the case. Obviously, not all decisions issued by the prosecutor can be contested in such a form. Besides those that preclude the possibility of delivering a judgment (e.g., the decision to discontinue preliminary proceedings) there is a large group of decisions that can be contested. Among these are decisions on search and seizure (Article 236 CCP) as well as decisions imposing coercive measures other than detention on remand (Article 252 § 2 CCP).

C. *Parties*

587. Article 299 § 1 CCP provides that **in preliminary proceedings the aggrieved person and the suspect are the parties**. This means that when a natural person or a legal entity (e.g., a company) becomes the aggrieved party by law, regardless of this person's or entity's will, it can execute all powers that are granted to a party to preliminary proceedings. The suspect becomes a party from the moment when charges against him are officially presented. The positions of the suspect and the aggrieved party have been discussed in Chapter 1 (see *supra*, paragraphs 547–551 and 556–561 respectively).

§2. Commencement Of Preliminary Proceedings

I. Information on an Offence and Its Verification

588. Criminal investigative bodies can use their own means to uncover an offence that has been committed (e.g., an offence may be detected by officers patrolling the streets or intelligence about an offence can be gathered through undercover operations) or receive information on an offence from victims or from witnesses. Generally, there is no legal obligation to inform the police or any other body that an offence has been committed. It is seen more as a moral duty (Article 304 § 1 CCP). Only in the case of some grave felonies it is an offence not to report the offence to criminal justice bodies (see Article 240 CC). Additionally, public and local government institutions that learn of an offence having been committed, are obliged to report this immediately (Article 304 § 2 CCP).

589. The information on an offence having been committed will not always result in the immediate initiation of preliminary proceedings. Even though the Polish criminal justice bodies, and in particular the prosecutor, are bound by the principle of legality – understood as an obligation to investigate and prosecute all offences (Article 10 CCP) – this principle is not absolute. Polish criminal procedure differentiates between **offences that are prosecuted upon complaint** (*przestępstwa ścigane na wniosek*) and **offences that are prosecuted without complaint** (*przeste pstwa bezwnioskowe*). Criminal justice bodies carry out proceedings and undertake actions ex officio, unless, by virtue of the law, a complaint from a specified person, institution, or authority, or permission from an authority, is required (Article 9 § 1 CCP). Therefore, commencing preliminary proceedings in the case of offences investigated upon complaint is possible only if the aggrieved person files an official complaint with a criminal investigation body. The examples of such offences are: criminal threat (Article 190 CC) or theft committed to the detriment of next of kin (Article 278 § 4 CC). Since the prosecution of such offence is possible only upon the complaint of the aggrieved party, the criminal justice body must contact the aggrieved party (if this is not the person that reported the offence) and is obliged to inform it of the consequences of filing or not filing a complaint (Article 12 § 1 CCP). If the aggrieved party decides not to file a complaint, the case must be immediately discontinued (Article 17 § 1 paragraph 10 CCP). However, if the complaint has been filed, the aggrieved party loses control over the case. Only upon the consent of the prosecutor withdrawal of the complaint will be possible (Article 12 § 3 CCP), e.g. when the suspect reconciles with the aggrieved party. The aggrieved party may also withdraw the complaint at a later time, during court proceedings, but only until the commencement of the evidentiary phase of the trial and at this point in the course of proceedings it will be for the court, and not the prosecutor, to decide whether it accepts this withdrawal or not.

590. Both offences – those investigated upon complaint and those done so without –, belong to a large group of **offences investigated** ex officio (*przestępstwa ścigane z urzędu*). However, Polish criminal law also provides for a second, quite a small group of **offences prosecuted by private accusation** (*przestępstwa ścigane z oskarżenia prywatnego*). It consists of four offences: causing minor bodily harm or a minor impairment to health (Article 157 § 2 and 3 CC), slander (Article 212 CC), insult (Article 216 CC) and breach of personal inviolability – Article 217 CC). It is solely the aggrieved party's responsibility to investigate and prosecute these offences. What they have in common is the assumed lack of public interest in investigating and prosecuting them. However, the prosecutor who decides that the public interest does indeed demand investigation of any of these offences, can commence such preliminary proceedings ex officio or join the proceedings conducted by the aggrieved party (Article 60 § 1 CCP). This option must be considered rather rare, however. Criminal proceedings with regard to offences prosecuted by private accusation are regulated in Articles 59–61 and 485–499 CCP (see *infra*, paragraphs 751–761).

591. The competent criminal justice body or prosecutor must **immediately** issue a decision to commence preliminary proceedings when **justified suspicion that an offence has been committed** (*uzasadnione podejrzenie popełnienia przestępstwa*) is established (Article 303 CCP). However, the law provides for **exceptions**. The first exception is regulated in Article 307 CCP and provides for the conducting of **preliminary examination** (*czynności sprawdzające*) if verification of information on an offence is necessary. The second exception occurs when there is an urgent need to secure forensic traces and evidence against loss, as provided in Article 308 CCP regulating so-called **immediate procedures** (*czynności w niezbędnym zakresie*).

592. **Preliminary examination** (*czynności sprawdzające*) is carried out to verify information on an offence having been committed, regardless of the source of this information. The scope of actions that can be undertaken is very limited. The police cannot conduct any evidentiary procedures that require being recorded in the form of written record (the long list of such procedures is provided in Article 143 CCP and contains, among others, interviews, searches, seizures, crime scene examinations, body searches, taking of witness statements, etc.). The only possible procedures are: the taking of an oral report on an offence or a complaint (the latter in cases of offences prosecuted upon complaint), and taking of a statement from a witness who has reported an offence (Article 307 § 2 CCP). The preliminary examination may last thirty days at most. After this time, a decision to initiate or to refuse the initiation of preliminary proceedings must be issued.

593. The **immediate procedures** (*czynności w niezbędnym zakresie*) are regulated in Article 308 CCP. This type of proceedings allows for the preliminary proceedings not to commence immediately, if issuing of a formal decision is considered a waste of time in cases when the situation demands the immediate securing of forensic traces and the gathering of evidence that will otherwise be lost or destroyed, e.g. the necessity to conduct an urgent crime scene examination. The evidentiary procedures that can be conducted as part of these proceedings are not limited in their scope, as they are in the case of preliminary examination, i.e. evidentiary procedures requiring written record (Article 143 CCP) may also be conducted. These proceedings may last only five days and they are considered part of the preliminary proceedings from the moment when the first evidentiary procedure is undertaken.

II. Decision to Initiate Preliminary Proceedings

594. Preliminary proceedings can be officially and formally commenced when, according to Article 303 CCP, the **justified suspicion that an offence has been**

committed (*uzasadnione podejrzenie popełnienia przestępstwa*) **has been established**. This decision must be undertaken by a competent body **immediately** (Article 305 § 1 CCP) taking into account the exceptions discussed above (see Articles 307 and 308 CCP). 'Immediately' means altogether six weeks at most. If the person that reports an offence has not been informed within six weeks of either the commencement of preliminary proceedings or of the refusal to initiate preliminary proceedings, that person has the right to an interlocutory appeal against the inaction of the criminal justice bodies (Article 306 § 3 CCP).

595. The decision to initiate an investigation (*śledztwo*) can be issued only by the prosecutor (Article 305 § 3 CCP). If a report received by the police concerns an offence for which an investigation is mandatory, the police are obliged to submit it immediately to the prosecutor who must issue a decision (Article 304 § 3 CCP). On the contrary, the decision to initiate an inquiry (*dochodzenie*) can be issued by the police (Article 325e § 1 CCP) but the possibility that the prosecutor may also issue such a decision at his or her own initiative, in the exercise of his or her general competence to supervise the preliminary proceedings, as such is not excluded. The initiation of preliminary proceedings (investigation or inquiry) is always issued in the form of a decision (*postanowienie*). **The decision to initiate preliminary proceedings** should meet the general requirements for every decision, as prescribed in Article 94 § 1 and 98 § 1 CCP (it must identify the body as well as the person issuing the decision, its date, the case and matter the decision concerns, and describe the conclusion reached together with the legal grounds for it and justification). Moreover, it must consist of additional elements, such as the description of an offence that has been committed as well as its legal classification (Article 303 CCP). In this decision the information on the suspected offender is not provided. Only upon issuing a decision to charge a suspect should the name of the suspect be provided (Article 313 CCP).

596. There is no right to interlocutory appeal against a decision to initiate preliminary proceedings. Nevertheless, someone who has reported an offence to the police, as well as the identified aggrieved party, must be informed that the decision has been issued (Article 305 § 4 CCP).

III. Decision Refusing the Initiation of Preliminary Proceedings

597. In the case of a **lack of the justified suspicion that an offence has been committed** (*uzasadnione podejrzenie popełnienia przestępstwa*) a decision to refuse the initiation of preliminary proceedings must be issued (Article 303 CCP). Moreover, even if justified suspicion that an offence has been committed exists, the criminal justice body must make sure that none of the **negative grounds for the conduct of criminal proceedings** (*negatywne przesłanki procesowe*) provided in Article 17 § 1 CCP exist, such as, decease of the defendant or expiry of the prescribed statute of limitations. The existence of any negative condition results in the immediate termination of criminal proceedings at every stage of the criminal process, including during a trial (see *infra*, paragraph 649).

598. A decision refusing the initiation of an investigation (*śledztwo*) can be issued by the prosecutor or by the police, but in the latter case it must be confirmed by the prosecutor (Article 305 § 3 CCP). In the case of preliminary proceedings conducted in the form of an inquiry, the decision can be issued by the police and it does not have to be confirmed by the prosecutor at all (Article 325e § 2 CCP). The decision to refuse the initiation of preliminary proceedings should contain the same elements as the decision to initiate preliminary proceedings e.g. the description of an offence and its legal classification.

599. The decision refusing the initiation of preliminary proceedings is considered one of the decisions precluding the possibility of delivering a judgment and therefore is subject to interlocutory appeal (Article 466 § 1 CCP in connection with Article 459 § 1 CCP). This is due to the fact that validation of that decision makes a case final if not appealed by the person entitled to do so. Those that are entitled to submit an interlocutory appeal must receive a copy of the decision (see Article 306 § 1 in connection with Article 305 § 4 CCP) and are given the right to acquaint themselves with materials gathered by the police up to that point in time. This group consists of:

- the identified aggrieved party;
- the state, local government or social institution that reported an offence;
- the person that reported an offence if that offence resulted in the violation of the rights of this person.

Others that reported an offence must only be informed that a decision has been issued (Article 305 § 4 CCP) and they have no right to interlocutory appeal.

§3. Conduct Of Preliminary Proceedings

I. General Issues

600. Preliminary proceedings are conducted in a very formal and official way. Criminal justice authorities mainly focus on establishing whether an offence has been committed, on identifying the perpetrator and on gathering evidence necessary to verify grounds for the submission of an indictment, or for concluding the proceedings in another way (see Article 297 § 1 CCP). What must be noted is that **materials and information collected during preliminary proceedings are considered evidence** and treated as such. Moreover, **the rules that govern the conduct and recording of evidentiary procedures are common for preliminary proceedings and court proceedings**. This stage even resembles court proceedings to some extent, although it is not conducted in an open court but in camera and not before a judge but by a prosecutor or other criminal justice body. The prosecutor and police are obliged to undertake all necessary evidentiary procedures, such as interrogating witnesses, appointing expert witnesses in order to receive their opinions, as well as conducting searches, seizures, etc. At this stage the admissibility of evidence is decided by the prosecutor or the police, similar to how it is usually done by a court during court proceedings.

601. Moreover, Article 143 § 1 CCP provides that all procedural actions (*czynności procesowe*) at this stage of criminal proceedings have to be documented for the record. Among these are: the taking of testimony ('examination') of the accused (suspect), a witness or expert witness; crime scene investigation and the physical inspection of a body and things, as well as autopsy and exhumation; the search of a person, place or object and seizure of objects, etc. The rules covering the composition of records are provided in Article 148 CCP and demand many formal requirements to be met that later will allow the court to reconstruct every evidentiary procedure that was recorded. The law also provides for other forms of recording evidentiary procedures i.e. an audiovisual record (Article 147 CCP). The findings from the preliminary proceedings are placed in the **dossier** (*akta poste powania przygotowawczego*).

602. Preliminary proceedings are conducted ex officio, which means that the proceedings are conducted regardless of the will or actions undertaken by the parties to the preliminary proceedings (the suspect and aggrieved person) (see Article 9 § 1 CCP). Therefore **during the preliminary proceedings most evidentiary procedures are triggered and conducted ex officio, although the parties have the right to file evidentiary motions requesting the conduct of certain procedures**, e.g. interrogating a certain witness or searching certain premises (Article 315 § 1 CCP). Moreover, the law provides for rules allowing parties and their representatives to participate in evidentiary procedures (Article 315–318 CCP). Generally, the party who has submitted an evidentiary motion, as well as defence lawyers and legal counsels, cannot be denied the right to participate in the examination of such evidence if they so demand (Article 315 § 2 CCP). However, the suspect who remains in custody (e.g. because of their detention on remand) is not brought to participate in the examination of such evidence if it would cause serious difficulties (Article 318 CCP), e.g. in terms of transporting the suspect from a detention facility that is far away from the place where the procedure is to take place. The parties and their appointed representatives should also, upon their demand, be allowed to participate in other procedural actions conducted during preliminary proceedings (Article 317 § 1 CCP). The prosecutor, in particularly justified cases, may also deny a party the right to participate in evidentiary procedure if such a denial serves an important interest of the preliminary proceedings (*ważny interes postępowania przygotowawczego*) or decline to bring the suspect who remains in custody to court if this would cause serious difficulties (Article 317 § 2 CCP). In particular, the participation of parties and their representatives in expert witness examinations, as well as notification of the content of expert witness' reports, is an obligation of the body conducting preliminary proceedings (Article 318 CCP).

603. The necessity to secure the presence of parties to the preliminary proceedings exists in particular in cases when the evidentiary procedures that are to be conducted (e.g., interrogation of a dying witness) cannot be repeated during the trial, (Article 316 § 1 CCP). In such case the parties should be allowed to participate in the procedure, unless a delay associated with informing parties of such a procedure might result in the loss or distortion of evidence. In particular, this applies to the suspect remaining in custody (Article 316 § 3 CCP). Moreover, both the body conducting the preliminary proceedings or the party (the suspect or an aggrieved person), may request that the examination of a witness is conducted before a court if there is a risk that it will be impossible to examine the witness during the trial e.g. due to the likely death of a witness (Article 316 § 3 CCP).

II. Duration

604. The Constitution of the Republic of Poland, in Article 45 paragraph 1, provides everyone with the right to a fair and public hearing, which should be held **without undue delay** before a competent, impartial and independent judge. Additionally, Article 2 § 1 paragraph 4 CCP states that one of the objects of criminal proceedings is that a case should be resolved within a reasonable period of time. The normative determination of the duration of preliminary proceedings implements the principle of speedy trial.

605. Preliminary proceedings conducted in the form of an **investigation** must be concluded within **three months** from the date of the decision to initiate investigation being issued (Article 310 § 1 CCP). However, it is usually not possible to conclude a case, which can sometimes be quite complicated, within such a short period of time. Therefore, the law allows for the extension of an investigation. In 'justified cases' an investigation can be extended for an additional time of no longer than one year and in 'particularly justified cases' for an additional time that is not limited in any way by the law (Article 310 § 2 CCP). In the former case, the decision to prolong the investigation must be issued by the prosecutor supervising the investigation or by the prosecutor directly superior (*prokurator bezpośrednio przełożony*) to the prosecutor directly conducting the investigation and in the latter case by the prosecutor of a higher level (*prokurator nadrzędny*) to the prosecutor conducting the investigation or supervising it.

606. Proceedings conducted in the form of an **inquiry** must be concluded within **two months** from the date of the decision to initiate inquiry (Article 325i § 1 CCP). The prosecutor supervising or conducting the inquiry can issue an extension for three months without cause and for one year in 'justified cases'. In 'exceptional cases justified by extraordinary circumstances' the prosecutor directly superior (*prokurator bezpośrednio przełożony*) to the prosecutor conducting or supervising the inquiry may extend the inquiry for additional time that is not limited in duration.

607. According to the above rules, theoretically an **investigation or inquiry can last almost infinitely** and the only end date arises from the statute of limitation of the investigated offence. However, if participants in preliminary proceedings think that the proceedings last too long, they may issue the court with a complaint against undue delay under the Act of 17 June 2004 on the complaint against a breach of a party's right to have a case examined in preliminary proceedings conducted or supervised by a prosecutor and court proceedings without undue delay (J.L. 2004, No. 179, item 1843 as amended). The same applies to court proceedings.

608. During preliminary proceedings a long-lasting impediment preventing the conduct of the proceedings can arise. In such cases the law provides for the **suspension of proceedings** (*zawieszenie postępowania*), as long as such an impediment exists (Article 22 § 1 CCP). The example of such an impediment is a situation in which the suspect cannot be apprehended or cannot participate in the proceedings due to mental illness or any other serious health disorder. In such cases, preliminary proceedings are suspended by virtue of a decision issued by the prosecutor or a decision issued by the police and approved by the prosecutor (Article 325 CCP). Each of the above decisions is subject to interlocutory appeal (Article 22 § 2 CCP). During the period of suspension, only measures to protect evidence against loss or distortion are allowed (Article 22 § 3 CCP). Whenever the impediment disappears, the proceedings must be immediately resumed. All the above also applies to court proceedings, however in this case all decisions will be, obviously, issued by the court.

III. Charging a Person with an Offence

609. The formal charge is a crucial moment during the course of preliminary proceedings. It can be done immediately at the beginning of preliminary proceedings or later after the careful collection of materials that allow for the identification of a suspect. The standard that has to be met is a **sufficiently justified suspicion** (*dostatecznie uzasadnione podejrzenie*) **that the offence was committed by a specific individual** (Article 313 § 1 CCP). From that moment, the case moves from the stage of preliminary proceedings in which the alleged perpetrator is officially unknown (Latin: in rem) into the stage where the suspect is officially named and notified on offences that he is charged with. Therefore, from the moment when a decision to charge a suspect with an offence is issued, one can speak about **preliminary proceedings being conducted against a person** (Latin: *ad personam*). As a consequence, since in Polish criminal proceedings the formal notion of the suspect is adopted, this is the very moment when he is granted with a wide range of rights that will protect him until the final conclusion of the proceedings (see *supra*, paragraphs 547–551).

610. The **procedure that governs the charging of a person with an offence** is provided in Article 313 CCP and **does not involve the court in any way**. The presentation of charges is the sole decision of the body conducting preliminary proceedings. Regardless of the form of the preliminary proceedings (investigation or inquiry) **the decision to charge a person with an offence can be issued by the police or other criminal justice body responsible for the conducting of preliminary proceedings** (Article 298 § 1 CCP and Article 325a § 2 CCP) **without any necessity to consult the prosecutor**. Since 2015 a prosecutor may reserve certain procedures to be carried out by him or her personally (Article 311 § 6 CCP), but if such a reservation has not been made, the police are free to issue a decision to charge a person with an offence. Practice shows that only in the most complicated cases does the prosecutor reserve that competence. The only exceptions are immediate procedures (*czynności w niezbędnym zakresie*) where, only a prosecutor can charge a person with an offence (Article 308 § 4 CCP).

611. The decision to charge a person with an offence must meet the general requirements set for a decision issued in criminal proceedings (Article 94 § 1 CCP) but does not have to be justified in writing (*a contrario* Article 313 § 3 CCP). However, upon the request of the suspect or his defence lawyer, the grounds and justification of the decision to charge must be provided first orally and subsequently within fourteen days in writing. The decision must indicate the suspect and provide the exact description of the offence as well as its legal classification (Article 313 § 2 CCP).

612. According to Article 313 § 1 CCP, charging a person with an offence demands, cumulatively, three actions:

(1) issuing a decision to charge a person with an offence;
(2) immediate announcement of the content of the decision to the suspect;
(3) interrogation of the suspect.

According to the currently adopted jurisprudence, only these three steps taken altogether result in the charging of the suspect. In exceptional cases, it is acceptable that the simple issuing of the decision, without the suspect being notified about its content or being interrogated, is enough to charge a suspect with an offence if he or she cannot be reached (see the Supreme Court decision of 24 April 2007, IV KK 31/07, LEX 262649 and the Supreme Court judgment of 2 June 2010, V KK 376/09, Lex 590304; and also the Supreme Court decision of 13 June 2012, II KK 302/11, Lex 1212980).

613. The charges form the basis of what the defendant will be finally accused of in the indictment filed with the court, and of what will be the subject of the trial. Therefore, if in the course of preliminary proceedings it transpires that the suspect should be charged with an offence not included in the charging decision already issued, with an offence in a significantly changed form, or that the offence should be classified under a provision that sets out a more severe penalty, a new decision should be issued immediately, announced to the suspect, and the suspect should then be interrogated (Article 314 CCP). Accordingly, whether the charges are of a not significant manner or an offence should be qualified under a provision that sets out a less severe penalty, it is solely the prosecutor's discretion to amend the charges on an indictment.

IV. Disclosure and Access to the Dossier

614. As a rule, **the parties have the right to obtain access to materials collected during preliminary proceedings kept in a dossier** (*materiały postępowania przygotowawczego*) **when a case is about to be sent to the court** (Article 321 § 1 and 322 § 1 CCP). The suspect's right of access to evidence collected during preliminary proceedings is a consequence of the premise that only a person who is aware of evidence gathered against him or her is able to properly defend himself or herself. The Polish CCP also grants the same right to the aggrieved party and its legal counsel, upon the conclusion of preliminary proceedings. Article 156 § 5 CCP provides that the parties also have the right to access the dossier during the preliminary proceedings, but this may be limited in the interest of the proceedings. Both of these cases will be discussed below.

615. **The right of access to the dossier** (Article 321 CCP), is only granted upon the conclusion of preliminary proceedings and only if the analysis and evaluation of the materials gathered during the investigation or inquiry result in a decision to bring a case to court. If preliminary proceedings are to be dismissed, there is no need to disclose the materials to anyone in this form (Article 322 § 1 CCP), although in compliance with general rules the suspect and aggrieved party can still obtain access to such materials.

The right of access is granted, upon the conclusion of preliminary proceedings, in equal manner to the suspect and his or her defence lawyer, as well as to the aggrieved party and his legal counsel. However, a prosecutor may limit the number of aggrieved parties that will be granted this right on a case-by-case basis, e.g. if the number of people who intend to read the materials is too big (Article 321 § 2 CCP). Both parties must be informed of their rights of access before their first interrogation (Article 300 § 1 and 2 CCP). The materials will be disclosed only upon the request of the party or its legal counsel. They can read the dossier either at a police station or at the prosecutor's office. The party requesting access must be informed of the date when access is granted at least seven days before this date (Article 321 § 3 CCP). Furthermore, since it is a right of the party, and not an obligation, the party's failure to appear and read the materials does not obstruct further proceedings (Article 321 § 4 CCP).

616. When a party obtains access to the dossier of preliminary proceedings, all gathered materials are revealed to that party; he or she is also informed of which documents will be sent to the court along with the indictment in the dossier (see Article 334 § 1 CCP) as well as of the right to submit additional evidentiary motions at this time (e.g., motions to examine witnesses, seize additional physical evidence, etc.). The parties must be also informed of the possibility of filing a motion requesting the supplementation of the dossier with additional materials that the prosecutor did not plan to include in the dossier that is to be sent to the court (Article 321 § 1 CCP). The party will have three days from the date when the disclosure took place to submit both motions. It is up to the prosecutor to allow additional evidentiary procedures upon such a request. The dismissal of the evidentiary motion can be based either on general causes, as provided in Article 170 § 1 CCP (see *infra*, paragraph

920), or upon the conviction that the goals of criminal proceedings as prescribed in Article 297 § 1 paragraph 5 have been met. Nevertheless, if failure to allow the evidentiary procedure would threaten the loss or distortion of evidence, the evidentiary procedures requested by the party must be conducted. If additional evidentiary procedures take place after the disclosure of the dossier, both parties subsequently have the right to also familiarise themselves with the new materials and the whole disclosure process must be repeated. If the prosecutor does not allow the evidentiary motion, he or she is obliged to transfer this motion to the court together with indictment and dossier and it will be up to the court to decide on the issue again during court proceedings. At the same time, the prosecutor has to comply with the party's motion to supplement the dossier by including in it all the requested materials that were gathered during preliminary proceedings and which the prosecutor did not intend to send to the court (see *infra*, paragraph 630).

617. After all these efforts, the preliminary proceedings can finally be closed. A formal decision on the conclusion of the preliminary proceedings is necessary in the case of an investigation (Article 321 § 7 CCP) but does not have to be issued in the case of an inquiry (Article 325g § 1 CCP).

618. The grant of access to the dossier upon the conclusion of preliminary proceedings is not the only way in which the suspect and aggrieved party can obtain access to the materials gathered during preliminary proceedings. Additional rules provide for a person's right to familiarise oneself with these materials even before the preliminary proceedings are concluded. This is a result of the application of the **principle of transparency of proceedings** (*zasada jawności postępowania*) to this stage of the criminal process (see *supra,* paragraphs 539–542). Generally, parties do have the right to access materials from preliminary proceedings. **This right can be limited but only if there is the need to ensure the normal course of proceedings or to protect an important state interest** (Article 156 § 5 CCP). Access can be granted, in the form of an order, by the prosecutor or another criminal justice body conducting preliminary proceedings. The authorised party can read the documents collected in the dossier and make their copies, including with the use of photo cameras and hand scanners. An interlocutory appeal against such an order can be filed by a party whose motion is denied. Also, persons other than the parties can be granted access to the dossier, but such orders can only be issued in exceptional cases and solely by the prosecutor.

§4. The Decision To Prosecute And Other Forms Of Conclusion Of Preliminary Proceedings

I. General Remarks

619. After all evidentiary procedures during the preliminary proceedings have been concluded the criminal justice body responsible for these proceedings freely evaluates the material gathered during this phase (Article 7 CCP), bearing in mind the presumption of innocence (Article 5 § 1 CCP) and the settling of doubts that have not been resolved in evidentiary proceedings exclusively in favour of the suspect (Article 5 § 2 CCP). The person who conducts the preliminary proceedings must decide whether to **discontinue a case** or to **send it to court** in one of the permissible forms.

620. The decision to bring a case to court must be made by a prosecutor. If the police or another criminal justice body which has conducted preliminary proceedings wants a case to be brought to court, they must submit it to the prosecutor, who will independently decide on the issue. Decisions to discontinue preliminary proceedings can also be issued by the police only with the approval of a prosecutor. In case of some inquiries in which a perpetrator has not been identified, a decision on discontinuation can be issued by the police even without notifying the prosecutor.

621. The Polish CCP provides for the following forms of conclusion of preliminary proceedings:

(1) **a decision to bring a case before a court**:
  (a) filing an indictment (Article 332–333 CCP);
  (b) filing an indictment together with a motion to convict a defendant without a trial (Article 335 § 2 CCP);
  (c) filing a stand-alone motion to convict a defendant without a trial (Article 335 § 1 CCP);
  (d) filing a motion for the conditional discontinuation of proceedings (Article 336 CCP);
  (e) filing a motion for the discontinuation of proceedings and the imposition of protective measures (Article 324 CCP),
(2) **a decision to discontinue a case;**
(3) **the decision to decline the initiation of preliminary proceedings.**

This last decision (to decline to initiate preliminary proceedings) is considered a form of concluding preliminary proceedings, but it is undertaken at an early stage of proceedings, at most after thirty days from the report of an offence (see *supra*, paragraphs 597–599).

622. It must be noted at this point that according to the Polish legal scholarship, the '***decision to prosecute***' is understood more broadly than in some other countries and is sometimes even considered to have equal meaning with '*sending a case to the court*'. Prosecuting, in this sense, means not only bringing a defendant before court – other forms of sending a case to court are included within the scope of the decision to prosecute. For example, a motion to sentence the accused without holding a trial in fact results in no trial at all, but the person named in such a motion is treated as defendant, in an equal manner to a person facing a full trial. The same applies to a motion for the conditional discontinuation of proceedings. In all situations where a case is sent to the court, with the notable exception of a motion for the discontinuation of proceedings and the imposition of preventive measures, the person named in the indictment or motion is called the defendant.

623. Accordingly, a decision to prosecute is not the same as a decision to file charges against the accused. In some countries these two decisions are seen as identical and by charging a person a prosecutor is automatically deciding to prosecute them. In Polish criminal procedure the latter decision takes place in the course of preliminary proceedings and is undertaken in an official form by either the prosecutor or the police. This can be done at the beginning, in the middle or at the end of preliminary proceedings. Moreover, a decision to prosecute can be reversed, which means that a case will not be sent to court. Therefore, these two acts must be seen as separate, and a decision to prosecute has little in common with a decision to charge the suspect with an offence.

II. Filing an Indictment

624. An **indictment** is the typical form of initiation of court proceedings. The decision to prosecute, understood as bringing a case before a court to commence a trial, is made by the prosecutor or by another authorised agency, e.g. the Border Guard or National Sanitary Inspectorate (Article 14 § 1 and 45 §§ 1–2 CCP). The cases in which bodies other than the prosecutor are able to prosecute a case before a court are very rare and are allowed to act only within the scope of competencies of those agencies. The police do not have the power to prosecute in any kind of case. An indictment being brought to court by an entity who is not authorised results in a court's decision to discontinue proceedings, since this is considered as being against the principle of accusatorial proceedings (Article 17 § 1 paragraph 9 CCP).

625. The deadline for submitting an indictment to a court is fourteen days from the moment when a decision on closing an investigation has been issued by the prosecutor or when the police, after closing an inquiry, have notified the prosecutor of their preference for bringing a case to trial by way of an indictment drafted by the police and approved by the prosecutor (Article 331 § 1 CCP). However, in a case in which the suspect has been detained on remand, the deadline for submitting the indictment is shortened to seven days (Article 331 § 3 CCP) and it must be submitted to the court no later than fourteen days before the expiry of the term of this measure (Article 331 § 4 CCP). From a practical perspective, the time limits specified in Article 331 CCP are only of indicative character and failure to comply with them will not entail any consequences for the non-complying authority.

626. When the police or another criminal justice body responsible for an inquiry drafts an indictment, the prosecutor may refuse to approve it. Instead, the prosecutor may issue a decision to discontinue proceedings or to prosecute a case not on an indictment but by bringing the case to the court in a different manner, for example through a stand-alone motion to convict a defendant without a trial. Moreover, the prosecutor may instruct the police to conduct further investigative actions (interrogate witnesses, conduct searches, receive expert witness' opinions) with the aim of supplementing the pretrial findings (see Article 326 CCP). The police cannot challenge the prosecutor's decision or appeal against prosecutorial orders. The discretionary power of the prosecutor with regard to the final decision in each case as well as the power to give all kinds of orders to the criminal justice bodies conducting pretrial proceedings is remarkable, but it is limited by the principle of legality of Article 10 CCP (see *supra*, paragraphs 525–527). The prosecutor is granted with almost unlimited supervisory powers but, unless the law allows otherwise, he or she must investigate and prosecute all cases in which offences have been committed.

627. The structure of an indictment is very formalised. It has to meet formal requirements provided in Article 119 § 1 CCP, which apply to all pleadings in criminal proceedings (the case number, the identification of the person that prepared the pleading, the date and the signature), as well as those provided in Articles 332–333 CCP. According to these regulations, the indictment should contain:

(1) the name of the defendant, his or her other personal details and information concerning preventive measures applied;
(2) a precise description of the offence with which the defendant is charged, including the time, place, method and circumstances of its perpetration, as well as its consequences, in particular the extent of the harm caused;
(3) indication whether the offence was committed under the circumstances referred to in Article 64 CC or Article 37 § 1 point 4 of the Fiscal Criminal Code (reoffending);
(4) indication of the legal classification of an offence (precise article, section and, if applicable, paragraph of CC or other statute that applies to the charged offence);
(5) indication of the court that has jurisdiction over a case and the mode of proceedings in which case will be tried;
(6) information about whether during the pretrial proceedings the aggrieved party filed a motion according to Article 59a CC (motion to discontinue case with restitution);
(7) **optionally**, a justification which cites facts and the evidence on which the prosecution is based, and, if necessary, an explanation of the legal classification of an offence which discusses the circumstances relied on by the accused in his statements;
(8) the list of evidence that the prosecutor wishes to call and examine during the trial with an indication for each piece of evidence of the circumstances to be proved, and, if necessary, with an indication of the manner and order the evidence will be called and examined; the list must be structured in separate lists according to the types of evidence:
    (a) list A – people, who are to be called and examined by the prosecution
    (b) list B – documents which are to be read, reproduced or presented by the prosecution
    (c) list C – real evidence that is to be examined
(9) a list of identified aggrieved parties together with their addresses and the addresses of people who are to be called and examined by the prosecution – this is only for the attention of the court.

628. The prosecutor, when sending lists of evidence that he or she wishes to examine before the court, can also indicate that some witnesses should not be called to testify and that the testimonies previously given by them should only be read out in the court room (Article 333 § 2 CCP), what remains in contradiction to the principle of oral and direct presentation of evidence during the trial. This applies to a strictly limited category of witnesses: those living abroad or those who testify with regard to the circumstances that have not been disputed by the accused. Moreover, it can be done only in cases when testimonies of a witness are of such a low level of importance that the direct examination of witness during trial seems unnecessary.

629. Since 2015 the prosecutor is obliged to **provide in an indictment solely evidence that he or she wants to examine during the trial**, i.e. evidence against the accused, and not exonerating evidence. Nevertheless, the prosecutor must send the court the **dossier** of the preliminary proceedings (*akta postępowania przygotowawczego*) with all materials gathered during preliminary proceedings, both that which incriminates and that which exonerates the accused. **The dossier containing materials gathered during preliminary proceedings related to the issue of criminal liability of the accused must accompany the indictment** (Article 334 § 1 CCP). Therefore, if witness A questioned during preliminary proceedings testified in favour of the accused by giving him an alibi, this testimony, transcribed for the record, should be included into the dossier but the prosecutor most likely will not want to examine the witness during the trial and witness A will not be mentioned in the indictment.

630. Article 334 § 1 CCP provides in detail what exactly should be included in the dossier that the prosecutor sends out to the court. The dossier should contain:

(1) decisions and orders issued during preliminary proceedings (by the prosecutor or the police, but also those issued by the court) referring to the accused (e.g., a decision on commencing preliminary proceedings, a decision on charging the accused, a decision on the detention on remand of the accused);
(2) official records of all evidentiary procedures that demand this form of recording (Article 143 § 1 CCP provides a list of actions that need to be made for the record); records (transcripts) of witness testimonies that are to be called during the trial should be included in a separate folder (Article 334 § 3 CCP), since they will become part of the court file only after they are read out in the courtroom, for example to refresh the memory of a witness or to confront a witness with his or her, previously different, testimony(see Article 391 CCP);
(3) exhibits attached to official records (e.g., voice or image recordings);
(4) information on the disclosure of the dossier to the aggrieved party;
(5) expert witness' opinions;
(6) official and private documents (e.g., official database information on prior convictions of the accused, medical documentation, etc.),
(7) information on sources of income of the accused, his or her properties, and also tax information; this information cannot date back to more than thirty days from before an indictment is filed with the court (see Article 213 § 1a CCP).

631. The decision on the contents of the dossier remains in the hands of the prosecutor. Nevertheless, the accused, his or her defence lawyer, the aggrieved party and his or her legal counsel are granted some impact on the shape of the materials that are sent out to the court. The parties and their representatives have the right to familiarise themselves with the full dossier and to receive information concerning which materials out of those presented will constitute the dossier filed with the court (Article 321 § 1 CCP). Subsequently they can request the inclusion into the court dossier of materials left out by the prosecutor, and the prosecutor cannot oppose this (Article 334 § 2 CCP).

632. An indictment is sent out to the court together with the dossier (Article 332–334 CCP). The accused, the aggrieved party and the person or institution that provided initial information of the commitment of the offence must be informed of this fact by the prosecutor (Article 334 § 5 CCP). Parties must be informed of some of their rights, i.e. the course of proceedings with regard to motion of the prosecutor (Article 343 CCP) or of the accused (Article 343a CCP) to convict the accused without holding a trial (motion to convict a defendant without a trial) and the aggrieved party's rights to file with the court a motion to order the accused to redress the harm caused (Article 49a CCP) and to file with the court an entry of appearance as an auxiliary prosecutor (*oskarżyciel posiłkowy uboczny*).

III. Filing an Indictment with a Motion to Convict the Defendant Without a Trial

A. *General Observations on Negotiated Justice*

633. Polish criminal procedure provides for the possibility to resolve dispute between the state and the accused in a negotiated form (*porozumienia procesowe, konsensualne formy zakończenia postępowania karnego*). The objective is to expedite the criminal process and lower its cost by avoiding a trial or full examination of the evidence at trial and even sometimes to avoid complete preliminary proceedings (see Article 335 § 1 CCP). It is obvious that it is impossible to hold full trials for all cases that are to be prosecuted in court, and the number of cases to reach court proceedings is quite high due to the principle of mandatory prosecution (Article 10 CCP). Therefore, it was inevitable that new ways of resolving disputes had to be found. Since 1997, when for the first time some forms of proceedings resembling Anglo-Saxon plea bargaining were introduced in Poland, the growth of negotiated justice mechanisms can be observed.

634. Currently five distinct procedural modes can be identified that are based on the premise that criminal proceedings can be resolved in a way other than by holding a full trial. These are:

(1) a prosecutor's indictment with a motion to convict a defendant without a trial (Article 335 § 2 CCP);

(2) a prosecutor's stand-alone motion to convict a defendant without a trial (Article 335 § 1 CCP);
(3) a defendant's motion to receive a conviction without a trial, filed before the commencement of the evidentiary phase of a trial (*otwarcie przewodu sa̜dowego*) (Article 338a CCP),; (4) a defendant's motion to receive a conviction without a full trial, filed before the conclusion of the testimonies of all defendants during the trial (Article 387 CCP);
(5) an aggrieved party's motion to discontinue the proceedings (Article 59a CC).

Only the first and the second are connected with a case being sent to court by the prosecutor after the conclusion of preliminary proceedings. The two regarding a defendant's motions (voluntary assumption of criminal liability) will be discussed in Chapter 3 – Court Proceedings and Remedies (see *infra*, paragraphs 685–690), and an aggrieved party's motion will be discussed below as a form of discontinuation of preliminary proceedings (see *infra*, paragraph 653).

635. The use of negotiated justice mechanisms in criminal proceedings is becoming more and more popular. Currently, around 51% of indictments are being sent out to court together with a motion to convict the defendant without a trial (Article 335 § 2 CCP). The introduction into the CCP, after the amendments of 2015, of the stand-alone motion (without the necessity of it being accompanied by an indictment) provided in Article 335 § 1 CCP will possibly increase this figure even more.

B. Procedure

636. The **requirements** that allow a prosecutor **to send to the court an indictment together with a motion to convict a defendant without a trial** are provided in Article 335 § 2 CCP:

- the offence must be a misdemeanour;
- the circumstances of the offence as well as the guilt of a defendant cannot raise doubts;
- the statements of a defendant may not contradict the findings;
- the defendant must consent to the proposed penalties, penal measures and other measures provided for the alleged offences, as well as for incurring the costs of proceedings.

It must be strongly pointed out that obtaining a **guilty plea from the accused is not necessary** during preliminary proceedings. It is enough to achieve an agreement between the prosecutor and the defendant with regard to the penalty and to be sure that the defendant does not contradict the evidence gathered throughout the investigation or inquiry with regard to the circumstances of an offence.

637. The mechanism avoids a full trial (*rozprawa*). The case is resolved during a hearing (*posiedzenie*) where no evidence is examined. Therefore, the agreement between the prosecutor and the defendant results in expediting proceedings and makes them less expensive. What is equally important is the fact that the defendant has the chance to bargain with the prosecutor on penalties, penal measures and other measures provided for the alleged offence. The principle of legality **does not allow bargaining over a charge**. Therefore, the offence that the defendant is accused of will remain as stated by the prosecutor and only negotiations over possible penalties, etc. are allowed.

638. Since July 2015, the prosecutor, when making the decision on whether to offer the defendant privilege to be sentenced without a trial, must take into account the interest of the aggrieved party. It is provided that **the aggrieved party may oppose resolving a case without holding a trial** (Article 343 § 2 CCP). Therefore, it is expected, although not enforced by law, that the prosecutor, before deciding whether to send a motion to the court, would consult the aggrieved party on the issue.

639. Achieving agreement between prosecutor and defendant is the first step that opens the door to sentencing the defendant without holding a trial. The agreement is most often achieved during the interrogation of the accused in preliminary proceedings. It must be noted that the police are not allowed to negotiate with the defendant and solely the prosecutor is given the competence to decide on this matter. However, in practice the person conducting preliminary proceedings usually makes an agreement with the accused at the police station and the prosecutor simply confirms it over the telephone, then later does so officially by sending an indictment together with the relevant motion to the court.

The law is silent on whether an agreement achieved according to Article 335 § 2 CCP is binding on the prosecutor. Therefore, without any consequences the prosecutor might first offer the suspect a beneficial agreement and later, after reaching his consent, not send the motion to the court at all. However that should be perceived as a lack of procedural loyalty and it should not happen in practice.

640. The indictment which is accompanied by the motion to convict the defendant without holding a trial is constructed similar to the one that is filed to the court without such a motion (Articles 332–333 CCP). However, it does not need to contain a list of evidence that the prosecutor wishes to present and examine during the trial (Article 333 §§ 1–2 and Article 335 § 2 CCP). Without a trial, no such list is necessary. However, if the court does not accept the agreement, the prosecutor will be asked to supplement the indictment with all the typically required elements (Article 343 § 7 CCP). The motion should contain all the necessary elements of the agreement reached between the prosecutor and the defendant and should be substantiated with available evidence. This evidence should justify that the established circumstances of an offence and the defendant's guilt raise no doubts and that the objects of criminal proceedings will be achieved even without holding a trial (Article 335 § 2–3 CCP). The dossier, constructed according to the provisions of Article 334 CCP, should be attached to the indictment. The court proceedings regarding the motion are presented in Chapter 3 – Court Proceedings and Remedies (see *infra*, paragraphs 679–682).

IV. Filing a Stand-Alone Motion to Convict a Defendant Without a Trial

641. A stand-alone motion to sentence a defendant without holding a trial (Article 335 § 1 CCP) is a novelty in Polish criminal procedure, introduced in 2015. It looks quite similar to the motion that is filed to the court together with an indictment (Article 335 § 2 CCP). The main difference is **the obligation to admit guilt by a defendant** as a prerequisite for the stand-alone motion. The defendant does not need to testify and explain the reasons for having committed an offence or its circumstances. It is enough that he or she pleads guilty and achieves an agreement with the prosecutor with regard to the penalty and other measures.

642. If an agreement has been achieved, the prosecutor and other criminal justice bodies conducting the criminal investigation do not need to conduct all the normal evidentiary procedures. Nevertheless, it is essential to gather evidence that **sufficiently justifies the suspicion that the offence was committed** (*dostatecznie uzasadnione podejrzenie popełnienia przestępstwa*) by the defendant (Article 313 § 1 CCP), which is the necessary standard to be met in the case where a person is to be charged with an offence. Additionally, it is mandatory to gather evidence that will allow the evaluation of the credibility of a defendant's statements, or if the evidence might be lost or destroyed. In particular, crime scene investigation and examination of evidence must be conducted, including the collection of blood, hair and bodily secretions, according to Article 74 § 2 paragraph 1 CCP (see Article 335 § 1 CCP).

643. The procedure in which a stand-alone motion is filed with the court also resembles the one for an indictment with a motion to convict the defendant without a trial. Again, agreement must be reached between the prosecutor and the defendant, which usually takes place during the questioning of the defendant. However, as this motion is of an independent character, it does not have to be submitted with the indictment. Therefore, this accusation is considered to be clearly less formal. The motion has to contain some elements that are normally included in the indictment according to provisions of Article 332 § 1 paragraph 1–5 CCP (e.g., personal data regarding the accused, the precise description of an offence that the defendant is charged with, indication of the legal classification of an offence, etc.). It also has to meet the formal requirements provided in Article 119 § 1 CCP, which apply to all pleadings. The independent motion must be substantiated and outline the facts of the case, evidence proving that the circumstances of an offence and the defendant's guilt do not raise any doubts, and also stating that the aims of criminal proceedings will be met even without holding a trial (Article 335 § 3 CCP). The prosecutor must submit a stand-alone motion together with a dossier of preliminary proceedings (Article 335 § 3 CCP). The court proceedings regarding the motion are presented in Chapter 3 – Court Proceedings and Remedies (see *infra*, paragraphs 679–682).

V. Filing an Motion for the Conditional Discontinuation of Proceedings

644. The Criminal Code sets out the requirements to allow the court to conditionally discontinue proceedings. But even before the initiation of court proceedings the requirements have to be met by the prosecutor in order for a motion to receive such decision from the court to be filed. According to Article 66 §§ 1–2 CC, these are:

- an offence must carry a penalty of not more than five years' imprisonment;
- the guilt and the social harm (*społeczna szkodliwość*) presented by the offence are not significant;
- the circumstances of an offence must not raise any doubts;
- the defendant has not been convicted for an intentional offence;
- the attitude of the defendant, his or her personal characteristics and way of life to date must provide reasonable grounds to assume that even if the proceedings are discontinued, he or she will observe the legal order, and particularly that he or she will not commit an offence.

The motion can be seen as beneficial from the defendant's perspective since as a result **the decision to conditionally discontinue of proceedings is not considered as conviction**.

645. The prosecutor holds discretion whether to file the motion or indictment. However, the court, during the court proceedings, may also exercise some degree of discretion. Even if the prosecutor decides to file indictment, the court may still rule that conditional discontinuation of proceedings is appropriate and issue a judgment to this effect (see Article 339 § 1 paragraph 2 CCP and Article 342 CCP).

646. The motion for the conditional discontinuation of proceedings is seen as an accusation of the defendant and to some extent formally resembles an indictment, as it contains some of its elements (Article 332 § 1 paragraphs 1, 2 and 4–5 CCP read in conjunction with Article 336 § 2 CCP). It may contain suggestions regarding a probation period, duties that should be imposed on the defendant and suggestions concerning supervision (*dozór*). The prosecutor must justify the decision by pointing out that the requirements have been met and also the circumstances in favour of the conditional discontinuance of the proceedings. The motion is filed to the court together with the dossier. The court proceedings regarding the motion are presented in Chapter 3 – Court Proceedings and Remedies (see *infra*, paragraphs 691–693).

VI. Filing a Motion for the Discontinuation of Proceedings and the Imposition of Protective Measures

647. Insanity is one of the defences understood to exclude the culpability of an offender (see Article 31 § 1 CC). In the case of the insanity of a defendant confirmed by two officially appointed psychiatrists (see Article 202 § 1 CCP) he or she cannot be held criminally liable for an offence and the proceedings against such a defendant must be discontinued (Article 17 § 1 paragraph 2 CCP). In some cases, the prosecutor makes the decision to discontinue the proceedings, but when it is necessary to prevent the defendant from reoffending and when other measures as provided in law are not sufficient, the court may **discontinue the proceedings and impose protective measures** (*umorzyć postępowanie i zastosować środki zabezpieczające*) (see Article 324 CCP and Article 93b § 1 CC). Therefore, if the defendant is insane and there are grounds to impose protective measures, the prosecutor may file a motion with the court. Imposing protective measures, among which are a committal to addiction therapy and the placement of the defendant in a psychiatric institution, is the sole prerogative of the court.

648. The prosecutor has no discretion in deciding whether to discontinue the case or to file a motion for discontinuation of proceedings and the imposition of protective measures with the court. If the requirements to impose protective measures are met, the prosecutor must file a motion that resembles an indictment (see Articles 332, 333, 334 CCP in conjunction with Article 324 § 1a CCP). The court proceedings regarding the motion are presented in Chapter 3 – Court Proceedings and Remedies (see *infra*, paragraphs 746–750).

VII. Discontinuation of Preliminary Proceedings

649. Polish criminal procedure is bound by the principle of mandatory prosecution: offences must be investigated and prosecuted and the prosecutor does not hold any discretion over the matter. However, in some cases the investigation and prosecution is impossible and in these situations preliminary proceedings must be discontinued. Generally, Article 322 § 1 CCP provides that **if there are no grounds to file an indictment or motions with the court** (understood as motions provided in Articles 324, 335 § 1 and 336 CCP, i.e. motions to initiate the court proceedings as discussed above) **the preliminary proceedings must be discontinued**. The CCP gives some guidance as to what kind of circumstances exclude the possibility of sending a case to the court, with some additional regulations justifying the discontinuation of proceedings:

(1) existence of one of the so-called negative grounds for the conduct of criminal proceedings (*negatywne przesłanki procesowe*) provided in Article 17 § 1 CCP, which results in the immediate termination of criminal proceedings regardless of the stage (preliminary proceedings, trial, appellate proceedings) in which they occur; accordingly, the proceedings will end if:
   (1) the act imputed to the defendant has not been committed or there are insufficient grounds to suspect that it was committed (i.e., lack of evidence);
   (2) the act does not contain all necessary elements of a prohibited act or the law provides that even though the perpetrator has committed the act, he or she has not committed an offence (e.g., in the case of insanity, self-defence, etc.);
   (3) the degree of social harm presented by an act is negligible;

(4) the law states that for certain, strictly provided reasons the offender cannot be subject to a penalty (e.g., when a perpetrator voluntary ceases a prohibited act or prevents the consequences of the act – see Article 15 § 1 CC);
(5) the defendant is deceased;
(6) the statute of limitations has expired;
(7) criminal proceedings that concern the same act committed by the same person have arrived at a final judgment or, if previously instituted, are still pending;
(8) the offender does not fall under the jurisdiction of the Polish criminal courts;
(9) the accusation that commenced court proceedings has not been filed by an authorised person (usually by the prosecutor);
(10) permission from an authorised body to conduct an investigation against a person who holds immunity has not been filed (e.g., members of Parliament, judges, prosecutors, etc.) or the aggrieved party did not file a complaint to investigate a case in cases of offences investigated upon a complaint (see Article 12 CCP)
(11) other grounds excluding the possibility of investigating a case (e.g., amnesty or abolition);

(2) law enforcement authorities fail to identify the offender;
(3) it is established that an offence falls in the category of the offences prosecuted by private accusation and there is no public interest in investigating and prosecuting such an offence (Article 60 § 1 CCP).

650. Discontinuation of preliminary proceedings is a formal decision that must be issued by a competent body. Usually it is issued by the prosecutor or the police (Article 305 § 2 CCP). However, in the latter case, besides The police decides after inquiries in which charges are not presented to the suspect. In all other situations, the decision issued by the police must be confirmed by the prosecutor, who may overrule it (Article 325e §§ 1–2 CCP). The decision on the discontinuation of preliminary proceedings, beside elements typical for any decision (Article 94 § 1 CCP provides that every decision must at least identify the body and person issuing the decision, the date, the matter which the decision concerns, the solution with legal grounds and justification, unless otherwise provided by law), must include an exact description of an offence, its legal classification and grounds for discontinuation, usually one of the reasons from Article 17 § 1 CCP (Article 322 § 2 CCP). If preliminary proceedings were conducted against a person (i.e., after the suspect is officially charged) the decision on discontinuation should additionally contain information identifying the suspect (Article 322 § 3 CCP).

651. Beside the 'ordinary' discontinuation of preliminary proceedings, the decision to conclude proceedings and not to send the case to court may be also made under other specific circumstances:

(1) in the event of discontinuation of preliminary proceedings due to the absorption of an offence by conviction in other proceedings (*umorzenie absorpcyjne*) (Article 11 CCP);
(2) in the event of discontinuation of preliminary proceedings in the situation when a defendant has offered to redress the harm done (*umorzenie restytucyjne*) (Article 59a CC);
(3) in the event that preliminary proceedings are discontinued and the case recorded in the register of offences (*umorzenie rejestrowe*) (Article 325f CCP) (see *infra* paragraph 654).

It must be noted that the first two decisions may also be issued during court proceedings by the court, if any of their requirements have been met. However, the third one is only a form of concluding preliminary proceedings. They will be presented below accordingly.

652. The decision to discontinue preliminary proceedings due to the **absorption of an offence** by conviction in other proceedings against the same accused (Article 11 CCP) is seen as an exception from the principle of legality. In summary, a case might be discontinued if there is no purpose in holding proceedings against the defendant for a lesser offence (a misdemeanour punishable by a penalty of imprisonment for up to five years) in view of another penalty already imposed on that defendant for some other offence. The offence for which the defendant has already been sentenced should be of a graver manner and the penalty imposed for that offence would foreseeably most likely absorb the penalty that could be imposed for the offence in which the proceedings were discontinued. The interest of the aggrieved party must be taken into account. However, this does not mean that he or she may actually oppose such a decision. The prosecutor always makes the final decision. It is also possible to suspend preliminary proceedings pending the conclusion of other proceedings in which the penalty for the graver offence might be imposed (Article 11 § 3 CCP). The suspended proceedings should be discontinued or resumed within three months of the date at which the judgment concerning the other offence becomes final.

653. The decision to discontinue preliminary proceedings in the case of the **perpetrator remedying** the **harm** done by the offence (Article 59a CC) was introduced in 2015. It is another exception to the principle of legality, imposing on the prosecutor (or the court during court proceedings) an obligation to discontinue a case when the aggrieved party has reconciled with the perpetrator and is satisfied with the damages paid by the defendant. It is also considered a negotiated justice mechanism, since the discontinuation of proceedings demands that the aggrieved party and the suspect will achieve agreement how to compensate for the harm done by the offence.

Even though the grounds to prosecute an offence exist, the case must be discontinued if the aggrieved party submits a request to do so. It is possible only with regard to some misdemeanours (punishable by a penalty of imprisonment for up to three years and in the case of offences against property punishable by a penalty of imprisonment for up to five years and also offences prescribed in Article 157 § 1

CC) and only if the defendant was not previously sentenced for an intentional offence with the use of violence. The prosecutor has only limited discretion, since the law gives him the opportunity to continue preliminary proceedings and not comply with the aggrieved party's motion only if extraordinary circumstances exist justifying that the discontinuation of the case would be against the aims of imposing a penalty (Article 59a § 3 CC).

The only body that has the right to discontinue preliminary proceedings based on the above arguments is the prosecutor (Article 29b §§ 1–2 CCP) – the police have no discretion in the matter. The aggrieved party's request can also be filed with a court that will rule on the issue during court proceedings, but only if it is submitted before the **commencement of the evidentiary phase of the trial** (*otwarcie przewodu sądowego*).

654. Another specific form of discontinuation of preliminary proceedings is the **discontinuation of preliminary proceedings and the recording of a case in the register of offences** (Article 325f CCP). This is possible only in the case of preliminary proceedings conducted in the form of an inquiry (*dochodzenie*). It is the sole competence of the police without any prosecutorial involvement. If information acquired in the course of preliminary verification of an offence having been committed or in the course of an inquiry conducted for at least five days does not give sufficient grounds to uncover the offender in the course of further preliminary proceedings, the proceedings may be discontinued and the case may be entered into the register of offences (Article 325f § 1 CCP). This refers in general to situations when there is almost no prospect of finding a perpetrator, which usually happens in pickpocketing thefts, etc. The discontinuation of the case does not mean that the case is totally dropped. The criminal justice bodies are obliged, although in practice this is just a theoretical obligation, to conduct activities directed at revealing the perpetrator and in the case that he or she is discovered the inquiry may be reopened (Article 325f § 3 CCP).

655. All decisions on the discontinuation of preliminary proceedings can be subject to **judicial review** in the form of an interlocutory appeal (*zażalenie*). Those who are given the right to file an interlocutory appeal with a court (among others, the aggrieved party and the suspect, if identified, and also some of those who provided information about an offence having been committed listed in Article 306 § 1a CCP, e.g. state or local government institutions) must receive the decision. Other participants of preliminary proceedings, e.g. those who have provided information that an offence has been committed, other than those mentioned in Article 306 § 1a CCP, will be only notified that the case has been closed. Those who can appeal are are entitled to familiarise themselves with the dossier containing evidence gathered (Article 306 § 1b CCP). The rules on filing an interlocutory appeal will be discussed in Chapter 3 – Court Proceedings and Remedies (see *infra*, paragraphs 792–796).

656. Polish criminal procedure provides for a mechanism that allows an **aggrieved party to prosecute a case before a court even if the prosecutor has decided not to do so** (Article 55 and Article 330 CCP). If the prosecutor issued the decision to discontinue and the aggrieved party's interlocutory appeal was successful, the prosecutor must reopen preliminary proceedings. The court cannot force the prosecutor to prosecute a case, only to continue to conduct preliminary proceedings. If the prosecutor issues a second decision on the discontinuation, the aggrieved party cannot subject it again for judicial review and may only prosecute the case through so-called **subsidiary accusation** (*skarga subsydiarna*). This type of accusation should not be confused with a private accusation (*skarga prywatna*) for offences subject to a private prosecution, e.g. defamation or insult to a person. After two consecutive decisions on the discontinuation of proceedings, the aggrieved party must submit a subsidiary indictment (*subsydiarny akt oskarżenia*), in a form similar to the public indictment, prepared and signed by either an attorney or a legal counsel, within one month from receiving the second decision and also pay a fixed fee of 300 PLN (see Article 640 CCP and the Regulation of the Minister of Justice of 28 May 2003 on the lump sum equivalent of expenses incurred in cases involving a private prosecution (J.L. of 2003, No. 104, Item 980). If the court accepts the indictment, the dossier is sent to the court by the prosecutor and, if it is demanded by the aggrieved party, additional evidentiary procedures must be conducted by the police upon the court's request.

Besides **reopening preliminary proceedings** through overturning a decision on the discontinuation of preliminary proceedings with an interlocutory appeal, this may also happen **through a decision taken on the prosecutor's own initiative**. This may be the result of some new information on an offence being revealed, or when it is established that the discontinuation was based on wrong premises. Preliminary proceedings can be reopened at any time if they are not directed against a former suspect (Article 327 § 1 CCP). If preliminary proceedings are to be resumed against the same suspect, the decision must be issued by a prosecutor of a higher level (*prokurator nadrzędny*) than the prosecutor that issued or approved the decision on the discontinuation, and only if new facts or evidence have been revealed (Article 327 § 2 CCP). Under extraordinary circumstances the Prosecutor General (*Prokurator Generalny*) may annul a final and binding decision to discontinue preliminary proceedings against the same suspect party, if it is discovered that the decision was groundless (Article 328 § 1 CCP). However, after six months from the date on which the decision on discontinuation of preliminary proceedings becomes final, this annulment may be issued by the Prosecutor General only in favour of the suspect.

Chapter 3. Court Proceedings and Remedies

§1. Court Of The First Instance

I. Parties and Their Statutory Representatives

A. Public Prosecutor

657. In cases of offences prosecuted by public accusation, it is a public prosecutor *(oskarżyciel publiczny)* who is a party to the proceedings. In the overwhelming majority of cases, the role of a public prosecutor is performed by a prosecutor *(prokurator)* employed by the Prosecution Service. The Polish legal system contains no specific rules on which public prosecutor can argue a case in court. This means that, at least theoretically, a criminal case may be argued by any prosecutor, regardless of which branch of the Prosecution Service he or she is employed at.

658. Also, other authorised entities can act as public prosecutors in criminal courts. However, such situations are very rare in practice. Among these authorised entities are the following:

(1) the Trade Inspection Authority;
(2) the State Sanitary Inspection Authority;
(3) the Fiscal Office and Fiscal Audit Inspectors;
(4) the President of the Office of Electronic Communications;
(5) the Border Guard;
(6) the Forestry Guard;
(7) the State Hunting Guard.

Each of these bodies may prosecute strictly designated cases, acting under statutory authorisation. For example, the Border Guard may exercise such authority in cases that involve the illegal crossing of the border.

B. Subsidiary Prosecutor, Auxiliary Prosecutor, Private Prosecutor and Their Legal Counsels

659. Unlike in preliminary proceedings, in court proceedings an aggrieved person does not become a party by *ex lege*. However, before the evidentiary phase of a trial commences, an aggrieved person may submit a statement (in writing or verbally) informing the court that he or she intends to act as an **auxiliary prosecutor** (*oskarżyciel posiłkowy uboczny*). In this way, the aggrieved person assumes the rights of a party to the proceedings and retains this status even in a situation where the public prosecutor withdraws an indictment. In such an event, an aggrieved person who previously has not exercised the rights of a subsidiary prosecutor, may, within fourteen days from having been notified of the withdrawal of the indictment by the public prosecutor, declare that he or she will join the proceedings as an **subsidiary prosecutor** (*oskarżyciel posiłkowy subsydiarny*).

660. The adjudicating court may limit the number of auxiliary prosecutors if this is necessary for safeguarding the proper conduct of the proceedings. The court determines the number of auxiliary prosecutors and authorises the aggrieved persons' entry to the proceedings according to the order of submitted declarations.

Persons who cannot take part in proceedings may submit a written statement to the court within seven days from the date of the receipt of the court's decision to deny their entry to the proceedings.

661. In proceedings that involve offences prosecuted by public accusation, an aggrieved person may, in exceptional circumstances, perform the role of the prosecutor who submits an indictment to the court; in doing so, the aggrieved person assumes the status of 'a subsidiary prosecutor' *(oskarżyciel posiłkowy subsydiarny)*.

662. In proceedings that involve offences prosecuted by private accusation (see *infra*, paragraph 751–761), an aggrieved person, by submitting a private indictment or joining the proceedings initiated with an indictment filed by another aggrieved person, becomes a party to the proceedings known as the 'private prosecutor' *(oskarżyciel prywatny)*.

663. In the course of the proceedings a subsidiary prosecutor, auxiliary prosecutor and private prosecutor may be assisted by a legal counsel (*pełnomocnik*). A maximum of three such legal counsels may be appointed. An attorney or a legal advisor may act as a legal counsel. It is the prosecutor's discretionary decision whether or not to appoint a legal counsel. If a subsidiary, auxillairy or private prosecutor does not have a privately retained legal counsel, he or she may apply for the appointment of an ex officio (court-appointed) legal counsel. Such an application may be submitted irrespective of the prosecutor's financial situation. It is exclusively at the stage of preliminary proceedings that the appointment of an ex officio legal counsel depends on whether or not the aggrieved party is able to bear the costs of defence without prejudice to his or her necessary maintenance or to that of his or her family.

C. *The Defendant, Defence Lawyer and Statutory Representative*

664. The defendant (the accused) is a party to court proceedings. A person against whom a charge has been filed with a court, and also a person with respect to whom a public prosecutor has submitted a motion for the conditional discontinuation of proceedings, is considered the accused (Article 72 § 2 CCP).

665. In the course of court proceedings, the defendant may be assisted by a defence lawyer *(obrońca)*. The defendant may have no more than three defence lawyers at the same time. In principle, it is the defendant who selects a defence lawyer. An attorney or a legal advisor may act as a defence lawyer.

666. As a rule, the defendant has the right, not the obligation, to be assisted by a defence lawyer. However, in exceptional circumstances, the defendant is legally obliged to have a defence lawyer. This rule applies if:

(1) the defendant is under the age of 18;
(2) the defendant is deaf, mute or blind;
(3) there is a justified doubt as to whether the defendant's ability to comprehend the meaning of his or her actions or to control his behaviour was not, at the time of committing the offence, significantly reduced, or non-existent;
(4) there is a reasonable doubt as to whether the defendant's mental state allows him or her to participate in the proceedings or conduct a defence in an independent and reasonable manner;
(5) the court considers that the assistance of a defence lawyer is necessary due to circumstances impeding the defence (i.e., the complexity of the case, the defendant's inability to handle his or her own affairs).

Moreover, the defendant must have a defence lawyer in proceedings before a regional court when charged with a felony.

If the defendant has not retained a defence lawyer of his or her choosing, an ex officio defence lawyer will be appointed.

667. Under Article 80a CCP, a provision introduced in order to implement the principle of equality of arms in criminal court proceedings, the defendant has the right to apply for the appointment of an ex officio defence lawyer, who will represent the defendant in the course of the entire proceedings or will be appointed to perform a particular procedural act (such as the filing of an appeal against the first instance court's judgment). The defendant is advised of this right, and also of the obligation to pay the ex officio defence lawyer's costs, which may be imposed on the defendant, depending on the outcome of the proceedings.

668. In a situation when a defendant is a juvenile (a person under the age of 17) or an incapacitated person, a statutory representative or a person under whose care the defendant remains can perform any action that serves the interests of the defendant (e.g., file an appellate measure, make an evidentiary motion or appoint a defence lawyer).

II. Bringing a Case to Court and Preparations for Its Adjudication

669. In cases of offences prosecuted by public accusation, if there are sufficient grounds for doing so, a public prosecutor (or other authorised body) brings the case to court after the conclusion of preliminary proceedings. As a rule, a public prosecutor has four options for initiating the ordinary type of court proceedings. This can be done by submitting:

(1) a stand-alone motion to convict a defendant without a trial (Article 335 § 1 CCP);

(2) an indictment with a motion to convict a defendant without a trial (Article 335 § 2 CCP);
(3) a motion for the conditional discontinuation of proceedings;
(4) an indictment.

670. The first two options are linked with a preceding agreement, made between the public prosecutor and the suspect, in respect of the judgment to be delivered in a criminal case (a consensual manner of concluding criminal proceedings). The third option enables the quick conclusion of the case without evidentiary proceedings in a situation where a probative measure (conditional discontinuation of proceedings) can be applied. On the contrary, the submission of an indictment in principle initiates full proceedings in a trial. However, if the court so decides, it can conduct simplified proceedings that involve the issuance of a penal order *(tryb nakazowy).*

671. Apart from the above modes of initiation of court proceedings, the following types of motions can be submitted to court:

(1) A motion for the examination of the case in the accelerated mode (see *infra*, paragraphs 736–745).
(2) A motion for the discontinuation of proceedings and application of a protective measure (see *supra*, paragraphs 647–648).

672. Exceptionally, court proceedings may be initiated by an aggrieved person (or a person exercising the aggrieved person's rights, for instance the next of kin), who files what is known as a 'subsidiary indictment' (Articles 55 and 330 CCP). In such a case the matter is sent to trial and requires the conduct of evidentiary proceedings.

673. Most frequently, judicial proceedings in criminal cases are instigated by the filing of an indictment. In 2014 courts received 297,836 cases, including:

(1) 282,347 cases launched upon indictment (in 131,936 cases, the indictment was accompanied by a motion to convict a defendant without a trial, submitted in respect of all defendants);
(2) 14,129 cases in which a motion for the conditional discontinuation of proceedings was filed;
(3) 1,111 cases in which a motion for the discontinuation of the proceedings and application of a protective measure was filed;
(4) 249 cases in which a motion for hearing a case in accelerated proceedings was filed.

674. After an indictment (or any of the above motions) is filed with a court, the President of the court (head of a division) reviews it from a formal standpoint. The formal review includes the verification of whether the formal requirements set for a given pleading has been complied with and whether the party filing an indictment (a motion) has discharged other duties related to the submission of a case to a court (e.g., the public prosecutor's obligation to deliver selected documents and evidence from the preliminary proceedings or the final discovery of documents and evidence from the preliminary proceedings, if a proper motion has been filed). If any of the above requirements is not satisfied, an indictment (a motion) is returned to the prosecutor for supplementation. The prosecutor should remedy formal defects within seven days from having been notified to do so. If the obligation to effect the final discovery of documents and evidence from the preliminary proceedings has not been performed, the court sets a time limit for the completion of this action.

675. If the indictment or motion submitted to the court satisfies formal requirements, then, depending on the circumstances, the case is either sent to trial for the full proceedings to be conducted, or allocated to a hearing, which allows for the avoidance of full proceedings and a quick conclusion of the case. In all situations where a case is allocated to a hearing, no evidentiary proceedings are conducted before the court. The court adjudicating a case at a hearing makes its decision on the basis of the evidence collected during preliminary proceedings. Theoretically, the scenario in which a case is sent to trial is a model and typical solution. In practice, however, the majority of criminal cases (approx. 65%) are concluded without the conduct of full proceedings.

III. Simplified Forms of Case Processing Before First Instance Courts

A. Conviction Without Trial

676. The simplified modes of the processing of criminal cases include, first of all, the so-called consensual ways to conclude criminal proceedings: these are cases in which the parties come to an agreement as to the manner of resolving the case, as approved by the court.

677. The first type of plea bargaining agreement in the Polish criminal process is the **conviction without trial**, regulated by Article 335 §§ 1–2 CCP. This measure was introduced by the 1997 Code of Criminal Procedure. Since then, its applicability has been gradually extended. The essence of the measure adopted in Article 335 CCP is the enabling of the conclusion of an agreement between a suspect (suspect's defence lawyer) and law enforcement authorities or a prosecutor, at the stage of preliminary proceedings.

The agreement concerns the penalties handed down for offences committed and other measures provided in the Criminal Code, including penal measures, as well as rulings issued in respect of the costs of the proceedings. The concluded agreement may relate to any case that involves a misdemeanour. The conclusion of such an agreement is prohibited only in cases that concern a felony.

678. The Polish Code of Criminal Procedure does not provide for any special rules concerning the mitigation of penal sanctions imposed as part of plea bargaining agreements. Everything therefore depends on the arrangements made in a given case. As a rule, it is possible to arrive at a compromise, whose boundaries are determined by the statutory limits of a given penalty. However, Article 60a CCP allows the application of extraordinary mitigation of a penalty (hence, imposition of a penalty below the statutory minimum or a more lenient type of penalty). The provision also gives the court the option to refrain from the imposition of a penalty and to instead order only a penal measure, forfeiture or a compensatory measure, if the misdemeanour attributed to the defendant carries a penalty of not more than five years of imprisonment. In practice, however, in the majority of cases the imposed penalties or other penal measures of are not subject to such extensive mitigation.

679. A conviction under Article 335 CCP can be secured in two ways. The first option is to **submit a stand-alone motion to convict a defendant without a trial under Article 335 § 1 CCP**. A prosecutor can submit that motion if the following conditions are met:

(1) the defendant admits guilt in the course of the preliminary proceedings;
(2) the prosecutor decides that the circumstances of the case relevant to the admission of guilt raise no doubts;
(3) and it is considered that the defendant's attitude suggests that the objects of the proceedings will be achieved.

Upon receiving a case, the court reviews the prosecutor's assessment of the above circumstances of the case and decides whether or not the prosecutor's motion to convict a defendant without a trial had merits. Furthermore, the following requirements have to be satisfied so that a conviction can be obtained:

(1) the case must involve a misdemeanour; and
(2) the aggrieved person, duly notified of the date of the hearing on the conviction without trial, does not oppose such a conviction (Article 343 § 2 CCP).

Obviously, the court also assesses whether the agreed penalty and other measures of penal response are just and deserve acceptance.

680. The following persons are allowed to take part in a hearing of a court that rules on a motion to convict a defendant without a trial: a professional prosecutor or another public prosecutor, the defendant and his or her defence lawyer, and the aggrieved person and his or her legal representative.

During the hearing, the motion can be amended. This can be done on the aggrieved person's initiative or even on the court's initiative. In any case, the new version of the motion must be approved by the defendant and the public prosecutor.

If the court decides that a motion to convict a defendant without a trial can be accepted, it issues the conviction in accordance with the agreed terms. Conversely, if the motion is denied, the court returns the case to the prosecutor.

681. The second option of initiating court proceedings with the purpose of securing the defendant's conviction without trial is **the submission of an indictment with an appended motion to convict a defendant without a trial** (Article 335 §

2 CCP). In this event, a case is also examined during a hearing. Before a conviction can be secured, the court must check whether the following conditions are satisfied:

(1) the case involves a misdemeanour;
(2) an agreement on the length of penalty and other measures described in the Criminal Code and, if applicable, the cost of the process, have been validly concluded between the suspect and the body that conducts or supervises the preliminary proceedings; the agreement should take into account the legally protected interests of the aggrieved person;
(3) the circumstances of the commission of the offence and the defendant's guilt raise no doubts, and that the explanations of the defendant do not contradict the established facts of the case;
(4) the aggrieved person, duly notified of the date of the hearing on the conviction without trial, does not oppose the conviction without trial (Article 343 § 2 CCP).

Clearly, the court also assesses whether the agreed penalty and other measures of penal response are just and whether the objects of the proceedings will be achieved.

682. The court's decision-making in respect of an indictment with a motion to convict a defendant without a trial is governed by the same rules as those applicable to a stand-alone motion to convict a defendant without a trial submitted under Article 335 § 1 CCP. The only difference is that if the court denies a motion submitted together with an indictment, the motion is not returned to the prosecutor, and the case goes to trial and is examined under the general rules.

683. Notably, plea bargaining agreements in Poland cannot be based on the findings of fact that contradict reality; parties to such agreements may not determine a legal classification that does not reflect the findings of fact made in the case, an agreement cannot reduce the number of charges pursued against the defendant or make arrangements concerning a resolution of matters other than the type and length (or value) of the imposed penalty, measures provided under the Criminal Code or awards of costs.

684. The table below presents the frequency of the practical application of the institution under Article 335 CCP.

Year	*Convictions*	*Convictions under Article 335 CCP*
2015	286,472	115,907
2014	322,703	123,033
2013	374,691	150,810
2012	413,263	179,501

B. Voluntary Assumption of Criminal Liability

685. The other consensual procedure in the Polish criminal process is the **voluntary assumption of criminal liability** *(dobrowolne poddanie się odpowiedzialności karnej)*. The difference between the voluntary assumption and conviction without trial is that in the case of the former it is the defendant (and not the prosecutor) who submits the relevant motion. If the defendant files such a motion after the case is submitted to court, the motion can be examined at a hearing (as opposed to a trial). This situation will be discussed in more detail below.

686. As a rule, the voluntary assumption of criminal liability is permissible in all cases, including in felony cases. However, if the motion to assume criminal liability is filed in a felony case, the Code of Criminal Proceedings provides that it must be examined only in a trial.

687. In the event that a motion for the voluntary assumption of criminal liability is filed, a case will be allocated to a hearing if the motion is filed in a case that involves a misdemeanour, and the motion is filed before the defendant is served with notice of a trial date.

688. A conviction can be obtained at a hearing if:

(1) it is established that the circumstances in which the offence was committed raise no doubts;
(2) it is established that the defendant's attitude suggests that the objects of the proceedings will be achieved;
(3) the prosecutor and the aggrieved person, duly notified of the date of the hearing on the conviction without trial, do not object to conviction.

689. If the above conditions are met, the court enters a conviction that incorporates the proposal made by the defendant. Similar to a conviction without trial, the defendant's proposal can be amended in the course of a hearing. Also, the length (value) of the penalty or other measures is determined by the limit of a statutory penalty set forth in acts of criminal law and Article 60a CCP. If any of the conditions of the voluntary assumption of criminal liability are not met, the court issues a decision to deny the motion and refers the case to trial.

690. The table below presents the frequency of the practical application of the institution under Article 387 CCP.

Year	*Convictions*	*Convictions under Article 387 CCP*
2015	286,472	24,708
2014	322,703	28,158

2013	374,691	30,880
2012	413,263	33,976

C. Conditional Discontinuation of Proceedings

691. The President of the court refers the case to a hearing if there is a need to consider whether or not the proceedings should be conditionally discontinued (Article 339 § 1 paragraph 2 CCP). A case may thus be referred to a hearing if a prosecutor submits a motion for the conditional discontinuation of proceedings or an indictment and the President of the court decides that there is the need to consider the conditional discontinuation of proceedings in the case. At a hearing, the court determines whether the conditions described in Article 66 §§ 1–2 CC appear in a given case and it also decides if conditional discontinuation of the proceedings will serve the purpose of an appropriate response to offence. If these conditions are satisfied, the court conditionally discontinues the proceedings. The defendant has the right to oppose the hearing of the case in an accelerated mode and may request that the proceedings be conducted in full. In such an event, the case is referred to trial. A case will also go to trial if the court considers that there are no grounds for conditional discontinuation of the proceedings. In these circumstances, a prosecutor's motion for conditional discontinuation of the proceedings replaces an indictment.

692. The prosecutor, the defendant and his or her defence lawyer, and the aggrieved person and his or her legal counsel are allowed to take part in a hearing on the conditional discontinuation of proceedings.

693. The table below presents the frequency of the practical application of conditional discontinuation of criminal proceedings.

Year	*Convictions*	*Proceedings conditionally discontinued*
2015	286,472	25,376
2014	322,703	26,161
2013	374,691	28,485
2012	413,263	28,938

D. Penal Order Proceedings

694. If an indictment is filed with a court, the case normally goes to trial. However, the Code of Criminal Procedure introduces a simplified mode of processing a case. It is one of the special modes of the criminal process, known as the 'penal order procedure' *(tryb nakazowy)*. After a case is filed with a court, the President of the court (or head of a criminal division) is authorised, under Article 339 § 3 paragraph 7 CCP, to refer the case to a hearing for the purpose of issuing a penal order. The penal order procedure is a significantly simplified mode of criminal adjudication. The penal order is issued at a hearing held in camera, without the parties present. It is based on the evidence collected in the preliminary proceedings, without any evidence being examined before the court.

695. In accordance with Article 500 CCP, the penal order procedure may be applied in cases that cumulatively satisfy the following conditions:

(1) an inquiry must have been conducted;
(2) in the light of the evidence collected in the preliminary proceedings the circumstances of the commission of the offence and the defendant's guilt raise no doubts;
(3) holding a trial is not necessary.

696. By way of penal order, the court may impose only a penalty of restriction of liberty (a community sentence) or a fine to the amount of up to 100 daily rates or PLN 200,000. This means that under the penal order procedure it is impossible to impose the penalty of imprisonment. The court may impose a penal measure in the circumstances described in a statute. Alternatively, the court may decide to impose only a penal measure, provided that provisions of substantive criminal law so permit.

697. The penal order procedure may not be applied:

(1) in cases brought by private accusation; or
(2) if the prerequisites of mandatory defence under Article 79 § 1 CCP are satisfied (the defendant is under the age of 18, the defendant is deaf, mute or blind; or if there is a reasonable doubt as to whether the defendant's capacity to understand the meaning of the act or direct their conduct was non-existent or significantly limited at the moment when the act was committed; or in cases where there is a reasonable doubt as to whether the defendant's mental state allows him or her to participate in the proceedings or conduct a defence in an independent and reasonable manner).

698. A penal order may not be reasoned. A copy of a penal order is served, together with a copy of the indictment, on the prosecutor, defendant and the defence lawyer.

699. The table below presents the frequency of the practical application of penal order proceedings.

Year	Convictions	Penal orders
2015	322,703	30,499
2014	322,703	38,164
2013	374,691	44,005
2012	413,263	41,639

III. Trial Before the First Instance Court

A. *Preparation for a Trial*

700. If a case cannot be resolved in any of the simplified modes of procedure, the President of the court or a court referendary, having reviewed the indictment from the formal standpoint, orders the delivery of a copy of the indictment to the defendant. The defendant also receives notice that he or she may file evidentiary motions within seven days from the date the indictment has been served on him or her. The defendant has absolute discretion whether or not to file such motions. If the defendant does not exercise this right, he or she will be able to do so at further stages of the court case. The defendant has the right to submit a written reply to the indictment, which guarantees that the proceedings are adversarial in nature at the initial stage of the examination of the case. The defendant is also advised of the right to submit a motion requesting the prosecutor to supplement the materials of the preliminary proceedings attached to the indictment with specific documents contained in the dossier of these proceedings, provided that this is relevant to the interests of the defendant (Article 381 § 2 CCP). This is to ensure the equality of arms between the parties and to prevent the inaccurate selection of evidence by the prosecutor.

701. A trial is sometimes preceded by a so-called status conference *(posiedzenie przygotowawcze),* regulated in Article 349 CCP. This article stipulates that the President of the court must immediately appoint a judge (or judges) and refer the case to a hearing. A status conference is:

(1) obligatory, if the expected scope of evidentiary proceedings justifies the assumption that at least five different trial dates will need to be set in the case;
(2) optional, if the President of the court decides that having a status conference may facilitate the proceedings due to the complex nature of the case or for other material reasons.

702. In setting the date of a status conference, the President of the court requests a public prosecutor, legal counsels and defence lawyers to submit written proposals for how the main trial should be conducted and managed, including information on the order of the presentation of evidence during the trial, within seven days of the delivery of the relevant notice.

A public prosecutor, defence lawyers and legal counsels may participate in a status conference. At the status conference, the court arranges the dates and the course of the trial.

B. Public Character of a Trial

703. As a rule, a trial is open to the public. This rule does not apply, obviously, to the court's deliberations and voting on the sentence. It is possible to conduct a trial closed to the public, for example because of an interest of a participant in the proceedings or a need to safeguard legally protected secrets, but even then the judgment is pronounced publicly.

704. Members of the public attending a trial must be adults (at least 18 years old) and unarmed (Article 356 § 1 CCP). In justified circumstances, the presiding judge may allow minors or armed individuals (e.g., police officers). Due to the need to respect the dignity of the trial and the court as a state institution, persons who are in a state that is contrary to the dignity of the court may not be permitted to attend a trial. This prohibition covers, in particular, persons who are intoxicated or inappropriately dressed.

705. As regards members of the mass media, the provisions of the Code of Criminal Procedure do not establish any restrictions on note-taking during a trial. Such leeway does not exist in the case of sound and video recording. Article 357 CCP grants a court the power to issue a relevant permission, provided that the recording of the trial serves a justified social interest, it will not hinder the conduct of the trial and there is no material interest of a participant in the proceedings that would oppose the recording of the trial. A court may also determine the conditions applicable to the recording of a trial (e.g., a limit on the number of cameras present in the courtroom).

706. A party can also record the conduct of a trial. If the court so approves, a party may record the conduct of a trial with a sound recording device only, unless this would adversely affect the accuracy of the proceedings.

707. If a trial is closed to the public, then – apart from the interested parties – only so-called trustworthy persons *(osoby godne zaufania)* may attend the trial (Article 361 § 1 CCP). The right to appoint such persons may be exercised only by the public prosecutor, subsidiary and auxiliary prosecutor and the defendant. If there are at least three prosecutors or defendants, each of them may request that one person be left in the courtroom. The court has no power to interfere with the appointment of the persons allowed to stay in the courtroom, unless this would lead to a violation of the Code of Criminal Procedure, for instance if a witness expected to testify in the case would be left in the courtroom.

C. The Adversarial Character of a Trial

708. The degree of the court's involvement in the conduct of proceedings, and in particular in evidentiary proceedings, is crucial. The law preceding the criminal process reform of 1 July 2015, (Article 167 CCP) gave the court unlimited discretion to examine evidence ex officio, and the presiding judge should ensure that all circumstances of vital significance to the case are explained, including, whenever possible, those favouring the commission of the offence (Article 366 § 1 CCP). Trial before a first instance court was rather inquisitorial. The court was explicitly obliged to comprehensively explain the circumstances of a given case. Therefore, although the burden of proof was placed on the prosecutor, it was the presiding judge who – in accordance with the principle of material truth adopted in the criminal process (Article 2 § 2 CCP) – had to explain these circumstances that were significant for the case and had not been sufficiently explained in the course of evidentiary proceedings initiated by the parties. As was accepted by case law, '*the obligation under Article 366 § 1 CCP, imposed on the judge presiding over a trial, is not merely the technical management of the trial which ensures its expeditious conduct, but also the accompanying necessity to pay attention to the explanation of all material circumstances of the case, a necessity which is realised not only by the examination of the evidence submitted by the parties, but also as a consequence of taking necessary initiative in examining the evidence*'.[19]

709. On 1 July 2015, the wording of the Code's Articles 366 § 1 and 167 § 1 was modified. The presiding judge is not obliged to pay attention to the explanation of all material circumstances of a given case and the court's ability to examine evidence ex officio has been limited (Article 167 § 1 CCP). These amendments were expected to make the criminal process more adversarial. However, the adopted model of court proceedings is not purely adversarial, but a mixed one, as the court retained the right to interfere with the evidentiary proceedings. Still, this right is significantly limited in scope. The court gets involved in the conduct of the proceedings only when such involvement is absolutely necessary for the purpose of providing a just sentence.

D. Participation of Parties, Defence Lawyers and Legal Counsels in a Trial

710. The defendant is **entitled** to participate in a trial. This significant change was introduced as from 1 July 2015; before that date the defendant's presence at a trial was mandatory. It has been argued that '*the introduced change is a consequence of the extension of the adversarial nature of court proceedings, an expression of a move away from an overly paternalistic approach to the defendant, thus making one of the elements of the right to defence more in line with reality. The elimination of the defendant's absolute obligation to be present at a trial and the*

19. Judgment of the Court of Appeal of Gdańsk of 22.01.2014, case no. II AKa 465/13, LEX no. 1430708.

associated duties imposed on the court is also designed to negate yet another source of the excessive length of court proceedings'.[20]

711. If a defendant is incarcerated, then upon being served a summons setting a trial date, he or she must be advised of the right to file a motion for being brought to trial. Such a motion should be submitted within seven days of the date of delivery of the notice or summons. Requests submitted after this deadline may be considered, provided that this will not cause the necessity to adjourn the trial.

712. Exceptionally, a defendant's presence at a trial is mandatory. This is the case when:

(1) the presiding judge or the court considers the defendant's presence (during the whole trial or a part of the trial) necessary (second sentence of Article 374 § 1 CCP);
(2) during the procedures mentioned in Articles 385 and 386 CCP, namely at the launch of the evidentiary phase of a trial and during the first examination of the accused, if the case involves a felony(Article 374 § 1a CCP).

713. Even if the defendant's presence is mandatory it is possible to conduct proceedings in his or her absence – if the defendant behaves in a way intended to prevent the conduct of the case in court, for instance by preventing himself or herself from being brought to trial or by rendering himself or herself unable to take part in the trial (Articles 376–377 CCP).

714. The presence of a defendant's lawyer during a trial largely depends on the nature of defence. Grounds for mandatory defence can appear and make a defence lawyer's presence mandatory. A defence lawyer is also obliged to be present at a trial if he or she has been appointed ex officio at the request of the defendant under Article 80a § 1 CCP. In situations other than those mentioned above, a defence lawyer's failure to appear does not have to stop the conduct of a trial. In such a case, the trial will be conducted if the defendant gives his or her consent (Article 117a § 1 CCP).

715. In cases of offences prosecuted by public accusation, the prosecutor's participation in the trial before a first instance court is mandatory. The provisions of the Code of Criminal Procedure do not establish the requirement of the mandatory presence of an auxiliary prosecutor or a subsidiary prosecutor at a trial. Such prosecutors may thus take part in a trial if they so decide. Their presence is desired in view of the adversarial nature of the proceedings. The same is true in respect of a subsidiary prosecutor's legal counsel.

716. An aggrieved person who has not yet assumed the rights of a party (and become a subsidiary or auxiliary prosecutor) may also participate in a trial before a

20. Sejm Record No. 870, statement of reasons, p 83.

first instance court. However, he or she must remain passive in the courtroom. The aggrieved person is notified of the place and date of a main trial.

It should nevertheless be noted that an aggrieved person who has not assumed the rights of a party in court proceedings has important rights that he or she can exercise during a trial. These rights include:

(1) the ability to submit at a main trial, before the end of the evidentiary phase of a trial, a motion for the adjudication of the obligation to redress the loss caused by the perpetrator (Article 49a CCP), and the
(2) ability to oppose a defendant's voluntary assumption of criminal liability at the trial (Article 387 § 2 CCP).

E. The Course of a Main Trial

717. A **main trial** *(rozprawa główna)* is conducted orally and begins with the calling of the case *(wywołanie sprawy)*. After the persons summoned and authorised to take part in the trial enter the courtroom, the presiding judge checks the attendance and makes sure there are no impediments that prevent the trial from proceeding. After this, the court commences the **evidentiary phase of the main trial** (*przewód sądowy*). The evidentiary phase of a trial is the fundamental part of a trial before the first instance court; evidentiary proceedings are conducted during this phase.

718. **The evidentiary phase of a trial starts with a concise presentation of charges by the prosecutor.** If a reply to the indictment has been submitted, the presiding judge describes its content.

719. The charges are laid by the prosecution, and then – if the defendant takes part in the main trial – the presiding judge advises the defendant of his or her basic procedural rights and then asks whether he or she pleads guilty and wants to offer explanations (testify). If the defendant wants to offer explanations or answer questions, he or she is heard.

720. Subsequently, the court examines the evidence put forward by the parties; also, if a statute so provides, evidence is examined ex officio (see *infra*, paragraphs 916–917).

721. As a rule, evidence in support of the prosecution's charges should, if possible, be presented and examined before the evidence of the defence, as the burden of proof is on the prosecutor. If a person gives testimony, the party presenting a piece of evidence asks this person questions first (Article 370 § 2 CCP). Then, the questions are asked by other participants in the trial, in the order established by Article 370 § 1 CCP: the public prosecutor, subsidiary prosecutor, auxiliary prosecutor, legal counsel of the subsidiary or auxiliary prosecutor, expert witness, defence lawyer, the accused and members of the adjudicating panel. If the court examines evidence ex officio, the members of the adjudicating panel are first to ask questions.

722. Either party to a trial has the opportunity to comment on evidentiary motions submitted by the opposing party. A party's evidentiary motion that is opposed by the other party is considered not solely by the presiding judge, but by the full adjudicating panel (Article 368 CCP).

723. The evidentiary proceedings before a first instance court are not subject to any passage-of-time bar to evidence. It its thus possible to file evidentiary motions during a trial. Such motions are governed by the general rules applicable to evidentiary motions (Articles 169–170 CCP). It is worth noting in this context that Article 170 § 1 paragraph 5 CCP provides that an evidentiary motion may be denied if it is clearly submitted for the purpose of extending the length of the proceedings. However, this basis for denial is very rarely invoked.

724. Since the principle of direct examination of evidence is of crucial importance to the criminal process, evidence, as a rule, should be presented and examined at a trial (e.g., by way of conducting a physical inspection of an item or hearing the testimony of a witness). However, the Code of Criminal Procedure gives the court extensive authority to order – during a trial – the reading out of records of evidentiary procedures carried out as part of preliminary proceedings or other proceedings (such as transcripts of witness testimonies). In principle, a party reads out the parts of these records that are material for the resolution of the case (e.g., if a witness' testimony given at the trial differs from that given in the preliminary proceedings).

After passages of the records are disclosed at the trial, the court incorporates the relevant record to the dossier of the case, making a note of the portion of a given record that has been read out (Article 391 § 1d CCP). As explained, after the conclusion of preliminary proceedings, the records (transcripts) of witness testimonies are sent to the court, albeit in a separate folder, and must be read out at the trial in order to become a basis for the judgment issued in the case.

725. It is also possible to read out during the trial any private documents created outside the criminal proceedings, in particular – statements, publications, letters or memos. Audio and video recordings can be played in court.

726. If the need arises, a trial can be put on hold by way of a recess (for a maximum period of thirty-five days) or adjourned (if a recess is not sufficient). After a recess, the trial is resumed and continued from the point immediately before the recess, whereas an adjournment results in the resumption of the trial from scratch.

727. The court adjudicating a case is bound by the scope of the charges laid down in the indictment. Exceptionally, it is possible to also jointly hear another case involving a prohibited act other than that charged in the indictment. This can be done provided that:

(1) new circumstances have appeared during the trial;
(2) the defendant has agreed to it;
(3) it is not necessary to conduct preliminary proceedings in this respect.

728. Having examined evidence admitted in a case, the presiding judge asks the parties if they are applying for *the supplementation of evidentiary proceedings* (admission of additional evidence). If the answer is negative, the judge issues an order to close the evidentiary phase of the trial.

729. **After the conclusion of the evidentiary phase of a trial,** the presiding judge allows the public prosecutor, subsidiary prosecutor, auxiliary prosecutor, defendant's defence lawyer and defendant to present **closing arguments** *(głos końcowy)*. If the counsels of parties other than the defendant take part in the case, they are allowed to present their arguments as well (each counsel speaks before the party he or she represents). After the closing arguments, the prosecutor is allowed to present a rebuttal argument; this is known as the right to reply *(prawo do repliki)*. However, in this case, the defence lawyer and defendant should also be given an opportunity to speak at the end.

730. Having heard the closing (and rebuttal) arguments of the parties, which present a kind of a summary of their case, the court immediately commences **deliberations** (Article 408 CCP). However, closing arguments of the parties may result in the adjudicating panel's contention that certain aspects of the case require additional explanation. In order to address such a possibility, the court can resume the evidentiary phase of a trial or allow the parties to present additional closing arguments (Article 409 CCP).

Deliberations and voting are strictly confidential, this obligation of secrecy cannot be waived (Article 108 § 1 CCP). The voting is held separately on the guilt and legal classification of an act, the penalty, penal measures, forfeiture, compensatory measures or the remaining issues. The case must be decided by a majority of votes. However, since the majority cannot always be attained, the Code of Criminal Procedure establishes the rules of the creation of what is known as the 'artificial majority' (*sztuczna większość*). If the votes are divided in such a way that no majority can be reached, the vote that is the least advantageous for the defendant is joined with the second least advantageous one, this procedure is repeated until a majority is obtained. If a professional or lay judge votes against holding the defendant guilty, he or she may abstain from voting on further issues, and his or her vote is joined with the vote that is the most favourable for the defendant.

731. After the conclusion of voting **a judgment is made.** The judgment is signed by all members of the adjudicating panel, also those who were outvoted.

The rules of criminal procedure provide for the option of entering **a dissenting opinion**. It is made together with the ruling and designated in what part and in what direction the dissenting judge opposes the issued ruling. A dissenting opinion can also comment only on the justification given to the ruling. In such a case, the opinion is communicated when the justification (*uzasadnienie* – sometimes referred to as the 'statement of reasons') is signed. In judicial practice, dissenting opinions are rare.

If a case is complex or another important reason appears, the court may delay issuing a judgment for a period of up to fourteen days.

732. After a judgment is signed, the presiding judge **pronounces it publicly**. When a judgment is pronounced, all those present, with the exception of the members of the court, should be standing (Article 418 § 1 CCP). The entry of a dissenting opinion is made public, and if the dissenting judge so agrees, his or her name is also made public.

After the judgment is pronounced, the presiding judge or a member of the adjudicating panel orally provides the key reasons for the judgment. Upon completion of these formalities, the participants in the proceedings are advised of their right to submit an appellate measure, of the time limit for this and the manner in which it should be submitted, or informed that the ruling is unappealable. The giving of this advice concludes the trial before a first instance court.

F. Shortening of Proceedings at a Main Trial

733. Provisions of the Code of Criminal Procedure provide a number of options to simplify proceedings at a trial. The first such option (Article 387 CCP) is embedded in one of the consensual procedures, namely the **voluntary assumption of criminal liability** (see *supra*, paragraphs 685–690). In each criminal case (involving a felony or a misdemeanour) the defendant can be convicted and sentenced to a specific penalty or a penal measure, or issued a forfeiture order or an order of a compensatory measure, and also can become subject to an arrangement made in respect of the costs of the proceedings without the conduct of evidentiary proceedings. However, this may happen only if the following conditions are satisfied:

(1) the defendant must submit the relevant motion before the end of the first questioning of all defendants at the main trial;
(2) the circumstances of the commission of the offence and the defendant's guilt raise no doubts;
(3) the objects of the proceedings must be accomplished despite the fact that a full trial is not conducted; and
(4) neither the prosecutor nor the aggrieved person, duly advised of the trial date and the defendant's right to submit such a motion, objects to the motion.

734. If the defendant so agrees (and the prosecutor and aggrieved person make no objection), the defendant's motion can be amended if its original version raises objections from the adjudicating panel. As a rule, a court imposes a penalty within the limits of the substantive criminal law. However, in admitting a motion from the defendant, a court may apply the extraordinary mitigation of a penalty, irrespectively of the grounds laid out in Article 60 §§ 1–4 CC (Article 60a CC). In felony cases the extraordinary mitigation of a penalty may be applied only where a motion has been filed prior to the delivery of notice of the trial date to the defendant. The latter solution is to favour those perpetrators who decide to cooperate with law enforcement authorities at an early stage of proceedings, thereby conserving the efforts and resources of the justice system, which would otherwise be used in bringing them to justice.

735. To accelerate and simplify criminal proceedings, **the court may, with the consent of the parties present, conduct evidentiary proceedings only partially**, provided that the explanations given by the accused who pleads guilty raise no doubts (Article 388 CCP).

IV. Accelerated Procedure

736. The accelerated procedure is the other special mode of conducting criminal proceedings (the first one is the penal order procedure). First introduced in 2006, it was intended to remedy the excessive length of criminal cases. Together with the simultaneously implemented provisions that established more restrictive rules governing the liability for misdemeanours involving antisocial behaviour, this procedure was designed to strengthen the preventive value of applicable regulations of the criminal law by ensuring that justice is served quickly and effectively. The changes were introduced amid much controversy, both political and purely legal in nature. This was connected, in part, to the negative historical connotations of the accelerated procedure that operated in the People's Republic of Poland, but also with the discussion about the actual need for an accelerated procedure and the cost of its introduction. Indeed, in the course of the lawmaking process in Parliament, the argument was made that this procedure does not allow to achieve the desired goals.

The proceedings conducted at a trial under the accelerated procedure do not materially differ from the standard proceedings.

737. The sponsors of the amendment forecasted that the accelerated procedure would be used in approximately 150,000 cases annually. Reality quickly showed these expectations were excessive. In 2007 the courts received 37,044 cases which included a motion for hearing the case in accelerated procedure. In 2008, the figure decreased to 8,097. For 2009 this number was 1,572, in 2010 it was 450, 2011 – 255, 2012 – 226, 2013 – 152, 2014 – 292, and 2015 – 218. The numbers show that from the practical perspective the accelerated procedure has failed to accelerate the administration of criminal justice.

738. The accelerated procedure can be launched provided that a number of certain unique positive conditions are met and several negative conditions are excluded.

739. The following types of cases can be heard under the accelerated procedure:

(1) cases in which preliminary proceedings were conducted in the form of an inquiry;
(2) cases of offences prosecuted by private accusation, if such offences involve antisocial behaviour *(przestępstwa o charakterze chuligańskim).*

In both situations, the defendant must be apprehended in the act of committing an offence or immediately afterwards, arrested within 48 hours and brought by the police to the custody of the court, together with a motion to hear the case under the accelerated procedure.

740. Article 517b § 3 CCP allows a waiver of the perpetrator's arrest and his or her forced appearance before the court, or the release of the arrested person on bail pending their appearance in court, which must take place within a maximum of 72 hours from the moment when the perpetrator was arrested or handed over to the police.

Each time an arrest is waived or the perpetrator is released from custody, a motion to hear the case must be submitted to the court, together with relevant evidence, within 48 hours from the moment the defendant was arrested or handed over to the police, and should this time limit expire on a holiday, on the next working day, in such a way, however, that the court may commence the examination of the case within 72 hours from the moment when the defendant was arrested or handed over to the police (second sentence of Article 517b § 3 CCP).

741. In cases heard under the accelerated procedure, the inquiry conducted by the police may consist only of interviewing the suspect and securing evidence to a necessary extent.

742. If the evidence gathered during the inquiry justifies bringing an accusation before the court, and the conditions that enable the hearing of the case under the accelerated proceedings are met, the police prepare the relevant motion and submit it to the court, together with the collected evidence, and immediately notify a prosecutor (Article 517d § 1 CCP).

743. After the case is brought to the court, the presiding judge first reviews the motion to hear the case from a formal standpoint. If it satisfies the formal criteria, the president (or the court itself) serves a copy of the motion on the defendant and his or her defence lawyer, designating a time frame for the mounting of a defence.

The defendant must be given the opportunity to confer with his or her defence lawyer in private. Attorneys and legal advisors have been obliged to hold duty hours in order to enable defendants to use the assistance of a defence lawyer in accelerated proceedings.

744. The court commences the examination of the case immediately. Before hearing a case under the accelerated procedure, the court reviews the conditions that enable the case to be examined at a trial (both positive and negative conditions).

745. If prior to or during the trial the court ascertains that the case cannot be examined under the accelerated procedure, it refers the case to a prosecutor for the purpose of conducting preliminary proceedings under the general principles of law, notifying the aggrieved person of this fact. It will act in the same way if the case cannot be examined within the maximum cumulative duration of recesses in the trial conducted under the accelerated procedure, which is fourteen days. The court will also decide to refer a case to a prosecutor for the purpose of conducting preliminary proceedings under the general principles of law in the following situations:

(1) the court decides, on the basis of information revealed after the commencement of the evidentiary phase of a trial, that additional evidence must be examined, and that performing the necessary procedural actions as part of court proceedings would cause significant difficulties (Article 517g § 2 CCP);
(2) based on the circumstances revealed after the commencement of the evidentiary phase of a trial, the court anticipates the possibility of imposing a penalty of more than two years of imprisonment; prior to the referral of the case, the court rules on a preventive measure (Article 517g § 3 CCP).

V. Discontinuation of Proceedings and Application of a Protective Measure

746. The application of protective measures (see *supra*, paragraphs 654–655) in the criminal process requires separate discussion.

747. If it is determined that a suspect has committed a prohibited act in a state of insanity and there are grounds for the application of protective measures, after the conclusion of the investigation (inquiry) the prosecutor must refer the case to the court together with a motion for the discontinuation of the proceedings and the application of protective measures (Article 324 § 1 CCP). Only a prosecutor can submit such a motion.

748. After a positive review of the formal requirements of the motion, the case can be handled in two ways. As a rule, pursuant to Article 354 paragraph 2 CCP, it is referred to a trial.

The trial is then conducted principally according to the same rules as those applicable to trials held in matters involving criminal offences. However, the case can be referred to a hearing, provided that in the light of the materials collected during the preliminary proceedings the suspect's commission of a prohibited act and the insanity at the moment of commission of the act raise no doubts, and the President of the court deems it is appropriate to examine the case at a hearing. The purpose of this option is to speed up the proceedings.

749. Proceedings initiated by a motion for the discontinuation of proceedings and for the application of a protective measure feature significant differences regarding the status of an aggrieved person. The provisions regarding a subsidiary and auxiliary prosecutor do not apply. In consequence, an aggrieved person has no capacity to take part in the case as a party, but is permitted to be present at the trial or hearing.

750. If a court decides that there is no basis for the ordering of a protective measure, the court refuses to admit the motion and refers the case to a prosecutor for further processing. This decision may be appealed. On the contrary, if the court holds that the case should be discontinued and that it is reasonable to order a protective measure, the court issues such adecision.

VI. Private Prosecution

751. One of the basic principles of the criminal justice system is that the investigation and prosecution of offences is delegated to specialist state bodies (the police and other law enforcement authorities, the public prosecution service). In Poland, however, this arrangement does not apply to all offences. On the contrary, it encompasses only and solely prohibited acts prosecuted by public accusation. In addition to this category of offences, there are the offences prosecuted by private accusation, or on the initiative of the aggrieved person (see *supra*, paragraphs 590).

752. In cases of offences prosecuted by private accusation, it is the aggrieved person who is given the discretion to demand that the perpetrator would be held criminally responsible. These cases directly relate to the private interest of the aggrieved person (in particular, personal honour and dignity). This private interest, and not a public one, is the dominant justification as to why the acts have been criminalised.

753. The first characteristic feature of the proceedings by private accusation is the absence of preliminary proceedings. Evidence is thus gathered by the aggrieved person who appears before the court as a private prosecutor; whether the perpetrator of an offence will be prosecuted or not depends on the initiative of the aggrieved person. However, if the aggrieved person is unable to obtain evidence of the offence on his or her own (e.g., cannot identify the person who defamed him or her online), they may request that the police secure such evidence (Article 488 § 1 CCP).

754. There are two avenues of initiating proceedings by private accusation. First, through the submission of a 'private indictment' *(prywatny aktu oskarżenia)* by the aggrieved person. The indictment is informal and should identify the defendant, describe the offence imputed to the defendant and identify the evidence on which the accusation is based (Article 487 CCP). The reduction, to a minimum, of the number of the formal requirements for a private indictment results from the fact that the pleading is submitted by a non-professional (the aggrieved person). Upon submitting the indictment, the aggrieved person must pay a lump sum equivalent of expenses (court fee) to the amount of PLN 300 (ca. EUR 70). Second, proceedings by private accusation may be initiated by making an oral or written complaint to the police. The accusation made orally is officially recorded. After the receipt of the accusation (and securing necessary evidence, if this is required), the police are tasked with sending it to a competent court.

755. After a private indictment is filed with (or sent by the police to) the court, the President of the court (head of a division, other authorised judge) or a court referendary verifies the accusation from the formal standpoint. If there are no obstacles to further processing the case, the indictment (accusation) should be served on the defendant.

Then the case is referred, as a rule, to a conciliatory hearing *(posiedzenie pojednawcze),* conducted by a judge or a court referendary. The purpose is to reach a settlement between the parties to the proceedings. Alternatively, the court may refer it to mediation, if the parties request this or agree to it. If the case goes to mediation, the court sets a reasonable time frame for the process.

756. If the parties reach a settlement, the proceedings are discontinued (Article 492 § 1 CCP). The settlement reached in the course of a conciliatory hearing or in mediation may also cover other cases brought by private accusation that are pending between the same parties (Article 493 CCP).

757. If no settlement is reached, the case goes to trial. In order to speed up the proceedings, the parties present at the conciliatory hearing should submit evidentiary motions during that hearing (Article 495 § 2 CCP). However, a failure to submit such motions at that point does not deprive the parties the right to do so at a later date, during the trial.

758. The course of a trial conducted under the private accusation procedure does not materially differ from that of standard proceedings. Nevertheless, there are relatively far-reaching restrictions on the public character of a trial. A trial that concerns a case of defamation or an insult to a person is closed to the public by law (Article 359 paragraph 2 CCP). It may be held in open court, but only if the aggrieved person so requests.

Proceedings can be conducted under the private accusation procedure if the accusation is supported by a private prosecutor. Conversely, where a private prosecutor refrains from prosecuting the case, the proceedings are generally discontinued. However, if the private prosecutor withdraws from the case after the commencement of the evidentiary phase of a trial, the defendant must give his or her consent for discontinuation (Article 496 §§ 1 and 2 CCP). Also, the unexcused absence of a private prosecutor (and his or her legal counsel) at the main trial is considered a withdrawal from prosecution and results in the discontinuation of the proceedings.

If the parties reach a settlement at the trial, the proceedings are discontinued (Article 499 CCP).

759. A special institution of the private accusation procedure is the so-called counter accusation (*oskarżenie wzajemne* – Article 497 CCP). This constitutes an exception from the general rule that prohibits a combining of the roles of a prosecutor and defendant. Until the end of the evidentiary phase of the main trial, the defendant may file a private counter-indictment against the private prosecutor, alleging the commission of a prohibited act prosecuted by private accusation, which is linked to the act the defendant was originally accused of. If a private counter-indictment is filed, the court examines both cases together.

760. Even though the acts prosecuted by private accusation and those prosecuted by public accusation are differentiated in substantive criminal law, this has not led to a complete separation of these two modes of prosecution. Article 60 § 1 CCP provides that in cases brought by private accusation a prosecutor must commence proceedings or join already commenced proceedings (e.g., in the course of a trial), if the public interest so requires. The prerequisite of the public interest is undoubtedly vague. Nevertheless, it should be assumed that it is in the public interest to prosecute those offences normally prosecuted by private accusation that present a high degree of social harm or concern a person with certain characteristics which justify private prosecution (e.g., defamation of a universally respected and renowned authority, an aggrieved person's inability to conduct his or her own affairs).

761. If a prosecutor initiates or joins proceedings that were already launched, the prohibited act is further prosecuted ex officio. A prosecutor who initiates proceedings, acts in the case as a public prosecutor. The aggrieved person may then appear before the court as an auxiliary prosecutor. If a prosecutor joins pending proceedings, the case is further heard under the standard procedure. Again, the aggrieved person acts as an auxiliary prosecutor.

§2. Appeals and the Remedies

I. Introductory Remarks

762. The right to appeal against first instance rulings issued in criminal cases (those concerning the criminal responsibility of the accused and other rulings, e.g. those on detention on remand) is partially regulated in the Constitution of the Republic of Poland. Article 78 of the Constitution provides that each party has the right to appeal against judicial rulings and administrative decisions made in the first instance. Exceptions to this principle and the procedure for such appeals are specified by a statute. Furthermore, Article 176 paragraph 1 of the Constitution states that court proceedings must have at least two stages.

If follows that a verdict on the criminal responsibility for a committed prohibited act (e.g., a conviction) must always be subject to an appeal. The Constitution excludes the possibility of introducing an absolute ban on the challenging of the legitimacy of first instance rulings that resolve the above issue through appellate measures. However, it is possible to limit the category of objections and defences that can be raised on appeal. It is also permissible to limit or even exclude the ability to use an appellate measure for rulings on other procedural matters (e.g., disqualification of a judge, presentation of charges).

763. In accordance with the Constitution, the right to challenge judicial rulings made in the first instance is exercisable by parties to the criminal process. The provisions of the Code of Criminal Procedure offer more detailed guidance on the issue, explaining what appellate measures are available to the parties. As a rule, the right can be exercised by both the defendant and prosecutors.

764. Poland is bound by the norms of international law governing the right to appeal in criminal cases, namely by Article 14 paragraph 5 of the ICCPR and Article 2 of Protocol No. 7 to the ECHR. These norms, however, present a standard that is not more strict than the safeguards enshrined in the Polish Constitution.

765. Polish legal scholarship generally distinguishes between ordinary and extraordinary appellate measures. Among the former, which can be brought against rulings issued in the first instance, the most important are the appeal *(apelacja)*, interlocutory appeal *(zażalenie)* and objection *(sprzeciw)*. There are two extraordinary measures, which can be brought to challenge final rulings: an appeal in cassation *(kasacja)* and a motion for the reopening of proceedings *(wniosek o wznowienie postępowania)*.

766. As a rule, appellate measures can be brought against different types of procedural rulings (judgments, decisions, orders). However, in certain situations the CCP allows for the challenging of actions taken as part of the proceedings (procedural acts) or omissions of criminal justice bodies (these are, for instance, the interlocutory appeal that can be brought against an arrest, or against the inaction of a body obliged to initiate or refuse to initiate preliminary proceedings).

II. Appeal

A. *Summary*

767. An appeal is an appellate measure that can be brought against a non-final judgment of a court of the first instance. An appeal can be filed against every judgment; as an exception, a penal order (which is also a judgment from the formal standpoint) may be contested by way of an objection.

768. An appeal is always examined on its merits by a court superior to the one that issued the appealed judgment (i.e., by a regional court or a Court of Appeal). The submission of an appeal always suspends the enforcement of the judgment. This does not exclude, however, preventive measures, including detention on remand upon the entering of a first instance judgment.

B. *Entities Authorised to File an Appeal*

769. The following entities are authorised to file an appeal:

(1) the parties (public prosecutor, subsidiary prosecutor, auxiliary prosecutor, private prosecutor, defendant);
(2) an aggrieved person who does not have the status of a party, but in this case only against a judgment conditionally discontinuing proceedings that is issued at a hearing.

An appeal can also be submitted by the defendant's defence lawyer, legal counsel of a private prosecutor, subsidiary prosecutor or auxiliary prosecutor, as well as by the statutory representative of the defendant or an aggrieved person.

C. *Extent of an Appeal and Pleas Raised*

770. Entities authorised to submit an appeal are entitled to contest a first instance judgment in whole or in part (Article 425 § 2 CCP). An appeal can also be made only against the justification of a judgment.

771. A party that submits an appeal may challenge only such adjudications or determinations that violate his or her rights or are detrimental to his or her interests (this is described by the Latin word ***gravamen***). Exceptionally, a public prosecutor (professional prosecutor or other authorised person) may also file an appellate measure for the benefit of the accused (Article 425 § 4 CCP).

A person submitting an appeal is obliged to indicate the **pleas** *(zarzuty)* raised against a given resolution contained in a first instance judgment (Article 427 § 1 CCP).

772. The challenge can be based on what is known as the **relative grounds for an appeal** (*względne przyczyny odwoławcze* – Article 438 CCP):

(1) a violation of the substantive law;
(2) a violation of the procedural law, if it might have influenced the content of the appealed ruling;
(3) an error in a fact accepted as the basis of the appealed ruling, if such an error might have influenced the content of the ruling;
(4) the gross disproportionality of the penalty, a penal measure, punitive damages or an unjust application of or a failure to apply a protective measure, forfeiture or another measure.

773. Article 439 CCP sets out what is known as the **absolute grounds for an appeal** *(bezwzględne przyczyny odwoławcze).* These are aggravated violations of law, whose existence always result in the overturing of an appealed ruling, regardless of the extent to which the ruling was contested, pleas raised or the influence of a defect in the content of a ruling issued in the first instance.

Accordingly, it can be argued in an appeal that the ruling is defective because:

(1) it was issued with the participation of an unauthorised person or a person without a capacity to adjudicate or a person who should have been disqualified by law;
(2) the composition of the adjudicating panel was inaccurate;
(3) any one of the members of the adjudicating panel was not present during the entire trial;
(4) a common court decided a case that falls under the jurisdiction of a special court and vice versa;
(5) a lower court decided a case that falls under the jurisdiction of a superior court;
(6) a penalty, penal measure, compensatory measure or protective measure, which has not been established in a statute, was imposed;
(7) a ruling was made in contravention of the majority vote rule;
(8) a signature of any of the members of the adjudicating panel is missing from the judgment;
(9) there are inconsistencies in the language of the ruling that prevent it from being enforced;
(10) a ruling has been issued despite the fact that the criminal proceedings related to the same prohibited act committed by the same person have already been concluded with a final ruling (the *res iudicata* principle);
(11) any of the negative grounds for the institution of criminal proceedings *(negatywne przesłanki procesowe)* described in Article 17 § 1 paragraphs 5, 6 and 8–11 CCP) has appeared (for instance, prosecution of an offence has become time-barred, an aggrieved person has not filed a motion to prosecute);
(12) the defendant has no defence lawyer in court proceedings if such legal representation is mandatory, or due to a defence lawyer's absence during procedures when his participation is obligatory;
(13) the case has been heard in the absence of the defendant whose presence is mandatory.

If any of the grounds enlisted above in items 11–13 above is present, a ruling can be overturned only for the benefit of the defendant.

774. It should be emphasised that on 1 July 2015 the legislator introduced three important limitations to a party's capacity to raise certain pleas as part of an appellate measure.

First, the appellant may designate in the appeal new facts or evidence, but only if he or she was unable to invoke them in the proceedings before the Court of First Instance (Article 427 § 3 CCP).

Second, Article 427 § 4 CCP provides that in court proceedings initiated by a party, the following pleas may not be raised in an appellate measure:

(1) the court's failure to examine a specific piece of evidence, if a party has not filed a relevant evidentiary motion;
(2) a piece of evidence was examined despite the absence of a party's relevant motion;

(3) a breach of provisions governing the court's involvement in the examination of evidence, including the examination of evidence which brings about conclusions other than those presented in the evidentiary allegation. The above proviso does not apply to the situation where it is obligatory to examine a certain piece of evidence, for instance in cases that expert witness evidence must be obtained (Article 193 § 1 CCP), or where it is necessary to obtain certain information on the accused (Article 213 CCP).

Third, in accordance with Article 447 § 5 CCP, an appeal may not be based on the pleas designated in Article 438 paragraphs 3 and 4 CCP (the plea regarding an error in a fact accepted as the basis of a ruling, if such an error might have influenced the content of the ruling, and the plea regarding the gross disproportionality of a penalty, penal measure, pecuniary sanction or an unjust application or a failure to apply a protective measure, forfeiture or another measure) connected with the content of an agreement concluded as part of consensual procedures – conviction without trial and voluntary assumption of criminal liability (Articles 335 and 387 CCP).

The above restrictions have different purposes. The first one clearly intends to expedite the proceedings and prevent the obstruction of process. The same objective is sought to be attained by the prohibition of contesting the arrangements made as part of consensual procedures. However, in the latter case it is also important that the conditions of the conviction have been agreed on and any challenge mounted by the accused in their respect would be a manifestation of procedural dishonesty. On the contrary, the second restriction shows that the legislator gives priority to the principle of material truth, assuming that the court's interference in pending evidentiary proceedings, even that effected in contravention of the rules of criminal procedure, leads to the fullest implementation of this principle.

D. Procedure for the Submission

775. An appeal must be submitted in writing. It designates the contested ruling, pleas raised in respect of this ruling and the remedy sought by the appellant (e.g., amending a judgment, remanding a case for retrial).

If an appeal originates from a public prosecutor, defence lawyer or legal counsel, it should also include a justification. When an appeal is submitted against the judgment of a regional court, it must be drafted and signed by an attorney or a legal advisor unless it is brought by a prosecutor. The submission of an appeal is free of charge.

776. After a first instance judgment is issued, one needs to file a motion for the drafting and delivery of a written justification of this judgment. It should be made in writing within the strict time limit of seven days from the date of the judgment's pronouncement, and, where a statute provides that a judgment must be delivered (generally, in the case where a person was not present during the pronouncement) – from the date of its delivery. A motion for the justification of a judgment should be submitted to the court that issued the judgment. A strict time limit is set for the submission, which means that the time limit may be extended only in a situation where the prescribed time frame has not been kept for reasons not attributable to a party (e.g., due to an illness).

The filing of a motion for the delivery of the judgment accompanied by a justification is generally a condition of the submission of an appeal. This means that a judgment becomes final after seven days have expired since it was issued. An exception to this rule has been established in Article 445 § 2 CCP, which enables the submission of an appeal before the end of the time limit for filing a motion for the drafting of a justification of a judgment. In such a situation, a submission of an appeal has principally the same consequences as the filing of a motion for the delivery of a justification of a judgment: the court prepares and delivers the justification; a person who submits an appeal can amend it within fourteen days; the submitted appeal will be examined even if no amendment is actually made.

Apart from the above exception, a person who has been delivered a copy of a judgment together with a justification may submit an appeal within the strict time limit of fourteen days from the date of its delivery. This time limit cannot be extended, regardless of the nature and complexity of the case. However, it may be reinstituted in a situation where the prescribed timeframe has not been kept for reasons not attributable to a party.

An appeal is submitted through the court that issued the contested judgment (Article 428 § 1 CCP).

777. These rules have been modified for the purposes of the accelerated procedure. A motion for the drafting and delivery of a written justification of a judgment may be submitted not only in writing, but also presented orally for the record of a trial or hearing. An authorised entity must do this within a strict time limit of three days. The court is obliged to prepare a justification of a judgment within three days from the date the motion for the drafting of a justification was filed. The strict time limit for submitting an appeal is seven days.

E. Judicial Examination

778. Upon submission, an appeal is first reviewed from the formal standpoint: the President of the court that entered the judgment in the first instance (head of a criminal division of this court, other authorised judge) checks whether the relevant pleading has been correctly drafted and filed. If these conditions are not satisfied, an appeal is rejected. Conversely, if an appeal is acceptable, it is sent, together with the dossier, to the appellate court (Article 448 § 1 CCP). A party may submit a written response to an appeal (Article 428 § 2 CCP).

If the appeal is brought against a judgment of a district court, a regional court operates as an appellate court. A judgment of a regional court is appealed before a Court of Appeal.

779. When a case is received by an appellate court, it in turn reviews the admissibility of the appeal. Pursuant to Article 430 § 1 CCP, an appellate court disregards the accepted appellate measure if the latter is inadmissible by law, has been submitted by an unauthorised person or after the expiry of a time limit, or if the measure was accepted due to the illegitimate reinstatement of a time limit.

After the second formal review of the appeal, it is examined on its merits. Proceedings before an appellate court are conducted, as a rule, at a trial (Article 449 § 1 CCP). An appellate court may, exceptionally, decide a case at a hearing. This is possible in the situations where there appear absolute grounds for an appeal (Article 439 § 1 CCP).

780. A prosecutor's and defence lawyer's participation in an appellate trial is mandatory; this rule also applies to a defence lawyer appointed at the request of a defendant (Article 80a § 1 CCP).

A defendant who is not detained has the right to take part in the trial unless the President of the court, or the court itself, decides that his appearance is mandatory (Article 450 § 2 CCP). A detained defendant's participation in an appellate trial is governed by Article 451 CCP. This provision states that an appellate court, upon the motion of a detained defendant filed within seven days from the date delivering the notice of the admission of the appeal, orders that he or she be brought to trial, unless the court decides that the presence of the defendant's defence lawyer is sufficient. Requests submitted after this deadline may be considered, if this will not make it necessary to adjourn the trial. The defendant must be advised of the right to file such a motion. If the court does not order the appearance of a defendant who has no defence lawyer, an ex officio defence lawyer will be appointed. According to the established jurisprudence of the Supreme Court, *In general, an appellate court is allowed to invoke the exception provided under Article 451 CCP only if an appeal concerns a question of law, and not a question of fact, and when the purpose of the appeal is not to assess the credibility of evidence given by persons, in particular explanations of the accused.*[21]

The remaining parties and their legal representatives have the right to choose whether or not to take part in the appellate trial unless the President of the court or the court decides that their appearance is mandatory (Article 450 § 2 CCP).

781. An appellate court's function does not comprise only of a review of rulings issued in the first instance. The court may examine evidence and establish facts of the case on its own, provided that it is not necessary to conduct evidentiary proceedings anew in their entirety (Article 452 § 2 CCP). The above proviso clearly indicates that an appellate court can only supplement evidentiary proceedings conducted before the first instance court, even if this supplementation is quite extensive.

---

21. Judgment of the Supreme Court from 17 Jun. 2009, case no. III KK 30/09, *Prok. i Pr.* 2009, Vol. 11–12, Item 18.

F. Limits of an Appellate Court's Examination of a Case

782. As a rule, an appellate court does not hear a case brought on appeal in full and *de novo*. It normally examines a case within the scope of the appeal and rules only on the pleas raised in the appeal (Article 433 § 1 CCP). The appellant determines the extent to which a case is appealed, designating whether the appeal is made against a ruling that affects all or some of the defendants and whether it addresses the entire ruling affecting a given defendant or a only certain elements of the ruling, e.g. the imposition of a penalty. The pleas raised in an appeal must indicate specific defects of the ruling.

783. Exceptionally, an appellate court may rule outside the limits of an appeal and the pleas raised. This is permissible only in four cases:

(1) under Article 435 CCP – an appellate court reverses or amends a ruling in favour of a co-defendant, even though they have not submitted an appellate measure, if it has reversed or amended a ruling in favour of a defendant affected by an appellate measure and the same reasons support the reversal or amendment in favour of the remaining co-defendant (this is known as the 'benefit of someone else's appellate measure' – *dobrodziejstwo cudzego środka odwoławczego*); notably, the legislator allows for a reversal or amendment of a ruling exclusively if it is in favour of the co-defendants.
(2) under Article 439 § 1 CCP – the court is obliged to review ex officio whether any absolute appellate grounds appeared in the case (see *supra* paragraph 773).
(3) under Article 440 CCP – if the affirmation of a ruling would be grossly unjust, it should be amended (but only in favour of a defendant) or reversed irrespective of the limits of the appeal and the pleas raised. After a judgment is reversed, it may be decided both in favour of or against a defendant.
(4) under Article 455 CCP – an appellate court is obliged to correct erroneous legal classification of a prohibited act irrespective of the limits of appeal or pleas raised; the correction of legal classification to the disadvantage of a defendant may occur only if an appellate measure has been submitted against a defendant.

784. An appellate court is obliged to consider substantially all pleas and motions indicated in an appellate measure (Article 433 § 2 CCP). There is an exception to this rule, when the examination of certain defects invoked by a party or considered ex officio is sufficient for the issuance of a ruling and the examination of the remaining defects would be premature or irrelevant for the further conduct of the proceedings. In such an event an appellate court may limit the scope of its examination of the case (Article 436 CCP).

785. It is important to determine whether an appeal has been submitted in favour of, or to the disadvantage of, the accused. **The prohibition of *reformatio in peius*** ensures that a defendant can freely submit an appellate measure to his or her advantage. A defendant who files such a measure should not fear an unfavourable appellate ruling. The prohibition has two forms. The direct prohibition concerns the extent to which an appellate court may rule against a defendant (Article 434 CCP). The indirect prohibition relates to the possibility of a first instance court's ability to rule against a defendant after a case is remanded by an appellate court for retrial (Article 443 CCP).

Article 434 § 1 CCP enables an appellate court to rule against a defendant only in a situation when an appellate measure is submitted to his or her disadvantage. If an appeal is filed solely in favour of a defendant, the appellate court cannot worsen the defendant's situation, even if the first instance ruling was incorrect. If an appeal is filed against a defendant, the appellate court may enter a ruling to his or her disadvantage, but only within the scope of the appeal and only if the court ascertains defects raised in the appellate measure. In view of the above, only these portions of a first instance ruling that have been contested can be changed to the disadvantage of a defendant on appeal. At the same time, the court may consider only the defects argued in the appeal in respect of the contested portion of the first instance ruling. To a limited extent, the court may rule against a defendant on appeal ex officio (see *supra* paragraph 783).

The prohibition of *reformatio in peius* is not absolute. Article 434 § 4 CCP provides that if a conviction is made under Article 60 §§ 3 or 4 CC or Article 36 § 3 Criminal Fiscal Code, the provisions that guarantee the extraordinary mitigation of a penalty in a situation where a defendant has commenced collaboration with law enforcement authorities, an appellate court may rule against the defendant (even outside the limits of and pleas raised in the appeal) provided that an appellate measure was submitted solely in favour of the defendant, who retracted or materially changed his or her testimony or explanations after the judgment was made. The above exception was introduced in order to exclude the applicability of the prohibition of *reformatio in peius* in situations where a defendant first enjoyed the benefits of the mitigation of his or her penalty in return for providing assistance to law enforcement authorities but later behaved dishonestly and contested the ruling issued in his or her case knowing that he or she would be protected by the prohibition of *reformatio in peius* because of the absence of a prosecutor's appeal.

The indirect prohibition of *reformatio in peius* was regulated in Article 443 CCP, which states that in the event of a case being remanded for retrial, the court may issue a ruling that involves a more severe penalty than the penalty imposed in the revoked ruling only if the ruling was contested to the disadvantage of a defendant, or if the ruling was contested in favour of a defendant in conditions described in Article 434 § 4 CCP. The restriction resulting from the indirect prohibition of *reformatio in peius* has the corresponding scope to the restriction under Article 434 CCP. At a retrial, the court thus may rule against a defendant only where the appellate court has accepted an appellate measure brought to the disadvantage of the defendant (subject to the exceptions designated in Article 434 § 4 CCP) and only within the scope of the appeal and pleas raised, unless a statutory provision allows adjudication outside these limits (cf. Article 439 § 1 and Article 440 CCP). Another important proviso is that the court's ability to adjudicate against a defendant is also limited by the scope in which the case was remanded for retrial. An appellate court may refuse to accept certain appellate pleas that may result in the issuance of a ruling against the defendant. In this is the case, such pleas may not effectively determine the scope in which the case will be retried by the first instance court.

786. Apart from the prohibition of *reformatio in peius*, an appellate court's authority to adjudicate is subject to the so-called ***ne peius*** **rules.**

Article 454 CCP describes two such rules:

(1) An appellate court may not convict a defendant who has been acquitted or whose case was discontinued or conditionally discontinued by the court of the first instance.
(2) An appellate court may not increase a penalty to life imprisonment.

The *ne peius* rules were introduced in order to strengthen the guarantees available in proceedings in which the Criminal Code's most severe penalty can be imposed or which otherwise might bring a radical change to the verdict on the defendant's guilt.

G. An Appellate Court's Authority to Adjudicate a Case

787. Under Article 437 § 1 and Article 456 CCP, an appellate court may decide the appeal in the following manner:

(1) It can affirm the contested judgment of the first instance court provided that the latter ruling is correct or that the pleas of the appeal are not accepted and there are no grounds for the appellate court to challenge the reviewed ruling ex officio; the first instance judgment may be affirmed in whole or in part.
(2) It can amend the contested first instance judgment (in its entirety or in part, subject to the appeal) provided that the latter is incorrect, if the evidence so permits.
(3) It may reverse there contested first instance judgment and remand a case for retrial to the first instance court in any of the following situations:
   - where there appear absolute grounds for an appeal (Article 439 § 1 CCP);
   - if it is established that it is legitimate to amend a ruling issued against a defendant in a manner prohibited by the *ne peius* rules (cf. the discussion above);
   - if it is necessary to conduct the entire evidentiary proceedings in a case anew;
   - if the court finds that the first instance ruling is grossly unjust (Article 440 CCP).
(4) An appellate court may also reverse a judgment of a first instance court and discontinue proceedings if the first instance judgment should not have been issued because conducting proceedings in a given case was inadmissable (e.g., after the prosecution of an offence became time-barred).

III. Objection

788. **An objection is an appellate measure that can be used to challenge a penal order** (Article 506 § 1 CCP).

An objection can be filed by a defendant (a defence lawyer), a prosecutor (a public or auxiliary prosecutor) or a legal counsel of an auxiliary prosecutor within the strict time limit of seven days from the date the judgment is served. It must be submitted, in writing, to the court that issued a penal order. An objection does not have to include specific pleas in support of a challenge. It is sufficient to make a statement expressing the intent to contest a ruling.

789. A submitted objection is subject to a review by the President of the court (head of a division, other authorised judge). The president will reject an objection that is filed after the expiry of a time limit or that is filed by an unauthorised person (Article 506 § 2 CCP). The effective submission of an objection renders the contested penal order ineffective. The order is invalidated by law, and the case is referred to a trial in accordance with the generally applicable rules of the criminal process.

790. If a case has been referred for examination under the general procedure, the court that decides the case is not bound by the content of the invalidated penal order. Arguably (though this is disputed by some legal scholars), the prohibition of *reformatio in peius* does not apply to proceedings conducted after the effective submission of an objection. Consequently, if an accused sentenced to, say, a fine objects to a penal order, then a more severe penalty may be imposed in the proceedings conducted in accordance with the general rules. The above is true in respect of both penalties that are more severe in terms of a measure (e.g., a higher fine) and type (e.g., a prison sentence may be imposed in lieu of a fine).

791. **An objection can also be submitted against decisions** *(postanowienia)* **or orders** *(zarządzenia)* **issued by a court referendary** *(referendarz sądowy)* **where a statute so provides** (Article 93a § 3 CCP). Court referendaries are judicial officers appointed to decide matters that are uncomplicated or incidental to the merits of a case. For example, referendaries may request a party to remedy formal defects of a pleading or order the appointment of an ex officio defence lawyer or a legal counsel.

An objection to a decision or order of a court referendary can be submitted by a party or a person directly affected by the decision, unless a statute provides otherwise. The time limit for the submission, the requirement for it to be in written form and the procedure for processing the objection are the same as those applicable to the objection against a penal order. The only difference is that after the successful submission of an objection against a decision or order of a court referendary, the relevant decision or order is issued by the President of the court, or by the court itself, and not by a court referendary.

IV. Interlocutory Appeal

792. An interlocutory appeal *(zażalenie)* is an appellate measure that may be submitted against rulings issued in the criminal process other than judgments (decisions and orders), procedural acts and the inaction of criminal justice bodies (e.g., an arrest or the inaction of a body obliged to initiate preliminary proceedings).

An interlocutory appeal, similar to an appeal proper, can be filed against the above rulings issued in the first instance. Not all decisions and orders can be contested. This issue is regulated by the provisions of the Code of Criminal Procedure. An interlocutory appeal can be submitted in the case of all procedural rulings that materially affect the situation of parties or other participants in criminal proceedings: e.g. decisions on the application of a preventive measure, decisions in respect of security against property, decisions ordering a search, arrest and the compulsory appearance before a court or a prosecutor, decisions concerning a court's jurisdiction or decisions on the costs of proceedings.

793. An interlocutory appeal may be submitted by parties or by a person directly affected by the decision (an order, or an action), for example, a person who is not a party but whose premises were searched, unless a statute provides otherwise (Article 459 § 3 CCP).

794. Unlike the 'ordinary' appeals that are heard only by a court, interlocutory appeals in preliminary proceedings can also be heard by a prosecutor. Article 465 § 3 CCP states that an interlocutory appeal against a decision of a body conducting preliminary proceedings, other than a prosecutor, is examined by the prosecutor supervising the proceedings in question. If preliminary proceedings are conducted by a prosecutor, the rule is that the appellate instance is the court having jurisdiction to hear the case (Article 465 § 2 CCP). The Code of Criminal Procedure establishes a few exceptions from this rule.

795. An interlocutory appeal is of a relative suspensory character, which means that the submission of such a measure does not suspend the enforcement of the contested decision. Still, the court that issued the decision or the court appointed to examine the interlocutory appeal *may* suspend the enforcement of the contested decision. The enforcement of a decision may be ordered at the request of the appellant, or be ordered ex officio.

An interlocutory appeal is of a relative devolutive character, which means that a court (other body) whose decision has been appealed against, may accept the appeal in its entirety provided that it adjudicates on the matter of the interlocutory appeal in the same composition as did the one that issued the contested decision.

796. The general rules of submission and examination of interlocutory appeals are the same as those applicable to appeals proper. The time limit for filing an interlocutory appeal is different, however. Pursuant to Article 460 CCP, an interlocutory appeal must be submitted within a strict time limit of seven days from the date when the decision was pronounced, and, if a statute requires that a decision be served, from the date that it is served. Sometimes this time limit is shorter (e.g., decisions regarding making witness' data anonymous must be appealed against within three days). Interlocutory appeals are examined at a hearing.

V. Cassation

797. An appeal in cassation (*kasacja*) is an extraordinary appellate measure to challenge final judgments (and, exceptionally, also decisions). For this reason an appeal in cassation may be used in strictly limited circumstances.

798. **An ordinary (or common) appeal in cassation** *(kasacja zwykła/zwyczajna)* may be filed by a party to court proceedings, but only against the final judgment of an appellate court that concludes proceedings, and also against a final decision of an appellate court on the discontinuation of the proceedings and application of protective measures. It is thus impossible to use this measure to challenge, for instance, a judgment of a first instance court that became final as no appeal was submitted.

Articles 521 and 523 CCP impose further restrictions on the ability to contest the ruling of an appellate court by means of an appeal in cassation. First, as a rule, an appeal in cassation can be submitted provided that a first instance judgment has previously been contested with an appeal in regular form. A party who has not submitted an appeal may file an appeal in cassation against a ruling of an appellate court only if this ruling has been amended on appeal to the party's disadvantage or where one of the absolute grounds of appeal under Article 439 § 1 CCP exists. Second, an appeal in cassation may be submitted only in a case where a defendant receives the penalty of unconditional imprisonment. It is therefore impossible to use an appeal in cassation in the event that a non-custodial penalty is imposed or a custodial penalty which is conditionally suspended. On the contrary, an appeal in cassation that seeks a resolution unfavourable to a defendant can be submitted only if the latter was acquitted or when the proceedings were discontinued on the grounds listed in Article 17 § 1 paragraphs 3 and 4 CCP (an offence presents negligible social harm, the perpetrator is not subject to a penalty) or due to the insanity of the perpetrator. The two above restrictions do not apply to an appeal in cassation submitted because of the defects described in Article 439 § 1 CCP (the absolute grounds for appeal).

799. There is another type of an appeal in cassation: **the extraordinary appeal in cassation**. This measure may be submitted by the Minister of Justice, the Prosecutor General or the Commissioner for Human Rights. An extraordinary appeal in cassation can also be brought by the Commissioner for Children's Rights, but only in a case when the issuance of a ruling has violated children's rights. Each of the above bodies may submit an appeal in cassation against any final court ruling that concludes proceedings. In consequence, the submission of this measure is subject to no restrictions that apply to parties to the proceedings.

800. An authorised person or body can file an appeal in cassation in respect of the same defendant and the same ruling only once.

The Code of Criminal Procedure limits the number of pleas that can be raised in an appeal in cassation. Pursuant to Article 523 CCP, an appeal in cassation can be submitted only for the purpose of addressing the defects enumerated in Article 439 CCP (absolute grounds for appeal) or other gross violations of law that might have affected the content of a ruling in a material way. An appeal in cassation cannot be submitted only on the grounds of a disproportionate penalty or be based only on a plea invoking a grossly unjust ruling (violation of Article 440 CCP).

The time limit for the submission of an appeal in cassation is thirty days from the date when the ruling, accompanied by its justification, is served. A motion for the service of the ruling with justification should be filed in the second instance court that issued the ruling, within the strict time limit of seven days from the date of pronouncement of a ruling, and if a statute provides that the ruling be served, from the date of it being served. There is no statutory time limit for the submission of an extraordinary appeal in cassation. However, an appeal in cassation to the disadvantage of a defendant may not be considered after six months have expired from the date when the ruling became final.

If an appeal in cassation does not originate from a prosecutor, the Minister of Justice, the Prosecutor General, the Commissioner for Human Rights, or the Commissioner for Children's Rights, it should be drafted and signed by a defence lawyer or a legal counsel.

801. A party submits an appeal in cassation to the Supreme Court through the appellate court. The Minister of Justice, the Prosecutor General, the Commissioner for Human Rights or the Commissioner for Children's Rights submit an appeal in cassation directly to the Supreme Court.

802. The structure of the appeal in cassation as a pleading is similar to that of the regular appeal. However, there is a significant difference: an appeal in cassation, except the one filed by a prosecutor, must be accompanied by a receipt of payment of a court filing fee (this requirement does). The fee is PLN 450 (ca. EUR 105) in a case adjudicated by a district court and PLN 750 (ca. EUR 175) in a case decided in the first instance by a regional court. An appeal in cassation is processed and considered in a way similar to the appeal proper. The difference is that it is the Supreme Court that hears an appeal in cassation, and that a prosecutor submits a position statement on the appeal in the course of the proceedings, after the court has reviewed the appeal in cassation from the formal standpoint.

803. If an appeal in cassation is submitted, the Supreme Court may suspend the enforcement of the contested ruling, as well as any other ruling whose enforcement depends on the outcome of the appeal in cassation.

As a rule, the Supreme Court examines an appeal in cassation at a trial. An appeal in cassation can be considered at a hearing when the Supreme Court admits the cassation in its entirety in the event it is obviously legitimate, or when the Supreme Court dismisses the cassation as obviously groundless.

The Supreme Court examines an appeal in cassation within the scope of the appeal and pleas raised. It may expand the scope of adjudication on an appeal in cassation but only in the cases described in Articles 435, 439 and 455 CCP (see *supra* paragraph 783).

804. Having considered the case, the Supreme Court dismisses an appeal in cassation if it is groundless. On the contrary, when the Supreme Court admits the legitimacy of pleas raised or discovers any defects in a contested ruling that must be considered ex officio, it reverses the contested ruling in whole or in part and remands the case to the court that is competent to conduct the retrial (the first or second instance court). It may also reverse the ruling and discontinue the proceedings or, if a conviction is obviously unfair, acquit the defendant.

An appeal in cassation against a ruling of the Supreme Court produced as a consequence of the examination of another appeal in cassation is inadmissible.

VI. A Motion for the Reopening of Proceedings

805. **The reopening of court proceedings is a special measure, which,** similar to an appeal in cassation, **can be used to challenge a final ruling issued in a given case**. Due to its special character, the reopening of proceedings can be invoked on the basis of a strictly limited set of grounds.

The issue of the reopening of preliminary proceedings is regulated separately (see *supra* paragraph 656).

806. Court proceedings concluded by a final ruling may be reopened if an offence has been committed in connection with the proceedings and there are reasonable grounds to assume that this might have affected the content of the ruling (Article 540 § 1 CCP). The commission of the offence must in principle be determined by way of a final conviction. However, the absence of such a conviction does not always exclude the reopening of proceedings. Indeed, if the commission of an offence has not been determined because of the existence of negative grounds for the institution of criminal proceedings under Article 17 § 1 paragraphs 3–11 CCP (e.g., when prosecution of an offence has become time-barred, the perpetrator was protected by immunity, an aggrieved person has not filed a motion to prosecute) or because of the discontinuation of proceedings, then the court that reopens the proceedings independently decides on whether or not an offence that might have affected the content of the issued ruling has been committed. In that case, proceedings can be reopened both in favour of and to the disadvantage of the defendant.

807. Court proceedings can also be reopened if, after a ruling is issued, new facts or evidence are uncovered and these new facts or evidence suggest that:

(1) a convicted defendant has not committed a prohibited act or the act that he or she has committed did not constitute an offence or was not subject to a penalty;

(2) a defendant has been convicted for an offence carrying a more severe penalty, or when circumstances necessitating the application of the extraordinary mitigation of a penalty have not been taken into account, or when circumstances resulting in an extraordinary aggravation of a penalty have incorrectly been accepted;
(3) a court discontinued or conditionally discontinued criminal proceedings, incorrectly assuming that the defendant has committed the imputed offence.

All the situations mentioned above result in the reopening of proceedings only to the advantage of the accused.

808. Proceedings can also be reopened to the advantage of the defendant in the event that such a need results from the ruling of an international body operating under an international treaty ratified by the Republic of Poland (e.g. ECtHR).
A ruling of the Constitutional Tribunal declaring a legal provision, that was the basis for the contested ruling, to be contrary to the Constitution or to a ratified international agreement or a statute, serves as grounds for the reopening of proceedings to the advantage of a party (any party, not only the accused). However, proceedings may not be reopened in such a way to the disadvantage of the accused.

809. Court proceedings concluded by way of a final ruling can be reopened if a convicted defendant, whose penalty was extraordinarily mitigated in return for his or her cooperation with law enforcement authorities (under Article 60 §§ 3 or 4 CC or Article 36 § 3 Criminal Fiscal Code), did not confirm the disclosed information in criminal proceedings, or when proceedings were discontinued due to the absorption of an offence by other proceedings (see *supra*, paragraph 652) but the legal grounds for the discontinuation ceased to exist (Article 11 § 3 CCP). In the two cases above, proceedings are reopened to the disadvantage of the accused.

810. Court proceedings concluded by way of a final ruling may be reopened upon a motion of the accused, submitted within the strict time limit of one month from the date when the accused learned about the ruling issued against him or her, provided that:

(1) the case was heard in the absence of the accused, who was not served with notice of the trial or hearing date or who was served with this notice in a manner other than by being served with it personally, if the accused shows that he or she did not know about the date or about the possibility of the ruling being issued in his or her absence;
(2) the ruling was issued in the absence of the accused and was not served on the accused or was served in a manner other than by being served personally, if the accused shows that he or she did not know about the ruling's content and about the time limit and manner in which it must be submitted.

811. In all the situations designated above, proceedings are reopened at the motion of a party to court proceedings. In the case of a convicted defendant's death, a motion for the reopening of proceedings to the advantage of the defendant can be submitted by his or her next of kin.

812. A motion for the reopening of proceedings that does not originate from a prosecutor should be drafted and signed by a defence lawyer or a legal counsel.

813. The Code of Criminal Procedure also creates the possibility of reopening of proceedings ex officio, when the court establishes that absolute grounds for an appeal under Article 439 § 1 CCP exist. In such an event, however, proceedings cannot be reopened if the matter has been examined under the appeal in cassation procedure. It is not permissible to reopen proceedings ex officio to the disadvantage of a defendant more than six months after the ruling became final.

814. The reopening of proceedings concluded with a judgment of a district court is decided by a regional court; a Court of Appeal adjudicates on the reopening of proceedings concluded with a judgment of a regional court. The court decides the matter in a panel of three judges. The reopening of proceedings concluded with a ruling of a Court of Appeal or the Supreme Court is decided by the Supreme Court, also sitting in a panel of three judges. The court resolves whether or not to reopen the proceedings at a hearing held without the parties being present, unless the President of the court, or the court itself, decides otherwise.

815. By ruling on the reopening of proceedings, the court reverses the contested ruling and remands the case to a competent court for re-examination. This ruling is subject to no appellate measure. While reversing a contested ruling, the court may acquit the defendant by way of a judgment, if new facts or evidence suggest that the ruling is obviously unfair. Alternatively, the court may discontinue the proceedings. A judgment that acquits the accused or discontinues the proceedings may be contested by way of an appellate measure, unless the ruling in question is issued by the Supreme Court.

If a motion for the reopening of proceedings is groundless, the court will dismiss it.

VII. A Complaint Against the Excessive Length of Criminal Proceedings

816. A complaint against the excessive length of court and preliminary proceedings is governed by an Act of 2004 enacted in response to the ECtHR judgment of 26 October 2000 in *Kudła v. Poland.* It regulates the submission of a complaint against the excessive length of proceedings, not only in criminal proceedings, but also in civil or administrative proceedings.

817. A person may submit a complaint seeking to ascertain that his or her right to have his or her case heard without unreasonable delay was violated if the proceedings have lasted longer than it is necessary for the explanation of the factual and legal circumstances that are material for resolving the case.

818. It is assessed whether the court (or a prosecutor) has acted in the case in a timely and correct manner. This assessment should take into account the nature of the case, its factual and legal complexity, the significance of the case for the complainant, and the conduct of the parties, in particular that of the party who alleges that the length of the proceedings is excessive.

819. In criminal proceedings, a complaint can be submitted by a party, but also by an aggrieved person that is not a party.

820. The complaint is submitted in the course of the proceedings pending in the case. It cannot be submitted after the case is concluded. A complaint must be filed in writing. It should include a request for the ascertainment of the excessive length of the proceedings conducted in the case subject to the complaint and the description of the circumstances that substantiate the request.

It may also request that the court hearing the case or the prosecutor who is conducting or supervising the preliminary proceedings be recommended to initiate relevant actions within a prescribed time limit or the request to award the complainant an appropriate sum of money, from PLN 2,000 (ca. EUR 465) to PLN 20,000 (ca. EUR 4,650).

The complaint is subject to a fee of PLN 100 (ca. EUR 23), payable by each complainant.

821. The complaint should be filed with the court that is conducting the proceedings or to the prosecutor who is conducting or supervising the preliminary proceedings. The court or the prosecutor refers it immediately to the court competent to hear the complaint together with the dossier of the case subject to the complaint.

822. The court competent to hear the complaint is the court superior to the court before which the proceedings are pending (e.g., a regional court for a case pending before a district court). If the complaint concerns the excessive length of proceedings pending before a district court or a regional court, it will be examined in its entirety before a Court of Appeal. If the complaint concerns the excessive length of proceedings pending before a regional court or a Court of Appeal, it will be examined in its entirety before the Court of Appeal. If the complaint concerns the excessive length of proceedings pending before a Court of Appeal or the Supreme Court, the latter will have jurisdiction to examine it. Finally, if the complaint concerns the excessive length of preliminary proceedings, it will be examined by a court superior to the court that would have the subject matter jurisdiction over the case in the first instance.

The court sits in a panel of three judges to hear the complaint. The ruling should be issued within two months from the date when the complaint was submitted.

823. A court will dismiss a complaint that is groundless. Conversely, a complaint has merits, the court admits it and declares that the proceedings named in the complaint were excessively lengthy.

The court, acting upon the request of a complainant or ex officio, recommends that the court hearing the case on its merits or the prosecutor conducting the preliminary proceedings perform appropriate actions within the prescribed time limit unless the issuance of such recommendations is obviously superfluous. These recommendations may not interfere with the factual or legal assessment of the case.

At the request of the complainant, the court may award him or her a sum of money of between PLN 2,000-PLN 20,000, payable by the State Treasury. This sum is a specific lump sum compensation for the inconvenience related to the excessive length of the proceedings. Notwithstanding the above, a party whose complaint has been successful may seek the restoration of a loss resulting from the ascertained excessive length of proceedings by the State Treasury in a separate (civil) suit.

The ascertainment of the excessive length of the proceedings made in a decision admitting a complaint against the excessive length of proceedings is binding on a court in a civil suit for compensation (for a financial or moral loss).

824. To prevent that this complaint would be used as a tool to obstruct the course of proceedings, a complainant may submit a new complaint in the same case only after the expiry of twelve months (or in preliminary proceedings that involve the application of detention on remand, after the expiry of six months) from the date the court issues a ruling on the previously submitted complaint (Article 14 of the act).

Chapter 4. Coercive Measures

§1. General Overview

825. To effectively conduct the criminal process, both during preliminary proceedings and court proceedings, criminal justice bodies are equipped with so-called coercive measures (*środki przymusu*). Their aim is to secure the proper course of proceedings and reduce the possible obstacles that stand in a way of concluding a criminal process in an expeditious way. These coercive measures often limit the rights and freedoms of citizens and can present a substantial difficulties for the individuals affected. Detention on remand is probably the most extreme example. Therefore, coercive measures can be imposed on the participants of criminal proceedings, most often on the defendant, only in certain situations carefully prescribed by law and only in compliance with such principles as legality, proportionality and humane treatment. Finally, it must be taken into account that the Polish Constitution ensures 'personal inviolability and security' for everyone and, furthermore, provides that 'any deprivation or limitation of liberty may be imposed only in accordance with principles and under procedures specified by statute' (Article 41 paragraph 1).

826. The Polish CCP contains a separate part entitled 'Coercive Measures'. There are, however, other coercive measures provided in Part II Chapter 5 relating to evidence, e.g. seizure of property (Article 217 CCP), search (Article 219 CCP), surveillance and telephone tapping (Article 237 CCP). Moreover, additional provisions allow the court and the presiding judge to maintain the order of court proceedings (Articles 372 and 375 § 1 CCP).

827. The types of **coercive measures** referred to in the CCP are:

(1) arrest and detention (*zatrzymanie*);
(2) preventive measures (*środki zapobiegawcze*);
(3) search for the defendant and the issuing of a 'wanted' warrant (*poszukiwanie oskarżonego i list gończy*);
(4) letter of safe passage (*list żelazny*);
(5) procedural penalties (*kary porządkowe*);
(6) security against property (*zabezpieczenie majątkowe*).

828. The CCP provides for the following types of **preventive measures** (*środki zapobiegawcze*) in a strict sense:

(1) detention on remand (*tymczasowe aresztowanie*);
(2) financial surety (*poręczenie majątkowe*).
(3) surety of a social organisation (*poręczenie społeczne*);
(4) surety of a trustworthy person (*poręczenie osoby godnej zaufania*);
(5) police supervision (*dozór policyjny*);
(6) order to temporarily leave a premises (*nakaz opuszczenia lokalu*);

(7) suspension of the execution of official duties (*zawieszenie w czynnościach*);
(8) prohibition to leave the country (*zakaz opuszczenia kraju*).

829. Even though the framework of coercive measures raises controversy among Polish legal scholars, the coercive measures discussed below will be divided according to their definitions provided in the CCP.

§2. Arrest and Detention

830. In order to effectively hold a perpetrator criminally responsible, it may be required not only to identify him or her, but to also apprehend and potentially further detain the perpetrator in the course of the proceedings. Article 297 § 1 paragraph 2 CCP, states that the aim of preliminary proceedings is – among other things – to detect and, if needed, to apprehend the perpetrator. Hence, the Code of Criminal Procedure includes the possibility to detain the suspected person, the suspect and the accused (see *supra*, paragraphs 543–546).

831. The provisions of the CCP regulate the detention for the purposes of the criminal proceedings that are ongoing or are due to be initiated. However, it is important to mention that in the Polish legal system it is possible to detain a person for other reasons. First, detention is allowed in proceedings that are not strictly criminal (petty offences proceedings – Article 45 § 1 of Petty Offences Procedure Code of the 24 August 2001). Second, grounds for detention are also covered by the Police Act of the 6 April 1990 (J.L. 1990, No 30, Item 179 as amended). According to the act, the police have the power to:

(1) detain persons deprived of liberty (prisoners) who, on the basis of permission from relevant authorities, have left a remand centre or a prison and have not returned within the designated date;
(2) detain persons who clearly pose a threat to the health and life of other people, and a threat to property.

832. Moreover, pursuant to Article 40 paragraph 1 of the Act on raising minors in sobriety and counteracting alcoholism of 26 October 1982 (J.L. 1982, No 35, Item 230 as amended) there are grounds for the detention of an intoxicated person who, through their behaviour, may cause offence in a public place or in a workplace, or a person finds him – or herself in a situation posing a threat to their, or other people's, life and health, in order to bring such a person to a sobering-up station (a police unit), a healthcare institution or a place of residence or stay. Police or municipal police *(straż gminna)* are the authorities with power to do so. Such a person may be detained for up to 24 hours.

833. It should be emphasised that detention has quite broadly been regulated by the provisions of the Constitution. This is undoubtedly the result of negative experiences related to the functioning of law enforcement authorities before the political transition of 1989 and is aimed at the effective protection of the rights of persons who have been deprived of liberty in the new Polish democratic system.

Thus Article 41 paragraph 1 of the Constitution guarantees personal inviolability and personal freedom to all. Imprisonment or the restriction of liberty may be imposed only in accordance with principles and under procedures specified by the Constitution. In the case of detention for the purposes of criminal proceedings, relevant provisions are covered by the CCP.

Nevertheless, it is worth noting that the Constitution determines the most important rights of a person deprived of liberty. Article 41 paragraph 4 contains a general directive which requires that any person deprived of liberty (thus also a detained person) be treated humanely. Moreover, a person who was deprived of liberty not on the basis of a judgment (therefore, primarily detained persons, regardless of the reason for their detention) has the right to challenge the legality of detention before a court. The arrest and detention must immediately be disclosed to the family of, or a person designated by, the detained person (Article 41, paragraph 2). Moreover, Article 41 paragraph 3 of the Polish Constitution provides that every detained person must be informed, immediately and in a manner comprehensible to him or her, of the reasons for his or her detention. The person should, within 48 hours of detention, be given over to a court for consideration of the case. The detained person must be released unless a decision on detention on remand issued by a court, along with specification of the charges laid, has been served on him or her within 24 hours from the time they are given over to the court's disposal. Persons deprived of their liberty unlawfully also have the right to compensation (this is regulated by Chapter 58 CCP).

What is especially notable from the comparative perspective is the constitutionalisation of detention periods. This solution is universal and, without a prior amendment to the Constitution, prevents any changes to the legislation whose aim would be, for example, to extend the allowed detention period, including in a specified category of cases (e.g., terrorist crime).

Apart from constitutional provisions, Poland is also bound by ECHR standards on detention.

834. When it comes to detention for the purposes of criminal proceedings, the CCP provides first that anyone has the right to apprehend a person caught in the act of committing an offence, or seized in a pursuit undertaken directly following the commission of an offence, if it is feared that this person may go into hiding or if his or her identity cannot be established. The apprehended person must be surrendered immediately to the police (Article 243 §§ 1 and 2 CCP). It should be stressed that the right of persons who are not law enforcement personnel to apprehend a perpetrator of an offence is limited only to the above-mentioned scenarios. Apprehending a person under different circumstances – even if it appears that he or she has committed an offence – may result in criminal responsibility for unlawful detention (Article 189 of the Criminal Code).

835. The police are authorised to arrest a suspected person if there is reasonable grounds to suppose that he or she has committed an offence, and it is feared that such a person may go into hiding or destroy the evidence of his or her offence or if his or her identity cannot not be established, or there are reasons to carry out accelerated proceedings against this person. The suspicion that an offence has been committed is therefore not enough for detention to take place. There must be at least one further reason stipulated in Article 244 § 1 CCP.

836. The CCP regulates the issue of detaining perpetrators of domestic violence in a special manner. The police have the right to detain a suspected person if there are reasonable grounds to suppose that he or she has committed an offence involving violent acts perpetrated to the detriment of another person who lives with him or her and there is a compelling reason to believe that the suspected person will commit such an offence towards that person again, especially if he or she has threatened to do so (Article 244 § 1a CCP). The police have the duty to detain a suspected person if the above-mentioned offence was committed with the use of a firearm, knife or another dangerous item, and there is a compelling reason to believe that the suspected person will commit an offence involving violent acts towards another person who lives with the suspected person again, especially if he or she has threatened to do so (Article 244 § 1b CCP).

837. Apart from police officers, the power of arrest can be exercised in the above-mentioned scenarios by the officers of the Border Guard, Internal Security Agency, Customs Service, CAB and Military Police, but within the limits of the competencies of these agencies (Article 312 section 1 CCP).

838. Each person detained under the CCP has the following rights:

(1) to be informed of the reasons for the detention;
(2) to be heard (to make a statement or refuse to make a statement, for example on the circumstances of the detention or regarding the commitment of an offence);
(3) to consult an attorney or a legal advisor (cf. remarks below);
(4) to be assisted by an interpreter free of charge, if the detained person's command of the Polish language is not sufficient;
(5) in the case of foreign citizens, to contact, at the detained person's request, the competent consular post or diplomatic representation, and, in the case of stateless persons, to contact a representative of the state in which the detained person has his or her permanent residence;
(6) to access first aid;
(7) to inform his or her next of kin, or another designated person, including an employer or a representative of a school or university, a commanding officer, the manager of the detained person's company, or the enterprise he or she is responsible for, about the detention;
(8) to receive a copy of a detention report;
(9) to be released immediately if the reasons for the detention have ceased to exist, or to be released after the expiry of the statutory detention period (cf. remarks below);
(10) to lodge an interlocutory appeal against the detention to a court (cf. remarks below);

(11) to receive information on the above rights (delivered in writing, in a language the detained person understands).

839. At present, the Polish Code of Criminal Procedure does not guarantee free access to an attorney or a legal advisor by detained persons. Moreover, there is a lack of a systemic solution that would facilitate the detained persons' access to legal aid, for example through making available registers of attorneys and legal advisors providing services in the area where the detention took place. This is the reason why, in practice, the rule is that detained persons do not use professional legal aid. This situation has not changed although the time limit to implement the Directive 2013/48/EU of the European Parliament and of the Council of 22 October 2013 on the right of access to a lawyer in criminal proceedings and in EAW proceedings, and on the right to have a third party informed upon the deprivation of liberty and to communicate with third persons and with consular authorities while deprived of liberty has expired in 2016.

840. Another flaw in the detained persons' Letter of Rights is the lack of clear information about the right to remain silent (e.g., similar to the American *Miranda Rights*) and about the consequences of making a statement by the detained person, i.e. the possibility of using it as evidence against him or her.

841. The detention is documented in the form of a report, stating the given name, surname and the role of the arresting officer, and the given name and surname of the detained person. If it is impossible to identify the detained person, the report should state his or her description, the time, location and reason for the detention and the suspected offence. Any statements made by the detained person must be included in the report. It should also be indicated that the detained person has been informed about their rights. As already mentioned, a copy of the report is given to the detained person.

842. Detention linked to the above-mentioned constitutional regulations may last for up to 48 hours. On the expiry of this time limit, the detained person should be released, unless he or she is handed over to a court together with a motion to apply detention on remand. The court has 24 hours, counted from the moment the detained person is brought before a judge, to decide whether he or she should be detained on remand, and to serve a decision regarding detention on this person (Article 248 §§ 1 and 2 CCP).

843. In the case of an arrest carried out by the police (or other authorised authorities), the period of detention is calculated from the actual moment when the detention starts (and not from, for example, the moment when the detained person is brought to a police station). In the case of apprehension by a member of the public (Article 243 § 1 CCP), this period is calculated from the moment the apprehended person is handed over to the police.

844. The stipulated periods of detention are maximum periods. For the above reasons, even if the period has not expired, the detained person must be released as soon as the reasons for his arrest have ceased to exist (e.g., it has been established that he or she is not the perpetrator), or by order of the court or prosecutor. Importantly, Article 248 § 3 CCP forbids rearresting a suspected person on grounds based on the same facts and evidence.

845. The rights of an individual in the case of his or her detention are guaranteed by the mechanism of a judicial review. The detained person has the right to lodge an interlocutory appeal with the court, through which he or she may request an examination of the grounds of the legitimacy, legality and correctness of his arrest (Article 246 § 1 CCP). The interlocutory appeal is immediately referred to the district court that has jurisdiction over the place of detention or of criminal proceedings, which should examine the matter immediately. If the detention is found to be unjustified or illegal, the court orders the immediate release of the detained person (Article 246 §§ 2 and 3 CCP).

846. A detained person has the right to participate in the hearing on the interlocutory appeal of the detention. If a detained person has been imprisoned (e.g., he or she has been detained on remand), the court orders that the detained person be brought to the detention hearing, unless the court decides the presence of an attorney or a legal advisor is sufficient. If the court does not summon the detained person, and he or she is not represented by a professional counsel, the President of the court or a court referendary appoints an ex officio attorney or legal advisor.

847. A person who has been unlawfully detained for the purposes of criminal proceedings is entitled to seek compensation and redress from the State Treasury if he or she can prove that he or she suffered damages or harm as a result of the detention. A regional court rules on the motion for compensation or redress.

848. Apart from the reasonable grounds to suspect that an offence has been committed mentioned above, the necessity to secure the integrity of the criminal proceedings can also be the basis for detention. For the above reasons, similar to the case of detention on the basis of suspicion that an offence has been committed, a detained person can be a suspected person, a suspect or a defendant (especially if he or she fails to respond to summons of criminal justice bodies).

849. At the stage of preliminary proceedings, the prosecutor can order that a suspected person or a suspect be detained and forcibly taken to public prosecution office if:

(1) there is a compelling reason to believe that he or she will fail to appear as summoned for the purposes of the presentation of new or amended charges laid against this person, and also in order to undergo, for example, an inspection, fingerprinting, identity parade, or psychological and psychiatric examination;
(2) there is a justified concern that he or she may obstruct the proper course of proceedings by any other unlawful means;
(3) there is a need to apply preventive measures (e.g., detention on remand) immediately.

850. In the course of court proceedings, the court or the presiding judge is competent to order detention in order to forcibly take the defendant to court following his or her failure to attend a trial or hearing he or she was obligated to attend (Articles 75 § 2, 376 § 1 and 382 CCP).

851. Each decision to detain and forcibly take a person to court (public prosecution office) is subject to an appeal. Any interlocutory appeal against a prosecutor's decision is heard by a court.

852. Detention in the Polish territory can also take place in relation to criminal proceedings that are being or were conducted in a different state. Article 605a CCP provides for such a possibility if there is information that a person listed on the International Criminal Police Organisation database is wanted. It is also possible to detain a person in order to surrender them on the basis of an EAW. Regulations, discussed above, governing how these procedures are executed, along with the rights of a detained person, apply for these detentions.

853. The CCP allows for the possibility of detaining and forcibly taking to court (public prosecution office) a witness (and, in exceptional circumstances, also an expert witness or an interpreter). It is possible in situations in which he or she fails to appear as summoned or leaves the place where proceedings are taking place prior to their conclusion and without the court's leave. The authorities entitled to order compulsory appearance are the prosecutor (in preliminary proceedings) and the court (in court proceedings). One is entitled to interlocutory appeal against a decision on detention and compulsory appearance. Any interlocutory appeal against a prosecutor's decision is heard by a court.

§3. Preventive Measures

I. General Grounds for Imposing Preventive Measures

854. Pursuant to Article 249 § 1 CCP preventive measures may be applied:

(1) to secure the integrity of the proceedings;
(2) on an exceptional basis in order to prevent the commission of a new serious offence by a defendant.

Preventive measures may be applied only where **the collected evidence indicates a high probability that the defendant has committed an offence** – this is the so-called **general ground** for the application of preventive measures. This is also the first condition verified by the court.

855. Importantly, in the event of detention on remand, only the findings made on the basis of evidence that is open to the defendant and the defence lawyer may be used as the basis of a ruling on the application or extension of the detention on remand (in keeping with Article 249a CCP). This regulation does not generate any problems during court proceedings because the dossier of such proceedings is open to the defendant (Article 156 § 1 CCP). By contrast, during the preliminary proceedings where access to the dossier may be denied (Article 156 § 5 CCP), the access cannot be denied with regard to that part of the case files which contains evidence specified by the prosecutor in the motion for the application of detention on remand (Article 156 § 5a CCP).

In addition, in examining the motion for the application of detention on remand the court may rely exclusively on the evidence presented by the prosecutor (Article 249a § 2 CCP). Should the court wish to refer to other evidence, this may only be evidence favourable to the defendant and it has to be disclosed during a hearing. The court cannot issue a decision on detention on remand based on the evidence that is unfavourable and has not been disclosed to the defendant but is known to the court from the dossier which the prosecutor encloses with the motion for detention on remand.

856. Where it has been determined that there is a high probability of an offence having been committed by the suspect or by the defendant, the court must determine whether there is at least one of the **special grounds** for the application of a preventive measure.

The following are considered special grounds for the application of the preventive measures (Article 258 § 1 CCP):

(1) a justified concern that **the defendant (suspect) will abscond or go into hiding**, in particular where their identity cannot be established or when they have no permanent place of residence in the country;
(2) a justified concern that the **defendant (suspect) will attempt to induce others to give false testimony or explanations or to obstruct the proper course of proceedings by any other unlawful means**.

To justify the concern that the defendant would attempt to obstruct the proceedings, it is necessary to specify the facts that make such a concern probable (e.g., the accused or suspect has threatened witnesses). However, Article 258 § 2 CCP stipulates that the risk of the defendant obstructing the proceedings, which would justify the application of a preventive measure, may also result from the severity of the penalty which may be imposed on the defendant, **if the defendant is charged with a felony or a misdemeanour punishable with imprisonment with an upper limit of at least eight years or if they have been sentenced by a first instance court to imprisonment exceeding three years**. In this case, the CCP presumes that a defendant fearing a severe penalty may try to abscond or otherwise obstruct criminal proceedings. The presumption is rebuttable.

In exceptional situations, detention on remand may also be applied where there is **a justified concern that the defendant charged with an intentional offence** (not applicable to persons charged with an unintentional offence) **will commit an offence against life, health or public safety**, and especially where the defendant has threatened to commit such an offence (Article 258 § 3 CCP).

857. Despite the fulfilment of the above premises, Article 259 § 1 CCP requires that unless there are special reasons for such a decision, one should abstain from applying detention on remand for humanitarian reasons, in particular where imprisonment of a defendant:

(1) would create a serious threat to his life or health;
(2) would lead to exceptionally severe consequences for the defendant (suspect) or their closest family.

858. Detention on remand is not applied under the following circumstances, even if the premises referred to in Articles 249 and 258 CCP have been met:

(1) if the offence carries a prison term of up to two years;
(2) when the facts of the case permit the presumption that the defendant would be given a conditionally suspended prison sentence by the court, or a less severe penalty, or that the term of detention on remand would exceed the expected prison term without a conditional suspension.

However, these restrictions are not applicable if the defendant is in hiding, persistently fails to appear when requested, obstructs proceedings in any other unlawful manner or if the defendant's identity cannot be established.

859. The CCP regulations provide three modes of controlling the application of preventive measures. First of all, an interlocutory appeal may be submitted against the decision (Article 252 § 1 CCP). It is reviewed by a superior court. Where the detention on remand was applied by a Court of Appeal, the interlocutory appeal is reviewed by a panel of three judges in the Court of Appeal. The interlocutory appeal against the decision on a preventive measure is heard by the court immediately. However, when detention on remand is applied, the interlocutory appeal is heard not later than within seven days from the day when it is submitted to the court along with necessary parts of the dossier (Article 252 § 3 CCP).

Second, the application of a preventive measure is subject to control ex officio. A preventive measure shall be immediately revoked or changed if the reasons for its application cease to exist, or if any reasons justifying its revocation or change come into being (Article 253 § 1 CCP). This power is granted to the court, and also to the prosecutor during the preliminary proceedings.

Third, the person against whom a preventive measure is applied and his or her defence lawyer have the right to file a motion for having a preventive measure revoked or changed; such a motion may be filed at any time. The decision regarding the motion is taken by the prosecutor within three days. Once an indictment has been filed with the court, the decision is taken by the court which reviews the case (Article 254 § 1 CCP).

II. Detention on Remand

860. Detention on remand (sometimes referred to as 'pretrial detention') is a custodial preventive measure. Since it involves a deprivation of liberty, **it may only be applied by a court**. This is a last resort measure (*ultima ratio*) and it is not applied if any other (non-custodial) preventive measure is sufficient. When imposing detention on remand, the court may also direct that the measure will be changed once financial surety has been given.

861. Under detention on remand, a person is placed in a detention facility. It needs to be emphasised that the detention on remand regime is in general more strict than the prison regime. However, detention on remand may also take the form of placement in a suitable medical establishment, including a psychiatric facility if the defendant's state of health so requires.

862. Detention on remand may be applied during preliminary proceedings only if a decision has been taken to present charges to the person (the suspect). In court proceedings, detention on remand may be applied only against the defendant.

It may be applied during the entire criminal proceedings (even if they have been suspended): from the moment there is a decision to present charges until the beginning of the penalty, provided it involves imprisonment.

863. The period of detention on remand is counted from the day of the arrest. If a defendant is sentenced to imprisonment, restriction of liberty (a community sentence) or a fine, the period of detention on remand is counted towards those penalties. One day of actual deprivation of liberty is equal to one day of imprisonment, two days of restriction of liberty (community service) or two daily rates of a fine.

864. The district court responsible for the area in which preliminary proceedings are conducted has the competence to apply detention on remand during the preliminary proceedings; in urgent cases, detention on remand may also be applied by any other district court (Article 250 § 2 CCP). The court may apply detention on remand for a period not longer than three months. The first instance court competent to hear the case may extend the term of detention on remand beyond the three months, if necessary. The term of detention on remand may be extended to an aggregate period of a maximum twelve months (Article 263 § 2 CCP). Should it be necessary to continue detention on remand beyond that period, the decision should be taken by the Court of Appeal overseeing the area in which the investigation or inquiry is conducted; such a decision is required if:

(1) the criminal proceedings are suspended;
(2) actions are taken to establish or confirm the identity of the defendant;
(3) evidentiary procedures are taken in a particularly complex case or abroad; or if
(4) the defendant intentionally stalls the proceedings.

These situations are the only ones that can justify the application of detention on remand for a period longer than twelve months (Article 263 § 4 CCP).

Even so, the Court of Appeal may not extend detention on remand in excess of twelve months if the penalty in question does not exceed three years of imprisonment, unless the necessity of extending detention on remand results from the defendant intentionally stalling the proceedings.

During preliminary proceedings, detention on remand may be applied (extended) for a period not longer than three months at one time.

865. During court proceedings, the decision on detention on remand is taken by the court which hears the case (Article 250 § 2 CCP). However, if the total length of detention on remand imposed before the pronouncement of the first instance court's judgment (including any detention on remand during the preliminary proceedings) is to exceed two years, the decision on the extension of detention on remand is taken by the Court of Appeal overseeing the area in which the case is heard, at the request of the court reviewing the case; such a request is filed in cases listed above in relation to preliminary proceedings (Article 263 § 4 CCP).

The Court of Appeal may not, however, extend detention on remand in excess of twelve months if the penalty in question does not exceed five years of imprisonment, unless the necessity of extending detention on remand results from the defendant intentionally stalling the proceedings.

Once the decision on closing proceedings has been issued, the court which has issued the ruling will adjudicate on detention on remand; where the case is referred to the second instance, the matter will be adjudicated by the court of second instance.

866. Unlike preliminary proceedings, the maximum duration of detention on remand (extension) at one time during judicial proceedings has not been defined in the CCP as a rule. Only if it is necessary to apply detention on remand following the delivery of the first judgment by a first instance court, may such detention on remand be extended each time for a period of up to six months (Article 263 § 7 CCP).

Where detention on remand is requested by a prosecutor, the prosecutor shall file a motion to that effect with the court. It shall include evidence indicating the high probability that the defendant has committed an offence, facts supporting the existence of threats to the integrity of the proceedings or the possibility that the defendant will commit another serious criminal offence, as well as the specific basis for application of this preventive measure and the necessity of its application.

867. Prior to its decision, the court must hear a defendant, unless this is impossible due to the defendant's going into hiding or remaining abroad. The defence lawyers appointed to the case shall be admitted to be present if they appear. Notifying the defence lawyer of the date of questioning is not obligatory, unless requested by the defendant, provided that this does not render the questioning difficult. The court shall inform the prosecutor about the date of the questioning.

Where detention on remand is extended, only the prosecutor or the defence lawyer of the suspect (defendant) have the right to take part in the court hearing in that regard. However, at the request of a defendant who has no defence lawyer, an ex officio defence lawyer is appointed to take part in the detention hearing. The court will proceed with the matter even if the defence lawyer or the prosecutor, who has been duly notified of the court date, fails to appear at the hearing.

868. The decision on the application of a preventive measure should list the name of the person, the act imputed to them, its legal qualification, and the legal basis for the application of such a measure (Article 251 CCP).

It should also specify the duration of the preventive measure and the end date of the detention. The obligation to specify, in each case, the time limit for detention on remand applies until the ruling closing the proceedings becomes final.

The justification of a decision to impose a preventive measure should present evidence that the defendant has committed an offence and a description of facts that indicate that the integrity of the proceedings is at risk or that the defendant may commit another serious crime if the preventive measure is not imposed, as well as the specific grounds of, and the need for, the application of a given measure.

Furthermore, the justification must explain why the previous preventive measure was considered insufficient.

869. The court that applies detention on remand has several important duties. First of all, it is required to promptly notify the defendant's closest person that detention on remand has been imposed; this person may be designated by the defendant. Upon the request of the defendant, another person may also be notified instead of or in addition to the person referred to above. The court is required to promptly notify the defendant's employer, school or university, or in the event that the defendant is a member of the military, his or her commanding officer, and in the case of an entrepreneur or a member of a management body or an entrepreneur who is not an employee, upon a motion of that member, the person managing the enterprise, of the imposition of detention on remand. The court must also give notification of the detention on remand to the body conducting the proceedings against the defendant in another case, provided that the court has become aware of these proceedings (Article 261 CCP).

870. Pursuant to Article 262 CCP, the court who orders detention on remand is required to:

(1) notify the guardianship (family) court, if it is necessary to ensure custody of the children of the detainee;
(2) notify a social welfare authority, if care is needed for a disabled or an ailing person who has formerly been under the care of the detainee;
(3) take all measures necessary to protect the property and residence of the detainee.

III. Financial Surety (Bail)

871. **Three types of surety** may be demanded from the accused (suspect) whenever it is necessary to secure the presence of the accused (suspect) during criminal proceedings or to deter the accused (suspect) from obstructing the proceedings. These are:

(1) financial surety (bail);
(2) surety of a community organisation;
(3) surety of a trustworthy person.

Similar to detention on remand, they can be imposed only when the grounds for imposing measures provided in Articles 249, 258 and 259 CCP are met. In this subchapter the financial surety is discussed. The issues regarding the social guarantee and the guarantee of a trustworthy person will be presented below.

872. Financial surety (*poręczenie majątkowe*) is a non-custodial preventive measure. It can be imposed individually or alongside some other preventive measure, e.g. police supervision or the prohibition to leave a country. In some situations financial surety can be imposed by a court as an alternative to detention on remand (Article 257 § 2 CCP): if a defendant detained on remand provides the surety, he or she will be released from detention. However, predominantly financial surety may be imposed independently both by the prosecutor during preliminary proceedings and by the court during court proceedings.

873. Financial surety can be given in the form of money, securities (*papiery wartościowe*), a pledge (*zastaw*) or a mortgage (*hipoteka*). It can be posted either by the defendant or by another person (Article 266 § 1 CCP). The value, type and conditions of financial surety, and in particular the time limit within which it should be posted, should be defined in the decision ordering this measure, bearing in mind the financial situation of the accused (suspect) and of the person posting the financial surety, the extent of the damage and the nature of the offence committed (Article 266 § 2 CCP).

874. The person posting financial surety is notified every time that the defendant is summoned to appear before the court or the prosecutor (Article 267 CCP). This gives the person posting financial surety a chance to react and may be able to prevent forfeiture if a defendant is not willing to behave according to the conditions of the financial surety. The person posting financial surety is also obliged to inform the court or the prosecutor that the defendant has undertaken actions aimed at evading appearance when summoned or aimed at obstructing proceedings in any other unlawful way (Article 273 § 2 CCP).

875. Whenever the defendant behaves against the conditions imposed, the court may order (also during preliminary proceedings) the forfeiture of the financial surety. The forfeiture of assets and receivables that constitute financial surety is mandatory if the defendant flees or goes into hiding, and is optional if the proceedings are obstructed in any other way (Article 268 § 1 CCP). The decision on forfeiture is subject to interlocutory appeal (Article 270 § 3 CCP).

876. When financial surety is cancelled, any property or possessions that have been provided are returned and the sum of money is released. However, if the defendant is sentenced to a penalty of imprisonment, this occurs only when he or she begins serving the sentence (Article 269 § 2 CCP).

IV. Surety of a Community Organisation

877. Another preventive measure is the surety of a community organisation (*pore czenie społeczne*), which may be given for the defendant by his or her employer, the authorities of the school or university where the defendant studies or by a community organisation of which the accused (suspect) is a member (Article 271 § 1 CCP). The surety guarantees that the defendant will appear in the course of criminal proceedings whenever summoned and will not obstruct the proceedings in any unlawful way.

878. The relevant submission of a surety (which is a body corporate), must include a resolution on providing the surety (Article 271 § 2 CCP) as well as an indication of the person who is to perform the duties of the surety and a declaration by that person accepting these duties (Article 271 § 3 CCP). The decision is issued by the prosecutor in preliminary proceedings or by the court during court proceedings. At the time the surety is given, the surety or the person that accepts the surety duties is informed of the charges issued against the defendant, about the obligations arising from giving the surety and of the consequences of its violation (Article 273 § 1 CCP).

879. The organisations or persons providing are obliged to immediately inform the court or the prosecutor as soon as they know that the accused (suspect) has undertaken actions aimed at evading appearance in court when summoned, or at obstructing proceedings in any other unlawful way (Article 273 § 2 CCP). In the case of a breach of duties, if the defendant fails to appear when summoned or obstructs proceedings in another unlawful way, the prosecutor in preliminary proceedings, or the court during the court proceedings, notifies the surety of the violation. Moreover, the direct superior of the surety may also be notified if it is found that the duties arising from the surety of a community organisation have not been fulfilled (Article 274 CCP).

V. Surety of a Trustworthy Person

880. The so-called surety of a trustworthy person (*poręczenie osoby godnej zaufania*) can also warrant that the defendant will appear when summoned and will not obstruct proceedings in any unlawful way (Article 272 CCP). It is imposed by the court or by the prosecutor and may include obligations like those set forth in the police supervision decision as provided in Article 275 § 2 CCP (see *infra* paragraph 881). The regulation on the duties of the surety and the surety's conduct after the breach of surety obligations set forth for the surety of a community organisation (Article 273–274 CCP) also applies in the case of the surety of a trustworthy person.

VI. Police Supervision

881. As another type of a preventive measure, the defendant may be placed under the supervision of the police (Article 275 § 1 CCP). The defendant must fulfil the duties set forth in the decision of the court or the prosecutor, which may include:

(1) a prohibition to leave a defined place of stay;
(2) an obligation to report to a supervising body at specified intervals;
(3) an obligation to inform the supervising body of any intended departure and date of return;
(4) a prohibition from contacting the aggrieved party or other person;
(5) a restraining order – this is a prohibition to come closer to certain persons than an indicated distance;
(6) a prohibition to stay in certain places.

The list is not exhaustive: other restrictions necessary for the execution of supervision may be imposed (Article 275 § 2 CCP). If the defendant fails to comply with the requirements set forth in the decision, the supervising agency immediately notifies the court or the prosecutor who issued the decision (Article 275 § 5 CCP).

882. Police supervision can be imposed instead of detention on remand. This can happen if the conditions are fulfilled for applying the detention on remand of an accused person (suspect) charged with a violent crime or with making unlawful threats against his next of kin or other member of his household; in this case, supervision may be ordered instead of dentention on remand, provided that the defendant within a prescribed term leaves the premises occupied jointly with the aggrieved party and indicates his place of stay (Article 275 § 3 CCP).

883. The defendant on whom police supervision has been imposed also has a duty to:

(1) appear at a specified police station with a document confirming his identity;
(2) comply with the instructions given for the purposes of recording the conduct of the supervision;
(3) provide information necessary to establish whether he or she has fulfilled the duties imposed by the decision of the court or of the prosecutor (Article 275 § 4 CCP).

VII. Order to Temporarily Leave the Premises

884. As a preventive measure, an accused party (suspect) charged with a violent offence committed against a member of his household may be ordered to temporarily leave the premises occupied together with the aggrieved party (*nakaz opuszczenia lokalu*) if there is a justified concern that the accused (suspect) will commit a violent offence against this person again and in particular if he or she has threatened to do so (Article 275a § 1 CCP). This preventive measure was introduced in 2010 to strengthen the real protection of victims of domestic violence.

885. The order may be imposed on an accused party (suspect) by the prosecutor acting *proprio motu* or upon the request of the police (Article 275a § 2 CCP). It can be imposed for a period not exceeding three months. However, if the conditions in which the order was made have not ceased to exist, the Court of First Instance competent to hear the case may extend the application of the order for further periods, not exceeding three months (Article 275a § 4 CCP).

886. To provide full protection to victims, the CCP provides additional safeguards. If an accused party (suspect) is arrested pursuant to Article 244 § 1a and 1b CCP (see *supra*, paragraphs 836) and the conditions for ordering him to leave his premises are fulfilled, the police may immediately (not later than within 24 hours of the arrest) submit a request to the prosecutor to order this preventive measure, and this must be considered within 48 hours of the arrest of the accused or suspect (Article 275a § 3 CCP).

887. In the decision ordering a defendant to temporarily leave the premises, the defendant, upon his or her request, may be informed about the possibility of staying in an institution that offers accommodation; however, this cannot be an institution that provides accommodation for victims of domestic violence (Article 275a § 5 CCP).

VIII. Suspension in the Execution of Official Duties

888. The accused (suspect) may be suspended, as a preventive measure, from the execution of his or her official or professional duties or ordered to refrain from performing a certain activity (*zawieszenie w czynnościach*) or from driving vehicles of a certain type (Article 276 CCP). Later, if the accused is convicted, the above measures may be taken into account during sentencing phase.

IX. Prohibition to Leave a Country

889. The prohibition to leave the country (*zakaz opuszczania kraju*) can be imposed on the accused (suspect) whenever there is a justified concern that the he or she might flee Poland (Article 277 § 1 CCP). This may be also connected (and usually is) with the seizure of a passport or other document that would enable the accused (suspect) to cross a border or with a refusal to issue such a document (Article 277 § 1 CCP).

890. The decision to seize the documents and to impose the prohibition to leave a country is issued either by the prosecutor (during preliminary proceedings) or by the court (during court proceedings). However, until such a decision is issued, the criminal justice body conducting preliminary proceedings may seize documents temporarily. This temporary seizure cannot last longer than seven days (Article 277 § 2 CCP). General provisions regulating this seizure apply to the seizure of documents (see *infra*, paragraphs 952–955).

§4. Pursuit of the Defendant and the 'Wanted' Warrant

891. Neither the pursuit of the defendant (*poszukiwanie oskarżonego*) nor the 'wanted' warrant (*list gończy*) can be considered as typical coercive measures, since in these cases there is in fact no coercion. However, since both of these measures are directed against the defendant, it is probably best to regulate them within this scope.

892. **Pursuit** of the defendant, a suspect and even against a suspected person (Article 278 CCP) can be ordered whenever his or her whereabouts are unknown, and this can be considered quite a low threshold when compared to the 'wanted' warrant. To find a defendant, a search, according to Article 219 CCP, can be conducted. The provisions regulating arrest and surrender of a suspect (Article 247 CCP) apply accordingly.

893. The **'wanted' warrant** can be considered a 'higher level' of pursuit. It applies only to a defendant or a suspect – never to a suspected person, and only to those against whom a decision to detain on remand has been issued. Also, the threshold that has to be met to issue this warrant is higher. It applies only to situations when a defendant has gone into hiding (Article 279 § 1 CCP).

894. The 'wanted' warrant may be issued either by the prosecutor during preliminary proceedings, or by the court during court proceedings. It must contain (Article 280 § 1 CCP):

(1) the name of the court or the prosecutor issuing the warrant;
(2) information that may facilitate the pursuit of the defendant (or the suspect) – in particular personal details, a description, distinguishing features, place of residence and employment and, if possible, a photograph of the wanted person;
(3) information about the charges, about the decision regarding detention on remand or about the sentence carried by the defendant's (suspect's) offence;
(4) a call for every person who knows the whereabouts of the defendant to notify the nearest police unit, the prosecutor or the court;

(5) a warning about the criminal responsibility for aiding and abetting the defendant (suspect) to evade justice.

A warrant may contain a notice of a reward for apprehending or helping to apprehend the wanted person. It may also contain an assurance that the details of any informant will be kept confidential (Article 280 § 2 CCP). The warrant is distributed as required – by post, by being placed in public places or through public announcements, in particular in the press, or on radio or television (Article 280 § 3 CCP).

§5. Letter of Safe Passage

895. If a defendant residing abroad declares that he or she will appear in court or before the prosecutor on a specified day on the condition that they remain at liberty, the circuit court with jurisdiction over the case may grant to the defendant a letter of safe passage (*list żelazny*, Article 281 CCP). It may also decide to grant a letter of safe passage upon the posting of financial surety by a defendent (Article 283 § 1 CCP). If the defendant fails to comply with the conditions prescribed in the letter of safe passage or fails to answer a summons without justification, the court will revoke the letter (Article 282 § 2 CCP).

896. The letter of safe passage guarantees that a defendant will remain at liberty until proceedings are concluded with a final judgment, provided that the defendant:

(1) will appear on the specified day when summoned by the court or, in preliminary proceedings, by the prosecutor;
(2) will not leave a specified location within the national borders without the permission of the court;
(3) will not incite witnesses to provide false testimonies or explanations, or obstruct the proceedings in any unlawful way (Article 282 § 1 CCP).

§6. Procedural Penalties

897. Procedural penalties (*kary porządkowe*) have a specific place within the category of coercive measures. They can only be **imposed as a reaction to non-compliance with the procedural duties imposed on participants in proceedings, or issued with the aim of forcing a participant to perform such a duty**. In general, the prosecutor can impose disciplinary penalties during preliminary proceedings, and the court during court proceedings (Article 290 § 1 CCP). However, in some cases (e.g., thirty-day detention of an expert, an interpreter or a specialist, or a financial penalty imposed on a defence lawyer or a legal counsel) the power to issue the decision remains solely in the hands of the court, upon the request of the prosecutor (see Article 290 § 2 CCP and Article 285 § 2 CCP).

898. The first type of disciplinary penalty is a **financial penalty** (*kara pienię* *z'na*). A penalty of up to 10,000,00 PLN may be imposed on a witness, expert witness or a specialist who, without adequate justification, fails to answer a summons issued by the criminal body conducting proceedings or, has without permission departed from a designated place where procedural acts are performed before the procedure they are to be present for is completed (Article 285 § 1 CCP). The same applies to defence lawyers and legal counsels, however this measure can be imposed only in exceptional cases, when their behaviour has an impact on the course of proceedings (Article 285 § 2 CCP). In any case, if, within one week from receiving a decision imposing a financial penalty upon them, the person on whom it is imposed duly justifies his or her absence or unpermitted departure from the designated place, the financial penalty should be annulled (Article 286 CCP).

899. A financial penalty can also be imposed on a person, who, without any reason:

(1) refuses to give testimony;
(2) avoids performing the duty of an expert witness, an interpreter or a specialist,
(3) refuses to take an affirmation;
(4) refuses to surrender an object;
(5) refuses to fulfil the duties of a surety;
(6) refuses to fulfil any other duty in proceedings (Article 287 § 1 CCP).

A financial penalty of this kind may be also imposed on a representative or a manager of an institution, a legal person or an organisational unit without legal personality obliged to assist the agency conducting criminal proceedings who, without reason, refuses to provide assistance within the prescribed term (Article 287 § 1 CCP). However, this does not apply to parties, their defence lawyers and legal counsels, and also to persons who may refuse to give testimony, when it comes to the failure to surrender an object (Article 287 § 4 CCP).

900. Article 289 CCP also provides for so-called **charging with additional costs** (*obciążenie dodatkowymi kosztami*), even though this measure is not really a disciplinary penalty. According to this regulation, anyone, including a defence lawyer, legal counsel or prosecutor, who fails to perform the duties specified in Article 285 §§ 1 and 1a and in Article 287 § 1 CCP and thus causes proceedings to incur additional costs, may be obliged to cover these costs (Article 289 § 1 CCP). It is also possible to charge several persons jointly with these costs.

901. As well as the disciplinary penalties of financial character, the law provides for **arrest and forcibly bringing a person before a criminal justice body** (*zatrzymanie i przymusowe doprowadzenie*) and **detention** (*aresztowanie*). The former can be imposed on a witness who fails to answer a summons issued by the criminal investigation body conducting proceedings, or who has without its permission departed from the place of procedure before the procedure is completed and also, only exceptionally, on an expert witness, interpreter or a specialist (Article 285 § 2 CCP). The decision on detention for a period not exceeding thirty days can be imposed independent of a financial penalty if a witness, an expert witness, interpreter or specialist persistently refuses to give testimony or perform his or her duty, or if a person persistently refuses to surrender an object (Article 287 § 2 CCP). However, this does not apply to parties, their defence lawyers and legal counsels, and also to persons who may refuse to give testimony, when it comes to the failure to surrender an object (Article 287 § 4 CCP). The detention is cancelled if the detained person has fulfilled his duty, or whenever, at any stage, criminal proceedings are terminated (Article 287 § 3 CCP).

§7. Security Against Property

902. Security against property (*zabezpieczenie majątkowe*) is a coercive measure the aim of which is to ensure the feasibility of future judgments that sentence people to fines and other forms of financial penalties. It also allows for the execution of costs adjudicated against a defendant. The procedure is established in the Code of Civil Procedure, unless a statute does provides otherwise (Article 292 § 1 CCP).

903. The measure can be imposed on the accused (suspect) from the moment proceedings are commenced against him (i.e., from the moment when he is officially charged) until the moment when the judgment or decision concluding the court proceedings issued in the case becomes final. It therefore applies both to a suspect and subsequently to a defendant, but not to a suspected person.

904. The circumstances under which security against property can be imposed are as follows:

(1) if the defendant is charged with an offence liable to a fine, compensatory measure, punitive damages or forfeiture, the enforcement of the judgment may be secured ex officio on the property of the defendant, if there is a justified concern that without this security the enforcement of the judgment related to the penalty or penal measures will be impossible or significantly hindered;
(2) if the defendant is charged with an offence against property or an offence resulting in a loss in property, claims for the compensation of the loss may be secured ex officio, if there is a justified concern that without such security the enforcement of claims for the compensation of a loss will be impossible or significantly hindered;
(3) the execution of a judgment awarding costs may also be secured ex officio on the property of the defendant, if there is a justified concern that without such security the enforcement of the judgment in this respect will be impossible or significantly hindered (Article 291 §§ 1–3 CCP).

Moreover, a judgment concerning the restitution of material benefit that a defendant obtained from an offence may be secured ex officio on the property of an entity mentioned in Chapter 8a of the Criminal Code, if there is a justified concern that without such security the enforcement of the judgment in this respect will be impossible or significantly hindered (Article 291 § 4 CCP).

905. The forms in which security can be established are provided in Article 292 § 2 CCP:

(1) seizure of moveable property, receivables and other property rights;
(2) prohibition of a dispostion or encumbrance of real property;
(3) establishing receivership over real property or a business enterprise.

906. During preliminary proceedings the decision is issued by the prosecutor and during the court proceedings by the court. It should define the scope and method of securing the claim (Article 293 § 1 CCP). In most cases, determination of the exact amount of security is necessary (Article 293 § 2 CCP). The decision is subject to interlocutory appeal (Article 293 § 3 CCP).

907. Each decision on security against property can be executed only if it contains an **enforcement clause** (*klauzula wykonalności*). The procedure on appending an enforcement clause to the decision is provided in Article 293 § 5 CCP. The clause can be issued only by a court referendary or by the Court of First Instance competent to hear the case in which a decision has been issued, and if it has been issued in the course of preparatory proceedings conducted in the circuit of the court other than the court with the subject matter or territorial jurisdiction, by the court exercising general jurisdiction to hear a case, or by a refendary of this court. The enforcement clause is appended to the decision on security against property free of charge.

908. The CCP also provides for the temporary seizure of moveable property of a suspected person in cases when it is feared that this person might try to dispose of this property (Article 295 § 1 CCP). The police may conduct the temporary seizure of property, but such action must be authorised by the prosecutor in the form of a decision. The provisions regarding seizure in criminal process apply accordingly (see *infra*, paragraphs 952–956). If, within seven days of a temporary seizure, a decision establishing security for the claim has not been issued, the temporary seizure is annulled (Article 295 § 4 CCP).

Chapter 5. The Rules of Evidence

§1. Principles of Evidence

909. As pointed out in the doctrine of criminal process, evidence is any measure admissible under law which leads to the establishment of facts that are crucial for a given decision.

While the CCP contains provisions concerning specific types of evidence (the defendant's explanations, witness testimony and expert witness opinions), it does not specify the exact number of means of evidence, in accordance with the *numerus clausus* principle, that may be used in criminal proceedings. As a consequence, the general rule – although it has not been stated explicitly in the regulations and rarely in legal doctrine – is the freedom of evidence principle. This has two important consequences. First of all, it is possible to use evidence even if it has not been explicitly listed in the CCP (e.g., the ability to play a recording in any format). Second, there are no regulations that impose the duty to prove certain facts only by means of a specific piece of evidence (e.g., that the fact that a person was intoxicated with alcohol must be proved by means of a breathalyser or a blood test). Naturally freedom of evidence is not to be understood as complete freedom without any boundaries. This is because the CCP contains numerous restrictions on the admissibility of, and the procedure for taking, evidence in criminal proceedings (e.g., clergymen may not be questioned in respect of facts they have learnt of during confession).

910. In addition to the general principle of freedom of evidence, there are certain other important principles of evidentiary proceedings.

The first group regulates the position of the defendant during the process of gathering and taking evidence in a criminal trial. One of the most fundamental principles is the presumption of innocence, holding that a defendant is innocent until proven guilty and sentenced or until a decision is taken to conditionally discontinue proceedings (see *supra*, paragraph 511–512). It decides who shall bear the burden of proof: the prosecutor.

There are also other important consequences relating to the presumption of innocence. The principle of *in dubio pro reo* (when in doubt, for the accused) is regulated in Article 5 § 2. A defendant may not be convicted if there are any doubts concerning the facts of the case and the facts have not been eliminated from evidentiary proceedings. Consequently, if the criminal responsibility of the defendant was not proven as a result of the evidence presented by the parties and the permissible actions taken by the court, these doubts should be interpreted in favour of the defendant (see *supra*, paragraph 512).

The defendant is also granted the privilege against self-incrimination (Article 74 § 1 CCP): the defendant is not under any obligation to give evidence that might incriminate him. This rule is not absolute as Article 74 § 2 CCP provides for actions and tests that the defendant is required to undergo, and provides for coercive measures that may be applied to enforce them should the defendant refuse to comply. Both the *in dubio pro reo* principle and the privilege against self-incrimination have a material impact on the defendant's position during evidentiary proceedings. In general terms, together with the presumption of innocence they form a mechanism for balancing the positions of the parties to the trial – because there are no doubts that in the majority of cases, to say the least, a law enforcement agency and the public prosecutor have much more ability to gather evidence (including with the use of coercive measures) than the defendant and his defence lawyer.

911. The second major group of evidentiary principles includes the rules regulating the procedure for taking evidence: transparency of the proceedings, adversarial procedure and direct examination of evidence by the judge. Naturally, it needs to be kept in mind that the first two principles do not apply only to evidentiary proceedings; their scope is much broader.

The fact that the **proceedings before the court are transparent** is important in that it warrants that the evidence will be taken and evaluated by the court in a reliable manner.[22] The social scrutiny made possible by the public nature of the proceedings before the court does not warrant that the proceedings will be correct but it certainly makes any abuse more difficult.

The **principle of adversarial procedure** is closely related to the initiative in evidence-taking, as well as the sequence of, and procedure for, the taking of evidence (see *supra*, paragraphs 533–535).

The **principle of direct examination of evidence** by the judge has not been expressed explicitly in any provision of the CCP. However, its existence is confirmed by a number of provisions governing exceptions thereto. The principle of direct examination of evidence by the judge is most usually understood as a rule directing the court to:

(1) base its judgment solely on facts disclosed at the main trial (Article 410 CCP);
(2) have direct access to evidence;
(3) base its judgment mainly on primary evidence.

The principle does not apply only to court proceedings, but also to judgments rendered during preliminary proceedings (e.g., to discontinue preparatory proceedings).

The primary purpose of the principle of direct examination of evidence by the judge is to help the court arrive at the true facts of the case. It is for that reason that the CCP orders lawyers to use evidence that has the greatest potential, at least in theory, in terms of its ability to reconstruct facts material to the case. It is, however, obvious that the following of the directives arising from the principle of direct examination of evidence by the judge is not always feasible or desirable. As a consequence, Polish criminal law provides for several restrictions on this principle, and some of them are quite far-reaching. They include the ability to render a judgment on the basis of evidence gathered during preliminary proceedings according to abbreviated procedures (e.g., consensual forms of concluding criminal proceedings) and the ability to read out reports on actions taken during preliminary proceedings or any other proceedings before the court.

---

22. ECtHR addresses that issue. Cf. e.g. the ECtHR judgment in the case Barberà, Messegué and Jabardo v. Spain of 6 Dec. 1988 (application no. 10590/83), § 89.

912. The third group of principles is related to evaluation of evidence. One of the main principles in this group is **the principle of free evaluation of evidence** (Article 7 CCP): the authorities in charge of proceedings shall base their conclusion on all pieces of evidence they have examined and appraised freely, with due consideration to the principles of sound reasoning, standards of knowledge and life experience. Only evidence taken during the proceedings may be used as a basis for a ruling. The evaluation is free but not discretionary as it is limited by the principles of sound reasoning, standards of knowledge and life experience. The CCP does not provide definitions of these terms, which means that the courts are given very broad leeway in evaluating evidence in practice. There are also no regulations that would introduce exceptions to the free evaluation of evidence, and impose the specific evaluation of a given piece of evidence by way of a statute. In view of the above, the following assumptions are made, among others, in judicial interpretations:

(1) *under the regulations of criminal procedure, testimony given before the court is not given precedence over testimony given at an earlier stage of the procedure*[23]
(2) *there is no chronological gradation of the value of evidence in a criminal process. The fact that earlier explanations are revoked or changed only creates a piece of new evidence which is subject to evaluation, just as any other piece of evidence is. It is up to the court reviewing a case as to which piece of evidence it selects as true, and as to how it will prove it and justify it*[24],
(3) *Article 7 CCP does not reject a situation where the testimony of a witness is found fully credible, and to prove the perpetrator's guilt beyond reasonable doubt.*[25].

913. However, sometimes there are special requirements formulated in case law in respect of the evaluation of certain types of evidence, for example, unjust accusations as evidence. The Supreme Court is of the view that *the court is required to exercise extra caution when evaluating credibility of unjust accusations as they do not form fully valuable evidence, unless they are clear and consistent; furthermore, the accusations need to be corroborated by other direct or indirect pieces of evidence; the personality of the person making such accusations also needs to be taken into account. The truthfulness of unjust accusations may also be challenged due to the personal interest of the person making such accusations, for example when the person wants to shift the blame onto another person or even decrease his own guilt*[26].

The impartiality principle is another commonly recognised principle relating to the evaluation of evidence. Within the context of evidentiary proceedings, this principle orders criminal justice bodies to examine and consider facts that speak both in favour of and against a defendant. The case law specifies that it *is not about the duty*

23. Judgment of the Court of Appeal in Białystok of 3 Feb. 2015, II AKa 2/15, LEX no. 1651804.
24. Decision of the Supreme Court of 28 May 2015, II KK 123/15, LEX no. 1723771.
25. Judgment of the Court of Appeal in Warsaw of 19 Dec. 2014, II AKa 445/14, LEX no. 1630896.
26. Judgment of the Supreme Court of 11 Oct. 1977, VI KRN 235/77, LEX no. 21750.

to interpret evidence gathered in a case only in favour of a defendant. This principle orders judges to remain unbiased towards the parties to the trial and to evaluate all evidence gathered in a case in an objective manner.[27]

§2. Initiative in and Rules of Evidence-Taking

914. The parties have a dominant role during the evidentiary proceedings in an adversarial criminal process. This does not mean, however, that their activity is the same at each stage of proceedings and that criminal justice bodies have no ability to intervene in the evidence-taking.

Evidence may be brought forward on the motion of a party to the proceedings, but a criminal justice body may also decide to take evidence ex officio.

915. The decision on taking evidence in preliminary proceedings is generally taken by the criminal justice body in charge of the proceedings (e.g., the prosecutor, police officer). The evidence is taken by the same body (Article 167 § 2 CCP). This is related to the principle of legality (see *supra*, paragraphs 525–527) and actions taken ex officio (see *supra*, paragraphs 522–524). This does not exclude the right of a party to submit a motion for evidence. However, evidence is taken by the criminal justice body, even if it is requested by a party (Article 167 § 2 CCP). The party may naturally take an active part in the procedure, e.g. ask questions to witnesses. However, it is the body in charge of the proceedings that decides on the sequence of questions.

When filing a motion for evidence, a party may request to be granted the ability to take part in evidence-taking (e.g., take part during witness examinations). In such a case, the party may not be denied such a right. This does not, however, apply to a suspect who has been deprived of liberty if bringing in the suspect would cause serious difficulties (Article 315 § 2 CCP). In practice, it is quite rare that parties take the initiative in the examination of evidence during preliminary proceedings.[28]

916. During preliminary proceedings there are no strict rules as to the sequence of evidence-taking. This depends solely on the prosecutor or other law enforcement authorities. A party may take the initiative in that respect, but the decision is taken by the authority conducting or supervising preliminary proceedings.

As a rule, in judicial proceedings evidence is taken on the initiative of the parties. The presiding judge or the court should only review the motion, and then either admit it or reject it. The public prosecutor (as well as subsidiary, auxiliary and private prosecutor) formulates his motions for evidence primarily in the indictment (see *supra*, paragraph 629) However, this does not preclude, as in the case of other

27. Judgment of the Court of Appeal in Lublin of 20 Jun. 2012, II AKa 98/12, LEX no. 1216340.
28. This is the conclusion of empirical studies. Cf. K. Nowicki [in:] W. Jasiński, M. Kuźma, K. Nowicki, R. Ponikowski, J. Skorupka (ed.), S. Szołucha, *Jawność procesu karnego*, Warszawa 2012, pp. 443–459.

parties, the ability to submit motions for evidence in the course of proceedings. Only in exceptional cases, justified by extraordinary circumstances, may the court admit and examine evidence ex officio.

Where court proceedings are issued at the request of a party,[29] it is a rule that the evidence is taken by the parties. However, under Article 167 § 1 CCP, evidence is taken by the court if the court has admitted it ex officio. Where a party has filed a motion for evidence, the court takes the evidence if the party failed to appear in court and in exceptional cases that involve extraordinary circumstances.

The court may only do so in order to prove the circumstances indicated in the party's motion for evidence.

917. The above regulations came into effect on 1 July 2015. Under the pre-reform law, the court's role in the course of evidentiary proceedings was definitely more significant. Courts were awarded the unlimited power to order evidence-taking ex officio. Judges could also actively participate in the taking of evidence put forward by parties, e.g. ask questions to the witnesses. Most importantly, however, the court needed to explain any material circumstances of the case, even if the parties to the proceedings remained inactive. In practice, this often led courts to actually take on the whole burden of proving the defendant's guilt while the public prosecutor remained inactive during the proceedings.

918. The reform has significantly limited the court's evidentiary initiative and its involvement during proceedings. Judges must give reasons for the decision to consider a piece of evidence that has not been requested by parties and enables them to examine such evidence only in exceptional situations. A uniform judicial interpretation of that rule is yet to be formulated. Still, the legislator's intention is quite straightforward: criminal judges' ability to take evidence ex officio is to be significantly limited.

919. The Code of Criminal Procedure provides for certain general principles concerning the sequence of the presentation of evidence during court proceedings, which is unlike preliminary proceedings. Evidence in support of the prosecution shall, if possible, be taken before the evidence in support of the defence (Article 369 CCP). The legislator also established the sequence of questioning. Under Article 370 CCP, the party taking evidence first asks questions to the person subject to questioning. Other persons may ask questions in the following order: the public prosecutor, subsidiary prosecutor, auxiliary prosecutor, legal counsel of the subsidiary or auxiliary prosecutor, private prosecutor, legal counsel of the private prosecutor, expert witness, defence lawyer, the accused and members of the adjudicative panel. The latter may ask questions only in exceptional cases justified by extraordinary circumstances. If the court questions a person ex officio, the members of the adjudicating panel are the first ones to question the person.

29. This is a rule (e.g., when sending an indictment to a court, or a motion for the conditional discontinuation of proceedings). Court proceedings may be initiated ex officio only in exceptional cases (e.g., when the proceedings are reopened, or a cumulative judgment is issued).

920. To present a piece of evidence, a party must file a motion, in writing or verbally. The motion shall identify the evidence and indicate the circumstances to be proven. The manner of presenting evidence may also be determined (Article 169 § 1 CCP). The decision on the admission of evidence is taken by the criminal justice body (the one in charge of the preliminary proceedings or the presiding judge or the court). Under Article 170 § 1 CCP, a motion for evidence may be rejected if:

(1) the taking of such evidence is inadmissible;
(2) the fact to be proven is irrelevant to the resolution of the case;
(3) the fact to be proven has already been proven in accordance with the statement of the party who has submitted the motion,
(4) the evidence would be irrelevant to establish factuality of a given circumstance;
(5) it is impossible to take the evidence;
(6) the motion for evidence is manifestly aimed to lengthen the proceedings.

921. The grounds for the rejection of a motion for evidence are also presented in Article 201 CCP. If the opinion issued by an expert witness is incomplete or unclear, is self-contradictory, or there are contradictions between opinions on the same matter, the same expert witnesses may be summoned again, or another expert witnesses may be appointed. Thus, if an opinion of an expert witness has been presented in the case, the party challenging that opinion may demand that another expert witnesses is appointed only if the party has proven that at least one condition listed in Article 201 CCP was met.

922. Article 321 § 5 CCP contains special grounds for the rejection of a motion for evidence. During preliminary proceedings, the prosecutor may reject motions if they are filed while, or within three days as of, disclosure of the materials of preliminary proceedings to the parties, and if the prosecutor is of the view that an examination of that evidence will not contribute to the achievement of the objects of the preliminary proceedings under Article 297 CCP (see *supra*, paragraph 616). In such a case, the prosecutor should forward the motions for evidence together with an indictment to the court who will decide whether to admit or reject them. This solution aims at limiting the duration of the preliminary proceedings.

923. A motion for evidence must not be rejected only because previous evidence has proven the opposite of the fact which the motioning party now intends to prove (Article 170 § 2 CCP). As a consequence, neither the court nor the body in charge of the preliminary proceedings may anticipate what a piece of evidence will add to the case before it has been heard and a verdict has been given. It also needs to be added that the rejection of a motion for evidence does not preclude later admission of evidence, even if no new circumstances are disclosed (Article 170 § 4 CCP).

§3. Means of Proof

I. Classifications of Evidence

924. Polish criminal procedure law presents a number of distinct classifications of evidence. These can be generally divided into two groups – **sources of evidence** (*źródła dowodowe*) – a person or an object from which the evidence is obtained; and **means of proof** (*środki dowodowe*) – information on a fact that must be proven. Usually the notion of evidence is understood in the second meaning.

925. Furthermore, evidence can be split into two other groups: **testimonial evidence** (*dowody osobowe*) – derived from a living person in the form of testimony, and **real evidence** (*dowody rzeczowe*) – everything else besides the first group. A corpse is considered real evidence.

926. **Direct evidence** (*dowody bezpośrednie, pierwotne*) is given by a firsthand source i.e. an eyewitness or original document. **Indirect evidence** (*dowody pośrednie, wtórne*) is not obtained from a direct source but from other sources i.e. a hearsay witness, a copy of a document or an expert opinion.

927. The means of proof are listed in a separate part of the CCP, entitled 'Evidence':

(1) Statement of a defendant
(2) Testimony of a witness
(3) Opinion of an expert witness
(4) Inspection, autopsy and experiment
(5) Background interview (*wywiad środowiskowy*)
(6) Search and seizure
(7) Surveillance and telephone tapping.

II. The Statement of a Defendant

928. The defendant (and the suspect) as a source of evidence has a different position from any other person providing testimonial evidence. Even the wording that the CCP suggests that the defendant's statements (*wyjaśnienia*) are different from witness' testimonies (*zeznania*). The distinction is rooted in the **right of the defendant to remain silent** and the **right to provide a statement without a formal caution as to his or her obligation to tell the truth**. It does not mean that the defendant has 'a right to lie', but it is true that even his or her untruthful statements will not result in further proceedings directed against him. This is considered a manifestation of the right of a defendant not to be forced to prove his or her innocence or to self-incriminate (Article 74 § 1 CCP).

929. The defendant has the right to provide a statement (Article 175 § 1 CCP). However, without providing any reason, the defendant may refuse to answer certain questions or even refuse to give a statement. The criminal justice body that is to interrogate an accused during a trial as well as suspect during preliminary proceedings, must inform them of their rights. During an investigation or inquiry the suspect must be informed, in writing, of his or her rights, including those discussed above, and must confirm receipt of such information with his or her own signature (see Article 300 § 1 CCP).

930. As a rule, statements made by the accused (suspect) are given orally, both during preliminary proceedings and during a trial. Nevertheless, in the course of preliminary proceedings the suspect is allowed upon his own request (or the request of his defence lawyer) to provide the statement in writing (Article 176 § 1 CCP). In such a situation, the criminal justice body in whose presence the suspect is to provide the statement orally undertakes measures to prevent communication between the suspect and any another person while writing the statement. Only for important reasons may the person conducting the examination deny the suspect the right to provide the statement in writing (Article 176 § 2 CCP).

931. The defendant also has a right to comment, in the form of a statement, on evidentiary procedures conducted in his or her presence (Article 175 § 2 CCP). His behaviour is not limited to passive participation but, on the contrary, the comments must be recorded on every occasion and evaluated similar to the statements given during the questioning of the defendant.

932. The defendant also has some obligations. The defendant does not have to prove his or her innocence or self-incriminate (Article 74 § 1 CCP), yet is obliged to submit to:

(1) an external examination of the body and other tests not infringing his bodily integrity; in particular, fingerprinting and taking of photographs of his or her person and appear during an identity parade;
(2) a psychological and psychiatric examination (for more on psychiatric examination of a defendant, see *infra*, paragraph 949) and bodily examinations involving medical procedures, with the exception of surgical procedures, provided that they are carried out by authorised healthcare personnel in accordance with medical knowledge and without risk to the health of the defendant and providing also that such examinations are necessary; in particular, if the above conditions are fulfilled, the defendant subjects himself or herself to the collection of blood, hair and bodily secretions,
(3) collection by a police official of a buccal mucosa smear, if the collection is absolutely necessary and does not pose a threat to the health of the defendant or other people (Article 74 § 2 CCP).

III. The testimony of a Witness

933. **Every person summoned as a witness is obliged to appear before a questioning authority and testify** (Article 177 § 1 CCP). **This applies** to every person summoned as a witness **regardless of the stage of a criminal process,** including during preliminary proceedings, **and regardless of the summoning authority,** whether it is the court or the prosecutor or other criminal justice bodies conducting preliminary proceedings. A witness who cannot answer a summons for justified causes, e.g. illness, disabilities or other insurmountable obstacles, may testify in the place where the witness resides (Article 177 § 3 CCP). The examination of a witness may also be carried out with the use of technology that allows this procedure to take place remotely, with the simultaneous transmission of sound and vision (Article 177 § 2 CCP). If the absence of a witness is unjustified, a procedural penalty (*kara porządkowa*) of up to 10,000 PLN may be imposed on him or her (Article 285 § 1 CCP) or the witness may be arrested and brought before the questioning authority (Article 285 § 3 CCP). If the refusal to provide testimony is persistent, the witness may be detained for a period not exceeding thirty days, and this measure may be applied independently of a procedural penalty (Article 287 § 2 CCP).

934. Before the commencement of the examination, the witness should be informed of the criminal responsibility for giving false testimony or concealing the truth (Article 190 § 1 CCP). If interrogation takes place during preliminary proceedings the witness signs a declaration confirming he or she has been advised about this responsibility (Article 190 § 2 CCP, *see also* Article 300 § 3 CCP). If interrogation takes place during a trial, apart from being advised the witness also takes an affirmation (Article 188 § 1 CCP). As Article 189 CCP states, the affirmation is not taken when:

(1) the witness is not yet 17 years old;
(2) there is a justified suspicion that due to a mental disorder the witness is not fully aware of the meaning of the affirmation;
(3) the witness is suspected of having committed the offence in question or is suspected of another offence that is closely linked with the offence in question or was convicted of this offence;
(4) the witness was already sentenced for giving false testimony or making a false accusation.

In practice, however, the taking of an affirmation from a witness is an exception rather than a rule, because it can be waived if the parties consent (Article 187 § 3 CCP).

935. The examination starts with the witness being asked his name, surname, age, occupation and of any former convictions for false testimony or false accusations, as well as about his relation to the parties in the proceedings (Article 191 § 1 CCP). Since 2014, to protect witnesses and aggrieved parties, the place of residence of the witness is established through documents (Article 191 § 1a CCP) and is not revealed to the defendant during the course of criminal proceedings (Article 148 §§ 2a-2c CCP).

936. The relationship between the witness and the defendant must be established and confirmed at the beginning of questioning, since the level of intimacy between them has an impact on the right of the witness to refuse to give testimony or answer questions. The general rule is that the next of kin (*osoba najbliższa*) to the accused (suspect) may refuse to testify (Article 182 § 1 CCP). As 'next of kin' qualify (Article 115 § 11 CC): spouse, an antecedent, descendant, brother or sister, relative by marriage in the same line or degree, a person related by adoption, as well as his or her spouse and a domestic partner. The right to refuse to testify remains despite the fact that a marriage or an adoption has been dissolved (Article 182 § 2 CCP). A witness who is accused of being an accomplice to the offence in question in a separate trial that is in progress also has the right to refuse to testify (Article 182 § 3 CCP). Upon the request of a witness who has a particular close personal relationship with the accused (suspect), that witness may be released from the obligation to testify or to answer questions (Article 185 CCP). Finally, a witness may refuse to answer a question, if the answer might incriminate himself or herself or his or her next of kin for an offence or a fiscal offence (Article 183 § 1 CCP). The witness does not have to reveal the reasons why they deem the use of this right necessary. On a regular basis, receiving testimonies from a suspect before formally charging him or her with an offence and before the right to remain silent is guaranteed to them, is conducted according to the provisions of the Article 183 § 1 CCP. Although it must be clearly stated that **any testimony given by a defendant in the capacity of witness** before formally setting the charges against him or her **is not admissible as evidence** and will not be taken into consideration during a trial and cannot even be revealed during the trial upon the request of the defendant (Article 389 § 1 CCP, *see also* the judgment of the Supreme Court of 14 October 1970, IV KR 177/70, OSNKW 1971, No. 1, item 11).

937. The general rule is that a defendant should be aware of the identity of a witness to be able to confront this witness. According to current law, only the place of residence of a witness is not revealed to the defendant (Article 191 § 1a CCP). However, the CCP also provides for the possibility of **anonymous witness**. In the case of a justified concern of a danger to the life, health, freedom or property of considerable value of a witness or his next of kin, the identity of a witness and circumstances allowing disclosure of the identity of a witness can become confidential (Article 184 § 1 CCP). The decision is made either by the court during court proceedings or by the prosecutor during preliminary proceedings. The testimony by an anonymous witness is given in a place and manner precluding the disclosure of the identity of the witness (Article 184 § 3 CCP). The testimony can also be given by way of video link to totally exclude interaction between the witness and the defendant.

938. During preliminary proceedings, prosecutor or other criminal justice body examins the witness. The parties and their legal representatives have the right to participate in such proceedings and can ask questions. During court proceedings the examination will be conducted either by the party that filed the motion to question a witness during the trial. If the decision to question the witness was made ex officio, the court will do it itself (see more Article 167 § 1 CCP and *supra*, paragraph

916). However, in any event the court must control the conduct of examination. In particular, the presiding judge controls the questions posed by the parties. Suggestive, inadmissible, irrelevant or inappropriate questions must be overruled ex officio, without waiting for the reaction of the parties or any objections raised by them (see Article 171 §§ 4 and 6 and Article 370 § 4 CCP). Those questions that influence the statements of the testifying person by means of force or illicit threat are considered inadmissible (Article 171 § 5 paragraph 1 CCP). It is also prohibited to use hypnosis, chemical substances or technical means in order to influence physical processes in the body of the testifying person or to allow control of the unconscious reactions of the body in connection with the examination (Article 171 § 5 paragraph 2 CCP).

939. Questioning of a witness in Polish criminal process always commences with testimony given in a **narrative way** (Article 171 § 1 CCP). Giving a witness the possibility of expressing himself or herself freely does not mean that the witness is not limited in his or her freedom. These limitations are influenced by the purpose of the questioning (Article 171 § 1 CCP), which in turn is affected by the circumstances to be proven by the testimony (see Article 169 § 1 CCP).

940. Only after testimony given in a narrative way has ended can questions be asked. According to Article 171 § 1 CCP, they are only intended to supplement, clarify or control the testimony. However, in practice usually the first stage of examination of a witness is quickly terminated by the body or the party that examines the witness, since quite often the testimony given in a narrative way departs from the substance of the case and must be controlled through questions. Even though the witness testifying during a trial is treated as a 'witness of the court' and not of the party that requested his or her examination, both have a right to question the witness. The mode of questioning of a witness is provided in Article 171 § 2 CCP and Article 370 §§ 1–3 CCP. The questions are asked first by the prosecutor and then subsequently by the auxiliary prosecutor, the auxiliary prosecutor's legal counsel, the private prosecutor, the private prosecutor's legal counsel, the expert witness, the defence lawyer, the defendant (Article 370 § 1 CCP). In any case, the party that requested examination of a witness should ask questions first (Article 370 § 2 CCP). The judges of the adjudicating panel ask questions at the very end of examination. In rare situations when the court ex officio has called a witness to testify during a trial, the questions are posed first by the judges of the adjudicating panel (Article 370 § 3 CCP). The above scheme of examination of a witness is less frequently used during preliminary proceedings since only very rarely does anyone else besides the questioning authority (prosecutor or police officer) take part in questioning.

941. The law provides for a separate mode of examination of a witness in cases of minors (especially below 15 years of age) at the time of questioning. As a rule, a minor can testify only in the presence of their parents or legal guardians (Article 171 § 3 CCP). More specific provisions are laid down in for children under 15 years of age who are victims or witnesses of offences committed with the use of violence or illegal threats or those defined in Chapters XXIII, XXV and XXVI of the Criminal Code, namely offences against freedom, sexual freedom and decency, family and guardianship (Article 185a and 185b CCP). In such cases the rule is that a child should testify during the court hearing only once, and in the presence of a court-appointed psychologist acting in the capacity of an expert witness. This form of hearing can be also organised during the preliminary proceedings. At the same time, a defendant cannot be present during the examination but can be represented by his or her defence lawyer. The examination can be repeated only if important circumstances that must be clarified come to light, or unless a defendant who was not assisted by a defence lawyer during their testimony so demands. Similar provisions are adopted, regardless of the age of the victim testyfing as a witness, in cases concerning rape and some other offences regarding sexual freedom).

942. Examination of a witness can take the form of a so-called confrontation (*konfrontacja*). This procedure (Article 172 CCP) provides for the simultaneous examination of two witnesses with the purpose of explaining contradictions arising from their previous testimony. The conduct of the examination in the form of confrontation is based on the provisions regulating examination of one witness provided above (see Article 171 CCP).

943. The CCP, in the chapter regarding testimony, additionally also regulates the so-called line-up, (*okazanie*). A testifying person may be shown to another person for the purpose of recognition (Article 173 § 1 CCP). The line-up should be conducted in a manner that excludes suggestion and the person being presented should be placed in a group consisting of at least four persons. The same rules apply to the presentation of an image or an object.

944. The witness, as well as the delivering testimony, may be also the object of other evidentiary procedures. With the consent of the witness, physical examination, medical examination or psychological tests can be conducted on him or her for evidentiary purposes (Article 192 § 4 CCP). However, if the punishability of an act depends upon the state of health of the aggrieved party, he or she may not oppose physical examination or tests not involving a surgical procedure or observation in a medical institution (Article 192 § 1 CCP). Also, a witness cannot oppose the presence of a physician or psychologist when testimony is given by the witness, if there is a doubt as to mental state of the witness, his intellectual development, or ability to observe or recollect observations (Article 192 § 2 CCP). Those provisions do not apply to persons who refuse to testify or were released from the obligation to testify pursuant to Article 182 §§ 1 and 2 or Article 185 CCP.

IV. The Opinion of an Expert Witness

945. An expert witness can be defined as a person that is equipped with a 'special knowledge' that exceeds the knowledge available to an average person, including the judge (Article 193 § 1 CCP). An expert witness is called to give an opinion in cases when e.g. the signature on a document is questioned, the cause of death must be determined or the identity of the victim must be determined through DNA tests. In Polish criminal procedure an expert witness is, next to the defendant and the witness, another type of source of testimonial evidence, but this evidence is delivered in the form of an opinion, usually made in writting.

946. The expert witness is considered an expert of the court and not a partisan of any of the parties. Therefore, calling an expert witness remains in the hands of a criminal justice body, even if parties request it. It is an obligation of a criminal justice body to appoint an expert witness whenever the determination of circumstances vital for the solution of a case requires special knowledge (Article 193 § 1 CCP). The decision is issued during court proceedings by the court, usually upon the request of a party. During preliminary proceedings such a decision can be undertaken either by the prosecutor or by the police. In some cases police officers are not authorised to appoint an expert witness, e.g. when two psychiatrists must be appointed to deliver an opinion on the state of mental health of a defendant (Article 202 § 1 CCP) or when the external or internal examination of a dead body must be conducted (Article 209 CCP).

947. An expert witness can be chosen from a list that is maintained by the President of each regional court (Article 195 CCP). Expert witnesses are grouped according to their fields of expertise. Unfortunately, there is no procedure for the accreditation of such experts and, therefore, their level of expertise may vary. The law also allows for the appointment of a so-called ad hoc expert witness who is not on the list. The only difference between these two types of expert witnesses is that the 'expert from the court's list' undertakes an affirmation at the moment when he or she is placed on the list, while the 'ad hoc expert witness' does so every time their appointment takes place (Article 197 § 2 CCP). In practice, not much importance is attached to the undertaking of an affirmation by an expert witness. However, in every case an expert witness should be advised of the responsibility of delivering a false opinion. The level of expertise of expert witnesses is constantly criticised and the lack of a relevant regulatory framework of expert witnesses and the lack of an effective accreditation system for those wishing to enter the list of experts are considered reasons for this.

948. Typically, the opinion of an expert witness is delivered in written form, though this does not exclude the oral examination of the expert, which usually takes place only during a trial when one of the parties question the expert witness' findings. The scope of the opinion is prescribed by the appointing authority in the decision (Article 194 CCP). The opinion should contain:

(1) the name, surname, scientific title, specialisation and professional position of the expert;
(2) the names and surnames and the remaining details of the persons who participated in the issuing of the opinion, with an indication of the activities performed by each of them;
(3) in the case of the opinion of an institution, the full name and the registered premises of the institution;

(4) the timeframe for preparation of the expert witness' opinion and the date when the opinion was issued;
(5) a report on the activities performed, findings made and conclusions based thereon;
(6) signatures of all experts who participated in the issuing of the opinion (Article 200 § 2 CCP).

The expert witness' opinion is verified by the appointing authority based on its completeness, clarity and consistency (Article 201 CCP). The opinion cannot contradict other opinions delivered in the same case. If it does, the expert witness can be called again to clarify those issues in question, or another expert witness can be appointed.

949. A special type of opinion is that **on the mental state of a defendant**. The mental state of a defendant is crucial since criminal proceedings must be terminated if the insanity of the defendant is established. By law two expert psychiatrists are appointed by the court, or, in preliminary proceedings by the prosecutor, to establish the mental state of the defendant (Article 202 § 1 CCP). The experts may propose additional experts to participate in the examination of the defendant (Article 202 § 2 CCP). In cases concerning the mental state of the defendant with respect to a sexual preference disorder, it is compulsory that an expert sexologist participates in the examination and the issuing of the opinion (Article 202 § 3 CCP). The examination of the defendant usually takes the form of a conversation with the defendant. The opinion should contain information as to the mental state of the defendant at the moment the offence that the defendant is charged with was committed, as well as to the current mental state and in particular as to whether that mental state allows the defendant to participate in proceedings and defend himself or herself independently and reasonably (Article 202 § 5 CCP). They should also take a position with regard to the necessity of imposing protective measures on the defendant, according to Article 93b CC. If the examination of the defendant in accordance with Article 202 CCP appears to not provide an answer to questions concerning the mental state of the defendant, experts may request the examination of the defendant combined with committal to a medical institution for assessment (Article 203 § 1 CCP). This committal may be imposed only by the decision of the court, and only when the evidence collected indicates a high probability that the defendant committed the offence. The timeframe for the committal cannot exceed four weeks but may be prolonged for an additional period; the total length of committal cannot exceed eight weeks.

V. Documents

950. The CCP does not contain the definition of 'document', but the latter might be defined as any carrier of information expressed in written form and also in the form of a painting, drawing or a plan that is relevant to a case.

951. Since 2015 private documents, i.e. those created outside of the criminal process are admissible even if they were created directly for the purpose of criminal process (see Article 393 § 3 CCP). This is particularly important in the case of so-called private expert opinions. However, as was presented above (see *supra*, paragraph 946) an expert witness can be only appointed by the court (or the prosecutor during the preliminary proceedings). Therefore, a private opinion will be admissible, but it will be treated as just a private document and not as an opinion of an expert witness.

VI. Search and Seizure

952. Search and seizure are considered evidentiary procedures and therefore are regulated in Part V of the CCP entitled Evidence. However, at the same time they are also considered coercive measures (*środki zapobiegawcze*) in the broad meaning of the term, since they substantially limit the rights of a person (see *supra*, paragraphs 825–826). The procedures regarding the seizure of objects and search of premises, objects and persons, as well as the handling of their findings, are regulated jointly in Articles 217–236 CCP, while the seizure of persons (i.e., arrest) is considered a separate procedure regulated in Articles 243–248 CCP as part of the provisions regarding coercive measures. Search and seizure can be conducted both with and without a warrant (the body responsible for issuing warrants in preliminary proceedings is the prosecutor). The court only becomes involved when a person's rights were infringed by such actions, as such an infringement is subject to judicial review (see Article 236 CCP). The court also has a right to order search or seizure during court proceedings if it becomes necessary at this stage of criminal proceedings. However, in practice search and seizure are procedures typical of preliminary proceedings and are rarely ordered by the court and therefore will be discussed below, as conducted during preliminary proceedings under prosecutorial control.

953. The law regulating the **seizure of objects** does not provide for any threshold or standard that needs to be met. The relevant rule only provides that objects which may serve as evidence or which are subject to seizure in order to secure financial penalties, penal measures of financial nature or claims for compensation for a loss should be surrendered (Article 217 § 1 CCP). A person who is in the possession of such an object is first requested to surrender it voluntarily (Article 217 § 2 CCP) and in the case of refusal, the object may be seized by force (Article 217 § 5 CCP), which in fact means that a search to find the object must be conducted, if it is not visible at first sight. The seizure of the object may happen with a warrant, or in urgent cases without a warrant. In the latter case, the person surrendering the object or from whom the object was seized, may request the prosecutor to issue a decision approving the seizure within fourteen days of the seizure (Article 217 § 4 CCP). If the decision confirming seizure is not issued within seven days from the day the seizure took place, the seized objects must be immediately returned to the owner, unless the surrender was made voluntarily or the person has not submitted a request to receive the decision (Article 230 § 1 CCP).

954. Similar rules apply to the **search of premises or persons** (Article 219 CCP). It may be conducted whenever there are justified grounds for the belief that either a suspected person or specified objects are in a place or kept by the person that is to be searched. The aim of the search is described as the need to detect or arrest or forcibly bring a suspect to the prosecutor or other criminal justice body or to find objects which might constitute evidence in a case or which are subject to seizure in criminal proceedings. The search can be conducted with a warrant issued by the prosecutor or in urgent cases without a warrant by the police by simply presenting an order from the head of the police unit and an official identification (Article 220 § 3 CCP). In cases when the search is conducted without a warrant, the police, immediately upon the conclusion of the search, must in every case apply to the prosecutor to receive a decision confirming the legality of the search. The decision must be issued regardless of the will of the person whose rights were infringed by the search. Moreover, this decision must be delivered to the person who was searched or whose premises were searched whenever such a person requests this. If the search is not confirmed within seven days from the day it took place, the seized objects must immediately be returned to the owner, unless the surrender was made voluntarily or the person has not submitted a request to receive them (Article 230 § 1 CCP).

955. The law provides for the conduct of a search and specific rules regarding handling items that were seized. The search can be conducted only between 6 am and 10 pm, except in urgent cases (Article 221 § 1 CCP). However, this rule does not apply to premises open to public (Article 221 § 3 CCP). If a search is to be conducted in premises belonging to the state or local government, the head of the unit must be informed and can participate in the search (Article 222 § 1 CCP). The searches of private premises must be conducted in the presence of the owner, a person designated by the person conducting the search or at least one adult member of the household (Article 224 CCP). Search of a person and his or her clothing must be conducted by a person of the same sex (Article 223 CCP). A higher standard must be applied in cases when documents that are found or surrendered contain confidential information or other legally protected secrets. Generally, such documents must be handed over to the prosecutor in a sealed envelope (Article 225 § 1 CCP) and further procedures apply depending on the type of secret (strictly confidential, confidential, proprietary or privileged), according to Article 180 CCP. Special handling is also demanded in cases of documents related to the function of a defence lawyer or documentation of psychiatric treatment (Article 225 § 3–4 CCP). The seized objects must be subjected to physical inspection (*oględziny*) and a detailed description of them must be provided. The handling of these objects depends on their nature. They can be deposited with a trustworthy person, advised of the obligation to present them at every request of the criminal justice body conducting preliminary proceedings (Article 228 § 1 CCP). They can also be deposited with a competent institution, in the case of objects of artistic or historical value, or placed in judicial deposit if there are doubts concerning the title to the object (Article 231 CCP). Objects that are easily perishable, whose storage would be connected with disproportionate costs or excessive difficulty or would cause a significant decrease in their value, may be sold (Article 232 CCP). Finally, objects may be stored in a place and manner ensuring their adequate security, or even destroyed, if they are dangerous to life or health; this applies in particular to weapons, ammunition, explosives, flammable or radioactive materials, poison, asphyxiates or burning substances, drugs or psychotropic substances or their products and category one precursors (Article 232a § 1 CCP).

956. Separate regulations apply with regard to the surrender of correspondence, shipments and phone records (see Article 218 CCP). Offices, institutions and entities conducting postal and telecommunication activity, the customs office and transportation institutions and enterprises are obliged to surrender correspondence and packages. This surrender must be made upon the request of the court or the prosecutor, and only these bodies are authorised to open these items. The relevant institutions conducting telecommunication activity are also obliged, upon the request of the court or the prosecutor – expressed in the form of a decision, to immediately secure, for a definite period not exceeding ninety days, electronic data stored on hardware devices in an IT system or on storage media (Article 218a § 1 CCP).

957. Additionally, the law provides for secret methods of investigation. Surveillance and telephone tapping are regulated in Articles 237–242 CCP. Only the court, upon the request of the prosecutor, can order surveillance and recording of the content of telephone conversation by means of telephone tapping (Article 237 § 1 CCP). In urgent cases, the prosecutor may order telephone tapping without the court's permission. However, the prosecutor must request confirmation of such action from the court within three days (Article 237 § 2 CCP). Surveillance and telephone tapping may be ordered only with regard to the offences enlisted in the Article 237 § 3 CCP. Among offences on that list are homicide, trafficking in people, kidnapping and hijacking of an aircraft or a sea vessel.

958. The CCP is not the only legal basis for conducting secret methods of investigation. The Police Act of 1990 provides further instruments, such as control of correspondence, surveillance, controlled purchase and the activities of undercover officers.

§4. Improperly Obtained Evidence

959. The Code of Criminal Procedure does not contain any regulations that would comprehensively address the admissibility of improperly obtained evidence. There are, however, a few regulations that tackle the issue.

960. First of all, under Article 171 § 7 CCP, explanations, testimonies and statements made in conditions precluding freedom of expression or obtained in breach of the prohibitions listed in Article 171 § 5 must not be used as evidence. That article prohibits influencing the statements of the person subject to questioning by coercion or unlawful threats, and the use of hypnosis or chemical or technical measures influencing the psychological processes of the person subject to questioning or aimed at controlling the unconscious responses of his or her body. The ban is absolute.

961. Second, under Article 16 CCP if the participant in the proceedings is to be advised of his or her rights in the process, and has not received such advice, then the lack of such advice, or wrong advice, shall not result in any adverse consequences in the course of the trial for that person or any other persons concerned. That means that it is impossible to use evidence in a trial (such as testimony or explanations) that might give rise to adverse consequences for a given person or for any other person whom the evidence concerns. Hence, improperly obtained evidence will not necessarily be eliminated if the party has not received proper advice. Rather, the decision on whether to admit it or not depends on the effect the evidence may achieve.

962. Third, as of 1 July 2015, Article 168a states that evidence obtained for the purposes of criminal proceedings by means of a prohibited act, as referred to in Article 1 § 1 of the Criminal Code, is inadmissible. There have not yet been many interpretations of this provision. However, it does give rise to much controversy in the legal doctrine.

The person who obtained the evidence must have acted deliberately. Lack of intention – even if there was a violation of the criminal law – does not disqualify the evidence.

The reservation that the evidence is to be obtained by means of a prohibited act, as referred to in Article 1 § 1 of the CC, refers to conduct with elements described in the Criminal Code or any other act of law containing criminal provisions. However, it suffices that the statutory elements of a prohibited act were present. Therefore, it is irrelevant, for example, whether or not there were any circumstances in the case excluding criminal responsibility (such as necessity).

There are some doubts as to whether or not Article168a CCP only prohibits the use of evidence that is directly illegal, or whether it also extends to evidence that is indirectly illegal (so-called fruit of the poisonous tree). Opinions on this matter vary; however, the fact that there is no explicit statement referring to evidence obtained indirectly implies that it refers only to evidence that is in direct violation of criminal law.

963. In addition to these statutory regulations, decisions of the Supreme Court and of the courts of appeal have restricted the use of illegal evidence in criminal proceedings,. This concerns the ability to use evidence gathered by the police (and other authorised forces) pursuant to the Police Act (acts of law regulating the operations of other forces) as part of their operational activities (such as wiretapping).

Based on the constitutional provisions which provide for the principle of legality, the right to fair trial, and the right to privacy, the courts assume that '*while the police have the right to undertake investigative operations in order to investigate into, prevent and detect offences and petty offences, in order to consider the materials obtained as a result of such operations as evidence in criminal proceedings, it is necessary (..) to state that the material was obtained and recorded in a manner that is in compliance with the statutory restrictions applicable to the various categories of threats to the legal order in relation to which such operations are being taken.*'[30] In consequence, evidence is inadmissible if it has been obtained as a result of wiretapping without sufficient suspicion that an offence has been committed, which was the precondition for starting the wiretapping.

964. The ability to use evidence obtained improperly in cases other than the ones described above gives rise to certain doubts. There is no unanimous view on this matter in the legal doctrine. Some authors are of the opinion that the issue should be evaluated by the court, upon considering the impact on the ruling to be issued. Others argue that evidence obtained illegally should be banned as a rule.

965. The procedure for the elimination of evidence is yet another problematic issue. It has not been explicitly regulated in the Code of Criminal Procedure. Consequently, there are two views on the matter in the legal doctrine. According to some authors, the criminal justice body should issue a decision regarding the elimination of evidence, and such a decision should be issued at the request of a party or ex officio. Others are of the view that the court decides whether or not a given piece of evidence is inadmissible while evaluating the evidence prior to giving a ruling.

30. Supreme Court of 22 Sep. 2009, III KK 58/09, OSNKW 2010, Vol. 3, item 28.

Part III. Execution and Extinction of Sanctions

Chapter 1. Notion and Sources

966. The execution of sentences is regulated by the **executive criminal law** (*prawo karne wykonawcze*). This branch of law can be defined as the one that regulates the execution (enforcement) of judicial decisions that condemn offenders to penalties, penal measures and security measures and the execution of judicial decisions that refer to the detention on remand and the penalty of arrest (*kara aresztu*). The executive criminal law is not limited to the execution of measures provided in the substantive and procedural criminal law but also has effect in the fiscal criminal law (*prawo karne skarbowe*) and the petty offences law (*prawo wykroczeń*). The notion of executive criminal law must be differentiated from the notion of **penitentiary law** (*prawo penitencjarne*). In Polish understanding, the latter is limited solely to regulations regarding the execution of imprisonment, and does not include other forms of penalty (fines, etc.). It is probably more accurate to understand penitentiary law as a branch of law that regulates the execution of all measures that limit the freedom of a defendant or accused, including through detention on remand.

967. The main source of the executive criminal law is the CEC. It came into force on 1 September 1998, replacing the previous regulation that dated back to 1969. The new code was drafted and passed through Parliament together with new Criminal Code and Code of Criminal Procedure as a part of a great reform of the Polish criminal justice system.

There are several reasons why the new code was introduced instead of just incorporating the amendments to the old code:

- the dramatic change of the political system in Poland after 1989, which brought the state from the totalitarian and communist system to the new democratic state ruled by law. The change of the political system demanded changes in the law, in particular in the field of criminal law, which was used under the previous legal regime as a tool of oppression;
- the academic achievements of Polish researchers in the field of criminology and penitentiary law;
- national and foreign experience with regard to practice in the execution of penalties, both positive and negative;

- the need to increase the effectiveness of the execution of penalties, in particular of in the case of imprisonment;
- the growing need to respect the EU standards of criminal law[31].

The Criminal Enforcement Code is divided into four parts in the following way:

(1) General Part
 Chapter I. Scope of application
 Chapter II. Bodies of enforcement procedure
 Chapter III. Conviction
 Chapter IV. Enforcement procedure
 Chapter V. Penitentiary supervision
 Chapter VI. Expungement of conviction
 Chapter VII. Public participation in the execution of judicial decisions, assistance in the social readaptation of convicted persons and the Fund for Victim and Post-Penitentiary Support.
 Chapter VIIa. Electronic Monitoring System
(2) Special Part
 Chapter VIII. Fines
 Chapter IX. The restriction of liberty
 Chapter X. Imprisonment
 Chapter XI. The rights and duties of the court probation officer, the execution of supervision, conditional discontinuation of proceedings and the suspension of a sentence
 Chapter XII. Penal measures
 Chapter XIII. Security measures
 Chapter XIV. Court dues
 Chapter XV. Detention on remand
 Chapter XVa. Placement of persons detained on remand and those convicted for imprisonment in separate rooms, and rooms for the arrested
(3) Military Part
 Chapter XVI. General Part
 Chapter XVII. The restriction of liberty
 Chapter XVIII. Imprisonment and military confinement
 Chapter XIX. Penal measures
 Chapter XX. Detention on remand
(4) Final Part
 Chapter XXI. Explanation of Legal Expressions
 Chapter XXII. Final and Transitional Provisions

The specific issues relating to the execution of military penalties will be not be addressed in this monograph.

31. T. Szymanowski, J. Migdał, *Prawo karne wykonawcze i polityka penitencjarna*, Warszawa 2014, p. 35.

968. The executive criminal law is rooted in the Constitution of Republic of Poland of 1997 whose several provisions serve as the axiological basis of the executive criminal law. These are:

- Article 40 – No one may be subjected to torture or cruel, inhuman, or degrading treatment or punishment. The application of corporal punishment is prohibited.
- Article 41 paragraph 1 – Personal inviolability and security must be ensured to everyone. Any deprivation or limitation of liberty may be imposed only in accordance with principles and under procedures specified by statute.
- Article 41 paragraph 4 – Anyone deprived of liberty must be treated in a humane manner.

The above guarantees prescribed in the Constitution refer to all people deprived of freedom and sentenced to other forms of penalties and they are confirmed by regulations in Articles 4–8 CCE.

969. Ratified international agreements should be considered the second group of sources of executive criminal law. As its foundation, the following acts should be considered:

- Articles 1, 5 and 8 of the Universal Declaration of Human Rights
- Articles 7 and 10 of the International Covenant of Civil and Political Rights of 16 December 1966 (ratified in Poland on 13 March 1977);
- Articles 3 and 5 of the ECHR and Fundamental Freedoms of 4 November 1950 (ratified in Poland on 19 January 1993);
- Article 1 of the UN Convention against Torture and Other Cruel, Inhuman or Degrading Treatment or Punishment of 10 December 1984 (ratified in Poland on 21 October 1984);
- Articles 1 and 8 of the European Convention for the Prevention of Torture and Inhuman or Degrading Treatment or Punishment of 26 November 1987 (ratified in Poland on 1 February 1994);

The Recommendation Rec (2006) 2 of the Committee of Ministers to Member States on the **European Prison Rules** (EPRs) of 11 January 2006 also has meaningful impact on the Polish executive criminal law. The EPRs are not legally binding on the Polish territory and they should be treated more like guidance for shaping the law in a particular way. However, they are a reference tool for the Committee for the Prevention on Torture during visits that are conducted in each State-Party to the European Convention for the Prevention of Torture and Inhuman or Degrading Treatment or Punishment. Moreover, the ECtHR does refer quite often to these rules when examining individual applications from prisoners.

970. Beside the sources of law presented above, in particular the Criminal Enforcement Code, additional legal acts also consist of provisions relating to the executive criminal law. Among others, these are:

- The Prison Service Act of 9 April 2010;

- The Court Probation Officers Act of 27 July 2001;
- The Act on the employment of persons convicted to imprisonment of 28 August 1997;
- The Coercive Measures and Firearms Act of 24 May 2013.

971. It must be noted that issues concerning **conditional release** or **parole** (*warunkowe przedterminowe zwolnienie*) within the Polish criminal justice system are a part of the substantive criminal law and are regulated for the most part in the CC, discussed in Part I (see *supra*, paragraphs 440–447).

Chapter 2. Fundamental Principles

972. A visible tendency towards the shaping of principles of executive criminal law can be noted in Polish law. Perhaps the reason for this is the well-established tradition of determining the principles both of criminal law and criminal procedure.[32] Although there have been different attempts to categorise these principles, they may be summarised as follows:

(1) The principle of humanitarianism (Article 4 § 1 CEC): '*Penalties, penal measures, forfeiture, security measures and preventive measures must be executed humanely and with respect to the dignity of the convicted person. It is forbidden to use torture, inhuman or degrading treatment or punishment towards a convicted person*'.
(2) The principle of the limitation of rights and freedoms of the convicted person (Article 4 § 2 CEC): '*The civil rights and freedoms of the convicted person are preserved. Their limitations may be imposed only by means of statute and a final sentence based on that statute*'.
(3) The principle of subjective treatment of the convicted person (Article 5 § 1 CEC), which states that the convicted person is subject to the rights and duties prescribed in the CCE.
(4) The principle of the judicial review of the activity of non-judicial bodies of enforcement procedure. The convicted person has the right to appeal decisions of non-judicial bodies (Article 7 CEC). Moreover, according to Article 32 CEC, penitentiary supervision (*nadzór penitencjarny*) of the legality and propriety of the enforcement of penitentiary decisions is vested in the hands of the penitentiary judge (*sędzia penitencjarny*).
(5) The principle of social rehabilitation, re-education and social readaptation of persons convicted person of imprisonment (Article 67 CEC). Together with the principle of the individualised approach to the enforcement of penalties, these are aimed at bringing the convicted person back to society after having served the sentence. To achieve that goal, the executive criminal law, with particular regard to imprisonment, created a system of the classification of convicted persons and their assignment to certain types of prisons (e.g., open, semi-open and closed). Those issues will be discussed further in the next pages.
(6) The principle of public participation in the enforcement of judicial decisions and in social assistance with the aim of readapting the convicted person. One of the chapters of the CEC (Chapter VII) is devoted solely to those issues. These regulations provide for the wide participation of social groups (e.g., NGOs, associations, churches and religious groups) in the execution of criminal penalties. This principle is seen as one of the canons of contemporary penitentiary law and aims at the prevention of the negative consequences of isolation.

32. *See* on this topic A. Gerecka-Żołyńska, W. Sych, *Prawo karne wykonawcze. Zagadnienia procesowe*, Warszawa 2014, p. 48–55.

Chapter 3. The Prison System

§1. Organisational Structure

I. Prison Administration

973. According to Articles 68 and 208 CEC, the penalty of imprisonment is enforced in **prisons** (*zakłady karne*) while detention on remand takes place in **detention centres** (*areszty śledcze*). The administration of prisons and detention facilities is vested in the hands of the Prison Service (*Służba Więzienna*). It operates on the basis of The Prison Service Act of 9 April 2010. This uniformed and armed formation, is subordinated to the Ministry of Justice (Article 1 Prison Service Act). The Prison Service is therefore a government authority and is funded from the state budget (Article 6 Prison Service Act).

974. The structure of the Prison Service includes (Article 8 paragraph 1 Prison Service Act):

1. The Central Board of the Prison Service (*Centralny Zarząd Słuzby Wie ̨ziennej*);
2. Regional Inspectorates of the Prison Service (*okręgowe inspektoraty służby wie ̨ziennej*);
3. Prisons and detention centres;
4. The Prison Service General Education Centre, and Prison Service education centres and training centres.

The above remain under the supervision of the **Director-General of the Prison Service** (*Dyrektor Generalny Służby Więziennej*), who reports to the Minister of Justice (Article 10 paragraph 1 Prison Service Act). The Director-General of the Prison Service is the superior of every **Prison Service officer** (*funkcjonariusz Służby Wie ̨ziennej*). Each prison and detention facility is headed by a director. In 2015 there were eighty-seven prisons and sixty-seven detention centres.

II. Types of Prisons and Organisational Regimes

975. The penalty of imprisonment can be enforced in the following **types of prisons** (Article 69 CEC):

(1) prisons for young offenders;
(2) prisons for persons serving a first-time sentence;
(3) prisons for penitentiary recidivists (repeat offenders);
(4) prisons for persons serving a sentence of military confinement.

These types of prisons can be organised in the following **categories of prisons** (Article 70 § 1 CEC):

(1) closed prisons;
(2) semi-open prisons;
(3) open prisons.

Additionally the penalty of imprisonment can be enforced in one of the following **enforcement systems (regimes)** (Article 81 CEC):

(1) a system of planned influence (*system programowanego oddziaływania*),
(2) a therapeutic system (*system terapeutyczny*);
(3) a regular system.

All of the above will be presented below in the given order. The rules on the classification of convicted persons will be discussed in the next chapter.

976. In **prisons for young offenders** prison sentences are served by those who are not older than 24 years. In a justifiable situation, a prisoner who started his sentence in this type of prison can remain in here after reaching the age of 24, if he or she has been convicted for the first time and is distinguished by good behaviour (Article 84 CEC).

In **prisons for people serving a first-time sentence** those who are convicted for the first time and those who are not classified as penitentiary recidivists, e.g. convicted for a second time for an unintentional offence (Article 85 CEC) serve their sentences.

In **prisons for penitentiary recidivists** sentences of imprisonment are served by those who are convicted for the second time for an intentional offence (Article 86 § 1 CEC). Penitentiary recidivists can be directed to a prison for people serving first-time sentences if important rehabilitation reasons support this. The notion of 'penitentiary recidivists' and 'recidivist' in Article 64 CC differ significantly. This means that the group of penitentiary recidivists includes persons who do not meet the requirements of Article 64 CC (see *supra,* paragraph 461).

977. The **categories of prisons** are differentiated by the level of security, level of isolation of prisoners as well as their rights and duties with regard to freedom of movement inside and outside the facility.

In a **closed prison** a cell can be open during the day for a limited period of time; the convicted persons who are employed outside the prison must be securely transferred to and from work; cultural and sport activities can be held only inside the correctional facility; the convicted can use their own underwear and footwear, the rest of clothing is provided by the facility. Their movement inside the facility must be organised and supervised (Article 90 CEC).

In a **semi-open prison** a cell is open during the day and can be closed during the night; the convicted can work, study and take a part in educational or therapeutic meetings outside the prison; they can use their own clothing; and they can easily move inside the facility and once each two months but for not longer than in total fourteen days per year the convicted can receive a permit to leave the facility (Article 91 CEC).

In an **open prison** a cell is open 24 hours a day; the convicted can work, study, take part in educational and therapeutic meetings outside the prison; they can use they own clothing; they can move freely inside the facility; they can use their own money from the prison's deposit and once each month but for not longer than in total 28 days per year the convicted can receive a permit to leave the facility (Article 92 CEC).

978. The **system of enforcement of a penalty** is more complicated that the distinction provided in Article 81 CEC (the system of planned influence, the therapeutic system and the regular system). Inside of each of these given groups we can distinguish additional classes of those sentenced, such as women, alcohol or drugs addicts, high-risk prisoners and sex offenders. Nevertheless, these three systems of enforcement of a penalty have some common features that will be laid down below.

In the **system of planned influence** a sentence of imprisonment is served by young offenders and those adults who agree to cooperate in the creation and execution of an individual programme. In this system emphasis is placed on the work and education of the inmate, as well as his free time activities. Also, the importance of regular visits from relatives and maintaining contact with them is strongly stressed. Inmates serving a sentence in this system are evaluated periodically and the programme created for them may be modified and reconsidered or even annulled if it is not complied with. This system is considered to help the convicted return society in the best possible way.

In the **therapeutic system** sentences are served by those convicted who have non-psychotic mental disorders, including inmates convicted of offences specified in Article 197–203 CC (Offences against sexual freedom and decency) in connection with a disorder of sexual preference, as well as convicted persons who have mental disorders, are addicted to alcohol or drugs or to psychotropic medication (Article 96 CEC). This system is intended for convicts with physical disabilities if they require specialist treatment, especially psychological treatment or medical help and rehabilitation. Those assigned with the therapeutic system serve their sentence in this system as long as it is needed. While executing a penalty in the therapeutic system, the need to prevent the deepening of pathological personality traits, the restoration of psychological balance and the ability to shape social coexistence, as well as the preparation for independent living, are particularly taken into consideration (Article 97 § 1 CEC).

Finally, in the **regular system** sentences are served by those who are categorised as not eligible for any of the systems presented above. However, all those serving a sentence in the regular system are eligible to benefit from employment, education and cultural, educational and sport activities that are available in a prison (Article 98 CEC).

979. Polish law also provides for special **prisons for women**. These prisons are not divided into the different types presented above. Women serve their sentences separately from men (Article 87 § 1 CEC), usually in semi-open prisons. They have the right to a longer walk and to more frequent food shopping. Those who are pregnant or have small children are given special treatment and they can expect some exceptions from the typical regulations.

§2. PENITENTIARY TREATMENT

I. The Scientific Personalisation System

980. The execution of a penalty of imprisonment is conducted according to the **principle of personal approach**. Article 67 § 1 CEC provides that the execution of a penalty of imprisonment is aimed at inspiring in a convicted person the will to cooperate in developing his or her socially desirable attitudes, in particular a sense of responsibility and the need to respect the law and thus refrain from returning to crime. This should be understood as the ultimate goal of the influence of the system upon the convicted. Therefore, to achieve this objective, individualised action plans for convicted persons are carried out within the legal framework of systems of the enforcement of a penalty within different types and categories of prisons (Article 67 § 2 CEC). Primarily, these individualised action plans take the form of work – especially that which is conducive to obtaining relevant professional qualifications, teaching, cultural and educational activities and sports, maintaining contact with family and the outside world, and therapeutic measures (Article 67 § 3 CEC). All individualised action plans must be conducted while respecting the rights of the convicted.

981. Therefore, the classification of prisoners should be conducted with the aim to:

- create conditions conducive to the personalisation of treatment of prisoners;
- to prevent the harmful influence from disruptive inmates;
- to ensure the personal safety of all the convicted;
- to select the appropriate system of execution of a penalty, as well as type and category of prison and location of inmates inside a facility (Article 82 § 1 CEC).

The penitentiary law provides one additional aim for classifying the convicted, which is the protection of the community and assuring the security of a prison from inmates who generate a serious threat (Article 88 § 3 CEC).

II. Classification of Inmates

982. Inmates are classified based on several factors prescribed in Article 82 § 2 CEC, namely:

(1) gender;
(2) age;
(3) a history of imprisonment;
(4) intentional or unintentional nature of the committed crime;
(5) time remaining to serve of a sentence;
(6) physical and mental health, including the degree of addiction to alcohol, drugs or psychotropic medications;

(7) degree of disruptiveness or posed risk to society;
(8) type of offence committed.

This list is not exhaustive and body that decides on the classification of inmates can take into account other factors, such as the profession of an inmate, his family situation or education. Some of the above factors (1–5 and 8) are of formal character, which means that they can be determined objectively. But factors 6 and 7 are material in their nature. Therefore, to establish the physical and mental health of an inmate, as well as his degree of disruptiveness, it is necessary to conduct some examinations, since it is not sufficient to base a judgment solely on an inmate statements. In particular, prisoners in Poland are subjected to cognitive tests (*badania osobopoznawcze*) as well as psychological and psychiatric examinations, in which their participation is compulsory (Article 82 § 3 and Article 83 CEC).

983. The responsibility of classifying inmates is vested in the hands of the **penitentiary commission** (*komisja penitencjarna*) working in every prison (Article 75 CEC). The commission consists of Prison Service officers and other employees appointed by the director of the prison. Additionally, the commission may invite other people to work with an advisory role. These people may be representatives of organisations, associations or foundations, as well as institutions, churches and religious groups. The law provides a broad list of competencies for the penitentiary commission (Article 76 CEC), among which the most important are those connected with the classification of inmates.

984. The work of a penitentiary commission is carried out on the basis of materials made available to it. It is believed that the adequate and effective execution of a penalty is not possible without in-depth knowledge about a prisoner. Therefore, the administration of prisons is obliged to gather all necessary materials about a prisoner to allow the penitentiary commission to make a decision with regard to the classification of the prisoner. These documents include:

(1) a text of the judgment and sentence against the convicted;
(2) written reasoning of that decision, if available;
(3) information about an inmate that can be found in court materials (Article 11 CEC);
(4) other documents regarding an inmate, including from his previous periods of imprisonment;
(5) cognitive research about an inmate;
(6) psychiatric and psychological opinions about an inmate, etc.

985. After careful examination of available materials, the penitentiary commission classifies convicts into certain groups and subgroups. The system provides a code for each classification, according to which:

(1) types of prisons are marked with capital letters:
  (a) prisons for young offenders – M;
  (b) prisons for inmates serving first-time sentences – P;

(c) prisons for penitentiary recidivists – R–;
(d) prisons for inmates serving sentence of military confinement – W;
(2) categories of prisons are marked with numbers:
(a) closed prisons – 1;
(b) semi-open prisons – 2;
(c) open prisons – 3;
(3) systems of execution of a penalty are marked with small letters:
(a) system of planned influence – p;
(b) therapeutic system – t;
(c) regular system – z.

986. The first classification of inmates is made as soon as they arrive in a prison. However, this classification is not final, it can be modified whenever the situation of an inmate changes due to his or behaviour or state of mental or physical health. In particular, inmate's classification will change when he or she is moved from one facility to another or when the decision on permitting to work or study is being made, etc. Each decision regarding the classification of an inmate is subject to judicial review by the penitentiary court (Article 7 CEC).

§3. Penitentiary Regime

I. Introduction

987. Article 102 CEC provides rights of every inmate, among those are the right:

(1) to appropriate feeding, clothing, living conditions, rooms, healthcare and hygiene conditions;
(2) to maintain ties with family and loved ones;
(3) to religious freedom;
(4) to receive salary for work, and also social security, to the extent provided in separate regulations, as well as the right to receive help in obtaining disability benefits;
(5) to education and self-education as well as the right to creativeness and the right to produce and to sell items they have created upon the consent of the director of the prison;
(6) to use cultural, educational and sport equipment, and to participate in related activities, and the right of access to radio, television, books and newspapers;
(7) to communicate with an advocate, attorney, probation officer or a chosen representative;
(8) to communicate with representatives of associations, foundations, organisations and other institutions, including churches and religious groups;
(9) to be acquainted with opinions prepared by the administration of the prison which will constitute the basis of decisions regarding the inmate;
(10) to file motions, complaints and requests with an authority competent to consider them and the right to present them, in the absence of other persons, to

the administration of a prison, the head of organisational units of the Prison Service, a penitentiary judge, prosecutor and the ombudsman;

(11) to correspond with law enforcement agencies, the judiciary and other state bodies, local government bodies, the ombudsman, the ombudsman for children and other bodies protecting human rights.

II. Aspects of Living Conditions

A. *Healthcare*

988. Upon the arrival of an inmate in a prison, the administration is obliged to subject them to medical examinations as well as sanitary treatments. This is done with the aim of understanding the health condition and to provide the appropriate treatment. The reduction of the threat of spreading contagious diseases among the community, i.e. the protection of other inmates is also important here.

989. Every inmate has a guaranteed right to free healthcare, medication and sanitary articles (Article 115 § 1 CEC). Moreover, he or she has access to prostheses, orthopaedic instruments and aids, if their lack could worsen their state of health or prevent the execution of their penalty (Article 115 § 2 CEC). In the above cases this access is free of charge, in all other situations the convict will be charged for such assistance.

990. An inmate has no right to choose a doctor, a nurse, a primary care provider that offers outpatient services, or to choose a hospital (Article 115 § 1a CEC). Healthcare for all convicts is provided by doctors, nurses, hospitals, etc. for persons deprived of liberty (Article 115 § 4 CEC). Nevertheless, upon the consent of the director of the prison, the convict may choose his own doctor, other medication, etc., at his own expense (Article 115 § 6 CEC). In practice, frequently convicts are transferred to external medical facilities (e.g., hospitals) where they are treated medically, even for several weeks, due to the lack of treatment options in prison.

B. *Communication*

991. Communication of inmates with the outside world can be described as a direct communication with family through their visits and indirect communication through letters. Each inmate is granted the right to communicate not only with members of his or her family and close persons but also with other bodies (associations, religious groups, etc.) and with lawyers. Maintaining contact with family members is one of the most important elements of positive influence on an inmate. It is also treated as a part of a penalty and rewards system (see Article 105 § 1 CEC). Depending on the type and category of a prison, the scope and form of communication with the outside world may differ (Article 105 § 3 CEC).

992. Each visit can last up to 60 minutes. In closed prisons each convict has the right to two visits during every month and upon the consent of the director of the prison they can be held together (Article 90 § 6 CEC). Visits and conversations during visits in this type of a prison are always controlled by the administration of the prison (Article 90 item 7 CEC). In semi-open prisons each convict has the right to three visits during every month and upon the consent of the director of the prison they can be held together (Article 91 item 8 CEC). Visits are always conducted under the control of the administration of the prison but conversations may be conducted in privacy (Article 91 item 8 CEC). In open prisons a convict has unlimited access to visits (Article 92 item 10 CEC), which can be conducted under the control of the administration of the prison, though conversations cannot be overheard (Article 92 item 11 CEC). Young offenders have the right to one extra visit each month (Article 91a CEC). During each visit only two adults can be present at one time and an unlimited number of minors under 18 years of age, however they have to be accompanied by an adult (Article 105a § 2 CEC). Those convicts that exercise guardianship over children below 15 years of age are entitled to an additional visit from their children each month (Article 105a § 3 CEC). A visit from a person who is not a family member or a loved one of the convict is possible but only upon the permission of the director of the prison (Article 105a § 4 CEC).

993. Written correspondence and telephone calls in closed prisons are controlled by the administration (Article 90 item 8 and 9 CEC), while in semi-open prisons they can be controlled (Article 91 item 10 and 11 CEC) and in open prisons they are not controlled at all (Article 92 item 13 and 14 CEC). The convicted person is entitled to use a prepaid phone at his or her own expense or at the expense of their interlocutor (Article 105b § 1 CEC). The use of cell phones is prohibited. Interestingly, however, the director of the prison can temporarily deprive an inmate of his right to use a phone in the case of a threat to public order or a threat to the security of the prison (Article 105b § 3 CEC).

994. The general rule on communication with a lawyer is included in Article 8 § 3 CEC and states that the inmate can communicate with his or her lawyer in the absence of other people and that conversations with a lawyer during in-person meetings and through telephone calls are not subject to inspection. The same applies to a legal representative who is an attorney (*adwokat*) or legal advisor (*radca prawny*) and a representative approved by the Section President of the ECtHR, who is neither an advocate nor legal advisor, to represent a convict before this Court.

C. *Work*

995. Work is the right of every inmate. The general rule on work in prisons provides that an inmate, when possible, shall have access to employment (Article 121 § 1 CEC). The forms in which inmates may be employed are not limited to a contract of employment (*umowa o pracę*); they may also benefit from contracts for a specified task (*umowa o dzieło*) and others forms of employment (Article 121 § 2 CEC).

996. Employment of an inmate is subject to the consent of the director of a prison, and should take into account the process of the execution of a penalty (Article 121 § 3 CEC). Therefore, inmates can be employed inside and outside of a prison. An inmate serving a penalty of life imprisonment in a closed type of prison may be employed only inside the prison (Article 121 § 10 CEC).

997. Working is considered important in the process of an inmate's rehabilitation. Therefore, ensuring appropriate employment that suits the profession, education, interests and personal needs of a convict is essential (Article 122 § 1 CEC). In particular, work should be ensured to those that are obliged to pay alimony and those that have a particularly difficult material, personal or family situation (Article 122 § 2 CEC).

998. Inmates receive remuneration for their work (Article 123 § 1 CEC). However, the convict must perform, free of charge but not exceeding 90 hours in month, ancillary work at the facilities of the Prison Service or local government (Article 123a § 1 CEC). An inmate may also, upon his or her request or written consent, work without remuneration for public administration or charity (Article 123a § 2 CEC).

999. A convict cannot use his salary freely. By law, 10% of his or her remuneration is transferred to the Victim Aid and Post-penitentiary Assistance Fund, and 25% is transferred to the Fund for the Work Activation of Convicts. Additionally, some of the remaining salary is kept out of the reach of the inmate, so that it can be used after his or her prison term has been served.[33]

D. Security and Disciplinary Regime

1000. An inmate is obliged to respect the rules defining the principles and mode of execution of a penalty, to obey the order of the prison and follow the commands of authorised personnel (Article 116 § 1 CEC).

1001. The inmate and his clothing can be controlled in cases justified by public order and security. Similarly, cells and other rooms in which inmates stay, as well as items in their possession, can be searched (Article 116 § 2 CEC). A personal search should be conducted by a person of the same gender as the inmate and without the presence of other people (Article 116 § 3 CEC). Also lab tests for the presence of alcohol, drugs or psychotropic substances can be conducted (Article 116b § 1 CEC). There are no limitations with regard to the time in which a search can be conducted. The law provides for certain rules of engagement when it comes to the possession of dangerous or forbidden items. For security or medical reasons cameras can be installed and the image and sound is recorded (Article 116 § 5a CEC).

33. *See* on this topic A. Gerecka-Żołyńska, W. Sych, *Prawo karne wykonawcze. Zagadnienia procesowe*, Warszawa 2014, p. 143–144.

1002. Simultaneously, Article 116a CEC lists forbidden behaviours, which includes:

(1) participation in organised groups without the knowledge of a supervising officer;
(2) swearing or using words generally considered offensive or abusive, as well as using criminal slang;
(3) gambling;
(4) consuming alcohol and using drugs or psychotropic substances;
(5) refusing food or self-harming with the aim of forcing certain decisions or actions on the administration of a prison;
(6) tattooing another person or receiving tattoos;
(7) communicating with outsiders or inmates in a way that violates the order of the prison;
(8) arbitrarily leaving a cell or other place where an inmate is required to be;
(9) an inmate changing their appearance in a way that hampers their identification, in particular through shaving or growing their hair, beard or moustache or changing its colour, unless with the consent of the director of the prison.

Respect of the above regulations is taken into consideration by the penitentiary commission when the question of reclassification of an inmate is raised. Therefore, not obeying the rules may result in a tightening of the conditions in which an inmate will continue serving his or her sentence.

1003. A system of penalties and rewards is exercised in every prison. This is seen as a great educational tool. Rewards can be granted to an inmate distinguishes him or herself, or they can be used to encourage an inmate to correct his or her behaviour (Article 137 CEC). These rewards include: permission to receive an additional or prolonged visit, permission to receive a visit in separate room without any supervision, extinction of some penalties obtained in prison, commendation, as well as a pass (*przepustka*) that allows an inmate to leave a prison for a certain period of time (Article 138 CEC).

E. Leave from Prison

1004. A penalty of imprisonment may be postponed, interrupted or terminated early. This is possible by way of a postponement of the enforcement of a prison sentence (*odroczenie wykonania kary pozbawienia wolności*), an interruption in the enforcement of a prison sentence (temporary release from prison – *przerwa w wykonywaniu kary pozbawienia wolności*) and conditional early release from prison (parole – *warunkowe przedterminowe zwolnienie*).

1005. As a rule, a **penalty of imprisonment is postponed** by a court's decision. The following circumstances may serve as grounds for postponement:

(1) a mental illness or other severe medical condition that prevents a penalty from being enforced;
(2) the risk that the immediate enforcement of a penalty would cause excessively severe consequences to a convicted person or his or her family;
(3) the country-wide number of inmates in prisons or detention centres exceeds the general capacity of these facilities.

If any of the above applies, the court may postpone the enforcement of a penalty of up to one year – this will not be possible in the case of perpetrators of several serious offences and repeat offenders.

A postponement may be granted on multiple occasions, but its aggregate length may not exceed twelve months, unless it is granted to a single mother of a child aged up to three years.

Furthermore, the CCE enables further postponement of a penalty of imprisonment imposed on convicted persons who have already been granted the deferral of a prison term of no longer than two years. If such a person is granted a twelve-month postponement and he or she satisfies the criteria for the conditional suspension of a penalty defined in the CC, the penalty may be suspended pursuant to the conditions determined in Articles 69–75 CC (Article 152 § 1 CCE).

A postponement of the enforcement of a penalty of imprisonment may be revoked when the reasons for its application cease to exist or when a convicted person does not use the postponement according to its designated purpose or flagrantly violates the legal order or fails to perform obligations imposed by the court.

1006. **A temporary release from prison** is a measure similar to a postponement of the penalty of imprisonment. In granting a temporary release, the court is guided by the same criteria as those applicable to the postponement of the penalty of imprisonment. However, unlike postponement, under law a temporary release from prison may not be granted in order to relieve prison overcrowding, even if there is currently such a problem.

A temporary release from prison is granted by a penitentiary court. The court may impose on a convicted person the same obligations as those applicable in the case of the postponement of a penalty of imprisonment (e.g., a duty to report to a designated police unit or to undergo appropriate treatment).

In this case, the court may also revoke a temporary release from prison if a convicted person does not use the release according to its designated purpose or flagrantly violates the legal order or fails to perform imposed obligations.

1007. The institution of **parole,** which is governed by the CC and not the CCE, is discussed in Part I – Criminal Law (see *supra*, paragraphs 440–447).

F. Other

1008. Inmates are entitled to appropriate meals (Article 102 item 1 CCE). In fact, this is the first right that is mentioned in that rule, which suggests that this right is of particular importance. Three times a day, each inmate receives drink and food of sufficient nutritional value, including at least one hot meal; this should take into account the age, type of work performed by inmates, and, where possible, religious and cultural requirements (Article 109 § 1 CEC). The current norm for an inmate is 2,800 kcal for young convicts under 18 years old and 2,600 kcal for other male convicts. An inmate also has the right to make purchases of food and tobacco products and other items authorised for sale in prison at least three times a month (Article 113a § 1 CEC).

1009. Generally, inmates have the right to wear their own clothes but they can receive the appropriate clothing, including shoes and underwear, from the prison administration (Article 111 § 1 CEC). However, specific rules regulate this rule more extensively. Therefore, in closed prisons inmates may only wear private underwear, shoes and other clothing upon the consent of the director of the prison (Article 90 item 5 CEC). In semi-open and open prisons, the convicts have no restrictions with regard to private clothing (Article 91 item 6 and Article 92 item 7 CEC). While in transit between prisons or on the way to court, an inmate is entitled to his own clothing unless the clothing is not appropriate because of the weather, it is damaged, or if it should not be worn for security reasons (Article 111 § 2 CEC).

§4. Judicial Control

1010. Generally, the execution of judicial decisions within the criminal justice system is divided between distinct authorities of judicial and non-judicial character, including the Prison Service. This is true not only for the execution of the penalty of imprisonment (on which the Prison Service focuses) but also for the execution of other penalties, such as fines, the restriction of liberty and detention on remand. The following organs are listed in Article 2 CEC as executive procedure authorities (*organy postępowania wykonawczego*):

(1) court of the first instance or other court of equal rank;
(2) penitentiary court;
(3) president of the court or authorised judge;
(4) penitentiary judge;
(5) director of a prison, director of a detention centre, regional director of the Prison Service, General Director of the Prison Service or a person managing another facility prescribed in the executive criminal law and penitentiary commission;
(6) court probation officer (*sądowy kurator zawodowy*) and head of the court probation service (*kierownik kuratorskiej służby sądowej*);
(7) court or administrative executive authority (*sądowy lub administracyjny organ egzekucyjny*);
(8) fiscal office (*urząd skarbowy*);
(9) relevant local branch of government administration or local government;
(10) other authorities authorised by law to execute a judicial decision.

The authorities from the above list can be organised according to their function with regard to the execution of penalties, and we can therefore single out:

1. **Judicial authorities** (*organy sądowe*) - this means bodies that may issue judicial rulings (*orzeczenia*) in executive procedures (courts of the first instance or other courts of equal competency and penitentiary courts) as well as those that can only issue orders (*zarządzenia*) (president of a court or an authorised judge or penitentiary judge).
2. **Authorities with an organizational connection to the court** (*organy zwia ̨zane organizacyjnie z sądem*), which are: court probation officer and court executive authority, i.e. a court enforcement officer (*komornik*).
3. **Non-judicial authorities established to execute judicial decisions in criminal matters** (*organy pozasądowe powołane do wykonywania orzeczeń*) – a director of a prison, a director of a detention centre, a regional director of the Prison Service, the Director-General of the Prison Service and the penitentiary commissions.
4. **Non-judicial authorities established to execute judicial decisions in criminal matters only as an additional task** (*organy pozasądowe powołane do wykonywania orzeczeń jako zadaniem dodatkowym*) – a person managing another facility prescribed in the executive criminal law (e.g., director of a psychiatric hospital or director of a rehab facility where security measures are imposed), administrative executive authority, the fiscal office or the relevant local branch of the government administration or local government.
5. **Other authorities authorised by law to execute a judicial decision.**

1011. The **penitentiary commissions** (*komisje penitencjarne*) are located in prisons (Article 75 § 1 CEC) and are collective in character. They consist of Prison Service officers and other employees of the prison who are nominated by the director of the prison. However, other members can be added to the commission, i.e. representatives of associations, foundations, organisations and other institutions including churches and religious groups that have an advisory role. According to the Article 76 § 1 CEC, the powers that remain in the hands of the penitentiary commission include, among others, the power to direct an inmate to the appropriate type and kind of prison, as well as the management of systems for executing a penalty (see below) and the authority to give recommendations with regard to the possible rewards and punishments granted to a convict.

Chapter 4. Extinction of Criminal Liability

§1. Introduction

1012. The notion of the **extinction of criminal liability** (*wygaśnięcie odpowiedzialności karnej*) should be understood in broad terms as the situation where the actual or potential consequences of statutory criminal liability for a given offence are removed.

1013. Extinction of criminal liability may be caused by many different circumstances of various nature. The most obvious one, considering the personal character of criminal responsibility, is death of the accused. In Polish criminal process, the accused's demise results in the discontinuation of proceedings (Article 17 § 1 item 5 CCP). Criminal responsibility is also extinct if criminal sanctions imposed on a convicted person have been fully satisfied. However, Polish criminal law – both substantive and procedural – lacks a provision that would identify, in an exhaustive and explicit manner, what circumstances result in the extinction of criminal liability. The scholarship most often points to the following factors that bring this about:

(a) immunities (see *supra*, paragraphs 185–187);
(b) expiry of a limitation period for prosecution;
(c) expiry of a limitation period for the enforcement of a sentence;
(d) abolition;
(e) amnesty;
(f) pardon;
(g) expungement of a conviction.

1014. It should be emphasised that the above factors are different in their nature and eliminate the effects related to the assumption of criminal responsibility for a crime in a number of different ways. The available options for extinguishing criminal liability seek to prevent:

(1) the launch of criminal proceedings against the perpetrator of a prohibited act;
(2) the imposition of criminal sanctions on the perpetrator of a prohibited act;
(3) the enforcement of criminal sanctions imposed on a convicted person;
(4) keeping a criminal record in official registers.

In consequence, there is a whole spectrum of situations here – from those in which it is impossible to prosecute a person suspected of having committed an offence (which, e.g., had become time-barred), through those in which a convicted person avoids serving his or her sentence in full (e.g., amnesty, pardon), to a situation where only a defendant's criminal record is erased (expungement of a conviction).

§2. Expiry of a Limitation Period for the Prosecution of an Offence and Enforcement of a Sentence

I. Expiry of a Limitation Period for the Prosecution of Offences

1015. The Polish Criminal Code states the rules governing limitation periods for the prosecution of offences in Chapter XI (Articles 101–105). The length of a limitation period depends on how serious an offence is and on whether it is subject to a public or private prosecution.

1016. For offences prosecuted by public accusation, Article 101 § 1 CC stipulates that an offence is no longer punishable upon the passage of the following limitation periods:

(1) thirty years in the case of murder or voluntary manslaughter;
(2) twenty years in the case of other felonies;
(3) fifteen years in the case of misdemeanours that are subject to the penalty of imprisonment of more than five years;
(4) ten years in the case of misdemeanours that are subject to the penalty of imprisonment of more than three years;
(5) five years in the case of remaining misdemeanours.

1017. The prosecution of offences by private accusation becomes time-barred after the passage of one year from the date when a victim learns about the identity of the perpetrator of an offence in question, however, not later than after the passage of three years from its commission.

1018. The limitation period is counted from the date of an offence's commission. It must be noted, however, that if the commission of an offence depends on the presence of an occurrence defined in a statute, the limitation period starts running from the moment this occurrence actually appears. This rule prevents the premature expiry of a limitation period for the prosecution of an offence whose consequences, defined as an element of an offence (e.g., causing bodily harm), appear only after a prolonged period of time following the perpetration of an act.

1019. A special measure designed to protect the interests of minors (persons below the age of 18) was introduced in Article 101 § 4 CC. In accordance with this provision, limitation periods for the prosecution of the following types of offences may not expire before a minor attains the age of 30:

(1) misdemeanours committed against the life or health of a minor with the upper limit of statutory penalties exceeding five years of imprisonment;
(2) the offences described in Chapter XXV (offences against sexual liberty or decency) committed against a minor or those involving pornographic content that includes the participation of a minor.

1020. The aforementioned limitation periods are extended if proceedings have been initiated in a given case before the expiry of the initial limitation period (Article 102 CC). This extension is for ten years, counted from the end of the initial limitation period. Exceptionally, acts prosecuted by private accusation are extended by a further five years.

1021. As a rule, a limitation period runs continuously from point of the commission of an offence, which is the moment when an occurrence constituting a statutory element of an offence appears. However, Article 104 § 1 CC provides that the period of limitation does not run if a statutory provision precludes the initiation or further conduct of criminal proceedings. This applies to those situations in which legal impediments (in particular immunities) prevent prosecution. Had no such rule been established, the immunity granted to a perpetrator would enable them to also avoid criminal liability for those prohibited acts that were committed prior to the granting of immunity. It should be noted, however, that the rule allowing the suspension of limitation periods does not apply to the situation where a victim fails to submit an application for prosecution (which happens in the case of offences prosecuted upon complaint, and not ex officio) or in the case of offences prosecuted by private accusation. In consequence, a victim's inactivity may not cause the suspension of a limitation period.

1022. The general rule that criminal offences may be prosecuted only within certain limitation periods is subject to certain exceptions.

Article 105 § 1 CC stipulates that the provisions on limitation periods do not apply to crimes against peace, humanity and war crimes. This is primarily a consequence of the nature of the crimes concerned. The fact that these crimes are subject to no limitation period is also a consequence of the wording of Article 43 of the Polish Constitution, which reads that there is no statute of limitation regarding war crimes and crimes against humanity, and results from the Convention on the non-applicability of statutory limitations to war crimes and crimes against humanity ratified by Poland in 1969.

Furthermore, there is no limitation period for the offences of voluntary manslaughter, inflicting serious injury or grievous bodily harm or unlawful detention involving exceptional torment, committed by a public official in connection with the discharge of his or her official duties (Article 105 § 2 CC). This regulation is intended to prevent the expiry of limitation periods in respect of offences committed by public officials who are not prosecuted by competent state authorities for political reasons, and thus it avoids a situation in which perpetrators of such offences would be immune to any attempted criminal prosecution at a later date. Notably, Article 105 § 2 CC is more strict than the equivalent rule expressed in Article 44 of the Constitution, which stipulates that the limitation periods established for offences committed by, or by order of, public officials who have not been prosecuted for political reasons, should be suspended until such reasons cease to exist.

1023. A special regulation on limitation periods for the prosecution of criminal offences is established in Article 4 paragraph 1a of the Act on the Institute of

National Remembrance – Commission for the Prosecution of Crimes against the Polish Nation of 18 December 1998.[34] This provision stipulates that periods of limitation of 'communist crimes' that are not war crimes or crimes against humanity, defined as acts committed by officials of the communist state from 17 September 1939 to 31 July 1990 that involved, or were connected with, repression or other human rights violations targeting individuals or groups of the population that constitute criminal offences under the law applicable at the time of their commission, are counted from 1 August 1990. Such crimes become not punishable after forty years when the act in question is voluntary manslaughter, or after or thirty years in the case of other communist crimes. The above regulation was designed as a measure for bringing to justice the perpetrators of repression during Poland's period under communism; this could not have been done before 1990 for obvious reasons.

1024. Upon expiry of a limitation period for a criminal offence, a perpetrator of an offence may no longer be prosecuted. This effect is absolute. It is thus impossible to introduce a provision that would exclude limitation periods for certain types of offences whose limitation periods have already expired. However, a statute may be amended in a way that extends limitation periods that have not yet expired. Such a modification is not incompatible with the constitutional principle *nullum crimen sine lege.*[35]

II. Expiry of a Limitation Period for the Enforcement of a Sentence

1025. The Criminal Code stipulates limitation periods for the enforcement of criminal sentences. Article 103 § 1 CC provides that a sentence may not be enforced before the expiry of the following limitation periods, running from the date when a conviction becomes final:

(1) thirty years – in the case of a sentence imposing the penalty of imprisonment for a term of more than five years or a more severe penalty,
(2) fifteen years – in the case of a sentence imposing the penalty of imprisonment for a term of no more than five years,
(3) ten years – in the case of a sentence imposing other penalties.

Pursuant to Article 103 § 2 CC these periods also apply to penal measures, compensatory measures and forfeiture.

1026. Time limitation of the enforcement of sentences is governed by the rules on the suspension of limitation periods for prosecution (Article 104 CC) and on the exclusion of limitation periods (Article 105 CC) (see *supra*, paragraph 1022), applied *mutatis mutandis*.

34. J.L. 1998 No. 115, item 1016, as amended.
35. Judgments of the Constitutional Tribunal from 15.10.2008, Case No. P 32/06, published in OTK ZU Vol. 8/A/2008, item 138; and from 25.5.2004, SK 44/03, OTK ZU Vol. 5/A/2004, item 46.

§3. Abolition and Amnesty

1027. Abolition means the revocation of the punishability of a given offence, which occurs in connection with a prohibition of initiating criminal proceedings in a certain category of cases or with an obligation to discontinue such proceedings.

1028. Amnesty means the remittance of a certain penalty, in whole or in part, or another form of mitigation of such a penalty (e.g., a suspension of the enforcement of a prison sentence).

1029. Both amnesty and abolition are general acts (unlike a pardon, which is an individual act) and apply to certain categories of offences. They are applied on the basis of a universally applicable legal enactment, usually an Act of Parliament).

1030. Historically, legal acts with abolition and amnesty regulations have been adopted on a number of occasions in the period of the People's Republic of Poland (1945–1989). In principle, such laws were motivated by political factors, for instance the amnesties of 1964 and 1969 and those enacted to commemorate the twentieth and twenty-fifth anniversaries of Communist Poland. Some abolition and amnesty laws were guided by criminal policy factors and designed as measures mitigating excessively strict state penal policies. The last amnesty and abolition was enacted under the Amnesty Act of 7 December 1989.

§4. Pardon

1031. Pardon (*ułaskawienie*) is an individual rather than a general act that may be exercised by the President of Poland, who is a representative of the executive, and not the legislative branch of government. The power of pardon is established in Article 139 of the Constitution. The granting of the power of pardon to the President is an expression that follows a Polish constitutional tradition from the interwar period. The Constitutions of both 1921 and 1934 established the presidential power of pardon. Notably, in the era of the People's Republic of Poland, the power of pardon was granted to the Council of State, a body created in place of the office of President.

1032. As a rule, the President of Poland may pardon any person convicted in a criminal case. However, Article 139 of the Constitution stipulates that a pardon may not be applied to persons convicted by the Tribunal of State (*Trybunał Stanu*). The Tribunal of State is a special judicial body entrusted with hearing cases involving the criminal responsibility:

(1) of the President of Poland, the Speaker of the Sejm or the Speaker of the Senate, if either of the latter two is temporarily performing the duties of the president,
(2) of a member of the Council of Ministers for an offence committed in relation to his or her post.

1033. A pardon means the commutation or mitigation of a penalty or other penal measure. It may thus be applied to person convicted of having committed a criminal offence by a final court decision. It is disputable, on the contrary, whether a pardon can lawfully be given to a person accused of a crime, but not yet convicted by a final ruling. Arguably, the answer to the above question should be negative, most of all in the view of the separation of powers principle and the fact that a person who is not convicted by a final ruling benefits from the presumption of innocence. However, in 2015 such a 'pre-conviction' pardon was given in practice by the President Andrzej Duda.

1034. The president is not bound by the legal rules governing the imposition and conditions of criminal penalties. He is therefore autonomous in deciding how a mitigated penalty or penal measure will look.

1035. There are two options for initiating pardon proceedings: they may either be launched upon a relevant application submitted by an authorised entity or commenced ex officio.

Under Article 560 § 1 CCP, a pardon application may be submitted by a convicted person, a person authorised to submit appellate measures on a convicted person's behalf, a convicted person's relatives within the first degree of lineal consanguinity, a convicted person's adoptive parent or adopted child, or his or her siblings, spouse or cohabitee. The request for a pardon should be presented to the court that issued the first instance judgment. If a foreign judgment has been accepted as enforceable in Poland, a request for a pardon should be presented to the court that issued the first instance judgment. The request is heard by a panel that should consist of, if possible, the professional and lay judges who took part in the issuance of the conviction.

1036. In hearing a pardon request, the court should examine, in particular, a convicted person's behaviour in the period following the conviction, the length of the penalty already served, the convicted person's medical condition and family circumstances, the facts concerning the redressing of damage caused by the offence, and – above all – any extraordinary events that have occurred after the conviction was passed.

1037. If a case in which a pardon is requested was ultimately decided in the first instance, a negative opinion on a pardon request effectively concludes the proceedings. A positive opinion, together with the files of the case, is communicated to the Prosecutor General, who issues his or her own opinion and sends the case to the President of Poland. However, if the case in which a pardon is requested was decided by first *and* second instance courts, both courts must draw their own opinions. If both courts issue negative opinions, the pardon proceedings end. If the opinion of at least one of these courts is positive, the case is communicated to the Prosecutor General, who issues his or her own decision and sends the case to the President of Poland. Opinions issued in pardon proceedings by courts are not binding on the president. The president may therefore pardon a given person even if the Prosecutor General and one of the courts have issued negative opinions.

1038. Pardon proceedings can be initiated ex officio by the Prosecutor General or at the request of the President of Poland. In both cases, they may (but are not obliged to) ask for the opinion of the court that adjudicated the case of the person whose pardon is sought.

Former presidents of Poland (Lech Wałęsa 1990–1995; Aleksander Kwaśniewski 1995–2005, Lech Kaczyński 2005–2010, Bronisław Komorowski 2010–2015) have exercised their power of pardon with varying frequency. The relevant statistics are presented in the table below[36].

Year	*Number of pardons granted*
1991	423
1992	448
1993	569
1994	1077
1995	337
1996	735
1997	730
1998	759
1999	587
2000	384
2001	173
2002	198
2003	188
2004	233
2005	215
2006	53
2007	54
2008	61
2009	31
2010	54
2011	60
2012	80
2013	79
2014	70

36. www.prezydent.pl (accessed on: 2.10.2015).

§5. Expungement of a Conviction

1039. Although the expungement of a conviction (*zatarcie skazania*) does not apply to the possibility of holding a perpetrator criminally responsible or imposing a penalty on a perpetrator, entering an individual to the register of convicted persons is without doubt a very important consequence of the assumption of criminal liability. The expungement of a conviction is thus a measure that affects the broadly understood consequences of holding a person criminally responsible.

1040. The National Criminal Register (*Krajowy Rejestr Karny*)[37], is a register operated by the Minister of Justice that records final convictions for criminal offences (also convictions imposed by foreign courts), final rulings conditionally discontinuing criminal proceedings, and also rulings imposing protective measures and proceedings finally discontinued under an amnesty.

1041. The rule is that an entry into the National Criminal Register remains active for a period determined by a statute. The length of this period depends on the type of penal measure imposed on a perpetrator of an offence. The relevant regulation is laid down in Article 107 CC, which stipulates the following rules:

(1) if a conviction includes the penalty of life imprisonment, it is expunged by law after ten years from the date when the penalty is deemed enforced or commuted, or becomes time-barred;
(2) if a conviction includes the penalty of imprisonment or the penalty of twenty-five years of imprisonment, it is expunged by law after tenyears from the date when the penalty is enforced or commuted, or becomes time-barred;
(3) if a conviction includes the penalty of restriction of liberty, it is expunged by law after three years from the date when the penalty is enforced or commuted, or becomes time-barred;
(4) if a conviction includes the penalty of a fine, it is expunged by law after one year from the date when the penalty is enforced or commuted, or becomes time-barred;
(5) if a court refrained from imposing a penalty, a conviction is expunged by law after one year from the date of the final ruling.

If the court has imposed a penal measure, forfeiture or a compensatory measure a conviction may not be expunged before it is enforced or commuted, or becomes time-barred. Furthermore, a conviction may not be expunged before a protective measure is enforced.

1042. Upon expungement, a conviction is deemed non-existent. The entry of the conviction is then automatically removed from the register of convicted persons.

37. The Register operates under the National Criminal Register Act of 24 May 2000 (J.L. 2000, No. 50, item 580 as amended).

1043. The aforementioned rules of expungement can be subject to three exceptions. These exceptions either result in an earlier removal of an entry from the National Criminal Register or prohibit the removal of an entry despite the expiry of the periods in Article 107 CC.

First, a court may order the expungement of a conviction upon the motion of a convicted person, after the expiry of five years, provided that the convicted person has abided by the law in this period and the imposed penalty has not exceeded three years. In this case, a conviction is expunged not ex officio, but upon the motion of a convicted person (Article 107 § 2 CC).

Second, under Article 108 CC, in a situation where a perpetrator has been convicted of two or more non-continuous offences (where no aggregate penalty may be imposed), and also where a convicted person has reoffended during the period required for the expungement of a conviction, all convictions must be expunged simultaneously.

Third, under Article 106a CC, a conviction may not be expunged in the case of the imposition of an unsuspended penalty of imprisonment for an offence against sexual liberty or decency committed against a minor under the age of 15. In such cases, an entry on the National Criminal Register is not deleted. Notably, the above exclusion applies to all offences against sexual liberty and decency committed against minors under the age of 15 – e.g. rape, statutory rape, dissemination of pornographic content involving the participation of a minor, forced prostitution or procuring (cf. Chapter XXV CC).

1044. In Poland, access to the National Criminal Register is provided on a limited basis. A request for a criminal record check may be submitted by:

(1) everyone, in order to review one's own records;
(2) a state or local government institution (a government agency, courts, public prosecution service, the police);
(3) an employer, if the law requires that a prospective employee has no criminal record.

Index

The numbers here refer to paragraph nummbers.

Abolition, 100, 129, 649, 1013, 1027–1030
Accelerated procedure, 736–745, 777
Accused, 543–555
Aggregate penalty, 385, 472–476, 1043
Aggrieved party, 556–564
Aiding, 249, 253, 259–261, 466, 894
Amnesty, 1027–1030
Appeal
grounds for an appealabsolute grounds for an appeal, 773, 779, 787, 813relative grounds for an appeal, 772
ne peius rules, 786, 787
prohibition of *reformatio in peius,* 785, 786, 790
Associate judges, 35, 36
Attempt, 245–247
Attorney, 92–94, 105, 186, 391, 552, 554, 562, 656, 663, 665, 743, 775, 838, 839, 846, 987, 994

Cassation
extraordinary appeal in cassation, 799
ordinary (common) appeal in cassation, 798
Classification of inmates, 982–986
Coercive measures
arrest, 830–853
detention, 830–853
letter of safe passage, 895–896
preventive measures, 854–890
procedural penalties
search for the defendant and the issuing of a "wanted" warrant, 891–894
security against property, 902–908
Common courts, 29, 30, 37, 45–47, 84, 102, 148, 187, 478, 486, 773
Compensatory measures, 171, 375, 377, 383, 413–417, 429, 432, 435, 437, 439, 446, 467, 468, 730, 733, 773, 904, 1025, 1041
Complaint against the excessive length of criminal proceedings, 816–824
Complicity, 239, 249, 252–254, 260, 466, 468
Conditional discontinuation of proceedings, 96, 108, 408, 424–429, 440, 501, 530, 543, 621, 622, 644–646, 664, 669, 670, 673, 691–693, 967
Conditional suspension of a sentence, 430–439
Court proceedings, 657–761

Decision to bring a case before a court
indictment, 624–632
indictment together with a motion to convict a defendant without a trial 633-635
motion for the conditional discontinuation of proceedings, 96, 501, 621, 622, 644–646, 664, 673, 691
motion for the discontinuation of proceedings and the imposition of protective measures 621, 647-648
stand-alone motion to convict a defendant without a trial, 621, 626, 634, 641–643, 669, 679, 682
Decision to charge a person, 610–612
Decision to decline the initiation of preliminary proceedings, 597–599, 621
Defence lawyer, 552–555, 664–668, 710–716
Defendant's statements, 642, 928
Direct intention, 209–211, 245, 258, 323, 345, 354
Direct perpetration, 251

Index

Disclosure, 63, 520, 535, 542, 614–618, 630, 922, 937
Discontinuation of proceedings
decision to discontinue a case, 621
discontinuation of preliminary proceedings due to the absorption of an offence by other proceedings, 527
discontinuation of proceedings and imposition of protective measures, 501, 530
Dossier, 117, 500, 535, 549, 601, 614–618, 629–632, 640, 643, 646, 655, 656, 724, 778, 821, 855, 859
Drug offences, 369–372

Electronic monitoring, 380, 381, 394, 401, 448, 453
Evidence
direct evidence, 926
indirect evidence, 926
means of proof, 924–958
real evidence, 627, 925
sources of evidence, 924
testimonial evidence, 925, 928, 945
Excuses, 208, 216, 218, 226
Expert witness, 186, 329, 486, 493, 517, 571, 575, 600–602, 626, 630, 721, 774, 853, 898, 899, 901, 909, 919, 921, 927, 940, 941, 945–949, 951
opinion of expert witness, 945–949
Expungement of a conviction, 1039–1044
Extinction of criminal liability, 1012–1044

Fair trial, 514, 963
Felonies, 53, 54, 85, 145, 189, 212, 262–265, 468, 479, 487, 588, 1016
Forfeiture, 171, 352, 374, 375, 377, 383, 417, 418–423, 429, 435, 437, 439, 446, 467, 468, 585, 678, 730, 733, 772, 774, 874, 875, 904, 972, 1025, 1041

Grounds of justifications, 218–230, 238
Guilt, 170, 207–208

Hearing, 32, 87, 137, 148, 489, 500, 501, 518, 532, 539–541, 549, 604, 637, 673, 675, 679–681, 685, 687–689, 691, 692, 694, 701, 724, 737, 742, 744, 748, 749, 755–757, 769, 777, 779, 796, 803, 810, 814, 820, 823, 846, 850, 855, 867, 941, 1032, 1036

Immediate procedures, 591, 593, 610
Improperly obtained evidence, 959–965
Inquiries, 65, 69–73, 103, 115, 263, 439, 498, 501, 509, 542, 568, 569, 576, 581, 595, 598, 606, 607, 610, 615, 617, 620, 626, 636, 650, 654, 695, 741, 742, 864, 929
Insanity, 51, 218, 231–232, 250, 311, 423, 449, 647, 649, 747, 748, 798, 949
Instigation, 249, 256–258, 261, 335
Interlocutory appeal, 498, 499, 521, 530, 550, 583, 585, 586, 594, 596, 599, 608, 618, 655, 765, 766, 792–796, 837, 845, 846, 851, 853, 859, 875, 906
Investigations, 60, 103, 115, 179, 263, 477, 491, 498, 509, 522, 525, 533, 542, 559, 568, 569, 574–577, 581, 582, 589, 590, 595, 598, 601, 605, 607, 610, 615, 617, 625, 636, 642, 649, 747, 751, 864, 901, 929, 957, 958

Judges, 28, 34–37, 37, 41, 44–46, 76, 85, 87, 91–93, 103, 106, 118, 164, 174, 185, 187, 322, 444, 485, 487–490, 496, 498, 507, 516, 549, 568, 582, 600, 604, 649, 701, 704, 708, 709, 712, 717–719, 722, 728–732, 743, 755, 814, 822, 826, 842, 850, 859, 911, 913, 916–918, 920, 938, 940, 945, 972, 987, 1010, 1035

Lay judges, 37, 85, 106, 322, 487, 488, 730, 1035
Legal advisor, 37, 92–94, 186, 552, 554, 562, 663, 665, 743, 775, 838, 839, 846, 994
Legal counsel, 542, 552, 562–564, 571, 602, 614, 615, 631, 656, 659–663, 692, 702, 710–716, 721, 758, 769, 775, 788, 791, 800, 812, 898–901, 919, 940
Lex severior retro non agit principle, 166–168
Limitation period for the enforcement of a sentence, 1025–1026
Limitation period for the prosecution of offences, 1015–1024

Misdemeanours, 53, 54, 145, 189, 212, 262–265, 383, 461, 479, 568, 653, 736, 1016, 1019
Motion to reopen proceeding, 530

Necessity, 160, 202, 218, 220, 221,

224–227, 466, 468, 593, 603, 610, 635, 708, 711, 848, 864, 866, 949, 962
Negative grounds for the conduct of criminal proceedings, 597, 649
Negligence, 208, 214
Negotiated justice, 115, 263, 508, 633–635, 653
Nulla poena sine lege principle, 135, 162–165
Nullum crimen sine lege principle, 135, 150–162, 1024

Objection, 113, 734, 765, 767, 788–791, 938
Oblique intention, 209–211, 245, 261, 315
Offences
crimes against humanity, 138, 184, 189, 273, 275, 278, 279, 1022, 1023
crimes against peace, 273, 275, 276, 479, 1022
offences against business operations, 64, 348
offences against life and health, 290, 295, 392, 400, 412, 449
offences against property, 64, 270, 271, 342–344, 346, 347, 379, 461, 653
offences against public order, 64, 331, 334, 335, 337
offences against sexual liberty and decency, 310, 311, 396, 1043
offences against the activities of state and local government institutions, 321, 322
offences against the justice system, 64, 329
war crimes, 138, 184, 189, 273, 275, 279, 328, 479, 1022, 1023
Offences prosecuted upon complaint, 268, 367, 523, 525, 589, 592, 1021
Offences prosecuted upon private accusation, 531, 559
Offences prosecuted without complaint, 523, 589

Pardon, 1031–1038
Parole, 440–447, 452, 971, 1007
Penal measures, 388–412
Penal order, 501, 538, 670, 694–699, 736, 767, 788–791
Penalty
penalty of a fine, 378–379, 474, 1041
penalty of imprisonment, 91, 108, 197, 262, 293, 335, 362, 371, 377–379, 383–385, 387, 390–392, 412, 431, 435, 446, 462, 472–474, 652, 653, 696, 876, 973, 975, 980, 1004–1006, 1010, 1016, 1025, 1041, 1043
penalty of life imprisonment, 85, 197, 291, 384, 459, 473, 487, 996, 1041
penalty of the restriction of liberty, 380–383, 436, 473, 474
penalty of 25 years of imprisonment, 386
Police, 55–73, 580–581, 881–883
Preliminary examination, 591–593
Preliminary proceedings, 565–656, 565–656
Preparation, 241–244, 669–675, 700–702
Preventive measures
detention on remand, 860–870
financial surety (bail), 871–876
order to temporarily leave a premises, 884–887
police supervision, 881–883
prohibition to leave the country, 889–890
surety of a social organisation, 877–879
surety of a trustworthy person, 880
suspension of the execution of official duties, 888
Principle of active nationality, 180
Principle of guilt, 170
Principle of humanitarianism, 171, 972
Principle of individual and personal criminal responsibility, 169
Principle of limited objective nationality, 181
Principle of non-retroactivity, 104, 172
Principle of ubiquity, 179
Principle of universal jurisdiction, 183
Principles of criminal proceedings
in dubio pro reo, 507, 511–512, 910
presumption of innocence principle, 511–512
principle of accusatorial proceedings, 528–532, 624
principle of adversarial proceedings, 533
principle of conducting proceedings *ex officio*, 522–524, 537
principle of direct examination of evidence, 109, 536–538, 724, 911
principle of free evaluation of evidence, 912
principle of impartiality, 509–510

principle of inquisitorial proceedings, 533, 535, 567
principle of legality, 104, 499, 525–527, 567, 589, 626, 637, 652, 653, 915, 963
principle of material truth, 506–508, 534, 708, 774
principle of opportunity, 526
principle of the right to defence, 513–518
principle of transparency of proceedings, 539–542, 618
Prison administration, 973–974, 1009
Prisons, 89–91, 973–1011
Probation measures, 362, 371, 375, 424–447
Prosecutor, public prosecutor
auxiliary prosecutor, 502, 558, 563, 632, 659–663, 707, 715, 716, 721, 729, 749, 761, 769, 788, 919, 940
private accusation, prosecution, 186, 294, 317, 318, 524, 525, 531, 559, 590, 649, 662, 739, 751–754, 759, 760, 1017, 1020, 1021
private prosecutor, 659–663, 753, 758, 759, 769, 916, 919, 940
prosecution service, 37, 47, 74–83, 105, 106, 492, 580, 657
subsidiary accusation, prosecution, 531, 656
subsidiary prosecutor, 109, 659–663, 715, 721, 729, 769, 919
Protective measures, 448–455, 647–648, 746–750

Recklessness, 210, 214
Retroactivity of a "milder" statute, 173–174
Right to defence
ex officio defence laywer, 516, 517
formal defence, 514
mandatory defence, 515–517
optional defence, 515, 518
substantive defence, 514
Right to remain silent, 514, 544, 548, 840, 936
Royal principle, 182

Search, 58, 220, 491, 498, 512, 541, 585, 586, 592, 600, 601, 626, 792, 826, 827, 892, 927, 952–958, 1001
Seizure, 192, 220, 352, 498, 585, 586, 592, 600, 601, 826, 889, 890, 905, 908, 928, 952–958
Self-defence, 200, 218–223, 225
Supreme Court, 29, 30, 33, 39, 44, 45, 47, 88, 103, 106, 148, 161, 174, 187, 219, 220, 246, 260, 285, 520, 612, 780, 801–804, 814, 815, 822, 913, 936, 963
Suspect, 543–555
Suspected person, 146, 228, 545, 574, 830, 835, 836, 844, 848, 849, 893, 903, 908, 954

Temporary release from prison, 1004, 1006
Territorial jurisdiction, 481, 483, 486, 907
Territorial principle, 177–179
Testimony of a witness, 724, 912, 927, 933–944
Trial, 84–88, 478–490, 633–643, 676–684, 700–735

Voluntary assumption of criminal liability, 685–690

Made in the USA
Monee, IL
18 October 2026

66041405R10201